SOVIET ADMINISTRATION OF CRIMINAL LAW

Volume V

UNIVERSITY OF PENNSYLVANIA
LAW SCHOOL SERIES

SOVIET ADMINISTRATION OF CRIMINAL LAW

By

Judah Zelitch, LL. M.

OF THE PHILADELPHIA BAR

Sometime Gowen Fellow
University of Pennsylvania Law School

Philadelphia
UNIVERSITY OF PENNSYLVANIA PRESS
London: Humphrey Milford; Oxford University Press
1931

Printed in the United States of America

AUTHOR'S PREFACE

Thoughtful people throughout the world are keenly watching the colossal human drama played, actively or passively, by one hundred and sixty millions of people in the vast land of the Soviets. Irrespective of personal bias toward the startling economic, social and political innovations introduced by the Soviet régime, it is at least of cultural interest to examine as closely and impartially as possible the human values and relationships brought into being by these changes. The administration of criminal law reveals an important phase of those relationships as affected by prevailing economic doctrines, social ideals, and political philosophy.

This volume is an attempt to present an analytical and objective study of the rise and development of the Soviet judicial system, in its numerous ramifications, as it has actually been at work administering the criminal law. Emphasis has been laid upon the economic, social and political background, as well as upon the human elements composing the administration.

This work was prepared chiefly during the years 1927-1929, while the writer was a Gowen Memorial Fellow at the University of Pennsylvania Law School. After availing himself of the original material obtainable in this country, the writer visited the Soviet Union in the summer of 1928, and there spent approximately three months in further study, collection of material, and observation at close range. The work, covering all important legislation to date, was completed and presented to the Faculty of the University of Pennsylvania Law School in January, 1931, as a thesis for the degree of Master of Laws. Some additions and changes were later made to bring the investigation down to the time of publication. Too late for extended discussion in the body of the text, the writer learned of the publication in August, 1931, of a Project for a new Soviet Code of Criminal Procedure. A summary of this draft has been inserted as an appendix (No. 7, page 375).

The author wishes to express his deep gratitude to the Faculty of the University of Pennsylvania Law School, whose appointment to the Fellowship made this study possible; to Professor Edwin R. Keedy and Assistant Professor Layton B. Register, who freely gave their kind and invaluable aid through every stage of the work, and to Marion S. Kirk, Esq., who read the entire manuscript, offering valuable suggestions. The author also feels greatly indebted to Matthew Taplinger, Esq. and Nathan Bass, Esq., with whom parts of the manuscript were discussed; to the kind and helpful staff of the Slavonic Division of the New York Public Library, where a considerable part of the material was collected; to the persons and institutions in the Soviet Union who offered the writer, during his stay there, every facility for independent search and observation, including access to archives, protocols and other unpublished material; and to Peter Gregorev Olimov, member of the Commissariat of Justice of the R.F.S.R., who freely rendered the incalcuable assistance his high office could give.

Judah Zelitch

Philadelphia, November, 1931

TABLE OF CONTENTS

Introduction

Chapter I

The Rise and Development of Courts and Tribunals During the First Period

Page

Chapter II

Criminal Courts During the Second Period

Chapter III

Criminal Courts of the Union of Socialist Soviet Republics (U.S.S.R.)

Chapter IV

Procuracy, Preliminary Inquiry, Investigation and the Bar

Chapter V

Criminal Prosecution

Chapter VI

Proceedings Prior to the Trial

Chapter VII

The Trial

Chapter VIII

Some Outstanding Characteristics of the Soviet Trial

Chapter XII

Impressions and Observations

Appendix

ABBREVIATIONS

Cheka	—The initials of words meaning Extraordinary Commission to Combat the Counter-revolution.
G.P.U.	—State Political Bureau, the Soviet Secret Service.
Nep	—The initials of the words meaning the New Economic Policy.
R.S.F.S.R.	—Russian Socialist Federated Soviet Republic. The leading republic in the Soviet Union.
Tzeek	—The Central Executive Committee of the Union, the U.S.S.R.
U.S.S.R.	—The Union of Socialist Soviet Republics.
Vtzeek	—The All-Russian Central Executive Committee, the highest authority in the R.S.F.S.R.

SHORT TITLES USED IN FOOTNOTES

Code, 1922	—Code of Criminal Procedure. Collected Laws, Nos. 20 and 21, Article 230, 1922. (*Ugolovno—Protzesualnyi Kodex.* R.S.F.S.R. *Sobranie Uzakonenii* 20 and 21—153, 1922.)
Code, 1927	—Code of Criminal Procedure. Collected Laws, No. 7, Article 106, 1923. (*Ugolovno—Protzesualnyi Kodex.* R.S.F.S.R. *Sobranie Uzakonenii* 7—106, 1923.) The edition of 1927, which included all the amendments made to the Code of 1923, is cited.
Commentaries	—*Code of Criminal Procedure of R.S.F.S.R.* Text and Sectional Commentaries, by M. S. Strogovich and D. A. Karnitskii, 3rd edition, Moscow, 1928. (*Ugolovno Protzesualnii Kodex.* R.S.F.S.R. *Texst i Postateinii Kommentarii.*)
Cr. Code, 1922	—Criminal Code. Collected Laws, No. 15, Article 153, 1922. (*Ugolovnyi Kodex.* R.S.F.S.R. *Sobranie Uzakonenii,* 15—153, 1922.)
Cr. Code, 1926	—Criminal Code. Collected Laws, No. 80, Article 600, 1926. (*Ugolovnyi Kodex.* R.S.F.S.R. *Sobranie Uzakonenii* 1926, No. 80—600.)

First Decree —First Decree on Courts. Collected Laws No. 4, Article 50, 1917. *(O Sude—Dekret—Sobranie Uzakonenii i Rasporazhenii* 4—50, 1917.)

Fund. Laws —*Fundamental Laws of the Russian Empire.* A systematic compilation of laws by A. L. Saatchian, edited by A. A. Dobrovolskii, St. Petersburg, 1911.

Instructions —Instructions to the Supreme Court of the U.S.S.R. Systematic Compilation of the Existing Laws of the U.S.S.R., Book V, chapter XXI. *(Nakaz Verkhovnomu Sudu Soyuza Sovetskikh Respublik. Sistematicheskoe Sobranie Deistvuyuschikh Zakonov Soyuza Sovetskikh Sotzialisticheskikh Respublik. Kniga Pyataya.)*

Jud. Act, 1922—Judiciary Act. Collected Laws, No. 69, Article 902, 1922. *(Polozhenie O Sudoustroistve. Sobranie Uzakonenii* 69—902, 1922.)

Jud. Act, 1926—Judiciary Act. Collected Laws, No. 85, Article 624, 1926. *(Polozhenie O Sudoustroistve. Sobranie Uzakonenii* 85-624, 1926.)

Jud. Prac. —*Judicial Practice,* an official bi-weekly journal published by the Supreme Court of the R.S.F.S.R.

Krylenko, Jud. System—*The Judicial System of R.S.F.S.R.,* by N. V. Krylenko, Moscow, 1924. (*Sudoustroistve R.S.F.S.R.*) This book contains a series of lectures delivered by Mr. Krylenko to students of law at Moscow in 1923.

Krylenko, The Judiciary and the Law, 1927—N. V. Krylenko. *The Judiciary and the Law of U.S.S.R.* First Part, The Basis of the Judiciary, Moscow, 1927. *(Sud i Pravo v. S.S.S.R. Chast Pervaya Osnovy Sudoustroistva.)*

Krylenko, The Judiciary and the Law, 1928—N. V. Krylenko, *The Judiciary and the Law of U.S.S.R.* Second Part, The Basis of Criminal Procedure of the U.S.S.R. and the Constituent Republics, Moscow,

1928. *(Sud. i Pravo v. S.S.S.R. Chast Btoraya Osnovy Ugolovnovo Sudo Proizvodstva Soyuza S.S.R. i Soyuznych Respublik.)*

P.C. Act, 1918—People's Court Act, Collected Laws No. 85, Article 889, 1918. *(O narodnom Sude* R.S.F.S.R. *Polozhenie. Sobranie Uzakonenii* 85—889, 1918.)

P.C. Act, 1920—People's Court Act, Collected Laws, No. 83, Article 407, 1920. *(Polozhenie O Narodnom Sude* R.S.F.S.R. *Sobranie Uzakonenii* 83—307, 1920.)

Second Decree—Second Decree on Courts. Collected Laws, No. 26, Article 420, 1918. *(O Sude—Dekret* No. 2—*Sobranie Uzakonenii* 20—420, 1918.)

Sup.Court Act—Supreme Court and Procuracy Act, Collected Laws of the U.S.S.R. No. 50, Article 445, 1929. *(Polozhenie o Verkhovnom Sude Soyuza S.S.R. i Prokurature Verkhovnovo Suda Soyuza S.S.R. Sobranie Zokonov S.S.S.R.,* 50-445, 1929.)

Themashev —N.S. Temashev, Procedural Law. *The Law of Soviet Russia.* A collection of Essays, Prague, 1925. *(Protzesualnoe Pravo, Pravo Savetskoi Rosii.)*

Third Decree —Third Decree on Courts. Collected Laws, No. 52, Article 589, 1918. *(O Sude—Degret* No. 3—*Sobranie Uzakonenie* 52—589, 1918.)

Weekly, The —*The Weekly Journal of Soviet Justice. (Yezhenedelnik Sovetskoi Yustitzii.)* An official publication of the Commissariat of Justice of the R.S.F.S.R., since 1922.

INTRODUCTION

I. AN OUTLINE OF THE SOVIET GOVERNMENTAL SYSTEM

The judicial system in Sovietland is so directly connected with, and made an integral part of, the political system that some knowledge of the latter, if only in a general way, should prove advantageous to one reading of the criminal courts and the administration of the criminal law in those lands which are still indiscriminately called Russia.

The great Russian Empire of the Tzars has vanished as a single unit, both politically and geographically. The ten *Gubernias* (provinces) which formerly made up Russian Poland, together with some additional territory, now constitute part of an independent Poland; Bessarabia has been annexed to Roumania; while Finland, Esthonia, Latvia and Lithuania have become independent states, completely out of the Soviet circle. Even the rest of the vast territory of the old Empire no longer constitutes a single state, governed in every respect from a center, as it did before 1917.

The entire area embraced by the soviet, or council, form of government is composed of seven independent, sovereign republics which are united, for some purposes, into one political body called the Union of Socialist Soviet Republics (U.S.S.R.).

The Union was created by a treaty, or covenant, between four independent republics at a conference on December 30, 1922,[1] at Moscow. This treaty was incorporated into the Constitution of the Union, adopted July 6, 1923. Two years later, in 1925, two new independent republics were admitted to the Union;[2] in December, 1929, Tadzhik was accepted as an independent republic.[3] The Union, therefore, now consists of the following soverign republics:

1. Russian Socialist Federative Soviet Republic (R.S.F.S.R.).
2. Ukraine Socialist Soviet Republic (Uk.S.S.R.).
3. White Russian Socialist Soviet Republic (W.R.S.S.R.).
4. Transcaucasian Socialist Federative Soviet Republic (Trans.S.F.S.R.).

[1]Constitution, U.S.S.R. Part I.

[2]*Ibid.*

[3]Collected Laws, U.S.S.R., 1929, No. 75, Article 717. (*Sobranie Zakonov,* S.S.S.R., 1929, 75-717).

5. Turkoman Socialist Soviet Republic (Turk.S.S.R.).
6. Uzbek Socialist Soviet Republic (Uz.S.S.R.).
7. Tadzhik Socialist Soviet Republic (Tad.S.S.R.).

These individual sovereign republics do not represent homogeneous units. Within them will be found autonomous republics and autonomous territories *(oblasti)*.[4] These are semi-independent governments which sprang up in the early stages of the Revolution, and whose growth and development have been encouraged by the consistent policy of the Soviet régime which favors national self-determination, in the ethnographical sense. The autonomous republics and even territories, while not completely independent, have their own governmental machinery for the management of their own state affairs. They also have their schools, which usually employ their native language, and their own judiciary, directly supervised by their autonomous central authorities. They have their own congresses, central executive committees, and their presidia. Naturally, all the legislation and administrative policies of the autonomous republics must fit into the general framework of the sovereign mother republic.

At the present time there are, in the seven sovereign Soviet republics, fifteen autonomous republics and eighteen autonomous territories, the Russian Socialist Federative Soviet Republic alone having eleven autonomous republics and fifteen territories.[5]

The Constitution of the Union of the seven soverign republics specifically provides that the sovereign powers of these republics *(Souyznye Respubliki)* shall be limited only to the extent specified in the Constitution and only over subject matters within the purview of the Union.[6]

We have, therefore, a Union vested with authority over matters touching the entire land, and seven soverign republics which have voluntarily given up some of their sovereign powers as long as they remain a part of the Union, from which they may

[4]See Appendix No. 1, page 369 for diagram.

[5]Soviet Upbuilding (a monthly published by the *Tzeek* of the Union) 1931, No. 58-59, page 241 (*Sovetskoe Stroitelstvo*). In 1925 there were only thirteen autonomous republics and eighteen territories in the Union, the R.S.F.S.R. having nine such republics and thirteen territories. See *Cyclopedia of Government & Law,* Book 1, page 34, Moscow, 1925. (*Entziklopediya Gosudarstvo i Prava).*

[6]Constitution, U.S.S.R., section 3.

secede at any moment.[7] The latter important provision may not be changed or modified except by the unanimous consent of all the republics.[8]

While the Union may be said to be a government of enumerated powers, the Constitution confers upon it not only authority over such matters as we should call Federal, such as the power to make treaties, to declare war and make peace, regulate transportation, postal and telegraphic service, the coinage of money, etc., but also over matters which in the United States would be considered purely local. Thus, the Constitution grants to the Union the authority to lay down basic principles relating to the creation of the judiciary and its procedure, and governing criminal and civil legislation.[9] In accordance with this constitutional provision, the Union passed basic principles on the judiciary,[10] basic rules on criminal procedure in the Union and the constituent republics,[11] basic rules for criminal legislation;[12] and a statute of limitation for criminal offenses.[13] All these rules are, as the name indicates, mere basic outlines, leaving much latitude to the constituent republics for further legislation.

The governmental system of both the Union and the constituent republics is developed upon the fundamental base of the soviet. The word "soviet" does not signify any revolutionary idea, or any peculiar trait. It can be translated literally as "council", and has the same meaning in the Russian language. In the old régime there was the Imperial Soviet, a sort of "Upper House". There were medical and bee-keepers' soviets.[14] The word soviet began to be identified with proletarian movements after the

[7]*Ibid.*, section 4.
[8]*Ibid.*, section 2.
[9]*Ibid.*, section 1.
[10]Collected Laws, U.S.S.R., No. 23, Article 203, 1924. *(Sobranie Zakonov*, S.S.S.R., 23-203, 1924).
[11]*Ibid.*, No. 24, Article 206, 1924.
[12]*Ibid.*, No. 24, Article 205, 1924.
[13]*Ibid.*, section 10. See also amendment published in the *Isvesti* (News) No. 186, 1926. The "News" is the official daily publication of the Union Government where all the laws are published before they are compiled into the collected laws in pamphlet form, with number of pamphlet and number of article. This arrangement serves as permanent form for citing any law. Even in the systematic compilation of the Union laws where they are arranged according to the subject matter the established form of citation is inserted.
[14]Arthur Bullard, *The Russian Pendulum,* (1919), Chapter VI.

abortive Revolution of 1905. During the great general strike in October, 1905, the strike committee of St. Petersburg, at that time the capital, was composed of delegates from most of the large factories, and that body was known as the "Soviet of Workingmen's Deputies". This soviet was suppressed when the reaction once more gained the upper hand. But after the Revolution of March, 1917, such a body was organized and was known as the "Soviet of Workingmen's and Soldiers' Deputies".[15] Such soviets were organized all over the country during the reign of the Provisional Government, and when the Bolsheviks took over the reins of government, in November, 1917, it was through, and in the name of, these soviets that the All-Russian Congress was held at that time.

At the base of the soviet hierarchy is the village or city soviet. The deputies to these soviets are elected directly by the people having a right to vote, which is almost the entire population since the percentage of those not having the franchise is very small. The number of deputies varies with the size of the town. Thus, in a village of one thousand inhabitants it is one for every fifteen voters, while in a city of a population of one hundred thousand there is one deputy to every two hundred voters.[16] The city soviet elects a president and a presidium consisting of not more than eleven persons.[17] This small body constitutes the authority of the city in local matters, and is directly subordinate to the county soviet. The village and city soviets are the only bodies organized on the basis of direct representation. The next step on the soviet ladder is the county soviet assembly which is composed of delegates from all the local soviets—city, village, or *volost*—within the county. The assembly elects a county executive committee which is, in fact, the highest authority in the county.

The most important administrative division in the constituent republic—the province, circuit, or the region[18]—is governed in a

[15]The words "and peasants" were added later.

[16]City Soviets Act. Collected Laws of R.S.F.S.R., No. 91, Article 662, 1925, section 8. *(Polozhenie O Gorodskikh Sovetakh, Sobranie Uzakonenii* 91-662, 1925).

[17]*Ibid.*, section 16.

[18]The usual large administrative unit in pre-revolutionary Russia as well as in the R.S.F.S.R. has always been the province. But the soviet government gradually began to reorganize parts of the country into larger

similar way. It has its provincial, or regional, soviet assembly which is made up of delegates from the county soviets, city soviets, and the soviets of factories and mills which are situated outside the city limits.[19] The assembly of the province convenes once a year, and is the highest authority within the province, subordinate only to the authority of the constituent republic. In the constituent republic, the R.S.F.S.R., as undoubtedly in the other constituent republics, each provincial assembly elects a provincial executive committee consisting of not more than fifty persons.[20] The personnel of this powerful executive committee is so composed as to give representation to the county executive committees, as well as to those of the large industrial centers. The provincial executive committee elects its presidium, a kind of inner executive committee, of not more than seven persons, including the president of the provincial executive committee and his deputy.[21] All of these assemblies or executive committees are directly or indirectly subordinate to the highest authority within the R.S.F.S.R. In this Republic, the highest authority is the All-Russian Congress of Soviets and the All-Russian Executive Committee or its presidium.[22] This Congress is made up of delegates from the city soviets and circuit, provincial or regional assemblies of soviets.[23] It is convoked once a year by the All-Russian Executive Committee which is elected by the previous Congress, and constitutes the highest authority of the Republic in the intervals between the sessions of the Congress.[24] The Constitution of the Republic specifically designates the All-Russian Executive Committee, within the limits set by the Constitution, as the supreme legislative, executive, and controlling organ of the Russian Socialist Federative

units called regions, embracing an area formerly occupied by several provinces. Whenever this is done, the region is subdivided into circuits, each of the latter being a smaller unit than was the province. In the Ukraine and White Russian republics, the province as a unit was completely abolished and the largest unit is the circuit. See Appendix No. 2, page 370 for diagram.

19Collected Laws of R.S.F.S.R., No. 72 and 73, Article 907, 1922, Section 1.

20*Ibid.*, sections 12 and 13.

21*Ibid.*, section 40.

22*Ibid.*, section 8.

23Constitution of R.S.F.S.R., 1925, section 20.

24*Ibid.*, sections 21 and 22.

Soviet Republic.[25] The Executive Committee itself is convoked by its presidium, which exercises great authority between the sessions of the Executive Committee. The latter also institutes the Soviet of People's Commissars, which is responsible to the All-Russian Congress of Soviets as well as to its Executive Committee. The system of commissariats, with a People's Commissar at the head of each commissariat, is the same as the system of the Union, which will be mentioned later.

The commissariats have elaborate machinery of their own. If we examine the Act on the Commissariat of Justice,[26] we find that it provides for six separate departments, the most important of which are the departments of the judiciary and supervision, legislation and codification, the procuracy, and publication.[27]

Ascending to the highest sovereignity, the Union of Socialist, Soviet Republics (U.S.S.R.), we find that this has a political structure similar to that of the constituent republic, the province, the county and the city.

The Union is governed by a Congress of Soviets. This Congress, which convenes once in two years,[28] is the supreme authority of the land. It may not only legislate, but it is the executive branch and has complete control over the judiciary of the Union. Furthermore, the right to change the provisions of the Constitution of the Union is also exclusively within its powers.[29] The Congress, however, is too large a body to perform any executive duties, or even to legislate. In actual practice it merely listens to reports by the various departments, lays down general principles to be followed by the governmental departments, and elects the Soviet of the Union from among the representatives of the several constituent republics in proportion to their population. The exact number composing this Soviet is determined by the Congress itself.[30] In 1927 it was fixed at four hundred and fifty.[31]

[25] *Ibid.*, section 24.

[26] People's Commissariat of Justice Act. Collected Laws, No. 10, Article 120, 1923. *(Polozhenie O Narodnom Komisariate Yustitzii. Sobranie Uzakonenii*, 1923, 10-120).

[27] *Ibid.*, section 2. See Appendix No. 3, page 371 for diagram.

[28] Before 1927 the Congress met every year.

[29] Constitution of U.S.S.R., section 2.

[30] *Ibid.*, section 14.

[31] *Governmental System of the U.S.S.R. and R.S.F.S.R.* by A. M. Turubiner, Moscow, 1927, page 40. (*Gosudarstvennyi stroi S.S.S.R. and R.S.F.S.R.*).

Between the sessions of the Congress the supreme authority is vested in the Union Central Executive Committee, *the Tzeek,* which is, to all intents and purposes, the active, supreme governmental body within the Union. This all-powerful body, with practically unlimited authority, consists of two chambers—the Soviet of the Union, elected by the Congress, and the Soviet of Nationalities. The latter is composed of representatives of the sovereign republics as well as of the autonomous republics and territories which are part of these soviet republics. Irrespective of the size and relative significance of the republics, each sovereign and autonomous republic is represented equally by five delegates, while the autonomous territories send one representative each.[32]

All the laws passed for the entire Union must be approved by the Soviet of the Union as well as by the Soviet of Nationalities.[33]

The Union Central Executive Committee elects a presidium consisting of twenty-seven persons. This is made up of the persons comprising the personnel of the presidia of both the Soviet of the Union and of the Nationalities, consisting of nine members each, and nine additional members elected at a joint session of the Soviet of the Union and the Soviet of Nationalities.[34]

To demonstrate the equality of the independent republics, the Union Central Executive Committee, which is a sort of joint gathering of the two houses, elects seven presidents, equal to the number of constituent republics in the Union. Each of the republics is given the honor of having its own representative in the presidential chair. The presidents take up their duties in rotation, as arranged by the presidium of the Union Central Executive Committee.

The Union Central Executive Committee elects also the Soviet of People's Commissars. These commissars correspond roughly to the ministers or secretaries in other countries, and are the chiefs of the administration. This Soviet has larger powers than any European cabinet, since it may even pass emergency legislation and issue decrees, though they must be ratified later by the

[32] Constitution of U.S.S.R., section 15.
[33] *Ibid.*, section 22.
[34] *Ibid.*, section 26, as amended in May, 1925.

Tzeek. Each people's commissar is in reality a chairman of a small board called the Collegium of the Commissariat. The members of the board supervise the various departments of the commissariat and act as advisers to their chairman, the commissar. Each member of the board may appeal to the Soviet of People's Commissars from any act of the commissar.

All the people's commissars, as well as the members of the Union Supreme Court and of the military tribunals, are appointed by the Union Central Executive Committee or by its presidium.

This, then, is the political structure of the Soviet Union, a pyramid of councils, elected only at the base by the people, and each council selecting members to a higher council, until at the peak of the pyramid we have the Congress of the Union.

II. THE SCOPE OF THIS STUDY

In our discussion of criminal courts and the administration of the criminal law in Sovietland, we shall confine ourselves to the Union of Socialist Soviet Republics and to only one of the constituent republics—namely, The Russian Socialist Federative Soviet Republic. To do otherwise would mean to indulge in unnecessary repetitions. The R.S.F.S.R. is not only by far the most significant and largest republic in the Union, with a population of 110 million out of 161 million in the entire Union and an area of over ninety percent of all the sovereign republics combined,[35] but it is also, in a sense, the mother republic. It was the Moscow government which led the Revolution and fought the civil war, and it was again Moscow which was instrumental in creating all the independent republics, which have followed the model evolved during the early years of the Revolution in Central Russia. The Moscow-made laws were, as a matter of course, frankly adopted and incorporated into the codes of the other sovereign republics. Thus, the Code of Criminal Procedure, adopted by the Ukraine Socialist Soviet Republic of 1922,[36] stated in the preamble that its aim is to ensure a uniform system of procedure in all the Soviet republics, and therefore the Code of the

[35]Soviet Upbuilding, *op. cit., supra,* note No. 5. In 1927 the population of the Union was 147,013,609 and that of the R.S.F.S.R., 100,857,985.

[36]Code of Criminal Procedure of the Uk.S.S.R., 1922. Collected Laws of Uk.S.S.R., No. 41, Article 598, 1922.

R.S.F.S.R. was taken as a model. An examination of the Ukraine Code of 1922 reveals the fact that it is not only based upon that adopted by Moscow, but that it is indeed a complete, true copy of the latter, with the name of the republic changed, and somewhat different terms employed for the administrative divisions. The same fact is true with regard to White Russia. The Judiciary Act[87] of the latter is based upon, and differs very little from, the Judiciary Act of the R.S.F.S.R.

The writer has not examined all the present codes of the other five soverign republics. From an examination of codes of two of these five republics—namely, the Uzbek Judiciary Act of 1927 and the Georgian Code of Criminal Procedure of 1923—we learn that the former is an exact copy of the Code of the R.S.F.S.R., and the latter is also based entirely upon the pattern devised by the leading Republic. Although the recent codes of the more advanced constituent Soviet republics, especially that of Ukraine, made some departures from the similar codes in existence at Moscow,[88] those deviations are not of any real basic importance. There is little reason to suppose that any material differences will be found in the codes of those republics which were not examined, or that any serious differences are likely to develop, since all the codes of criminal procedure would have to be predicated upon the "basic principles" or "basic rules" worked out by the government of the Union which are binding on all the Soviet republics.

III. INTRODUCTION TO THE JUDICIAL SYSTEM

The present structure of a well-planned criminal judiciary erected by the Soviet régime, after a pattern clearly designed and strictly adhered to by its builders, passed through innumerable stages of forming, changing, and shaping until it finally culminated in the passage of the Judiciary Act of December, 1926,[89] which went into effect in 1927. But during the nine years of Soviet régime which lie behind the passage of this Act, the criminal

[87]Judiciary Act. Collected Laws of White Russian S.S.R. No. 49, Article 382, 1925.

[88]See new Code of Criminal Procedure of the Uk.S.S.R. Collected Laws, 1927, No. 28, Article 133.

[89]Collected Laws, No. 85, Article 624, 1926.

judicial system in its rise and development underwent a most emphatic metamorphosis. To look into the different and, not infrequently, contradictory steps taken while the planning and the building were going on and to analyze the ideas, theories and reasons which lie back of these, will be necessary for a proper understanding of the Soviet system of criminal courts and procedure which, it is to be observed, are far removed from our own, both in theory and practice.

The entire period between the beginning of the Soviet régime and the passage of the Judiciary Act of 1926 may conveniently and properly be divided into two separate parts—first, the period between November 1917, and November 1922, and second, the period between November 1922 and 1927.

a. *The Period between November, 1917 and November, 1922*

These five years may be described, so far as the building of a criminal judicial system is concerned, as a period of incessant searching and groping. The judicial system which existed prior to November, 1917, was, as we shall see, completely destroyed, thus necessitating the building of a totally new structure. The institution of criminal courts and tribunals was going on constantly, but there was apparently no clearly marked plan followed. The development proceeded in a rather hazy and zigzag manner. Courts were hastily established only soon to be discarded, and just as swift were the changes with regard to the basic ideas as to the nature of the courts, their jurisdiction, functions, and so on. Thus, to cite one striking example, the people's court was instituted as a lower court of original jurisdiction, but soon afterwards became the only ordinary[40] criminal court, only to undergo rapid and striking changes while descending to take again its place as a humble court of first instance.

This period also witnessed the birth, remarkable growth, far-reaching expansion and complete disappearance of the highly

[40]From the very beginning of the soviet régime there had existed two distinct types of criminal courts. One tried ordinary offenses and was, therefore, termed the ordinary (or normal) court, while the other, usually the revolutionary tribunal, dealt with what we would term "crime wave" incident to the Revolution and accompanying civil war, and the sharp change in the political and social order. These tribunals were called the exceptional or extra-ordinary courts.

centralized system of revolutionary tribunals, which have exerted a tremendous influence upon the process of shaping some of the policies of the Soviet judiciary as the administrator of the criminal law.

The revolutionary tribunals had also to undergo an evolution. During the four years of their existence they markedly changed their makeup and mode of procedure, as well as their attitude towards the defendants brought before them. In the course of their growth they developed striking peculiarities, which made them clearly distinguishable from the ordinary criminal courts. Some of the peculiar characteristics of the abolished tribunals may still easily be traced to, and found in, the differently-constructed, newly-organized types of courts, such as the important provincial *(gubernia)* court, and, to a certain extent, the Supreme Court. This period of vicissitudes finally terminated with the passage of the first complete Judiciary Act of 1922.[41]

b. *The Period between November, 1922 and 1927*

These four years witnessed the emergence of a clearly conceived system of criminal judiciary. While many important changes were eventually made by the Judiciary Acts of 1923,[42] 1924,[43] and other minor acts, the fundamental ideas and the general basic scheme were laid down in the first Act of 1922.

The entire period between the passage of the Act of 1922 and the enactment of the extended and clarified Judiciary Act of 1926,[44] which has repealed nine different prior acts dealing with the creation or organization of the judicial system, was devoted to the further development, clarification and stabilization of an already established system of criminal courts.

The main characteristics of the Soviet criminal judiciary as it finally emerged during the second period are:

1. A highly centralized system of criminal courts has been established which consists, with some exceptions, of three branches: The people's court, the provincial court, and a Supreme

[41]Collected Laws, No. 69, Article 902, 1922.
[42]Collected Laws, No. 84, Article 481, 1923.
[43]Collected Laws, No. 78, Article 782, 1924.
[44]Collected Laws, No. 85, Article 624, 1926.

Court. All these courts, except the people's, consist of a number of separate departments, *collegia*. In the reorganized administrative units, where the province has been replaced by the region, the judiciary consists of four branches, for the provincial court in these places has given way to a regional and a circuit court.

2. Each of these courts has original jurisdiction of various grades of offenses. As trial courts, they are made up of one permanent judge and two people's co-judges.[45] The co-judges sit for a limited period of time only, but while sitting enjoy all the rights and powers of the permanent judges.

3. The provincial, circuit and Supreme Courts are also, or rather mainly, courts of cassation and supervision, and in that capacity they sit without the participation of people's co-judges. Provincial and circuit courts are courts of cassation for cases tried at the people's court, while the Supreme Court has jurisdiction over cases originally heard at the provincial, circuit, or regional court.

4. The jury system, as it is known in our courts, is abolished.

5. Appeals, as distinguished from cassation, are discarded.

6. A highly centralized hierarchy of public prosecuting officials, called the procuracy, with tremendous powers and equally extensive duties, is instituted. The procuracy is not merely the agency for public prosecution. Its powers extend far beyond that. It is a peculiar institution entrusted with the authority to supervise the executon of the law of the land in the courts as well as outside of them. The procuracy is termed the "guardian of the Revolutionary law."

7. A well worked-out and clearly defined system is inaugurated consisting of two branches of officials for investigation and preliminary inquiry. The nature and scope of the pre-trial investigation or inquiry performed by these officials present a unique

[45]The Russian word is *Narodnii zasedatel* literally people's co-sitter. The term "co-judge" has been therefore selected. It is worth noting that the Russian word used to designate the present co-judge is the same as was used in pre-revolutionary days to denote a juror, only the previous prefix "sworn" is now supplanted by the word "people's". Thus instead of the sworn *zasedatel* there is now the people's *zasedatel*.

feature of the administration of Soviet criminal law. This inquiry is, in a sense, a preliminary inquisitorial trial of the case.

8. The ultimate control of the entire judiciary in all its phases is in the last analysis vested in the same central body which makes and executes all the laws of the land.

Chapter I

THE RISE AND DEVELOPMENT OF COURTS AND TRIBUNALS DURING THE FIRST PERIOD

I. THE FIRST SOVIET COURT AND REVOLUTIONARY TRIBUNAL

a. *The First Decree*

On November 7, 1917 (October 25, old style), the soviet organizations made their successful *coup d' état*. With the battle cry of "all power to the soviets", they overthrew the provisional government of Kerensky, and on November 24 the First Decree on Courts was signed.[1] With one stroke of the pen the entire judicial system of the Russian Empire was swept away. In unequivocal terms it was decreed "to abolish the existing branches of the General Judiciary,[2]—*i. e.*, the circuit courts, the judicial *palata*, the Governing Senate with all its departments, and the military and admiralty courts—* * * and to replace those courts by others organized on the basis of a democratic election."[3] This decree did not purport to create any courts to take the place of the so-called General Judiciary which was destroyed. But there was another group of courts, the justice of the peace type, which remained to be dealt with. What was to be the fate of these courts?[4] The decree provided that "The existing institution of the justices of the peace be discontinued and those judges who have been elected until now indirectly be replaced by a local permanent judge and two alternate co-judges invited to each session from a special list of persons who shall serve in rotation. The local judges shall be chosen on the basis of a direct democratic election."[5] The act then proceeded to provide for the temporary

[1]See *infra*, page 24 for facts on drafting of this Decree.

[2]See chapter on Criminal Court in Imperial Russia, Appendix No. 8, page 381.

[3]First Decree, section 1.

[4]The Courts of the Peace of Tzarist Russia included an Assembly of Justices of the Peace, which was a court of appeals. These courts of the peace must have gained in significance in the years immediately preceding the Revolution of 1917, since the *zemsky* type of courts was apparently given up. See Kornilov, *Modern Russian History*, Book II, page 334.

[5]First Decree, section 2.

appointment of these judges, until elections should be held, by the different *volosts,* district or city soviets of the workers', peasants' and soldiers' deputies. The same soviets were to compile lists of co-judges[6] and fix the time when they were to appear for service at the sessions of the court.

Although this decree did not determine the exact nature of the one court it undertook to create, nevertheless it outlined some of the basic characteristics which touched upon matters of principle. Thus, the former justices of the peace did not lose the right to be appointed and then elected as judges of the new court.[7] The jurisdiction of this court was limited to offenses punishable by not more than two years' imprisonment, provided the civil claim incident thereto was not above 3000 rubles.[8] The judgment was to be final and not subject to any appeal (as distinguished from cassation), but if the punishment inflicted was more than seven days' imprisonment or a fine of over 100 rubles a complaint by way of cassation was permitted.[9] The "local court", as it was to be called, was to decide cases in the name of the Russian Republic, but was to be guided by the laws of the deposed government in so far as they were not repealed or were not contradictory to the spirit of the Revolution and revolutionary justice,[10] whatever that might import. Since complaints by way of cassation were to be allowed, the decree provided that "the court of cassation shall be the county assembly of the local judges."[11]

If we bear in mind the political and social nature of the Revolution of November 17, 1917, its avowed class character, and its hostile attitude towards the principles of justice as enunciated by the western world, the First Decree will appear rather significant. While the old judiciary was discarded, the beginning of the new one was heavily tinged with "bourgeois prejudices", as was later declared by Soviet writers. Judges were to be elected directly by the people; the old, experienced judges were not to be

[6]It is not clear from the act whether the temporary method of appointment was also meant with regard to co-judges.

[7]First Decree, section 2.

[8]While normally the ruble is worth about 50 cents, it was then worth only a few cents.

[9]First Decree, section 2, last part.

[10]*Ibid.,* section 5.

[11]*Ibid.,* section 2.

barred from becoming candidates; the old system of a territorial assembly of judges was to be reestablished, and the decree laid down the rule that the "power to pardon those convicted for a crime shall henceforth belong to the judiciary."[12] This first legislation of the present régime was later vehemently assailed by one of the most important personalities within the Soviet judiciary, N. V. Krylenko.[13] He ridiculed the provisions enumerated above as being opposed to the very idea of a Soviet system and ascribed their enactment solely to Dr. Shteinberg, the Commissar of Justice, who represented the left Social-Revolutionary group which participated in the government immediately after the Revolution of November, 1917.

But while the influence of Dr. Shteinberg and his group must have been instrumental in shaping the policies of the government, the decree was nevertheless signed by such eminent leaders of the Bolsheviks (later communists) as Lenin, Trotsky, Stalin and Stuchka. Furthermore, Krylenko erred historically, for at the time of the issuance of the First Decree, the communist, P. Stuchka, was acting Commissar of Justice, Dr. Shteinberg taking that office a short time later. It is quite possible that the democratic tinge present in the act may be attributed to the fact that the Bolsheviks still remembered their old party platform which was committed "to the election of all judges by the people."[14] We must not, however, overlook the innovation promulgated by the First Decree, which survived all the stages of development,—namely, the institution of people's co-judges, and the abolition of the previous forms of appeals, as they had existed under the Russian law.[15] The First Decree, although it bore the influence of Tzarist Russia and the Western European system, carried within itself the seeds of the new peculiarly Soviet ideas with regard to the judiciary.

[12]*Ibid.*, section 7.

[13]Krylenko, *The Jud. System.*

[14]Programme of the Social Democratic Party, quoted by Krylenko, *The Jud. System*, page 6.

[15]Krylenko, *The Jud. System*, page 56, gives the following definition: "Appeal means a complaint against the decision or verdict as to the merits of the case. Cassation means a complaint against the permission of a formal violation of (substantive or procedural) law at the trial."

Except for the local courts and assembly of local judges, the First Decree laid the cornerstone for the building of revolutionary tribunals. With regard to the latter, an entirely different note was sounded. The concluding section of the decree reads: "To combat counter-revolutionary elements * * * , as well as to try cases involving marauding, plundering, sabotage and other abuses of the merchants, industrialists, officials and other persons, revolutionary tribunals of workers and peasants shall be established."[16] A tribunal was to consist of one president and six co-judges sitting in rotation, elected by the provincial or city soviets of workers', peasants' and soldiers' deputies. In these vague words the advent of the revolutionary tribunals was announced.

We have in the First Decree the starting points of two different systems,—courts and revolutionary tribunals, or ordinary and special courts—which immediately began to branch off and develop along different lines. We shall proceed to discuss their growth and development separately and attempt to follow their divergent trails until they meet again at one point at the close of 1922, when all the courts were blended into one harmonious whole.

II. CRIMINAL COURTS—1917 TO 1922

a. *Circuit Court*

The people's court is, at present, the judicial institution of the Soviet Union where the overwhelming majority of criminal cases are disposed of.[18] But before we take up our discussion of the people's court, let us digress for a moment in order to note the rise and disappearance of a judicial structure which was to be erected above the people's court.

As the people's court was originally conceived to be the minor judiciary only, a Second Decree on courts was issued in March, 1918,[19] instituting a people's circuit court to take jurisdiction over all offenses not within the authority of the local people's

[16] First Decree, section 8.

[17] The soldier's deputies were later discontinued, and in later enactments this word disappeared. See H. N. Brailsford, *How the Soviets Work,* page 62, New York, 1927.

[18] Commentaries, page 38.

[19] Collected Laws, No. 26, Article 420, 1918.

court.[20] Thus a court of original jurisdiction for more serious offenses was created.

The judges of the people's circuit court were to be elected by the circuit soviets, which had also the power to recall them.[21] An examination of the Second Decree will undoubtedly reveal the dominating influence of the pre-revolutionary Russian judicial system over an act signed by such revolutionaries as Sverdlov, who was then president of the All-Russian Executive Committee, and Lenin, the President of the Soviet of People's Commissars.

This decree provided that, at a general meeting of all the judges of the circuit court, the judges for the different criminal and civil divisions were to be assigned. Each of these divisions was to consist of a president and not less than two permanent judges. The judges themselves were also to elect their president and the chairmen of the various divisions. The most remarkable feature of this act was the provision that "In deciding criminal cases the court shall be made up of twelve people's co-judges[22] and two substitutes presided over by one of the permanent members of the court."[23] The people's co-judges were to decide not only matters of fact, but questions of law, and determine the punishment as well.[24] In the latter respect their powers were very extensive. They were invested not only with the power to fix the term and nature of the punishment to be inflicted, and to set it even below the norms prescribed by law, but they could go even so far as to "release the accused without any punishment at all"[25]—suspend sentence. All this clearly indicates that the highly cherished institution of trial by jury was practically re-established. True, the power of the co-judges was greatly extended over that exercised by the pre-revolutionary juries. But all the characteristics of the latter were, nevertheless, retained, since it was clearly stated that "in the deliberation of the co-judges the presiding judge partici-

[20]*Ibid.*, section 1.

[21]*Ibid.*, section 1 and last part of section 2.

[22]For an explanation of the term "co-judge", see *supra*, note 45 of the Introduction.

[23]Second Decree, section 3.

[24]This was a departure from the previous Russian system where the jury could not decide any question of law, though it had something to say with regard to inflicting the punishment.

[25]Second Decree, section 29.

pates only with the right to advise,"[26] while the decision was to be reached and voted on by the co-judges themselves. The presence of the judge as a mere adviser did not change the fundamental fact that the twelve persons were a jury to decide both the facts and the law.

The entire decree was permeated with a "liberal conception" of justice. The participation of the defense counsel, even in the preliminary investigations and inquiries, was provided for with some limitations. But even such apparently justifiable limitations were subject to an appeal to the people's court.[27] Each accused was to have counsel selected by himself or appointed by the court.[28] A rather interesting feature was the provision that, in addition to the prosecution and the defense, two persons from the public present at the trial could argue, one on behalf of the defendant and the other against him.[29] The latter provision was apparently inserted to give emphasis to the note of plainness and real democracy which was henceforth to prevail even in the dignified Temple of Justice.

Although the decree under discussion was passed in March, 1918, five months after the Bolsheviks and their adherents had seized the power, the act stated that "The procedure in the courts * * * shall be in accordance with the judiciary statutes of 1864 in so far as it was not repealed * * * and was not contradictory to the conscience of the toiling masses."[30] A similar provision was inserted with regard to the pre-revolutionary criminal law.[31] It also stipulated that the members of the Tzarist judiciary might be re-elected to judicial office.[32] These provisions were bitterly criticized later in Soviet legal writings, but, nevertheless, they indicate convincingly that the western idea of justice had at that time a strong grip upon Soviet leaders and that their own, different point of view was still slumbering.

[26] *Ibid.*, section 30. This section also states that the right of the presiding judge to sum up the case is abolished. He may state only his opinion as to the measure of punishment provided under the law.

[27] *Ibid.*, section 21.

[28] *Ibid.*, section 27.

[29] *Ibid.*, section 28.

[30] *Ibid.*, section 8.

[31] *Ibid.*, section 36.

[32] *Ibid.*, section 39.

b. *Territorial Court and Supreme Judicial Control*

The Second Decree undertook to erect a pyramid of higher tribunals from members of the lower courts. Thus the old scheme of the Russian assembly of justices of the peace, which was remodeled into the assembly, and later soviet, of people's judges, was further extended. The permanent members of the people's circuit court of a given territory *(oblast)* were to select from among themselves a number of judges who were to constitute a territorial people's court. The members of the latter court were to elect their own president and presiding judges for the various divisions. The territorial people's court was to be the court of cassation for cases originally decided by the circuit court.[33]

In the interest of a uniform practice of cassation, there was to be a Supreme Judicial Control *(Verkhovnyii Sudebnyii Kontrol)* at the capital, an institution made up of representatives of the territorial people's courts who were to be elected for a term of one year. The function of this third court on the pyramid was not to review cases decided in a lower court, but to render uniform decisions on matters of principle, after that principle was interpreted differently by the different courts of cassation. The decision, or rather interpretation, as laid down by the Supreme Judicial Control was then to serve as guidance for all the courts.[34] This intended system of cassation, supervision and interpretation was apparently never put into actual operation.[35] Such a complicated machinery was, it seems, bound to fail because the very idea of having a chain of courts springing out of each other, not created by the different executive committees and without any direct responsibility to them, was too repugnant to the Soviet system to survive. The Third Decree on Courts of July 18, 1918, evidently replaced this form of cassation by providing that "for cassational complaints against the decisions of the circuit people's court * * * instead of the Supreme Judicial Control, there shall be temporarily instituted at Moscow a Court of Cassation * * *, consisting of a president, vice-president * * * and eight members, the latter to be appointed by the All-Russian

[33] *Ibid.*, section 4.
[34] *Ibid.*, section 6.
[35] Temashev, page 213.

Executive Committee from the candidates nominated by the circuit people's court and the local soviets of the people's judges." The president and his deputies were to be appointed by the People's Commissariat of Justice and confirmed by the All-Russian Executive Committee.[36]

The circuit court, which was to serve as the generator for both the territorial court and the Supreme Judicial Control, did not strike any deep roots in the Soviet system,[37] although it functioned for a while. The discontinuance of the circuit court may be attributed to a number of causes, but it would seem that two factors were mainly instrumental in its abolition—on the one hand, the rapid growth of the different revolutionary tribunals, and on the other the growing idea that there should be only one type of criminal court, a people's court. With all this in mind, we may turn back to our discussion of the development of the people's court.

c. *People's Court*

1. The Third Decree on Courts

No court in Soviet Russia has traveled more diametrically opposite paths than has this court during the few years of its rise and growth. The First Decree, as we have seen, laid down mere rudimentary ideas of a lower court with limited jurisdiction. The Third Decree,[38] which was promulgated in 1918, gave a more important aspect to the nature of the people's court. The first section of this act, which was an addition to the First Decree, provided that the local people's court should have jurisdiction over "all criminal cases except those dealing with an attempt to kill, rape, robbery, counterfeiting," and several other grave offenses.[39] That the act intended to enlarge the powers of the local people's court is obvious from the provision that "The local people's court shall have the power to impose a sentence of five years' imprisonment,[40] * * *" while in the First Decree this power was limi-

[36]Collected Laws, No. 52, Article 589, 1918.
[37]*Cyclopedia Granat.* Book 41, Part III, page 200, Moscow. P. Lyublinkii *(Entzklopeiya. Granat).*
[38]Collected Laws, No. 52, Article 589, 1918.
[39]*Ibid.,* section 1.
[40]*Ibid.,* section 3.

ted to the imposition of sentences of two years. The upward march of the people's court was thus set in motion by the Third Decree, and was still to go on.

Only a few days after the publication of the Third Decree, which, as we have seen, added to the importance of the people's court, a lengthy order, or instruction, with regard to this court was issued.[41] In the historical development of the people's court this order occupies an intermediate position, standing, as it were, at the crossroads between the policies enunciated in the first three decrees and in the acts which were to follow. It provided that the judicial districts of the local people's court were to correspond with the previous districts of the justices of the peace.[42] The attitude of the first three decrees with regard to pre-revolutionary law was also re-affirmed. On the other hand, the order was the fore-runner of a number of important rules with respect to the qualifications of the judges, methods of procedure, and the election of judges and co-judges, which rules were incorporated in the later acts and especially in the very significant People's Court Act of December, 1918.[43]

2. People's Court Act of 1918

Soviet legal writers insist that the People's Court Act of 1918 is a landmark in the history of the Soviet judiciary. Proudly they boast that it was the beginning of the building of a judicial system along the lines of a purely proletarian *Weltanschauung*. Here for the first time the application of pre-revolutionary law was explicitly forbidden, and since there was a complete absence of any written law of Soviet origin, the judges were to guide themselves by the "revolutionary conscience".[44] Soviet writers maintain that such a change in the judicial policy was due to the fact that the act was the first to be drafted without the influence, devastating from their point of view, of the left Social Revolutionary group, which broke away from the communists in July, 1918. Such an explanation is, to our mind, not entirely correct. The Order of July, 1918, was signed, not by Dr. Shteinberg, but

[41]Collected Laws, No. 53, Article 597, 1918. (*Sobranie Uzakonenii* 53-597. 1918).
[42]Third Decree, section 1.
[43]Collected Laws, No. 85, Article 889, 1918.
[44]Temashev, pages 215 and 216.

by the new Commissar of Justice, Stuchka, a staunch communist, who is still an outstanding figure in the Soviet judiciary; nevertheless the order, as pointed out before, contained the general characteristics of the first three decrees. The truth, we venture to say, is that the communists themselves simply changed their attitude as the Revolution and the civil war proceeded.

This assumption is well supported in the interesting narrative by P. Stuchka of the history of the First Decree on Courts. Together with one Kozlov, he drafted a project for a decree on courts which contained a fiery revolutionary preamble.[45] The suggested decree provided for the appointment of judges who were to be guided, not by the laws of the overthrown government, but by those decreed by the soviets or by their own revolutionary conscience. The communists, however, were not willing to accept it. They said: "First new laws, and then new courts". Even after agreeing to a decree abolishing old and creating new courts, they insisted that not all the courts should be abolished at once.[46] It is evident that the Bolsheviks were not ready to adopt an entirely new course so far as the courts and the law were concerned. A complete change of attitude was manifested later. It is probable that the bitterness with which the civil war was being fought at that time, the end of 1918, made it perhaps necessary for the party in power to emphasize its complete departure from everything which showed the influence of pre-revolutionary days.

The first section of this People's Court Act of 1918, which was really a judiciary act and a code of criminal procedure combined, proclaimed the new principle that, within the territory of the Russian Socialist Federative Soviet Republic, there shall be a uniform system of people's courts consisting either of one permanent judge sitting alone, or of one permanent judge and two or six temporary judges, people's co-judges.[47] This act did not explicitly abolish the circuit court, but the inference to be drawn from the act leaves no room for doubt that the circuit court was discarded since the act stated "that the people's court, within its

[45] P. Stuchka, "Five Years of Revolutionary Courts," *The Weekly*, Nos. 45 and 46, 1922, page 1.

[46] *Ibid.*, pages 2 and 3.

[47] P. C. Act, 1918, section 1.

district, shall have jurisdiction over all criminal cases * * * ".[48] This sweeping jurisdiction was then somewhat modified by specifying a number of offenses of a specific nature, such as counter-revolutionary activities, espionage, sabotage, etc., which were to come within the jurisdiction of the revolutionary tribunals. In spite of these modifications, the important fact remains that the people's court was made the only ordinary criminal court of original jurisdiction. It was, however, divided into three different units:

(a) A single permanent judge. This judge was invested with some important powers. He could conduct, if he found it necessary, a preliminary inquiry in any criminal case which was to be tried by a court made up of one permanent judge and two people's co-judges; he was to supervise the investigations carried on by the police *(militzia)*. He had also the authority to set free all those unlawfully held under guard,[49] and to issue orders of arrest, subject, however, to confirmation by the full court.[50]

(b) One permanent judge and six co-judges. Such a court, composed of seven judges (since the co-judges while sitting had all the powers and rights of the permanent judges),[51] was the most important court of first instance. It had jurisdiction over such serious offenses as "attempts to take human life * * * , rape, robbery, counterfeiting, * * * bribery, speculation in * * * necessities",[52] all of which were previously under the jurisdiction of the circuit court.

(c) One permanent judge and two co-judges. This court took jurisdiction over all criminal cases not specifically assigned to the bench of seven judges.

The permanent judges were elected by the general assembly of the city or county soviets, and were subject to recall by the same body.[53] To be eligible for the office of permanent judges, it was necessary to satisfy the following requirements: One had to have (1) a right to vote in soviet elections, and the right to

[48] *Ibid.*, section 4.
[49] *Ibid.*, section 6.
[50] *Ibid.*, section 54.
[51] *Ibid.*, section 9.
[52] *Ibid.*, section 7.
[53] *Ibid.*, section 13.

be elected to the soviet;[54] (2) experience in the work of a number of proletarian institutions; and (3) a theoretical or practical training for the office of judge.[55] These vague qualifications were made more uncertain by the provision that one had to satisfy, absolutely, only the first qualification, which was really a political one, and at least one of the other two.[56]

To qualify as a candidate for co-judge, one need only have the right to vote and to be elected to the soviets. The co-judges were chosen by the local soviets, subject to the approval of the executive committee of the county.[57] Lists of the elected co-judges were compiled for a period of six months, the names of the persons to serve were drawn by lot, and each of these co-judges then served for not more than six sessions. His service was made obligatory, and any failure to appear, without good cause, involved a fine imposed by the court. As most of the people were employed by the government, the government would continue to pay the wages of the co-judge at his regular place of employment while he was performing judicial duty. But if the co-judge was an independent workman he was to receive the minimum rate paid for such work by the government.[58]

As the people's court mounted to the heights of the sole criminal court, its powers became great and impressive. Thus,

[54]The Constitution of 1918, section 64, provides that "The right to vote and be elected to the soviets is enjoyed by the following citizens, irrespective of religion, nationality, domicile, etc., of the Russian Socialist Federative Soviet Republic, of both sexes, who shall have attained their eighteenth year by the day of election:

(a) All who have acquired the means of living through labor that is productive and useful to society, and also persons engaged in housekeeping, which enables the former to do productive work, *i. e.,* laborers and employees of all classes who are employed in industry, trade, agriculture, etc., and peasants and Cossacks engaged in agriculture, who employ no help for the purpose of making profit. [The definition of productive work is omitted in the Constitution of 1925. See Collected Laws—in Russian—No. 30, Article 218, 1925.]

(b) Soldiers of the Soviet Army and Navy.

(c) Citizens of the preceding categories who have to any degree lost their ability to work."

The Constitution of 1918 was published in the *Nation* for January 4, 1919.

[55]P. C. Act, 1918, section 12.

[56]*Ibid.,* section 12, last part.

[57]*Ibid.,* sections 13 and 14.

[58]*Ibid.,* sections 16, 17, 18 and 20.

the court was given the power to inflict punishments, or "take measures for social protection", as the phrase runs, in accordance with its own conviction, and the authority to declare an absolute or conditional suspension of sentence.[59] In the same direction ran the provision which gave the court the power to liberate a prisoner before his term was over, on his own petition or that of his close relations.[60]

The predominant idea that the only system fit for a revolutionary government consists of a single criminal court was thus put into effect. The congress of the Communist Party, the organized body which shaped the principles of the government, triumphantly stated the new doctrine in the following words: "The Soviet Government has replaced the former endless series of courts of justice with their various grades by a very simplified uniform system of people's courts accessible to the people and devoid of useless delay".[61]

3. The People's Court Act of 1920

In October, 1920, a new People's Court Act was adopted.[62] The new act differed little from its predecessor of 1918, but the few changes that were made clearly indicate the prevailing tendency to shift the control over the judiciary from the local authorities to the more important and more dependable higher central bodies. Accordingly, the Act of 1920 provided that the number of people's courts in each district was to be determined by the provincial *(gubernia)* executive committee with the approval of the Commissariat of Justice,[63] and not by the county or city soviets as under the act of 1918. In line with the new tendency was the provision that the people's judges were to have their election confirmed by the provincial executive committee.[64] The power to recall a judge was still left with the local soviets, but an important restriction was introduced. The local soviets were to report any proposed recall of a judge to the provincial

[59] *Ibid.*, section 23.
[60] *Ibid.*, section 79.
[61] Programme of the Russian Communist (Bolshevik) Party, article 11, adopted at the eighth conference of the party in March, 1919, and published in English by the Third International, Moscow, 1919.
[62] Collected Laws, No. 83, Article 420, 1920.
[63] *Ibid.*, section 3.
[64] *Ibid.*, section 14.

executive committee with their reasons in detail and the latter was to decide the question after learning the opinion of its own department of justice.[65]

The idea of exercising authority over the judiciary from the provincial center began to make headway. To make the control more effective, a department of justice was organized, attached to each provincial executive committee. Such a department consisted of a group of associates *(collegium)* with a supervisor, who was a member of the provincial executive committee and the representative of the group. The members were appointed by the provincial executive committee, but the appointment of the supervisor was to be confirmed by the Commissariat of Justice. This department of justice was to guide and unify the activities of the local judicial institutions.[66] For similar purposes county bureaus of justice were instituted to perform the administrative functions of the provincial department of justice within the particular county. The county bureau was also given the additional duty of compiling and preparing the rolls of the people's co-judges.[67]

The procedure of preparing these rolls was described in great detail by a special act. The names of the prospective co-judges were to be sent into the county bureau by the different factory committees, trade unions, workers laboring at their own homes, *volost* executive committees, and so on, and were to be accompanied by appropriate observations as to fitness, members of the Communist Party being specifically noted.[68] From these lists the county bureau was to compile one general list and another special list containing the names of the more intelligent candidates for co-judgeship. The members of this special list were to be assigned for service in the more complicated and important cases.[69]

[65]*Ibid.*, section 15.

[66]Act on Departments of Justice attached to the Provincial Executive Committees, Collected laws, 1919, No. 2, Article 29, sections 1, 2, 3 and 4. *(Ob Otdelakh Yustitzi Gubernskikh Ispolnitelnikh Komitetov, (Polozhenie) Sobranie Uzakonenii*, 1919, 2-29).

[67]Instruction as to the manner of preparing the lists of the People's Co-judges, Collected Laws, 1920, No. 100, Article 542, section 1. (*Instruktziya O Poryadke Sostavleniya Spiskov Narodnikh Zasedateli, Sobranie Uzakenoneii*, 1920, 100-542.)

[68]*Ibid.*, section 2.

[69]*Ibid.*, sections 4 and 9.

d. *The Special Session and the Waiting Court*

Just as the principle of "judges elected by the people", proclaimed by the Bolsheviks of 1903, was denounced by them as "a formula of burgeois democracy" in 1919, so the new doctrine of a "very simplified uniform system of people's court" began to lose ground by the end of 1920.[70] True, the "single court" idea was still, at least nominally, retained, but new wings to the court's structure began to appear. By the Act of December, 1920,[71] two special branches of the people's court were created. One was the waiting court *(Dizhurnaya Kamera)*. This was a court to dispose of simple cases which did not require any investigation or preliminary inquiry. Such cases were tried on the day of arrest by a judge and two co-judges, provided the permanent judge on duty at the special court considered the facts and the the material of the case sufficiently simple and clear; otherwise he transferred it to the regular people's court, stating his reasons for so doing.[72]

The second new branch was designed, on the other hand, for particularly complicated cases. Both special courts were to function either at the provincial capitals, under the immediate supervision of the soviet of people's judges, or at the county seat, under the direction of the county bureau of justice.[73] The jurisdiction of the special branch for complicated cases was over a number of specified offenses, such as speculation on a large scale, offenses in public office, the manufacturing of liquor without a permit, and so on. In addition to these cases, the Commissariat of Justice, the soviet of people's judges, or the county bureau of justice, could transfer cases to this special branch whenever they considered a case of vital state or social interest.[74] Over it presided a member of the soviet of people's judges, or a member of the county bureau, but all the rules of procedure in the regular

[70]Krylenko points out that, strictly speaking, there has never existed a system of one criminal court only. For even by the Acts of 1918 and 1920, the people's court consisted of different branches which tried various kinds of offenses.

[71]Special Sessions of the People's Court Act, Collected Laws, 1920, No. 100, Article 541. *(Ob osobykh sesiyakh Narodnovo suda. Sobranie Uzakonenii*, 100-541, 1920.)

[72]*Ibid.*, Part II, section 5.

[73]*Ibid.*, Part I, section 1 and Part II, section 1.

[74]*Ibid.*, Part I, section 3.

people's court were, without exception, applicable.[75] In the sessions of the waiting court, all the people's judges in the district were to sit in rotation, as arranged by the soviet of people's judges, or the county bureau of justice.[76]

The sentences, decrees, and decisions of all branches of the people's courts were subject to a complaint by way of cassation to the soviet of people's judges.[77]

e. *The Soviet of People's Judges—The Courts of Cassation*

An assembly of people's judges was inaugurated, as we have already learned, by the First Decree, which retained for the new court the old term *siyezd* (assembly). This first act did not define the composition of the assembly, nor did it describe its powers and duties. It is quite conceivable that it was intended to have the county assembly of people's judges function on the same basis as had its predecessor before the Revolution, since the imperial laws were not totally wiped out. This assumption is supported by the fact that even the Order of July, 1918,[78] which devoted a number of sections to the county soviet of the people's judges, which was now no longer called the assembly, modeled it, in many respects, after the assembly of the justices of the peace of Imperial Russia. But the People's Court Act of 1918 gave to this court a new aspect, added to its vigor and prestige, and invested it with powers unknown to the similar assembly of justices of Tzarist Russia.

The local character of the old assembly was entirely discarded. The act provided[79] that "All the people's judges within a province, or similar territorial unit, shall comprise a judicial district". Within such judicial district there was to be instituted a soviet of people's judges whose function was to review, by way of cassation, cases originally heard at the people's court, and to have immediate control over the activities of the people's court.[80] Unlike the old system under which an assembly of all the local judges of a given territory sat as a higher court, the judges

[75] *Ibid.*, sections 4 and 5.
[76] *Ibid.*, Part II, section 2.
[77] P. C. Act, 1918, section 75.
[78] See *Supra*, note 41.
[79] P. C. Act, 1918, section 81.
[80] *Ibid.*, section 82.

would now merely participate in the creation and organization of such a court, which was to consist of (a) the president of the soviet of people's judges and his deputy; (b) from two to five permanent members of the soviet; (c) one temporary judge from among the people's judges in the district who sat in rotation. The president, his deputy, and the permanent members were elected at a conference of all the people's judges of the province, and in the cities of Moscow and Petrograd—now Leningrad—at a general meeting of the people's judges of the city, from among their own members, and these were to constitute the presidium of the soviet of people's judges. The members of the presidium were subject to recall by the provincial, or, in the case of Moscow and Petrograd, the city executive committee on its own initiative, as well as on the recommendation of the provincial or city soviet of the people's judges.[81]

By the People's Court Act of 1920,[82] the authority of the provincial executive committee over the soviet of people's judges was further extended. The election of the latter's presidium was henceforth to be subject to confirmation by the provincial executive body and, in the event that the provincial executive body failed to confirm, the latter was vested with authority to appoint a temporary presidium from among the people's judges of the province until another gathering of the judges was convoked. The obvious tendency to broaden the power of the provincial executive committee with regard to the judiciary was in evidence everywhere.

The soviet of people's judges had a number of divisions—civil, criminal, and so forth. Each division was supervised by a member of the presidium. When sitting as a court of cassation, or as a court to hear special complaints, *i. e.*, a complaint against an order or a decision other than a verdict or judgment, the court was composed of three judges, one member of the presidium and two judges from the people's judges of the province, who were to serve for a period of not more than two weeks. The task of arranging the system was left to the provincial soviet of the

[81] *Ibid.*, sections 83 and 84.
[82] P. C. Act, 1920, section 86.

people's judges.[83] The number of judges composing this tribunal was fixed at three by the Act of 1920, whereas by the previous Act of 1918 five judges (two of whom were members of the presidium) sat as a court of cassation, and three judges sat at the hearing of special complaints.

As a court of cassation, the powers of the soviet of people's judges were impressive. It had the power to reverse any judgment, verdict, or decision where it found a substantial violation or incorrect application of the law, or a violation of the established forms of procedure. All these were the normal powers of a court of cassation in the Russian system of jurisprudence. But the Soviet system added a new and extremely broad discretionary power to the court of cassation by providing that it might also reverse a verdict or sentence if it was manifestly unjust.[84] This important innovation was introduced by the Order of 1918, and has survived all the numerous changes in the Soviet judicial system.

The power of the court to look into matters which might warrant annulment of the verdict was unlimited. Thus it was provided that "The soviet of the people's judges, when reviewing a case, shall not be limited by the scope of the cassational complaint, nor by the reasons assigned therein."[85] When the verdict was reversed or annulled the case was sent to a different people's court within the district with a statement, explaining in what respect the law had been violated or misapplied, and these explanations were binding on the court retrying the case.[86]

f. *The Supreme Judicial Control*

A discussion of the ordinary courts during the first period would be incomplete without mentioning the special Act of March, 1921,[87] which created the court known as the Supreme Judicial Control. This act was a new and important step in the direction of

[83] *Ibid.*, section 88.
[84] P. C. Act, 1918, section 89.
[85] *Ibid.*, section 90.
[86] *Ibid.*, section 92.
[87] Supreme Judicial Control Act, Collected Laws, 1921, No. 15, Article 97. *(Polozhenie o vysshem sudebnom Kontrole. Sobranie Uzakonenii,* 15-97, 1921.)

rigorous centralization. In the words of a Russian writer,[88] "The act revealed the beginning of the centralization policy which was to permeate the soviet system in later years." Unlike the Supreme Judicial Control proposed by the Second Decree of 1918, the Control created by the Act of 1921 was not to be a high court springing up from the base, but an institution for supervision and control superimposed from above.

What were the functions of this new institution? The act stated that for the purpose of working out a correct and uniform system of supervision over all the judicial organs of the Russian Socialist Federative Soviet Republic, and to furnish them with the necessary interpretation of Soviet law, for which, we may safely assume, there was a crying need, the Commissariat of Justice should function as the Supreme Judicial Control. As such it was given the power to review any verdict or sentence which was not yet legally binding, that is, when the time for making a complaint from the verdict or sentence of the trial court had not yet expired; or, in exceptional cases, even those already binding,[89] but subject to be reopened, for example, on submission of newly discovered evidence, and so on. The act specified on what grounds a judgment might be "recognized", that is, reversed, by the Supreme Judicial Control, and under what circumstances a binding verdict might be reopened. The important feature of this Supreme Judicial Control was that it functioned at the administrative center, and that it could demand the record of any case on its own initiative or on the recommendation of a number of different central executive bodies. The grounds upon which the Supreme Judicial Control could take action were a clear violation of Soviet law or a failure to apply it, the taking of jurisdiction over a case which was not subject to judicial proceedings at all, of the rendering of a verdict which clearly contravened Soviet policies.[90] When the Supreme Judicial Control "recognized" a case, as the phrase goes, it was remanded to the proper court for retrial.[91]

The Supreme Judicial Control, as the word "Control" indicates, was not a court of cassation to which defendant or prose-

[88]Temoshev, page 218.
[89]Supreme Judicial Control Act, op. cit., *supra,* note 87.
[90]*Ibid.,* section 2.
[91]*Ibid.,* section 7.

cutor turned to seek redress. The soviet of people's judges remained the only court of cassation, even after the institution of the Supreme Judicial Control. Its purpose and power were to interfere when its attention was called by central executive bodies to cases requiring its intervention.

Such was the system of criminal courts on the eve of the judicial reform of 1922.

III. REVOLUTIONARY TRIBUNALS

(November 24, 1917 to January 1, 1923)

From a legal point of view, the historical significance of the revolutionary tribunals which for five years flourished in the vast territory of Sovietland, lies in their service as "experimental laboratories", where the theories of Soviet "class justice" went through stages of test and cultivation. One thing, however, is to be remembered. Notwithstanding the extraordinary conditions surrounding the revolutionary tribunals, they were, nevertheless, orderly judicial institutions, following prescribed procedure with definite powers, functions and jurisdiction. Besides these judicial tribunals there was the dreadful *Cheka,* which by the Act of June, 1919,[92] was given discretionary power to impose penalties, including death, in areas under martial law. The *Cheka* could exercise this formidable power against persons charged with political or semi-political offenses such as treason, espionage, participation in counter revolutionary activities, wilful destruction of railroad property, etc. There also existed non-judicial tribunals during the bloodiest period of the civil war, such as the special tribunal attached to the *Cheka,*[93] but these, as well as the *Cheka* itself, were clearly non-judicial, repressive commissions, and not part of the regular judicial system.[94]

[92]Collected Laws, No. 27, Article 301, 1919. *(Sobranie Uzakonenii, 27-301, 1919.)*

[93]Collected Laws, No. 53, Article 504, 1919. *(Sobranie Uzakonenii, 53-504, 1919.)* The trials before this tribunal were public, but there were no prescribed rules of procedure.

[94]It is a common fallacy to consider the cheka as ever being a part of the Soviet judicial system, as it has often been said to be by writers in our legal periodicals. Mr. Allan J. Carter in an article entitled "The Bolshevist Substitute for a Judicial System", *Illinois Law Review,* Vol. 16, page 345, states (at page 345) that in the place of the old imperial court system

a. *The Instructions of December, 1917*

The First Decree of November, 1917, as we have already seen, created the revolutionary tribunals, consisting of a president and six co-judges, and the same decree laid down in general terms the extent of their jurisdiction.[95] This decree was soon followed by another act, the Instructions of December, 1917,[96] which gave the tribunals some shape and form. This act is of the most arresting interest to any student of the history of Soviet judicial structure. It exhibits a dualism of antagonistic types of judicial institutions. The extra-normal judicial character of the tribunals is apparent in the very nature of their jurisdiction. They were to try cases dealing with organized insurrections, sabotage against the government, wilful destruction of necessaries, etc.[97] On the other hand, they were to be open, public courts, with both prosecution and defense participating in the trial, which was conducted by a permanent judge and six temporary people's co-judges whose names were drawn by lot from the general list of co-judges. A stenographic record of the proceedings was to be kept.[98] A harsh feature of these tribunals was that their decisions were final. If, however, established rules were violated, or the elements of a clearly unjust verdict were visible, the Commissar of Justice had the authority to turn over

the "Bolsheviks created three new types". The most important of the three, he says, was the "Extraordinary Commission, familiarly known as the * * * chaika". (Should be cheka.)

Professor Pitrim Sorokin, *Mich. Law Review*, Vol. 23, page 38, declares that "At that moment (before 1922) there practically existed almost no courts, and no trials excepting that of the cheka". Further: "In 1919 there appeared the people's courts, but they did not play any rôle and existed principally on paper."

Whatever one may think of the cheka, as a government agency, it had never been considered by the Soviet authorities as a court, or as a substitute for a judicial system. It was created for the obvious purpose of suppressing those who opposed the Bolshevik Revolution. After all, the vast majority of criminal cases have not been of any political significance at all. After the abortive revolution of 1905, the Tzarist government set up special field tribunals which tried and condemned people to death in absolute secrecy. No matter how abhorrent those field tribunals were to the liberals of Russia, no one pointed to them as being a part of the judicial system of Russia.

[95]First Decree, section 8.

[96]Instructions to the Revolutionary Tribunals. Collected Laws, No. 12, Article 170, 1917. *(Instruktziya Revolyutzionomu Tribunalu.)*

[97]*Ibid.*, section 1.

[98]*Ibid.*, sections 3, 4 and 6.

the case to the All-Russian Central Executive Committee with a recommendation that a new trial be granted.[99] In contrast to the denial of the right to a review, the pendulum swung toward moderation when the act provided that the tribunal was to be limited in its power of punishment to "imposing a fine, imprisonment, banishment from the capital, designated locality or the borders of the R.S.F.S.R., public rebuke, declaring the defendant an enemy of the people, depriving him of all or some of his political rights, confiscation of his property or forced public labor"[100] without imprisonment. Even upon those who might organize insurrections in times of revolution and civil war, capital punishment or even hard labor in Siberia (Katorga) was not to be imposed. Thus, two diametrically opposed tendencies—harshness and severity on the one hand and liberalism on the other—were brought to play in the same act.

The local soviets elected the personnel of the tribunals, which consisted of one president, his two permanent deputies, and forty co-judges. The president judge and his two deputies were subject to recall by the same soviets that elected them.[101]

The tribunals organized upon the basis of the Act of December, 1917, differed from the people's courts only with respect to the number of co-judges sitting, the tribunals having six, while only two sat at the court. Though they differed little from the courts, the tribunals sprang up everywhere. It is quite possible that the name itself—revolutionary tribunal—appealed to the imagination of the local soviets. Every village was anxious to have its own revolutionary tribunal, which sat sometimes even as a divorce court.[102] They were far from being stern—as one would expect. According to a Soviet writer, the tribunals were, at that time, so mild that "Their softness with regard to sentences discredited them completely."[103]

The situation just described was not to last long. The Act of May, 1918,[104] abolished the numerous local tribunals, and such

[99] *Ibid.*, section 11.

[100] *Ibid.*, section 2.

[101] *Ibid.*, section 3.

[102] Krylenko. *The Judicial System*, page 82.

[103] Krylenko, Soviet Law *(Sovetskoe Pravo)*, 1922, No. 3, page 55.

[104] On Revolutionary Tribunals, Collected Laws, No. 35, Article 471, 1918. *(O Revolyutzionykh Tribunalakh, Sobranie Uzakonenii*, 35-471, 1918.)

institutions were henceforth to exist only in the provincial capitals, at the county seats and in important industrial centers.[105] This was the first step towards making the tribunals organs of the central authorities.

b. *The Act of June, 1918*

Another important step was taken by the Act of June, 1918.[106] By this act a Special Revolutionary Tribunal attached to the All-Russian Central Executive Committee was created. It was a tribunal of original jurisdiction for very important cases which the president of the All-Russian Central Executive Committee, or the Soviet of the People's Commissars might take out of the jurisdiction of the ordinary tribunals.

The Special Revolutionary Tribunal was to consist of one president and six judges, all appointed by the All-Russian Central Executive Committee, and subject to recall by it. An investigating commission at the special tribunal was also provided.[107] There are two important changes to be noted. First, the highest central governing body was to have its own revolutionary tribunal for especially important cases, and second, this act instituted the first tribunal in which there was to be no participation of people's co-judges. The latter feature was soon to become general for all revolutionary tribunals.

As the civil war with all its horrors rose to unusual proportions, the liberal or humane tendencies of the first acts on revolutionary tribunals began to grow weaker, while their harsher aspects became more pronounced. The bar against the infliction of extreme punishments was lifted. The Act of June, 1918,[108] repealed the previous acts and provided that "The revolutionary tribunals, when selecting measures [punishments] to combat counter-revolutionary activities, sabotage, etc. * * * are not

[105] *Ibid.*, section 1.

[106] On the Revolutionary Tribunal attached to The All-Russian Central Executive Committee of the Soviets. Collected Laws, No. 41, Article 520, 1918. *(O Revolyutzionnom Tribunale Pri Vserossiiskom Tzentralnom Ispolnitelnom Komitete Sovetov. Sobranie Uzakonenii,* 41-520, 1918.)

[107] *Ibid.*, sections 1, 2 and 3.

[108] On Repealing all the Previously Issued Decrees on Revolutionary Tribunals, Collected Laws, No. 44, Article 533, 1918. *(Ob Otmene Vzekh donyne Izdannykh Tzirkulyarov o Revolyutzionnykh Tribunalakh, Sobranie Uzakonenii,* 44-533, 1918.)

bound by any limitations[109] * * *." Thus the coming of the new era of harshness and severity was heralded. In the opinion of Dr. Shteinberg, the first Commissar of Justice after the *coup d'état* of November, 1917, the introduction of capital punishment meant nothing less than the destruction of one of the Revolution's loftiest institutions—the revolutionary tribunals. These, the author of the Instructions on Tribunals of December, 1917, insists, were designed originally to serve during the difficult period of transition as instruments to develop "the revolutionary sense of justice", and a socially moral self-consciousness, and not as organs of vengeance, aiming at the physical destruction of an adversary.[110]

c. *The Act of April, 1919*

The sternness and determinedness of the new type of revolutionary tribunal became apparent with the passage of the Act of April, 1919,[111] which was to replace all the previous enactments on revolutionary tribunals.[112] This last act left no room for ambiguity with regard to the character of the tribunals. They were "instituted specifically for the purpose of trying cases involving counter-revolutionary activities and other acts [a sweeping inclusion] which were directed against all the achievaments of the Revolution, or were designed to weaken the authority of the Soviet government."[113] The tribunals were clearly given unlimited powers in deciding upon measures of repression. The tendency to limit the operation of the tribunals only to the larger centers was carried a step farther. The tribunals were now to exist in the provincial capitals, and in other cities of over 200,000 inhabitants,[114] which were considered very large cities. This act also

[109] *Ibid.*, section 2.

[110] Dr. Z. Shteinberg, *The Moral Face of the Revolution* (in Russian), Berlin, 1923, page 36.

[111] Revolutionary Tribunals Act, Collected Laws, No. 113, Article 132, 1919. *(O Revolyutzionykh Tribyunalakh, Sobranie Uzakonenii,* 13-132, 1919.)

[112] This Act was the result of a compromise between two opposing tendencies, represented by the *Cheka* and the People's Commissariat of Justice respectively. The former's views were incorporated by the establishment of a trial court of three judges instead of five without the participation of co-judges. The Commissariat of Justice on the other hand, had checked some of the ideas of the *Cheka.* See Krylenko, *Jud. System,* page 106.

[113] Revolutionary Tribunals Act, *op. cit., supra,* note 111, section 1.

[114] *Ibid.*, section 2.

provided for a special commission to conduct a preliminary inquiry, described the powers as well as the limitations of this commission, and created a Supreme Tribunal for cases of original jurisdiction, instead of the previous Special Revolutionary Tribunal attached to the All-Russian Central Executive Committee. All these points were incorporated in, and will be discussed in connection with, the Tribunals Act of April, 1920.[115]

d. *The Revolutionary Tribunals Act of 1920*

This significant and elaborate legislation was enacted as the basic law for all the revolutionary tribunals. It repealed all the previous acts pertaining to tribunals, and also provided for the outright abolition of all the non-judicial powers of the *Cheka,* and the All-Russian Special Revolutionary Tribunal. Henceforth all the tribunals, even the extraordinary military ones, were to comply with the provisions of the basic act or be abolished.[116]

This remarkable provision, to be sure, was not due to any rejuvenation of liberal ideas. Far from that! The counter-revolution had spent itself and the state of civil war was on the decline. The government apparently felt itself strong enough to dispense with the non-judicial commissions for oppression, while simultaneously strengthening the judicial revolutionary tribunals. The powers of the tribunals, as a consequence, became enormous. They had jurisdiction over cases of counter-revolutionary acts, speculation on a large scale, important cases of misfeasance in office, and so on. But the true scope of their jurisdiction is suggested by the provision that the tribunals could take jurisdiction over any case which they might recognize as dangerous to the Soviet Republic.[117] Their power to inflict punishment was also unrestricted for "they could fix any measure of repression".[118] The tribunals were to be instituted in the provincial capitals. The local soviets could establish a tribunal also in a city having a popu-

[115]Revolutionary Tribunals Act, Collected Laws, Nos. 22 and 23, Article 115, 1920. *(O Revolyutzionykh Tribunalakh, Polozhenie. Sobranie Uzakonenii,* 22 & 23-115, 1920.)

[116]*Ibid.,* section 5.

[117]*Ibid.,* section 2.

[118]*Ibid.,* section 1.

lation of over 200,000,[119] but only with the consent of the Commissariat of Justice, which was not required in 1919.

The revolutionary tribunals consisted of one president judge and two members. One of the latter had to be a member of the provincial department *(Collegium)* of the extraordinary commission *(Cheka)*. The judges were elected by the local and the provincial executive committee. The soviets electing the judges were to report the results of the election to the Cassational Tribunal,[120] since the latter had the right to challenge the fitness of the president judge elected, stating the reasons for the challenge. To facilitate the work of the tribunals, the provincial executive committee could organize one or more tribunals, consisting of three judges each, to go on circuit under the direction of its president judge.[121] All the judges were to be elected for the short period of three months and could be re-elected, but were also subject to recall.[122]

By this Act of 1920, the entire machinery was installed for the proper functioning of the special judicial institutions or tribunals. There were to be appointed special inquisitor-reporters, who were to conduct the preliminary inquiry and present the case to the administrative session of the tribunal. The latter was to appoint one of its judges to supervise the activities of the inquisitor-reporters.[123] The control of the tribunal over these quasi-judicial officers was so complete that even their decisions as to searches, seizures, fixing of bail, and so on, were binding only after approval by the president of the tribunal, on the advice of the supervising judge. In order to discontinue a case even greater restrictions were imposed. To accomplish this, the decision of the plenum, or full session of the tribunal, was required.[124] Every judge of a tribunal had the authority to visit a prison and set free those unlawfully held.[125]

Despite all their crudeness, the tribunals did not lack the characteristics of a normal judicial court. The sessions were open

[119] *Ibid.*, section 3.
[120] See *infra*, page 43.
[121] Revolutionary Tribunal Act, *op. cit., supra*, note 115, section 6.
[122] *Ibid.*, section 7.
[123] *Ibid.*, section 9.
[124] *Ibid.*, section 10.
[125] *Ibid.*, section 12.

and public; the defendant had to be present, except when he consented to be tried in his absence, or it was clearly proved that he had absconded; a protocol of all the important matters at the trial was to be made; the accused had the right to interrogate the witnesses, make statements at any moment during the trial, and was always to have the final word.[126] In contrast to the first acts on revolutionary tribunals, this Act of 1920 did away with the absolute right of the accused to have counsel. The tribunal was to determine at its administrative session whether this should be permitted. But if the prosecutor was allowed to participate, the defendant might engage his own counsel, or the court would appoint one.[127] In accordance with the general character of the tribunals, the act provided that "The judges rendering the decision are to be guided exclusively by the circumstances of the case, and the interest of the Proletarian Revolution.[128]

1. The Supreme Revolutionary Tribunal—A Trial Court

Besides the provincial tribunals, the Act of 1920 also instituted a Supreme Revoluntionary Tribunal, attached to the All-Russian Central Executive Committee. This tribunal was not, as the name might indicate, a court of appeal or cassation, but a high tribunal of original jurisdiction only. This tribunal was to consist of a president and two members, all appointed by the presidium of the All-Russian Central Executive Committee. It was to take original jurisdiction in very important cases directed to it by the president of the All-Russian Extraordinary Commission, the People's Commissariat of Justice, or the presidium of the Central Executive Committee.[129] This high tribunal was to have its own inquisitorial commission to investigate the cases to be tried by it. All other rules and regulations set forth in the

[126]*Ibid.*, sections 18, 21 and 23.

[127]*Ibid.*, section 17. There are many cases tried in the Soviet courts without the participation of either the procurator, as the representative of the State, or the private prosecutor. The person injured or aggrieved appears merely as a witness as any other witness for or against the defendant. In such trials there is no particular person to conduct the prosecution. The court examines the witnesses and then decides the case.

[128]*Ibid.*, section 24.

[129]*Ibid.*, section 39.

basic Act of 1920, with regard to revolutionary tribunals were also applicable to the Supreme Revolutionary Tribunal.[130]

The verdicts, decisions and decrees of all the revolutionary tribunals except the Supreme Revolutionary Tribunal were subject to a complaint by way of cassation.

e. *Cassation and Supervision*

1. Early Development in the Revolutionary Tribunals

At an early stage in the development of the revolutionary tribunals some method for reviewing their decisions was provided for. By the Act of February, 1918,[131] a Department of Cassation[132] to take up complaints against verdicts and decisions of the tribunals was created and attached to the Commissariat of Justice of the Republic. The authority of the Department was very limited. It could either dismiss the complaint as groundless, or forward it to the Central Executive Committee for further action. Such an arrangement was in harmony with the early Act of December, 1917, stating that there should be no cassational complaints against the verdicts of the tribunals.[133] The next step was taken by the Act of June, 1918,[134] which also provided for a Department of Cassation attached to the Central Executive Committee. This Department, which consisted of a president appointed by the Soviet of People's Commissars and approved by the Central Executive Committee, and two judges—one representing the Commissariat of Justice, and the other delegated by the Central Executive Committee[135]—had all the characteristics of a cassational institution. Whenever it found that the law had been violated or misapplied by the revolutionary tribunal at the trial, it could reverse the verdict or the sentence

[130] *Ibid.*, section 40.

[131] On the Cassational Division of the People's Commissariat of Justice, Collected Laws, No. 21, Article 314, 918. *(O Kassatzionnom OtDelenii Narodnvo Kommissariata Yustitzii, Sobranie Uzakonenii,* 21-314, 1918.)

[132] The first act on the Revolutionary tribunals did not allow any cassation.

[133] See *supra,* note 96.

[134] On instituting of a Cassational Department at the All-Russian Central Executive Committee of the Soviets. Collected Laws, No. 45, Article 545, 1918. (*Ob Uchrezhdenii Kassatzionnovo Otdella Pri Ispolnitelnom Komitete Sovetov Sobranie Uzakonenii,* 45-545, 1918.)

[135] *Ibid.*, section 2.

and remand the case for retrial to a different tribunal.[136] But if no law, either substantive or procedural, was violated, but the sentence was unjust, the Department could refer the case to the Central Executive Committee with appropriate recommendations, the latter having the power to reduce the punishment or discontinue the case without ordering a new trial.[137] The provisions of this act were, with a few unimportant modifications, incorporated in the Act of 1919,[138] and thereafter such a form of cassation was in effect for some time.

2. The Cassational Tribunal

The Cassational Department was not yet a high tribunal empowered to supervise and guide the provincial tribunals. A tribunal entrusted with such functions was created by the already discussed basic Act of 1920.[139] A Cassational Tribunal was instituted by that act for the purpose of organizing a uniform procedure in all the revolutionary tribunals, supervising their activities, determining procedural and other questions, as well as reviewing cassational complaints against verdicts and decisions of the provincial revolutionary tribunals.

The Cassational Tribunal, which was not a mere department, as heretofore, was to consist of a president, chosen by the Central Executive Committee from among the members of the Commissariat of Justice, and two judges. The president of the Revolutionary Military Tribunal, and the President of the Supreme Revolutionary Tribunal were to be members *ex-officio*.[140] There was also to be a special member-reporter, who was to prepare the cases and state his conclusions but could not participate in the deliberations in the consulting chambers[141] where the verdict was decided upon.

The Cassational Tribunal had the same authority as the former Cassational Department with regard to the granting of a new trial where rules of law or forms of procedure were violated. But unlike the Department, the Cassational Tribunal could also

[136]*Ibid.*, section 7.
[137]*Ibid.*, section 8.
[138]Revolutionary Tribunals of 1919, *op. cit., supra*, note 111.
[139]Revolutionary Tribunals of 1920, *op. cit., supra*, note 115.
[140]*Ibid.*, section 28.

act, instead of merely offering recommendation, where the verdict was regarded as unjust. The decision in the latter instance would, however, have to be sent to the Central Executive Committee for confirmation.[142]

The member-reporter was to take charge of the supervisory functions within the authority of the Cassational Tribunal. He was to report the activities of the provincial and other revolutionary tribunals, recommend necessary changes, and suggest the transfer of any case when he thought advisable to the Cassational Tribunal for review, irrespective of whether a complaint by way of cassation had been entered.[143]

f. *The Unification Act of 1921*

The entire scheme of supervising and controlling the tribunals was perfected by the Unification Act of 1921.[144] This Act did not repeal the previous enactments on revolutionary tribunals. It merely developed some parts of the Act of 1920, leaving the latter basic law intact. All the provincial or other local revolutionary tribunals, also the military and the military transport tribunals, the Supreme Revolutionary Tribunal connected with the Central Executive Committee, and the Cassational Tribunal, were united into a comprehensive system consisting of two units only—the provincial revolutionary tribunals and the Supreme Revolutionary Tribunal. As the provincial tribunals were left practically unchanged by the Act of 1921, we shall concern ourselves only with the newly instituted Supreme Revolutionary Tribunal.

1. The Supreme Revolutionary Tribunal

The numerous functions of the Supreme Revolutionary Tribunal were alloted to (a) the plenum, (b) four different departments—the cassational, the judicial, the military, and the mili-

[141] *Ibid.*, section 30.
[142] *Ibid.*, section 35.
[143] *Ibid.*, section 37.
[144] An Act concerning the uniting of all the Revolutionary Tribunals of the Republic. Collected Laws, No. 51, Article 294, 1921. *(Ob Ob'edinonii Vsekh Revolyutsionykh Tribunalov Respubliki. Sobranie Uzakonenii,* 51-294, 1921.)

tary transport—and (c) the territorial branches of the Supreme Revolutionary Tribunal.[145]

(a) *The Plenum*

The Plenum consisted of all the presidents of the various departments of the Supreme Revolutionary Tribunal, a special member-reporter and a representative of the All-Russian Extraordinary Commission.

The president of the Supreme Revolutionary Tribunal and his deputy, who was also the member-reporter, were elected by the Central Executive Committee, the president being selected from among the members of the Commissariat of Justice,[146] thus assuring the highest tribunal usually of a legally trained man as its head.

The underlying purpose of the Act of 1921, complete centralization, found its full expression and reached its summit in the provisions dealing with the plenum. In the plenum were concentrated all the powers of complete control and of absolute revision in matters relating to any revolutionary tribunal of the Republic.[147] All the powers of control which were vested in the Cassational Tribunal by the basic Act of 1920 were now transferred to the plenum of the new Supreme Revolutionary Tribunal. In a similar way the authority of the member-reporter of the previous Cassational Tribunal was shifted to the member-reporter of the plenum.

The idea of having a high court of original jurisdiction, such as the Supreme Revolutionary Tribunal prior to 1921, whose decisions would be absolutely final, was given up. The judicial department of the Supreme Revolutionary Tribunal, analogous in the scope of its jurisdiction to the Supreme Revolutionary Tribunal attached to the Central Executive Committee, was deprived of the attribute of infallibility. Its verdicts and decision, as indeed the verdicts and decisions of all the departments of the Supreme Revolutionary Tribunal, including even the Department of Cassation, were subject to reversal by way of supervision by

[145] *Ibid.*, section 2.
[146] *Ibid.*, section 3.
[147] *Ibid.*, section 6.

the plenum. The latter was subordinated only to the presidium of the Central Executive Committee, and the People's Commissariat of Justice, acting as the Supreme Judicial Control.[148]

(b) *The Four Departments*

1. The Department of Cassation

The most important among the departments of the Supreme Revolutionary Tribunal was undoubtedly that of cassation. It was made up of the president of the plenum or his deputy, a member-reporter (not the one holding this office in the plenum), and two members from among the judges of the Supreme Revolutionary Tribunal who sat in rotation as arranged by the plenum at its administrative sessions.[149] The department of cassation, like its predecessor, the Cassational Tribunal, was to take up complaints against verdicts or sentences of the provincial revolutionary tribunals, or the military or the military transport tribunals. All the rules laid down in the basic Act of 1920 with regard to the Cassational Tribunal were now applicable to the cassational department.[150]

2. Judicial Department

The judicial department was composed of a president, his deputy and four judges, all appointed by the All-Russian Central Executive Committee.[151] This department was to try originally cases of exceptional importance directed to it by the Central Executive Committee, the All-Russian Extraordinary Commission, or the People's Commissariat of Justice. The order of the Central Executive Committee to try a certain case was binding upon the judicial department, but it could refuse to take jurisdiction of a case if sent by the other above-mentioned authorities. In case of such refusal the judicial department transferred the case to the appropriate tribunal.[152]

3. The Military and the Military Transport Departments

The military and the military transport departments were organized like the judicial department. These two departments

[148] *Ibid.*, section 6.
[149] *Ibid.*, section 4.
[150] *Ibid.*, section 7.
[151] *Ibid.*, section 5.
[152] *Ibid.*, section 8.

were to supervise the lower military and the military transport tribunals, respectively, and try certain cases of a military character. The significance of these tribunals was rapidly declining. The Unification Act of 1921 provided for the abolition of almost all military and military transport tribunals, leaving only a few here and there. The Central Executive Committee acted thus after "considering the decline of the civil war."[153]

(c) *Territorial Branches*

These branches carried out the functions of the Supreme Revolutionary Tribunal within certain restricted areas. They were also instituted in the autonomous republics with the consent of the latter's higher authorities, upon the approval of the All-Russian Central Executive Committee.

To supply the finishing touch to the entire elaborate scheme of centralization, the Act of 1921 provided that the president, or the deputy president, of the provincial revolutionary tribunals might not be recalled or dismissed by the provincial executive committee (as provided by the Act of 1920) without the sanction of the Supreme Revolutionary Tribunal.

Thus a perfected system of revolutionary tribunals was completed by June, 1921. There were, to be sure, two more acts dealing with the branches of the Supreme Revolutionary Tribunal in the autonomous republics or territories.[154] These acts did not, however, add anything to the fundamental principles or basic structure of the revolutionary tribunals. Even in the autonomous republics the branches of the Supreme Revolutionary Tribunal were to be established with the consent of the all-powerful plenum.[155]

[153] *Ibid.*, section 10.

[154] The Organization of the Supreme Judicial Centers for the Exclusive Courts (Revolutionary Tribunals) in the Independent Republics * * * Collected Laws, No. 62, Article 442, 1921. The other Act is in Collected Laws, No. 11, Article 98, 1922, and is entitled: An Act Concerning the Authority of the Central Executive Committee of the Autonomous Soviet Republics with Regard to Local Revolutionary Tribunals. *(Ob organizatsii Vysshikh Sudebynkh Tsentrov dlya isklyuchitelnykh Sudov * * * vnezavisimykh Sovetskikh Respublikakh * * * Sobranie Uzakonenii,* 62-442, 1921.)

[155] The Act of 1921, *op. cit., supra,* note 144.

IV. SUMMARY

By the end of 1922, after five years of the Soviet régime, the structure of the criminal judiciary presented the following picture:

A decentralized system of normal courts, with some advancement in the direction of centralization but at the most not reaching higher than the provincial authorities. Even the soviet of people's judges, the only court of cassation and supervision, was not subject to the control or influence of the authorities at Moscow. The people's co-judges, two or six, as the case might be, always had the power to override the decision of the permanent judge, since a majority decided.

The Supreme Judicial Control, established in 1921, had only limited powers and could not exercise pressure upon the election or recall of judges.

The entire ordinary court system, as distinguished from the revolutionary tribunals, was apparently very feebly controlled by the ruling party. From the point of view of soviet authorities, this was an intolerable situation and conclusively proved the ineptitude of the entire system. "The best evidence of its sorrowful position", writes N. V. Krylenko, "was the fact that of all the presidents of the soviet of people's judges [the highest office within the ordinary judiciary] forty-nine per cent, were non-party people."[156]

In complete contrast to the ordinary courts, the revolutionary tribunals, which tried political or semi-political offenses, had even the lowest degree in their pyramidal structure, the provincial tribunal, under the control of the provincial executive committee, with some additional supervision from the central authorities. But the tribunal to try important cases originally, and the Supreme Revolutionary Tribunal, which had an absolute power of cassation, supervision and interpretation, were directly and completely under the surveillance of the highest authorities of the Federated Republic. The judges, who were subject to recall at any moment, were the only persons to decide matters of law and policy, since the institution of co-judges was entirely barred from the revolutionary tribunals.

With this picture in mind, we now enter the second period.

[156]Krylenko. *The Jud. System,* page 50.

Chapter II

CRIMINAL COURTS DURING THE SECOND PERIOD

A. The Judicial Reform of 1922 and the First Judiciary Act

The year 1922 will go down in the annals of Soviet judicial history as distinguished for its great judicial reforms. The various scattered decrees and the innumerable regulations and acts were brought together, revised, and arranged in a concrete, judicial system. Codification became the order of the day. Thus, in May, 1922, the first criminal code was signed;[1] the first code of criminal procedure was put into effect in July, 1922;[2] and in November of the same year the first judiciary act was passed.[3]

The latter act, which is of immediate moment to us, and which, more than any other of the above-mentioned codes, effected fundamental changes, was enacted after a thorough discussion in the Soviet legal press, and was, in many respects, shaped at the meetings of the fourth Congress of Soviet Judicial Workers held in 1922 at Moscow. The Judiciary Act, says its promulgator, fully realized the principles laid down at that gathering.[4] The gist of the new policy heralded by that Congress was complete centralization of the entire judicial system, while the principles of a unified court, and a unified system of cassation[5] were to govern.

The general political situation in the country at the end of 1922 necessitated drastic changes in the criminal judicial apparatus. The new economic policy, the *nep*,[6] introduced by Lenin in 1921, was becoming more than a mere temporary retreat of militant Bolshevism; it had, apparently, come to stay. The revo-

[1]Cr. Code, 1922.
[2]Code, 1922.
[3]Jud. Act, 1922.
[4]Krylenko, *The Jud. System*, page 158.
[5]*Ibid.*, page 163.
[6]This word is made up from the initials of the New Economic Policy, which was put in effect in 1921. This new policy consisted mainly in permitting private trade, and giving concessions to private enterprises and capital. The person who avails himself of this opportunity to engage in business or trade was termed the *nepman*.

lutionary tribunals became a dissonance in the new economic chorus in which the voice of the *nepmen,* the new bourgeois class, was far from negligible. On the other hand, this very situation gave impulse to the movement among Soviet leaders which determinedly strove for a more rigid control by the central authorities over the judiciary as a whole. For over three years the ordinary judiciary, in contrast to the revolutionary tribunals, received little attention from Soviet authorities, party and trade union organizations.[7] The existing situation became, from the point of view of Bolshevik leaders, intolerable. The growth of the *nepman* and the concessions which he steadfastly wrung from the hands of the hitherto uncompromising rulers, called for a change in the attitude of soviet leaders towards the criminal courts. The Soviet legal periodical of that period is permeated with the alarming cry "the *nepman* be upon thee, proletariat". "The judicial organs ought to fight with harsh repression those spoliators [i. e. the nepmen] who permit themselves to misuse our new economic policy", writes a member of the Commissariat of Justice.[8] The danger that the *nep* might wipe out even the very nature and proletarian character of the court itself was perceived. That "fear has big eyes" is an old Russian saying. But it is quite possible that the new political situation resulting in the increased activities of the bourgeoisie warranted the apprehension that the Bolsheviks were running "the risk of being drowned by the petty bourgeois wave, and, therefore, the courts must carry through their class encroachment and preserve their own proletarian essence."[9]

The revolutionary tribunal, as already mentioned, had outlived itself. It was frankly admitted that the tribunal was not a court that should be preserved, because it appeared "as the extraordinary organ in a period of transition".[10] The inference was clearly drawn, and Krylenko, the apostle of "class justice", came even at the beginning of 1922 to the conclusion that it was absolutely necessary to "abolish the functions of the extraordinary

[7]Ya. Brandenburgski quoted by Temoshev, page 219.
[8]Ya. Brandenburgski. *The Weekly,* No. 9, 1922.
[9]I. Slavin. "The Courts and the New Economic Policy", *The Weekly,* No. 1, 1922.
[10]A. Lunin, *The Weekly,* No. 15, 1922.

courts", that is, the revolutionary tribunals.[11] The remedy proposed by all Soviet writers was to strengthen the ordinary courts. The proletarian class was to have its own courts and be able to hold them firmly in hand. This was the *leitmotif* of the entire judicial reform of 1922.

The new policy to pay more attention to the working of the judicial machinery found its most characteristic expression in the provision inserted in the preamble of the Judiciary Act of 1922 which stated its purpose "To make it obligatory upon the People's Commissariat of Justice and the chief committee on professional, technical education to submit within a short time to the Soviet of People's Commissars a plan for opening during the year of 1923 not less than ten schools of jurisprudence, and one higher school of jurisprudence at Moscow, in order to prepare a sufficient staff of trained judicial workers".[12]

The Judiciary Act of 1922 did not merely introduce changes or modifications in the judicial structure. The entire judicial system was thrown into a crucible, melted and then remolded into something new and different. True, an experienced assayer would easily find that the new composition contained most of the elements of the previous system; nevertheless, its shape and form were markedly different, and some characteristics—notably the trial of serious cases without the sitting of people's co-judges—had actually disappeared.

A glance at the judicial structure created by this act discloses that the system was to be without any revolutionary tribunals; the people's court, with six co-judges, was dropped, and the special people's session, together with the waiting court, was discarded, (although the retention of the latter was recommended by the fourth Congress of Soviet Judicial Workers which has been mentioned before).[13] The result of all this was that henceforth there was to function a unified system consisting of the following courts: 1. A court with one people's judge sitting; 2. a court composed of one people's judge and two people's co-

[11]About Reforming the Existing Judicial System, *Ibid.*, No. 5, 1922. *(O. Reforme Deistvuyushcshikh Sudebnoi Sistema.)*

[12]Jud. Act, 1922, Preamble, section 3.

[13]*The Weekly*, No. 5, 1922, page 13.

judges; 3. a provincial court; 4. a Supreme Court.[14] While the complete uniformity was somewhat shattered by later legislation, the fundamental framework of the first act has survived to this day. We shall now proceed to describe the Soviet judiciary as it has developed since January 1, 1923, the day when the new act was to take effect.[15]

B. The System Existing in 1930

I. The People's Court

The idea that one type of court, a people's court, should take jurisdiction over all criminal cases began to lose ground, as we have seen, in 1921,[16] and was totally discarded in the Judiciary Act of 1922. The people's court was henceforth to function as a lower court of original jurisdiction akin to the pre-revolutionary court of the peace. This court was now to try criminal cases either (a) by a single judge sitting alone or (b) by one people's judge and two people's co-judges.[17]

a. *The Power and Functions of the Single Judge*

The permanent judge of the people's court when acting alone has a number of important duties to perform. He affirms or disaffirms measures taken by the organs of investigation to prevent absconding;[18] he presents to the administrative session of the full court which consists of one judge and two co-judges, the question of holding the accused for trial;[19] the judge supervises the preparations for holding a court session, and appoints defense counsel whenever it is necessary.[20] In addition, the single judge is vested with the power to conduct a preliminary inquiry in cases in which an inquiry is not absolutely required by law, whereas a preliminary inquiry, if required, is almost always conducted by

[14] Jud. Act, 1922, section 1.

[15] *Ibid.*, Preamble.

[16] See, *supra*, page 29.

[17] Code, 1927, section 24.

[18] *Ibid.*, section 247, subsection 4. See also *infra*, page 162.

[19] By the amendments of October, 1929, the question of holding the accused for court is presented to the administrative session of the court in certain exceptional instances only, for the function of holding for court is transferred to the inquisitor or the procurator.

[20] Code, 1927, section 250.

the inquisitor; the single judge is to conduct an investigation in cases which do not require a preliminary inquiry, to hold persons for court in those special cases which come to the people's court directly and not through the investigating or inquisitory agencies, and to adopt measures to insure the presence of the defendant at the trial.[21]

Besides the innumerable duties and powers of an administrative character vested in the single judge, he is also to act as a court and to dispose of simple, minor criminal cases by way of "judicial order". This innovation in the Soviet system was introduced by the first Code of Criminal Procedure of 1922,[22] which provided that the single judge was to try certain specific offenses in the criminal code. An examination of the criminal code in effect at that time[23] shows that these offenses covered a wide range of violations against public health, public safety and order none of which was punishable by more than three months' forced labor, without imprisonment, or by a fine exceeding three hundred rubles. In addition to this group of offenses, the single judge under the Act of 1922 was given jurisdiction over offenses against labor laws which were punishable by imprisonment not exceeding one year. The jurisdiction of the single judge over the latter offenses was, however, excluded from the Code of Criminal Procedure of February, 1923.[24] This Code became necessary since the passage of the First Judiciary Act of 1922 made the previous codes of criminal procedure unworkable. By later amendments,[25] which are still in effect today, a different group of offenses have been assigned to the jurisdiction of the single people's judge sitting alone. The nature and seriousness of the crimes, however, have not been changed, for none of these violations is punishable by more than three months' forced labor or by a fine exceeding 300 rubles.

b. *Jurisdiction of the People's Court*

The people's court, made up of one permanent judge and two temporary people's co-judges, is the trial court of the Soviet

[21]*Ibid.*, section 247. There is quite a difference between investigation and inquiry as will be explained later. See, *infra*, pages 130, 135-138.
[22]Code, 1922.
[23]Cr. Code, 1922.
[24]Code, 1927.
[25]Collected Laws No. 78, Article 784, 1924 and No. 78, Article 623, 1926.

judiciary which has jurisdiction over the vast majority of criminal cases. In 1924, there were 2,018,246 cases on the trial list at the people's court,[26] while the provincial courts, which try certain more serious cases, as will be explained later, had only 131,888 cases.[27]

The jurisdiction of the people's court is prescribed in an indirect way. The law provides[28] that the people's court is to try all criminal cases within its district except those assigned by law to other branches of the judiciary. Such a method of prescribing the jurisdiction of the people's court was probably intended to preserve the prestige of the court which but recently occupied the high position of the only ordinary criminal court, but it does not alter the material fact that the more important and serious cases are specifically assigned to other courts. The tendency is, however, to enlarge and broaden the scope of the jurisdiction of the people's court, by transferring to it cases previously assigned to the provincial court. By the amendment of October 1, 1924,[29] the jurisdiction of the people's court was considerably increased. In 1925 it was reported that 3251 criminal cases which would have been tried at the provincial court under the original act were transferred as a result of this amendment to the people's court.[30]

c. *Appointment and Recall of People's Judges*

The permanent people's judges are elected for the period of one year, and are eligible for re-election, by the provincial executive committee, and in some specific instances by the city soviets,[31] on the nomination of the provincial court or the people's Commissariat of Justice of the Republic. The judges may be recalled before their term expires by the same authorities that elected

[26] *The Weekly,* No. 30, 1926.
[27] Tarnovski, *Ibid.,* No. 36, 1926.
[28] Jud. Act, 1926, section 6.
[29] Collected Laws No. 78, Article 784, 1924.
[30] *The Weekly,* No. 46, 1925, page 1422.
[31] City Soviets Act. Collected Laws No. 91, Article 662, 1926, section 23, subsection (a). *(Polozhenie O gorodskikh Sovetakh)* provides: "The city soviets of the main cities—capitals—of the autonomous republics, regions, territories, and provinces shall approve and recall people's judges and inquisitors who are in charge of city districts."

them, on their own initiative or on the suggestion of the People's Commissarist of Justice. While the provincial executive committee is made the usual agency to elect and recall the people's judges, its authority to recall has been considerably limited, and made subordinate to that of the central authorities at Moscow. If a provincial executive committee decides to dismiss a judge it must immediately inform the Commissariat of Justice of the Republic of its decision, stating in detail its reasons therefor. This requirement undoubtedly affords the Commissariat an opportunity to supervise and disaffirm any unjustifiable removal of a judge. The dependency of the people's judges on the executive authorities was obviously intended; nevertheless, the absolute power of the central authorities to dismiss a judge at will would seem a bit curtailed by the following provision: "The removal of a people's judge because of his judicial activities may take place exclusively by a verdict of a court or by a decision in a disciplinary proceeding as provided by this Judiciary Act."[32]

d. *Eligibility for People's Judgeship*

In consequence of the new attitude of the higher authorities towards the judiciary, more attention has been paid to the working of the judicial machinery; the fitness of the judicial personnel has markedly improved, and the qualifications requisite for the office of judge have been broadened. To be eligible for election as judge of the people's court a person must have, besides the constitutional right to vote,[33] a record of two years' service in a "responsible" position[34] in a governmental institution, or in a workingmen's, peasant's, social or professional organization, or the candidate must have served, prior to his appointment or election as a member of the Soviet judiciary for a period of three years in a position not lower than that of people's inquisitor.[35]

[32]Jud. Act, 1926, section 16.

[33]Constitution of the R.S.F.S.R. Collected Laws No. 30, Article 218, 1925. (See *supra* note No. 54 of chapter 1.)

[34]There are certain government positions which are designated as "responsible *(otvetstvenie)* positions". In an office or bureau where several scores of people are employed, there are but few persons whose duties are termed "responsible". There is more responsibility as well as prestige attached to certain offices.

[35]Jud. Act, 1926, section 15.

e. *People's Court Districts*

The people's court functions within a certain district fixed by the provincial executive committee on the recommendation of the provincial court. The final arrangement of districts is submitted to the Commissariat of Justice, which has the authority, in the event that it disagrees with the arrangement, to demand a change. The Commissariat of Justice may also determine the minimum number of people's court districts for a given province.[36] The court must have its permanent seat within the limits of its judicial district. A deviation from this rule is permissible only by a special allowance of the provincial court.[37]

f. *People's Co-judges*

The people's co-judges (or "juror judges" as Soviet leaders themselves translate the term into English) are an integral part of the people's court so long as they sit on the bench. The law clearly provides that "in relation to their judicial rights and duties, as well as with regard to their judicial and disciplinary responsibilities for offenses and violations committed by them in connection with the performance of their duties as co-judges, they shall be on the same footing as the [permanent] people's judges."[38]

Though the co-judges are to decide matters of law on equal terms with the judges, there are no specific qualifications required for the office of a co-judge in a people's court. Each Soviet citizen who has a right to vote, according to the Constitution of the R.S.F.S.R., is eligible for the office of co-judge. But "A person has no right to be a co-judge, if he has been expelled from a social or professional organization for a disgraceful offense or conduct, for a period of three years from the day of expulsion * * *."[39]

The last judiciary act, the Act of 1926, describes at great length the methods of preparing the rolls of co-judges, and the manner in which they are called to serve. A special commission

[36] *Ibid.*, section 17.
[37] *Ibid.*, section 33.
[38] *Ibid.*, section 27.
[39] *Ibid.*, section 18.

in each county *(Uyezd)* or district *(raion)* is created,[40] composed of a member of the local county executive committee, who is also the chairman of the commission, the local assistant provincial procurator, and one people's judge of the county or district. The commission distributes the number of co-judges to be elected by the various occupational groups in such a manner as to give fifty per cent to the workingmen, thirty-five per cent to the inhabitants of the villages and *volosts* (that is, to the peasants), and fifteen per cent to the members of the military.[41] The various factory committees, *volost* executive committees, etc. are informed by the commission of the exact number of co-judges to which their group or territory is entitled, whereupon they proceed to elect them at a general meeting of their respective village, factory, and so on, and the names of those elected are forwarded to the people's court.[42] The authority of the commission extends beyond a mere preparation for the election of co-judges. The people's judges must send copies of the names of prospective co-judges to the commission for confirmation, though the people's judge may immediately make use of the rolls without awaiting the approval of the commission.[43] The latter provision was apparently inserted to facilitate the business of the people's court, which might be handicapped for lack of co-judges.

When the commission receives the list for the entire county or district it prepares a general list of co-judges—two hundred for each judicial district—to serve at the people's court, and a special list of co-judges for service at the provincial court in the county when the provincial court is on circuit. The commission is also empowered to strike out the names of those who lack the qualifications required for people's co-judges.[44] Persons so excluded may, however, appeal to the presidium of the county or district executive committee, whose decision is final.[45]

[40]The *raion* (district) embraces a much larger area than the *Volost*, and smaller than the county and is to be found usually where the provinces, (*Guberniyas*) were abolished. In such places we have instead of the province, county and *volost*, the region, circuit and district. See appendix No. 2, page 370.

[41]Jud. Act, 1926, section 21.

[42]*Ibid.*, section 22.

[43]*Ibid.*, section 23.

[44]*Ibid.*, sections 20 and 24.

[45]*Ibid.*, section 25.

It is noteworthy that the ultimate power of supervising the selection of the people's co-judges is taken out of the hands of the judges, although the latter are represented on the commission, and placed in the hands of the executive authorities of the county or district. The effect of this, without, perhaps, any intention on the part of Soviet legislators, should be to make co-judges independent of the judges in rendering a verdict.

The people's co-judges, as we have seen, perform all the functions and exercise all the powers of judges. Nevertheless the law does not prescribe any special training or experience for co-judges. The law states merely that the people's judge is bound to explain to the co-judges who report for service their rights and duties, and have them sign a statement that they have received the necessary explanations. The co-judges must also give a solemn promise to judge according to their conscience.[46] The practice, however, is to invite the co-judges to conferences, or even to evening classes, in preparation for their duties. As early as 1924, a number of provinces began to conduct such conferences.[47] The writer was told by people's judges that a part of the permanent judge's work is to meet the prospective co-judges for a general discussion of problems with which they will be confronted in their rôle as temporary judges.

The co-judges sit no more than six days consecutively in one year. Where, however, a case on which they serve is, for some reason, continued they may be summoned again to complete the case, in which event the six-day limit is not applied.[48]

g. *Special Session on Labor Cases—Branch of the People's Court*

Special sessions on labor cases are instituted only in the capitals of the autonomous republics, in the centers of the regional and territorial administrative units, at the provincial seat, which is always the largest city in the province, and at the industrial centers. These sessions are organized by order of the plenum of the highest court within any given administrative unit.

[46] *Ibid.*, section 26.
[47] Official report about the activities of the Judiciary for the first half of 1924, Moscow, 1924, page 47.
[48] Jud. Act, 1926, section 19.

The jurisdiction of the special session must not extend beyond the limits of the city or industrial center in which it has its seat.[49]

The special session on labor cases consists of three judges, one of whom is a regular people's judge. A second member is chosen by the provincial soviet of the trade unions, and the third is appointed by the executive committee of the territory or province, as the case may be, from among those employed in the institutions in charge of public economic affairs. All the judges are elected for a period of one year. The powers and duties of the special session as well as the disciplinary and other responsibilities are equivalent to those of the regular people's judges.[50] Except that these courts (or sessions) deal with one type of offense—violations of the code on labor—they function on the same basis, and follow the same regulations as the general sessions of the people's court.[51]

The Soviet Code on Labor, which defines the jurisdiction of this special session of the people's court, states: "All violations of the code of laws on labor * * * so far as they are prosecuted criminally are to be tried at the special session of the people's court."[52] Although the special session has some features which would seem to classify it as a separate court, such was not the intention of the framers of the Judiciary Act. "This court", says a Soviet legal writer in referring to the special session on labor cases, "is not a new court but a part of the ordinary people's court."[53]

h. *Waiting Court (Deshurnaya Kamera)*

The waiting court is not a separate court instituted at certain special places, as was the case with the special court of the same name created in 1920, but simply a session of the court provided "for the speediest trial of the clearest and least complicated cases",[54] and it seems to function when necessary at each people's court.

[49] *Ibid.*, section 34.
[50] *Ibid.*, section 35.
[51] *Ibid.*, section 35.
[52] Labor Code of R.S.F.S.R. Collected Laws No. 70, Article 903, 1922, section 169. *(Kodex Zakonov o Trude. Sobranie Uzakonenii* 70-903, 1922.)
[53] S. Oskarkhanov. *The Weekly,* No. 48, 1926.
[54] *Commentaries,* page 341.

The fact that this waiting session is not considered as a special court or even a special branch of the people's court probably accounts for the fact that it is mentioned only in the Code of Criminal Procedure (sections 360 to 365) and not at all in the Judiciary Acts. The promulgator of the First Judiciary Act of 1922, Krylenko, clearly stated (in 1923) that that act wiped out the "waiting court",[55] and, indeed, neither the Judiciary Act of 1922, the later additions to that act, nor the new Judiciary Act of 1926 provided for such a court or branch of a court. The sections of the Code of Criminal Procedure,[56] enacted before the First Judiciary Act, dealing with the waiting court were, however, re-enacted in the later Code of Criminal Procedure, and those sections have not been modified up to this day.

This court functions in the same manner as the general people's court, with one judge and two people's co-judges sitting. The law specifically prohibits the trying of a case in the waiting court unless the facts of the case are absolutely complete and the case entirely clear.[57] Cases are sent there for trial either "when, in the opinion of the organs which arrested the accused, no investigation is necessary, or when the defendant admits his guilt."[58] But should the defendant at the trial point to facts which require an investigation, "the trial must be discontinued and the case forwarded for disposal in the general manner * * *."[59]

The verdicts or decisions of the people's court, in all its branches or sessions, are subject to complaint by way of cassation to the division of cassation of the provincial court.[60]

II. THE PROVINCIAL COURT

This court, "the strong judicial fist",[61] most strikingly reveals the blending of a number of judicial institutions into a single judicial unit. Elements, characteristics and functions of

[55]Krylenko. *The Judicial System*, page 158.
[56]Code, 1922, sections 397—402.
[57]Code, 1927, section 362.
[58]*Ibid.*, section 361.
[59]*Ibid.*, section 364.
[60]*Ibid.*, sections 344, 365 and 370.
[61]Krylenko, as quoted by Temoshev, page 220.

the former people's court with six co-judges, the soviet of people's judges, and the provincial revolutionary tribunal have all been brought together as raw material for the building of this new type of judicial institution. Furthermore, the new provincial court inherited the administrative functions of the old provincial departments of justice, which were abolished as a result of a compromise effected at the Fourth Conference of Judicial Workers in 1922.[62]

a. *Personnel*

The permanent personnel of the provincial court consists of a president, two deputy presidents—one for the criminal and one for the civil division—and a number of permanent judges. As the provinces of the vast Federated Republic vary greatly in size and population, the number of judges for each provincial court is under the Judiciary Act of 1926 determined by special statute or regulation *(shtatami)*. By the Judiciary Act of 1922 the number of judges for each province was fixed at twelve.[63] The present act states: "The temporary personnel of the provincial court shall consist of people's co-judges who shall be elected and convoked for service in the manner provided by law."[64]

The president of the provincial court and his two deputies comprise the presidium of the court. The latter body, which exercises great power and is a very important link in the chain of judicial control and supervision, was first established by the Judiciary Act of 1924.[65]

b. *Election and Recall of Judges*

The president, his deputies, and the permanent judges are elected by the provincial executive committee for the period of one year, subject to the approval of the People's Commissariat of Justice, which has also the right to nominate candidates. All the

[62]By the compromise the judicial administrative functions of the abolished provincial departments of justice were transferred to the presidium and plenum of the provincial court and the administrative powers to the People's Commissariat of Justice at Moscow. See Krylenko, *The Judiciary and the Law*, 1927, page 70.

[63]Jud. Act, 1922, section 40.

[64]Jud. Act, 1926, section 39.

[65]Collected Laws No. 78, Article 782, 1924, sections 6 and 7.

judges are eligible for reelection, but they may also be recalled by the provincial executive committee before the expiration of their term. No recall is effective without the sanction of the Commissariat of Justice at Moscow, except where the removal of a judge is included in a court sentence or decreed in disciplinary proceedings.[66] All this pointedly demonstrates the authority of the central government of the R.S.F.S.R. in controlling the election and, still more, the recall of provincial judges.

To be eligible for election to permanent judgeship of the provincial court a person must have all the qualificiations required for a judge of the people's court. In addition, the candidate for the office of provincial judge must have a record of Soviet judicial service in a position not lower than people's judge[67] for a period of three years, in the case of the president and the deputy president, and two years in the case of the other judges of the provincial court.[68] This rule would seem to place on the provincial bench judges who have had some experience. But the effect of the rule is weakened by a special note inserted under the section which provides: "Deviation from the stated rule [requiring a fixed period of judicial experience] is allowed only with the permission of the People's Commissariat of Justice."

Besides the regular permanent judges, the provincial court may also have judges in reserve. The latter are at the disposal of the president of the court to sit in place of absent judges of the provincial or of the people's court. These judges also perform certain functions of the provincial court, such as conducting investigations and inspections in judicial institutions subordinate to the provincial court.[69] The judges in reserve must possess all the qualifications required for regular, permanent, provincial judges, but are elected in the manner fixed for the election of judges of the people's court.[70] In other words, the sanction of the Commissariat of Justice is not necessary.

[66]Jud. Act, 1926, section 41.

[67]"Or a judge in a revolutionary tribunal", as it was specified by the first Judiciary Act of 1922. But the Act of 1926, for obvious reasons, dropped that phrase.

[68]Jud. Act, 1926, section 40.

[69]*Ibid.*, section 57.

[70]*Ibid.*, section 58.

c. *People's Co-judges of the Provincial Court*

The people's co-judges for the provincial court, who are also termed by the act rotating judges, are selected with great care. The principle of "inducing all workmen without exception to perform judicial duties", which was boastingly proclaimed as the programme of the Communist Party of 1919,[71] was now boldly rejected. The co-judges for each (provincial) court, not less than two hundred in number, are selected from a special list of citizens of both sexes who have had not less than two years' experience in the work of certain state, social or professional organizations. The rolls of co-judges are compiled and prepared by a special commission consisting of a chairman, elected by the provincial executive committee from its own members, two judges of the provincial court appointed by its president, one representative of the provincial procuracy, and three members of the provincial soviet of trade unions, elected by the latter. The persons named on the list by the commission to serve as co-judges are subject to the approval of the provincial executive committee. The latter may strike out any name, and its decision in this respect is not subject to appeal.[72] The provincial executive committee, therefore, absolutely controls the actual choosing of people's co-judges for the provincial court, while the special commission is merely a body for the performance of the necessary preparatory work.

d. *Functions of the Provincial Court*

The functions of the provincial court are divided into three parts: (1) It is the judicial center of the province and exercises direct supervision over all the judicial institutions within the province. (2) It is a tribunal for reviewing by way of cassation and supervision cases originally tried at the people's court. (The difference between the powers of cassation and supervision will be explained presently.) (3) It is a court of original jurisdiction for cases specifically designated by the Code of Criminal Procedure.[73]

[71]See, *supra*, chapter 1, note 61.
[72]Jud. Act, 1926, section 43.
[73]*Ibid.*, section 38.

The numerous functions of the provincial court are not performed by the same personnel, but are distributed with great care and exactness among the different departments and divisions of the court. The somewhat complicated scheme was planned to insure a harmonious functioning of every part of the powerful judicial machine. The entire apparatus is divided into the following parts: (1) The plenum; (2) the presidium; (3) the president, (4) the criminal division which in turn is divided into separate judicial and cassational branches, and (5) disciplinary department (collegium). The composition, jurisdiction, powers and duties of each of these divisions is described in great detail by the Judiciary Act.

1. Plenum of the Provincial Court

The plenum of the provincial court is, of course, the most significant single unit of this judicial body. It consists of all the judges of the court, at least half of whom must be present at a session. The participation of the provincial procurator or his deputy at the sessions is required. The plenum, in session, decides all questions concerning the arrangement of the territorial divisions of the people's court and the election, transfer and recall of the people's judges, fixing the limits of the territorial districts for the people's inquisitors and the dismissal of the inquisitors (although the latter are elected by the presidium of the court), and finally all questions concerning the appointment and recall of the county representatives of the provincial court. It listens to reports made by a member of the court specially appointed by its president concerning the activities of the people's judges. It also receives reports regarding the investigations and inspections conducted at the people's courts and the offices of the people's inquisitors. These investigations and inspections are ordinary, normal proceedings, and are made part of the supervisory authority exercised by higher courts over those subordinate to them. In addition to the various reports mentioned, the plenum hears periodic reports submitted by the presidium of the provincial court, the heads of the separate divisions of the court, (criminal, civil, cassational, etc.) the people's judges, the union (collegium) of advocates of the province, and so on.[74]

Although there is a department which has special disciplinary jurisdiction over members of the judiciary, nevertheless it is the plenum which has the authority to suspend persons from office, or remove them from certain judicial duties, when disciplinary proceedings are pending against them.

In the realm of interpretation, the powers of the plenum of the provincial court are extensive. It may interpret the law of a concrete case whenever such law is uncertain or incomplete. Problems of this sort may be submitted to the plenum by the president of the provincial court, the presidents of the judicial or cassational divisions, or by the provincial procurator. A copy of the interpretation as laid down by the plenum is forwarded to the Supreme Court of the R.S.F.S.R. and to the People's Commissariat of Justice.[75] The plenum is not bound to interpret; it may, if it deems it advisable, transfer the entire question to the Supreme Court for interpretation. It is required to transfer the question if the provincial procurator disagrees with its interpretation. This power of interpretation was first vested in the plenum of the provincial court by the Judiciary Act of 1926, in conformity with the prevailing tendency to strengthen the powers of the court and at the same time to leave to the Supreme Court the power of inquiry and reversal. By the First Judiciary Act of 1922, the provincial court could merely state its opinion on the question of law raised and then transfer the question, with its opinion, to the Supreme Court.[76]

The marked tendency to increase the power of the provincial court is also revealed by the provision conferring upon its plenum the authority, by way of supervision as distinguished from cassation, to reverse a people's court verdict or decision which has become legally binding.[77] It is to be borne in mind that the opportunity for cassational complaint ceases after the verdict becomes of legal force. This immense power of judicial supervision over verdicts was first delegated to the pro-

[74]*Ibid.*, section 49, subsection a.
[75]*Ibid.*, section 49, subsections b and c.
[76]Jud. Act, 1922, section 50.
[77]For a definition of the term "legally binding" see *infra*, pp. 231, 305.

vincial court by the Act of 1924,[78] and was incorporated in the Act of 1926.[79]

This description of the powers of the plenum affirms the truthfulness of the epithet, "the strong judicial fist", applied to the provincial court which is also provided with the necessary facilities to exercise its powers. By means of the periodic and special reports which it receives from every judicial institution, touching upon every activity going on throughout the province, the plenum is furnished with information which enables it to exercise its colossal supervisory powers promptly and effectively.

2. Presidium

The functions of the presidium are to assign the judges of the court to the various divisons, to petition the Commissarist of Justice of the Republic to enlarge, when necessary, the fixed personnel of provincial judges, to arrange for investigations and inspections of the people's court, and to elect and dismiss the people's inquisitors. (The question of dismissing must also be decided at the plenum.) To facilitate the work of the plenum, the presidium has a preliminary discussion of the questions which must be finally decided by the former.[80]

3. President of the Court

The president of the provincial court is the administrative head who serves as a link between the provincial court and the other judicial as well as non-judicial agencies of the government. He must submit to the provincial executive committee, for appointment, the names of candidates for people's judges and people's inquisitors; he must furnish the Commissariat of Justice of the Republic and the provincial executive committee with reports on the activities of the provincial court and the judicial institutions subordinate to it. The president of the court is also charged with the duty of convoking the sessions of the plenum, at which he presides, and of submitting to the presidium all the problems which require a preliminary discussion. The author-

[78]Additions and amendments to the Judiciary Act. Collected Laws No. 78, Article 782, 1924, section 11.

[79]Jud. Act, 1926, section 49, subsection d.

[80]*Ibid.*, section 48.

ity of the president, as the head of the court, is not confined to any particular division. The law specifically provides that "the president [or his deputy] may preside in any case at the judicial or cassational division".[81]

4. The Criminal-Cassational Division

The division of cassation consists of a number of permanent judges of the provincial court, three of whom sit as a court of cassation in each case.[82] The plenum of the provincial court, with the special permission of the Commissariat of Justice of the Republic, may appoint one judge of the people's court to sit as a judge in the division of cassation.[83]

The jurisdiction and powers of this cassational division are not new in the Soviet system of jurisprudence. The powers exercised by the soviet of people's judges before 1923 were transferred to the cassational division of the provincial court. It is noteworthy that the chapter *(Glava)* of the Code of Criminal Procedure dealing with the cassational functions of the provincial court is identical with the chapter describing the functions of the soviet of people's judges in the Code of Criminal Procedure which was in effect before 1923.[84] The cassational division takes up a case only when a cassational complaint, or protest, which is the term used when the procurator is the complaining party, is filed.[85] Once a complaint or protest is made, however, the court is not limited to the particular points raised. On the contrary, it is bound to review the entire case, and if any ground for reversal is found, it must remand the case for retrial.[86] Grounds for reversal by way of cassation are the incompleteness and incorrectness of the investigating proceedings, a material violation of established forms of procedure, a failure properly to apply the law, or a verdict or judgment which is clearly unjust. Whenever a reversal takes place, the case is sent for

[81] *Ibid.*, section 47.
[82] *Ibid.*, section 51.
[83] *Ibid.*, see note to section 51.
[84] Compare Code, 1922, chapter XXVI, sections 355—372 and Code, 1923, chapter XXIX, sections 409—426. The term "soviet of people's judges" is substituted by the words "provincial court".
[85] Code, 1927, section 411.
[86] *Ibid.*, section 412.

new trial to a different people's court or to the same court which tried it. But in the latter instance different judges are to sit on the retrial. This rule, obviously based on the theory that no judge of original jurisdiction should sit on the same case more than once is a re-enactment of the pre-revolutionary Russian law.

In ordering a reversal the division of cassation transmits its directions with regard to the case to the people's court retrying it, and these directions are absolutely binding on such court.[87] By a later amendment,[88] the cassational powers of the provincial court have been so extended as to make it unnecessary to return a case for new trial if the reversal of the verdict is based on an improper application of the law by the trial court, or if the punishment imposed is out of proportion to offense committed. In all such cases the cassational court may either dismiss the case or modify the sentence. The sentence imposed must, however, be neither more severe than the one imposed originally nor milder than that prescribed by law.

The decision rendered by the court of cassation is final, so far as the parties are concerned, but the case may be taken to the Supreme Court of the Republic by way of supervision, which will be later explained, through the plenum of the provincial court.[89] The power to demand that such a case be sent to the Supreme Court is vested in the president of the Supreme Court, his deputy, the Procurator of the Republic, or his assistant who is attached to the Supreme Court.[90]

5. The Criminal-Judicial Division—Original Jurisdiction

This division is the instrument through which the provincial court exercises its functions as a court of original jurisdiction. The entire structure of the court, with all its tremendous powers in the realm of cassation and supervision, would indicate that its original jurisdiction is of an exceptional nature, somewhat analogous to the Imperial Russian Judicial Palata,[91] or even to

[87] *Ibid.*, sections 420 and 423.

[88] *Ibid.*, section 419a (as amended in 1924 by Collected Laws No. 78, Article 784, 1924).

[89] *Ibid.*, section 426.

[90] *Ibid.*, section 440.

[91] See chapter on Criminal Courts in Imperial Russia, page 375.

the Special Revolutionary Tribunal of June, 1918.[92] But such is not the judicial position of the provincial court. The latter, through its criminal-judicial division, is vested with such widely extended original jurisdiction as to make it resemble, roughly speaking, the Imperial Russian Circuit Court *(Okruzhnoi Sud)*, or the assize and quarter sessions courts of England.

The section of the Code of Criminal Procedure concerning the original jurisdiction of the provincial court has undergone six different changes and modifications since February, 1923, the time of the adoption of the Code which is with some changes still in force today. But the general scope and nature of the court's jurisdiction have hardly been affected by all those changes. The court now has jurisdiction over the following offenses:[93]

(a) Counter-revolutionary crimes designated by specific sections of the Criminal Code representing a great variety of counter-revolutionary offenses, the penalty for which ranges from capital punishment to not less than three months' imprisonment.

(b) Offenses against the public administration. These include participation in mass disorders, predatory raids and robberies by organized bands, refusal to carry out duties and obligations of a military nature in time of war, conducting propaganda and agitation for the purpose of inciting national[94] or religous animosity, etc.

(c) Crimes committed by officials in the exercise of their duties, such as exceeding the bounds or abuse of authority, failure to exercise authority in certain instances, pronouncement of an unjust sentence from avaricious or other personal motives, etc.

Almost all the offenses covered by the (a), (b) and (c) were, previous to the creation of the provincial court, under the jurisdiction of the revolutionary tribunals.[95] The provincial court inherited not merely some of the characteristics of the revolu-

[92]See chapter 1, note 106.

[93]Code, 1927, section 26.

[94]The word "national" is employed here to denote the different national groups that inhabit the soviet republics.

[95]Code, 1922, section 28. Compare it with the enumerated sections of the Cr. Code of 1922.

tionary tribunals, as we have seen, but the latter's entire jurisdictional powers as well.

(d) Economic offenses designated by specific sections of the Criminal Code. These embrace malfeasance or misfeasance in office by persons in control of state institutions, failure to fulfill obligations under a contract entered into with state institutions, where deliberate bad faith is charged, etc.

(e) Crimes against life, health, liberty, and personal reputation, as designated by six specific sections of the Criminal Code. These include the ordinary type of serious crimes, as premeditated killing, premeditated or wilful infliction of grievous bodily injury, causing the loss of sight, hearing, or the use of any other organ, sexual intercourse with immature persons, the corruption of minors, by the commission of vicious acts in relation to them, rape,[96] coercion of a woman into sexual intercourse with a man by force of her financial dependence on or employment by him.

(f) Crimes against property, as open assault with intent to steal or wilful destruction of property belonging to others, causing thereby suffering or the loss of human life. Almost all the offenses covered by paragraphs (e) and (f) were formerly tried by the abolished people's court with six co-judges.[97]

The tendency to enlarge the jurisdiction of the people's court at the expense of the provincial court, as we have stated before, becomes clearly evident upon an examination of the different codes on the subject of jurisdiction of various crimes. By the original Code of Criminal Procedure of 1923, which immediately followed the creation of the provincial court, the latter's jurisdiction qver crimes against life and property was made much broader than it is today. For example, by this Code, the provincial court was given jurisdiction over cases of deliberate killing under the influence of strong emotional excitement,[98] or by exceeding the limits necessary for self-defense, also cases

[96]Neither the Tzarist nor the Bolshevist system of jurisprudence knew of such one-word terms to cover specific crimes to compare with our terms of murder, manslaughter, rape, etc. The statute simply describes a homicide committed under certain circumstances, and so on.

[97]Code, 1922, section 26.

[98]This would probably be manslaughter, but see *supra*, note 96.

where death was caused through lack of precaution, etc.[99] These crimes, together with a number of others, are not included in the sections of the present Code of Criminal Procedure which prescribe the jurisdiction of the provincial court, and are, therefore, automatically shifted from the jurisdiction of the provincial court to that of the people's court, for the latter is given jurisdiction over any criminal case not specifically assigned to the jurisdiction of another court.

The provincial court, so far as original jurisdiction goes, is the heir of both the revolutionary tribunal and the people's court with six co-judges. In procedure, while the provincial court maintains the institution of co-judges, it resembles in the more striking instances the revolutionary tribunals. It is, therefore, not at all surprising that the sections of the Code providing the procedure at the provincial court are almost identical with those sections of the first Soviet Code of Criminal Procedure which laid down the procedural rules for revolutionary tribunals.[100] A characteristic illustration of this is the provision that the participation of defense counsel at the trial is not always required or even permitted. The entire question is left to the discretion of the court, the only restriction being that it must permit the participation of counsel, or appoint such, if the prosecution is to take part in the case.[101] The general nature of the procedure in the provincial court is, with a number of specified exceptions, the same as that in the people's court.[102]

All decisions and verdicts of the criminal-judicial division of the provincial court, usually referred to as the provincial court, are subject to complaint by way of cassation to the Cassational Department of the Supreme Court of the Republic.[103]

6. Disciplinary Departments

The disciplinary department of the provincial court consists of three judges, including the president of the court, or

[99]Code, 1927, section 26. See also Cr. Code, 1922, sections 144, 147 and 148.

[100]Compare the Code, 1923 with the amendments up to June, 1927. Collected Codes of R.S.F.S.R., 4th edition, 1927, sections 380-383 and the Code, 1922, sections 413 and *seq.*

[101]Code, 1927, section 381. See chapter 1, note 127.

[102]*Ibid.*, section 388.

[103]*Ibid.*, sections 400 and 401.

one of his deputies, elected by the plenum of the court for that purpose.[104] (The functions of this department will be discussed in another connection.)

7. County Representatives of the Provincial Court

The scheme by which the provincial court functions as a mighty organ of judicial supervision is in a measure effectuated by means of county representatives of the provincial court. This idea, to be sure, is not a novel one in Russian legal history. The Imperial Russian circuit court, which was formerly the important court of original jurisdiction, also had its county members, although their office differed somewhat from that of the county representative of the provincial court. The county bureau of justice in the early years of the Soviet régime was, to a degree at least, a reflection of the same idea.

The organization of county representatives of the provincial court was first established at the beginning of 1923 by an order or regulation issued by the Commissariat of Justice of the Republic,[105] and as this arrangement proved of value, the system was incorporated in the Judiciary Act of 1923, which defines the functions of the county representatives.[106] By subsequent acts, their position has been greatly enhanced and their powers and scope of their authority considerably enlarged.

The function of the county representative is to strengthen the interrelation between the provincial court and its subordinate local judicial organs in matters of judicial administration. These representatives are appointed by the plenum of the provincial court from among the people's judges of the county.[107]

The duties of the county representatives are described at great length. The most important of these are to supervise all the judicial institutions in the county, including the bureau of advocates, notaries, etc., to participate in the compilation of the rolls of co-judges, to call county meetings and preside over them for the purpose of discussing judicial problems, to investi-

[104]Jud. Act, 1926, section 52.

[105]*The Weekly*, Nos. 25 and 26, 1923, page 577.

[106]Additions and amendments to the Judiciary Act. Collected Laws No. 48, Article 481, 1923, sections 75—77.

[107]Jud. Act, 1926, section 53.

gate the activities of the people's judges and people's inquisitors when specially directed by the plenum of the provincial court. The last important duty was assigned to the county representative by the Judiciary Act of 1924.[108] By this act, the county representative was also given the authority with the approval of the presidium of the provincial executive committee and the Commissariat of Justice of the Republic to exercise the judicial functions of a provincial judge particularly in remote counties. Like other judicial officials of the province, the county representative must report to the provincial court all of his activities.[109]

III. THE SUPREME COURT

To complete the plan of absolute centralization of the judicial system, the Supreme Court of the Republic was instituted. This court very much resembles the Supreme Revolutionary Tribunal created by the Unification Act of 1921.[110] To substantiate this statement, a comparison between the Codes of Criminal Procedure of 1922 and 1923 is instructive. The sections of the former Code which describe the cassational power of the Supreme Revolutionary Tribunal were, with a mere change of name of the court, incorporated into the Code of 1923.[111] But while the Supreme Revolutionary Tribunal of 1921 was made the supervisor of only one branch of the judiciary, the revolutionary tribunals, the Supreme Court of today has control over every phase of judicial activity within the vast territory of the Russian Socialist Federative Soviet Republic.

This court was created, as is the case with almost the entire Soviet judicial structure of today, by the Judiciary Act of 1922, but many important changes were made by subsequent judiciary acts. The general position of the court is thus stated: "The Supreme Court of the R.S.F.S.R. through its direct guidance of the entire judicial practice and its unified policy over the entire territory of the R.S.F.S.R. shall be the organ of supreme judicial supervision over all judicial institutions. It shall like-

[108]Collected Laws No. 78, Article 782, 1924, section 13.
[109]Jud. Act, 1926, section 54.
[110]See chapter 1, note 144.
[111]Code, 1922, sections 442—447, and Code, 1927, sections 434—439.

wise be the court of cassation for the superior courts of the autonomous republics, the regional, territorial, provincial and circuit courts, and a court of original jurisdiction in cases, as provided by law, of special importance to the state."[112]

The proclamation that the Supreme Court is the organ of supreme judicial supervision within the Republic is in accord with the fundamental principles adopted by the Union of the Soviet Republics.[113] This provision settled a long drawn-out dispute as to what should be the relation between the Supreme Court and the Commissariat of Justice of the Republic. The latter was by this act deprived of its former purely judicial functions, which were henceforth left entirely and exclusively to the Supreme Court. This separation of powers, we are told, was instituted out of considerations of efficiency.[114] We are, however, justified in entertaining some doubt as to whether depriving the Commissariat of its judicial functions was merely an adherence to the principle of specialization, the "division of labor", or whether more profound reasons, which we shall mention later, influenced such a division.

a. *Appointment of Judges*

The president of the Supreme Court, his deputy, and the presidents of the departments are appointed directly by the presidium of the All-Russian Central Executive Committee, while the other judges are appointed by the latter body on the presentation of the Commissariat of Justice with the consent of the president of the Supreme Court. Neither the president nor the other judges of the court may be recalled except by order of the presidium of the All-Russian Central Executive Committee,[115] the *Vtzeek*. To be eligible for election to the Supreme Court bench a person must satisfy the same requirements for candidates for president of the provincial court[116]—namely, three years' service as judge of the people's court.

[112] Jud. Act, 1926, section 8.

[113] Basic principles on the Judiciary, Collected Laws of U.S.S.R. No. 23, Article 203, 1924, section 10.

[114] Krylenko, *The Judiciary and the Law*, 1927, pages 71 and 81.

[115] Jud. Act, 1926, section 176.

[116] *Ibid.*, sections 177 and 178.

b. *Functioning Agencies of the Supreme Court*

The Supreme Court is divided into the plenum, presidium, judicial and cassational departments, and disciplinary department.[117] By the Act of 1922 there were also military and military transport departments, but these were later placed under the jurisdiction of the Union, and their functions will be discussed in connection with the Supreme Court of the Union.

1. The plenum

The plenum is composed of all the judges of the Supreme Court, and at least half of the entire membership must participate in any session; the presence of the Procurator of the Republic, or his first assistant, is made obligatory. The plenum, thus constituted, exercises great authority over all judicial matters of the Republic. In the realm of interpretation it may, unlike any other court, interpret all questions of procedure or substantive law, whether presented by litigants or by the various departments, the presidium of the Supreme Court or the Procurator of the Republic or his assistant. Judicial problems may also be submitted to the Supreme Court for interpretation by the plenum of the superior court of any of the autonomous republics, which is the highest court in such republics, and by the plena of the territorial, regional, provincial and circuit courts. The explanations and interpretations of the plenum of the Supreme Court are binding on all judicial institutions in the territory of the R.S.F.S.R.[118]

In the field of supervision, the power of the plenum is no less impressive. It is the body which reviews and affirms regulations and rulings of the presidium of the Supreme Court annulling or modifying verdicts, sentences, decisions, or orders of any department of the Supreme Court, or of any other court, including the highest court of any autonomous republic; it must give its approval of all circulars containing instructions and regulations sent out by the presidium of the Supreme Court to the subordinate judicial institutions. The plenum is also vested with the authority to elect the judges of the disciplinary department

[117] *Ibid.*, note to section 177.
[118] *Ibid.*, section 180, subsection 2.

of the Supreme Court.[119] Many of the powers of the plenum described above were not included in the Judiciary Act of 1922, but, in accordance with the general trend towards centralization, were added by later acts.

2. The Presidium

The presidium is made up of the president of the Supreme Court, his deputy, and the presidents of the cassational and judicial departments of the court.[120] The act designates its powers and duties as administrative and supervisory. As an administrative body it is charged with the duty of assigning judges for service in the various departments and appointing their deputy presidents, examining and affirming reports submitted concerning the activities of particular departments. The real significance of the presidium is revealed in the scope of its supervisory powers.

The presidium has the power to arrange for special investigations and inspections of the departments of the Supreme Court, the territorial and provincial courts, and also of the superior courts of the autonomous republics, on its own initiative or at the suggestion of the Procurator of the Republic, to present to the Commissariat of Justice plans for conducting the regular inspections of the same courts, and to suggest the necessary changes in their personnel.

While the plenum of the Supreme Court generally gives its approval before a verdict, sentence or decision of a department of the Supreme Court or of any other court can be annulled by way of supervision, all questions of annulment will, however, be preliminarily discussed and decided upon by the presidium, whose opinion, we may safely presume, will carry great weight with the plenum. (This power was assigned to the presidium by the Act of 1926.) We might add that a final decision is required to be made by the plenum only when a matter of legal principle must be decided in rendering a decision in a given case. In the absence of such a necessity, the presidium may reverse the verdict by way of supervision and return it for a new trial without obtaining the approval of the plenum.[121] A remarkable feature,

[119] *Ibid.*, section 180, subsections b, c and d.
[120] *Ibid.*, section 179.
[121] *Ibid.*, section 179, subsections b, c and d.

which throws some light on the connection between the judicial and the legislative departments of the government, is noted in the provision that the presidium is to prepare, on the basis of the data it obtains from the practical experience of the Supreme Court, bills for legislation on subjects connected with its work, and submit them to the Commissariat of Justice.[122]

The presidium, as the administrative and supervisory organ of the Supreme Court, may institute disciplinary proceedings against members of the Supreme Court, the presidents, and the deputy presidents of the superior courts of the autonomous republics, the territorial, regional, provincial and circuit courts, whenever this becomes necessary either as a result of an investigation and inspection or at the suggestion of the Department of Cassation of the Supreme Court or the Procurator of the Republic. The presidium is also to convoke the sessions of the plenum, and prepare all the materials necessary for the deliberations of the latter. To make the huge machinery entrusted to the presidium run more smoothly, the assistant procurator of the Republic, and, in certain instances, the superintendent of the Judicial Department of the Commissariat of Justice also, must participate with an advisory vote at the sessions of the presidium.

3. The Cassational Department

While the plenum and the presidium exercise an immense authority in judicial administration and supervision, the ordinary, normal functions of a higher court, the power of judicial review, are carried out by the Department of Cassation. This Department of the Supreme Court, sometimes referred to as the Supreme Court, is composed of a president and twelve judges, six of whom are assigned to the criminal and six to the civil division of the court. Three judges, the president of the department included, constitute a cassational bench, under the direct supervision of the president of the Supreme Court, who may assume the duties of presiding judge in any of the sessions of the department.[123]

The sessions of the Cassational Department are open, and the participation of interested parties is permitted if they so

[122] *Ibid.*, section 179, subsection 2, f.
[123] *Ibid.*, sections 181 and 182.

desire.[124] It may reverse a verdict or judgment for proper cause; and, generally speaking, it is governed by the same rules of procedure as prescribed for the cassational divisions of the provincial court.[125]

Unlike the provincial division of cassation which may not reduce a sentence below the minimum set by law the Cassational Department of the Supreme Court may, if it deems it necessary, reduce the sentence even below the limits fixed by the Criminal Code, submitting its opinion for the approval of the presidium of the All-Russian Central Executive Committee.[126]

The decisions rendered by this Department of Cassation are final so far as the parties are concerned for they have no further avenue of complaint, but the president of the Supreme Court or the Procurator of the Republic may protest the decision and thus bring it before the plenum of the Supreme Court. To make the latter provision more effective, the law has been amended so as to give any dissenting judge of the Cassational Department the right to submit a written minority opinion to the president of the Supreme Court. The latter may either dismiss it or protest (appeal from) the majority decision to the plenum.[127]

4. The Judicial Department[128]

The Judicial Department of the Supreme Court, which is the highest court of original jurisdiction within the Republic, consists of a president and four judges. Each bench of the court is made up of the president of the Department, or one of its judges who presides, and two people's co-judges, selected for a term of one year from a special list of forty-eight candidates, approved by the presidium of the *Vtzeek*. By the Judiciary Act of 1922, the Supreme Court, like the abolished Supreme Revolutionary Tribunal, did not have any people's co-judges.[129] But the institution of co-judges became so generally favored that Soviet legal writers demanded their introduction even in the purely military tribu-

[124]Code, 1927, section 435.
[125]*Ibid.*, section 436.
[126]*Ibid.*, section 437.
[127]*Ibid.*, note to section 438.
[128]The Judicial Department is subdivided in the criminal and the civil departments.
[129]Jud. Act, 1922, section 64.

nals.[130] The Act of 1923 amended the previous act and removed the exception provided originally for the Supreme Court.[131] Thus, the system of co-judges was henceforth to prevail in every court of the Republic, although in the case of the Supreme Court the strikingly rigid control of the Central Executive Committee, through its presidium, was not relaxed.

The original jurisdiction of the Judicial Department of the Supreme Court is not specified as it is for the provincial court by reference to particular sections of the Criminal Code; as a trial court it does not occupy a normal, clearly-defined position. It takes jurisdiction either over specific persons, irrespective of the nature of the crime, or over such criminal cases as certain high authorities may, in specific instances, refer to it. The Code of Criminal Procedure provides: "The Judicial Department of the Supreme Court as a court of first instance, shall take jurisdiction (a) over cases of exceptional importance, when sent to it for trial by the presidium of the All-Russian Central Executive Committee, the plenum of the Supreme Court, * * * the Procurator of the Republic, or the chief of the State Political Bureau." In the last two cases, the court may refuse to take jurisdiction and may send the case for trial to any provincial court;[132] (b) over cases involving offenses in office committed by members of the All-Russian Central Executive Committee, the people's commissars and members of its departments, * * * judges of the Supreme Court, the assistant procurator of the Republic, and the members of the *collegium* of the State Political Bureau;[133] (c) over offenses in office charged against the provincial procurators and their assistants, the members of the presidium of the provincial executive committee, the president, or deputy presidents of the provincial court." Assumption of jurisdiction over the persons in the latter group is not mandatory upon the Supreme Court, which may transfer such cases, if it refuses to take jurisdiction, to any provincial court.[134]

[130]Yak. Berman, "Military Tribunals and Co-judges". *The Weekly*, Nos. 19 and 20, 1924, p. 442.

[131]Collected Laws No. 48, Article 481, 1923 changed sections 64 to 103 and amended them accordingly.

[132]Code, 1927, section 449, subsection 1.

[133]*Ibid.*, section 449, subsection 2.

[134]*Ibid.*, section 449, subsection 3. See Appendix No. 5, page 373 for diagram.

5. Disciplinary Proceedings

The idea of having a perfected machinery for disciplinary proceedings against members of the judiciary, as it now exists in all the courts of the Republic except the people's court, is not novel in the Russian Judicial system. The Imperial Governing Senate, the Supreme Court of Tzarist Russia, had its supreme disciplinary sessions made up of the presidents of the cassational departments and all the senators or judges of the united session of the first and cassational departments, for the purpose of deciding disciplinary cases involving members of the judiciary subordinate to the Governing Senate.[185]

Disciplinary proceedings may be instituted not later than one year after the grounds for the complaint have arisen. Such proceedings may be started either by a private person, who cannot withdraw a complaint once made,[186] or by certain judicial officials. The authority of the latter to institute disciplinary proceedings is worked out according to a smoothly-designed, symmetrical plan. The president of a given court may bring before the disciplinary department any judicial worker of his own court or of courts subordinate to it except the procurator and assistant procurator of the court over which he presides. The procurator of the court is vested with a similar power except as to the president of the court and the president's deputy.

In accordance with this plan the Procurator of the Republic and the president of the Supreme Court may institute disciplinary proceedings against all persons, with the exception mentioned, connected with the judicial organs of the R.S.F.S.R.[187] Following the same method, the act provides that the president of the superior court and the procurator of any autonomous republic may set in motion disciplinary proceedings against all judicial officials within the autonomous republic, with the same exceptions.[188] The same scheme is embodied in the sections of the Code defining the authority of designated officials to bring

[185]Statutes on the Judiciary. *Fundamental Laws of the Russian Empire*, Volume XVI, section 119.

[186]Jud. Act, 1926, sections 194 and 195.

[187]*Ibid.*, section 187.

[188]*Ibid.*, section 188.

a case before the disciplinary sessions of the regional and provincial courts.[139]

The Disciplinary Department is made up of three judges of the Supreme Court with a member of its presidium presiding. The judges are assigned for this department by the plenum of the Supreme Court.

This department, unlike other departments of the same court, has both original and cassational jurisdiction. The law provides that the decisions of the disciplinary departments of the superior courts of the autonomous republics, the territorial, regional, and provincial courts shall be subject to review by a complaint filed with the Disciplinary Department of the Supreme Court either by the defendants, or by the person who instituted the proceedings, or by the procurator.[140]

The original disciplinary jurisdiction of this Department is over all persons connected with the Supreme Court, the central procuracy, certain high officials of the Commissariat of Justice, all judges of the regional and provincial courts, including the presidents and their deputies, and the procurators of the latter courts and their deputies.[141]

The grounds for instituting disciplinary proceedings against members of the judiciary are (a) acts of commission or omission either within or without the scope of their official duties which, though not subject to criminal prosecution, are inconsistent with the dignity or position of judicial officials; (b) rendering of verdicts or decisions by judges in plain contravention of the general spirit of the law of R.S.F.S.R. and the "interest of the toiling masses",[142] provided the Supreme Court has reversed the verdicts or decisions on these grounds.

The measures which may be invoked by the disciplinary courts are restricted to a remark, a rebuke, a transfer to a different position or a demotion, removal from office coupled with disqualification for any judicial position during a period of two years. In the case of advocates, they may be barred from practicing before the courts for a period of six months.[143]

[139] *Ibid.*, sections 189 and 190.
[140] *Ibid.*, section 199.
[141] *Ibid.*, section 191.
[142] *Ibid.*, section 192.
[143] *Ibid.*, section 193.

IV. ADDITIONAL COURTS

If there need be any substantiation of the proposition that a well-defined theory and its practical application do not always run together, one may point to the constant deviations of Soviet legislators from their once highly cherished principle that any judicial arrangement which tolerates a system of courts for offenses of various grades should be discarded. There is no doubt, in our mind, that the principle of a "very simplified uniform system" of courts, as proclaimed by the communist programme of 1919, was abandoned only under the pressure of hard, every-day actualities which collided with a well-meant principle based purely on abstract theory. The "three-story" judicial structure designed by the judicial reform of November, 1922, was apparently too simple to meet the needs of so vast a country as the Russian Socialist Federative Soviet Republic.[144]

First, there are the autonomous territories which have their own courts. The problem of these republics was, however, solved with comparatively little difficulty. The law provides: "In the autonomous territories territorial courts shall be organized which shall function on the same basis as the provincial court."[145] Thus, there was only a change in the name of the court; the unity of the system was not impaired, for in the autonomous territories there were still to be a people's court, a territorial court, and above these the Supreme Court of the Federated Republic. Second, there are the autonomous republics with a judiciary of their own. Third, and most significant, are the new administrative units, the regions, which, not infrequently, embrace a number of former provinces and even autonomous territories. Here a clear deviation was made and the system became more involved, since the new act decreed that "In the regional and territorial administrative units regional and circuit courts instead of provincial courts shall be organized and shall function."[146] We have, therefore, in the regions and territories two separate courts dividing between them the jurisdiction and authority of the one tribunal of the province, the provincial court. But the complication of the judicial system

[144] Krylenko, *The Judiciary and the Law*, 1927, pages 31 and 32.
[145] Jud. Act, 1926, section 3.
[146] *Ibid.*, section 2.

in the regions goes beyond the mere addition of another court, as we shall observe as we proceed.

a. *Regional and Circuit Courts*

The institution of the regional court was the natural outcome of the creation for administrative or economic reasons of very large territorial units. By the end of 1923, a large Ural Region was established, embracing an area of four former provinces which were now reorganized into fifteen circuits.[147] Soon after, a regional, or territorial, court *(Oblastnoi Sud)* was instituted for this region by a special act,[148] which was followed by another act on the judiciary in the Ural Region.[149] The latter act provided that all judicial and investigating organs of the region should function on the same basis as provided by the general Judiciary Act of 1922 for the provincial court.[150] Similar regional judiciary acts were enacted for the North-Caucasian Region,[151] and a little later for the Siberian Region.[152] The important provisions of these acts, wherein the structure of the regional judiciary was designed and its jurisdiction and powers outlined, were, with some important modifications, incorporated into the Judiciary Act of 1926, which explicitly repealed all former enactments.

1. The Regional Court

The regional court, following the general scheme of the Soviet judicial structure, is the administrative center of the judiciary of the region and also a court of the first instance for certain cases.

The organization and functions of the regional court are similar to those of the provincial court. The provisions of the Code regulating the composition of the court, the qualifications required of its judges and the manner of their election, the divi-

[147]Act on the Ural Region Collected Laws Nos. 103 and 104, Article 1027, and 1028, 1923, section 2. *(Polozhenie ob Uralskoi oblasti. Sobranie Uzakonenii,* 103 and 104—1027 and 1028, 1923.)

[148]Collected Laws No. 18, Article 181, 1924.

[149]Collected Laws No. 20, Article 194, 1924.

[150]*Ibid.*, section 2.

[151]Collected Laws No. 77, Article 595, 1925.

[152]Collected Laws No. 82, Article 619, 1925. All of the above mentioned regions are, of course, a part of the R.S.F.S.R.

sion of the court into the plenum, the presidium, the president, the judicial and disciplinary departments, the functions of each division (with the exception of the plenum), are all identical with corresponding provisions for the provincial court.[153]

There are, however, a few important distinctions to be noted between the provincial and the regional courts. First, the latter has no department of cassation. It is, therefore, the only court in the Soviet system which exercises great authority in matters of supervision and interpretation, and none at all in the realm of cassation. Second, the plenum is divided into an ordinary and enlarged session. The former convenes not less than twice a month, and at least one-half of all the judges of the court must be present, while the enlarged plenum, which meets at least once in six months, is made up of the judges of the regional courts and the presidents of all the circuit courts in the region.[154] This innovation was apparently introduced to create a more direct contact between the two higher courts, the regional and the circuit courts, functioning in such a large territory as the region. The act also provides that for the purpose of creating a uniform judicial policy throughout the region a representative of the territorial courts of any autonomous territory which may be included in the region may participate in the plenary sessions (apparently both the ordinary and the enlarged session) with an advisory vote.[155] The latter provision was necessary, for otherwise the territorial court of an autonomous territory, which is a national unit, would have absolutely no connection, even indirectly, with the highest judicial institution in the region, since the act provides that the territorial courts of the autonomous territories which function on the same basis as the provincial court, are not a part of the judicial institutions subordinate to the regional court.[156]

(a) *Ordinary and Enlarged Plenum*

The ordinary session of the plenum of the regional court considers in general the same sort of questions and problems

[153] Jud. Act, 1926, sections 109—117. See Appendix No. 6, page 374 for diagram.
[154] *Ibid.*, section 118.
[155] *Ibid.*, note to section 118.
[156] *Ibid.*, section 129.

as the plenum of the provincial court. The enlarged session, on the other hand, hears reports on the ordinary investigations and inspections, or special investigations carried on in the circuit and other courts. The chief difference between the plenum of the regional and the plenum of the provincial court appears in their respective powers in the field of interpretation. The ordinary session of the plenum has the authority to interpret the law of a concrete case, where it is not clear or complete. So far its powers are analogous to those enjoyed by the plenum of the provincial court. But unlike the latter, the ordinary session of the plenum of the regional court is not generally required even to send a copy of its interpretation to the Supreme Court; its decision becomes immediately final, and binding on all the courts in the region. If, however, the president or the procurator of the regional court is dissatisfied with the interpretation laid down by the plenum, the question is submitted to the Supreme Court for final action.

The interpretative power of the enlarged plenum of the regional court is far greater than that of the plenum of the provincial court. The former may interpret any question of substantive or procedural law, where it is not clear or complete, although it is not connected with any concrete case. Moot questions may be presented to the enlarged plenum by the president of the regional court, the presidents of the various divisions, the regional procurator, or the plena of the circuit courts. The interpretation reached by this enlarged plenum requires the approval of the plenum of the Supreme Court of the Republic.[157] The machinery of interpretation is intended to work so that each part is connected somehow with all the other parts. For example, the Supreme Court, before approving of the interpretation laid down by the enlarged regional plenum, is to be informed of the opinion of the circuit court where the question has been raised. In case the latter is dissatisfied with the interpretation of the enlarged plenum of the regional court, it must of its own motion send its opinion to the Supreme Court, before the latter reaches its final decision.

[157] *Ibid.*, sections 119, 120 and 122.

(b) *Judicial and Disciplinary Departments*

The judicial and disciplinary departments of the court are organized and function on the same basis, with few minor exceptions, as similar departments of the provincial court.[158]

The disciplinary department takes jurisdiction over all the judges of the circuit courts, including the presidents and their deputies, and the procurators and all other officials, except the judges, of the regional court. This department is also a court of review for cases originally heard by the disciplinary departments of the circuit courts.[159] This is the only field in which the regional court exercises cassational jurisdiction.

The judicial department of the regional court has jurisdiction over (a) counter-revolutionary crimes, such as those assigned to the provincial court, (b) crimes committed by officials in the exercise of their duties, such as pronouncement by judges of unjust sentences from venal or other personal motives, or confinement of a person in custody as a precautionary measure, from personal or venal motives, (c) all other crimes in office, as well as economic crimes, if committed by certain designated judicial and other officials.[160] The original jurisdiction of this court is not very extensive, but it has the authority to transfer to itself for trial any case normally within the jurisdiction of the circuit court.[161]

2. The Circuit Court

This court is the only Soviet judicial tribunal which was established for the first time by the Judiciary Act of December, 1926, and its establishment clearly created a four-story judicial structure. That the regional court could not properly take care of the judicial affairs of such a vast territory as the region was apparently realized at the very beginning. The act creating the Ural Regional Court, in 1924, provided for a large personnel consisting of a president, two deputies, and forty judges, and

[158] *Ibid.*, section 124.

[159] *Ibid.*, section 150.

[160] Code, 1927, section 26a as amended by Collected Laws No. 26, Article 175, 1927. For an explanation of the term "economic crimes", see *supra*, page 70.

[161] *Ibid.*, note to section 26a.

special circuit representatives of the court.[162] The act providing for the North-Caucasian Regional Court went a step further. This court was to consist of seventy-seven judges and was to have six divisions of its cassational department sitting in six different cities within the region.[163] In a similar way an act established a court for the Siberian Region.[164] By this latter act the powers and duties of the circuit representatives were considerably extended and more elaborately defined. Between the system of having special divisions sitting in different cities, with circuit representatives at the regional court, and a system of completely separate circuit courts there was but a narrow gap to bridge, and that was accomplished in December, 1926. The creation of the circuit court was strenuously opposed by many, and it was declared undesirable, from the point of view of simplicity, by two commentators on the Code of Criminal Procedure.[165]

The circuit court in its general make-up resembles the provincial court, though its authority and powers were greatly curtailed by making it subordinate to the higher judicial branch, the regional court. The circuit court's organization and its method of functioning is governed by the rules laid down by the Judicial Act for the provincial court with a few specified exceptions.[166] The judges are elected by the circuit executive committee subject to the confirmation of the regional executive committee, which acts only when it has before it the recommendation of the regional court.[167] A similar method is prescribed for dividing the circuit into territorial districts of the people's courts and of the people's inquisitors.[168]

Although the circuit court is built upon the same plan as the provincial court, it has no presidium; the law provides that "All the duties placed * * * by this Act on the presidium of the provincial court shall be carried out by the plenum of the circuit court."[169]

[162]Collected Laws No. 20, Article 194, 1924.
[163]Collected Laws No. 77, Article 595, 1925, section 12.
[164]Collected Laws No. 82, Article 619, 1925, section 14.
[165]*Commentaries,* page 35.
[166]Jud. Act, 1926, section 132.
[167]*Ibid.*, section 136.
[168]*Ibid.*, section 137.
[169]*Ibid.*, section 133.

The cassational powers of this court are similar to those exercised by the provincial court, since its superior, the regional court, has no cassational authority. The original jurisdiction of the circuit court, exercised by its judicial division, is the same as that of the provincial court, except over the offenses specially assigned to the jurisdiction of the regional court.[170]

In matters of judicial interpretation, the power of the circuit court is restricted to the preliminary discussion of questions raised as to the lack of clearness or completeness of the law of a concrete case. The problem raised together with the court's opinion must be forwarded to the plenum of the regional court for a final decision.[171]

The circuit court is, thus, a judicial tribunal of lesser importance than the provincial court, though the form of its organization is almost the same. This fact is indeed compatible with the relative significance of the two different territorial units; the province is usually a much larger, and more important administrative division than the circuit. We have observed that the Ural Region was divided into fifteen circuits, whereas previously four provinces embraced the same area.[172] The tendency to reorganize the country into regions is growing constantly. This will, naturally, increase the importance of this new, more complicated judicial arrangement; the "four-story" system with a people's, circuit and regional court in the region and the Supreme Court at Moscow, will, we may predict, cease to be the exception. The rapid growth of this new territorial unit may be seen from the fact that in 1927 there were only twenty-six circuit courts, while in 1928 their number had increased to sixty-one.[173]

b. *The Development of the Regional and Circuit Courts*

These regional and circuit courts have emerged from the Judiciary Act of 1926 as a compromise between two opposing tendencies. But prior to that they had already undergone an interesting development of their own. The creation in a few sections of the country of large units thereby abolishing the

[170] Code, 1927 (as amended in March, 1927).
[171] Jud. Act, 1926, sec. 134.
[172] See *supra*, note 147.
[173] *The Weekly*, No. 17, 1928.

former provinces, immediately called for some changes in the judicial structure, since the form constructed by the Judiciary Act of 1922 become plainly inoperative. In what direction was it to be changed? Here two different tendencies strove to direct the inevitable modification of the system.

There were those who insisted that the "three-story" system of courts must be preserved at all events. Therefore, the logical solution, from their point of view, was to substitute the regional court for the provincial court with the latter's structure, functions, and authority remaining unchanged. But to facilitate the work of the court in the enlarged area, the regional court was to have a number of divisions with original and cassational jurisdiction situated at the former provincial centres. These divisions were to be devoid of any administrative power. Cases originally tried by these divisions were to be taken by cassation directly to the Supreme Court of the Republic. As this theory prevailed at the beginning, the first acts were framed accordingly. But no matter how persistently the adherents of the three-story system clamored for its maintenance, it soon proved to be unsatisfactory. Hence, the other theory, which could not make itself felt at the beginning, came to the foreground. It proposed to create circuit courts, standing between the regional and the people's courts, entrusted with original and cassational jurisdiction. The regional court, under this plan, was to be the highest tribunal of the region, invested with cassational power in all cases tried originally at the circuit court. In other words, the aim was to erect a completely new addition to the judicial structure, and to effect a "four-story" judicial system for the regions.

Both tendencies strove for expression when the draft of a new judiciary act was being discussed. The Act of 1926, as finally passed by the All-Russian Central Executive Committee, was a compromise between these two opposing tendencies. A distinctly new court, the circuit court, was instituted in all the new regional units. But the adherents of the "three-story" system yet consoled themselves with the idea that no fourth wing had been really created, since the power to review, by way of cassation and supervision, cases tried at the circuit court was under this Act of 1926 still lodged with the Supreme Court of the Republic.[174]

[174]Krylenko, *The Law and the Judiciary*, 1927, pages 86 and 87.

This compromise was evidently recognized as a mere temporary solution, and, in the words of Krylenko, it could not boast of "its constructiveness or of its logic."[175] That the tendency is drifting rapidly towards investing the regional courts with cassational powers, was correctly observed by Mr. Krylenko even immediately after the passage of the Act of November, 1926.[176] Now, this seems to be a certainty. As soon as the project for a new Code, which is now being discussed, will pass through the legislative channels, the judiciary will consist of four complete branches in all the sections of the country where the region has been made the administrative unit. When this occurs the Soviet authorities will be confronted with a new problem concerning the powers and functions of the Supreme Court of the Republic as a court of cassation and supervision over courts of the region. The granting of cassational jurisdiction to the regional court will necessarily deprive the Supreme Court to a considerable extent of its most important function of directing and unifying the judicial policies of the courts through the exercise of its powers of cassation and supervision.

It is noteworthy that not only is there a complete four-story judicial system in prospect, but the possibility of further subdividing the criminal, as well as civil, jurisdiction may be witnessed in the near future. The Commissariat of Justice has already approved a project for a new court of the peace or chamber of reconciliation, attached to the village soviets.[177]

V. COURTS IN THE AUTONOMOUS REPUBLICS

The structure of the criminal courts in the autonomous republics within the R.S.F.S.R. does not, in any real sense, interfere with the general scheme of the three-story judicial system.

[175] *Ibid.*, page 157.
[176] *Ibid.*, page 158.
[177] *The Weekly*, No. 9, 1928, page 279. This project intends to create a village court consisting of a chairman elected from the members of the village soviet, and twelve judges elected at a general meeting of all the voters of the village. A court session would consist of the chairman and two judges out of the twelve elected. Such court would take jurisdiction in cases of assault and battery, slander, etc., if both parties live within the territory under the jurisdiction of the village soviet. The court's duty would be to attempt a reconciliation, but it would also have the power to impose a fine up to 10 rubles, or give a sentence of 7 days' imprisonment.

The autonomous republic has its people's courts, and a superior court. Where the Republic is divided into provinces, its judicial apparatus is to consist of a people's court, provincial court, and, in any case where the sanction of the presidium of the *Vtzeek* is obtained, a branch of the Supreme Court.[178]

a. *Superior Court*

The superior court was first created by the Judiciary Act of 1924, which stated that this court shall function in the autonomous republics on the same basis as the provincial court.[179] The Act of 1926 dropped the analogy between the two courts, and has greatly extended the powers of the superior court. The sections in the special chapter of the Code devoted to the judiciary in the autonomous republics are framed so as to make the court resemble, in many ways, the Supreme Court of the R.S.F.S.R.

The president and the deputy president of the superior court are elected for the term of one year by the central executive committee of the autonomous republic, while the other judges are nominated by the people's commissariat of justice of the autonomous republic and confirmed by the same committee.[180] The president, his deputies, and all the judges of the superior court, must, to be eligible for election, possess all the qualifications required for judges of the provincial court.[181] The fact that the central authorities at Moscow are not required, even as a mere formality, to confirm the election of the superior court judges is indicative of the autonomous character of the republics, but is not, in any sense, a relaxation of the central control over the judiciary. The central authorities of the autonomous republics take the place of the Moscow authorities in the case of the provincial, regional, and the Supreme Court. To the extent that the autonomous republic is not absolutely independent of Moscow, the latter has a grip also on the superior court. For example, the People's Commissariat of Justice of the R.S.F.S.R. may protest to the central executive committee of the autonomous

[178]Jud. Act, 1926, section 151.
[179]Collected Laws No. 78, Article 782, 1924, section 1.
[180]Jud. Act, 1926, section 158.
[181]*Ibid.*, section 157.

republic the election of the president, or deputy president, of the superior court.[182] So also there are provisions that the president of the superior court must submit a report on the activities of his court to the Supreme Court,[183] and that a copy of every decision of the plenum of the superior court on any question of uncertainty or incompleteness of the law must be forwarded to the commissariat of justice of the autonomous republics and to the Supreme Court of the R.S.F.S.R., while questions of interpretation, mentioned above, are decided finally by the plenum of the superior court, and if the president of the latter court or the procurator of the autonomous republic is dissatisfied with the interpretation, he may cause the entire question to be transferred to the Supreme Court for final determination.[184]

1. Functions of the Court

The superior court, in accordance with the general scheme of the Soviet judiciary, has a plenum, presidium, and judicial, cassational, and disciplinary departments,[185] which are made up in the same way as are similar divisions and departments of the other courts. Thus, the court exercises the functions of supervision, cassation, and original jurisdiction as do the Supreme, regional, or provincial court. The cassational jurisdiction of the superior court extends, of course, to all the cases tried at the people's courts within the autonomous republic. Its original jurisdiction, however, is not defined either directly or indirectly, the act merely stating that it shall be a "court of first instance for all cases assigned to its jurisdiction by law."[186] This jurisdiction is apparently fixed separately either by the law of the autonomous republic itself, or by special legislation of the R.S.F.S.R. since the Codes of the latter are silent on that point.

2. Status of the Superior Court

The exact status of the superior court is by no means permanently settled. The entire question as to its position within the

[182] *Ibid.*, section 158.
[183] *Ibid.*, section 161.
[184] *Ibid.*, section 165.
[185] *Ibid.*, section 155.
[186] *Ibid.*, section 154.

Soviet legal system is inseparably connected with the general status of the autonomous republics within the political framework of the constituent soviet republics.

There are two opposing tendencies struggling to control the highly complicated mechanism of the Soviet state. The general desire for complete centralization of political authority and strict uniformity in matters political and socio-economical is obvious everywhere. On the other hand, there is present the equally persistent idea of national self-determination and cultural autonomy. The Soviet political philosophy flatly repudiates any doctrine based upon the slogan "One nation, one language". True, all the autonomous republics are to be linked and welded together in the Union by a harmonious striving for a definite economic and social order. But as the people of the innumerable ethnographic entities within the Union of the Soviets are imbued with the idea of national self-determination, and are constantly encouraged to work for the development of their national culture, it will prove quite difficult to keep their awakened national consciousness within the strict bounds of the cultural sphere. The tendency to cultivate a desire for self-expression also in matters not purely cultural must inevitably follow, even if undercurrent.

This indefinite, but nevertheless real, striving for self-expression is also evident so far as the judiciary is concerned though the communist "orthodoxy" may be relied upon to check any excessive separatistic tendencies. The idea prevalent at the present time, however, among representatives of the autonomous republics is that the superior court is to be in the nature of a supreme court for the autonomous republic. At the third conference of the commissariats of both the R.S.F.S.F. and its autonomous republics, we are told, there "were expressed such opinions as, if carried to their logical conclusion, would inevitably lead to the separation of the commissariats of justice of the autonomous republics from that of the Federated Republic, and consequently the separation of the autonomous republics themselves from the U.S.S.R."[187]

But even those who would not consider any proposal that the superior court occupy the position of the highest and final

[187] *The Weekly* No. 25, 1927, page 754.

judicial authority in the autonomous republics concede, however, that "The superior courts should be vested with greater original and cassational power than the provincial or regional courts. The authority of the superior courts in matters of judicial control must also be extended."[188] We may safely conjecture that whatever changes will be made concerning the superior court will be towards increasing rather than diminishing the powers of this tribunal at the expense of the Supreme Court of the Federated Republic.

b. *People's Court*

The organization and functions of the people's courts of the autonomous republics are governed by the sections of the Judiciary Act dealing with other people's courts.[189] The names of the executive bodies and territorial divisions differ so as to correspond with the governmental structure of the autonomous republic.[190]

[188]Krylenko, *The Law and the Judiciary,* 1927, page 83.

[189]Jud. Act, 1926, section 173.

[190]Except the different courts described in this chapter there is also a separate, special network of disciplinary courts functioning throughout the R.S.F.S.R. As early as 1919 there were established special workmen's disciplinary "comradely" courts, to keep up the morale of the enterprise. In 1923 a Special Disciplinary Court Act was passed (Collected Laws No. 54, Article 531, 1923) which enactment was replaced by the Act of 1926. (Collected Laws No. 36, Article 294, 1926.) This act, as its predecessor of 1923, did not apply merely to workingmen, but to all government officials. It was instituted "for the purpose of combating negligence in office, misconduct, or improper actions by officials entrusted with responsible duties, if such actions do not carry with them criminal responsibility." The last sentence explains why these courts are not to be treated as criminal courts; they step in *when there is no ground for criminal prosecution.* Such courts were organized at the All-Russian Central Executive Committee, as a supreme disciplinary court, at the autonomous republics, regional, territorial, provincial and circuit executive committees. Among the punishments they were authorized to inflict there was also a "home arrest" up to one month. These courts apparently fell into disfavor and were displaced by "comradely courts" created by the Act of 1930. (Collected Laws, 1930, No. 4, Article 52.) The latter Act was superseded by the enactment of 1931, published in *Soviet Justice,* No. 10, 1931, establishing the so-called "Industrial-Comradely" courts. *(Proizvodstvenno-Tovarishcheskii Sud.)* These courts which function within the limit of industrial enterprise consist of a chairman and three members elected by the workers from among their own number. It is worth noting that this court has jurisdiction also over larceny of property not exceeding 50 rubles committed within the factory or similar unit. The sentence of this court which may consist of a warning, public reprimand, a fine not exceeding 10 rubles, or an order to compensate for damages up to 50 rubles, is not subject to any complaint.

Chapter III

CRIMINAL COURTS OF THE UNION OF SOCIALIST SOVIET REPUBLICS (U.S.S.R.)

The judicial system of the Union consists of a Supreme Court, with its numerous departments, and military tribunals which are an integral part of the Union Judiciary. When we realize that the military tribunals, as the name plainly indicates, are courts which function only in a restricted sphere, and can hardly be considered a part of the ordinary criminal courts, it becomes clear that the Union is practically without courts of original jurisdiction to enforce its numerous laws and regulations. These laws are actually enforced by the courts of the constituent republics, or their autonomous parts. It is characteristic of the general nature of the Union government that the criminal statutes covering offenses against the Union, such as counter-revolutionary acts or military crimes, enacted by the Union Central Executive Committee, have been incorporated into the Criminal Code of the R.S.F.S.R. by the legislative authorities of the latter.[1]

I. THE SUPREME COURT OF THE UNION

This is the only court in Sovietland created by the Constitution of the Union. The latter provides not only for the establishment of the Supreme Court, but outlines in a general way its jurisdiction and authority, the composition of the court and its relation to the other branches of the Union Government and to the constituent republics.[2] It was in pursuance of the Constitutional provisions that the acts dealing with the organization and powers of the Supreme Court were passed.

The Supreme Court consists of a president, deputy president, and thirty judges.[3] It carries out its functions through the president of the Court, the plenum, the Criminal Judicial De-

[1]Cr. Code, 1926, Part IX.

[2]Constitution, U.S.S.R., sections 43-47.

[3]The law nowhere states the exact number of judges, but this may be inferred from the number fixed for the various departments.

partment and the Special Session for criminal cases, and lastly the Military Department.[4] In its general frame work this court differs from the Supreme Court of the R.S.F.S.R. in that it has neither a presidium nor a separate cassational department, although it is not completely without cassational jurisdiction, as we shall presently observe. All the judges of the Union Supreme Court, except the representatives of the supreme courts of the constituent republics, are appointed by the presidium of the Central Executive Committee of the Union *(Tzeek)*.[5] It is rather interesting to note that the judges of this court are not subject to any arrest or search, nor can they be held for trial without the knowledge and consent of the Presidium of the *Tzeek* of the Union.[6]

a. *The President of the Court*

As the Supreme Court has no presidium, its president is vested with great powers and is charged with the performance of important duties. He looks after the activity of all the departments of the Court and directly supervises its administrative functions.[7] He, of course, presides over the sessions of the plenum, but he may also preside at the sittings of the Judicial Department.[8] In the absence of the regular judges, he appoints the presiding and other judges of the Judicial Department.[9]

The president has also the power to request the presidents of the supreme courts of the constituent republics to forward to the proper judicial authorities, for review, and by way of supervision, any verdict or judgment violative of the general legislation of the Union or prejudicial to the interest of another constituent republic. He may simultaneously petition the presidium of the Union *Tzeek* to suspend such verdict or judgment,[10] a power introduced by the Act of July, 1929. In line with the

[4]Sup. Court Act, section 9.
[5]*Ibid.*, sections 10-13.
[6]*Ibid.*, section 15.
[7]*Ibid.*, section 24.
[8]*Ibid.*, section 26.
[9]*Ibid.*, section 24, subsection c.
[10]*Ibid.*, section 27.

tendency to increase his powers, he was given the right to participate by an advisory vote in the sessions of the powerful presidium of the *Tzeek,* as well as in the sessions of the Soviet of the People's Commissars of the Union.[11]

The president convokes the plenum and may participate, by an advisory vote, in all sessions of the Court's different departments. He must also report and defend the plenum's position in all matters removed from the Supreme Court to the presidium of the Union Central Executive Committee for final determination. All questions and problems are laid before the Supreme Court through the president.

b. *The Plenum*

1. Composition

One of the outstanding structural features of the plenum of the Supreme Court of The Union is the fact that unlike the plena of the courts which have been discussed not all the judges of the Supreme Court are included in its membership, although it is often referred to by the statutes as the Supreme Court.

The plenum consists of sixteen judges.[12] It comprises the president of the court, his deputy, three presidents of the departments of the court, four other judges (all of whom are appointed by the presidium of the Central Executive Committee of the Union), and the presidents of the supreme courts of the seven constituent republics.[13] That it is so composed strikingly illustrates the intention to interrelate the Supreme Court of the Union and those of the constituent republics. While the former is unquestionably supreme in matters affecting the Union, the supreme courts of the republics are made parts of the plenum and thus become participants in decisions which may affect their interests. That the Supreme Court of the Union represents the interests of every republic, and not exclusively those of the Union as a distinct political entity, is stated as follows: "The Su-

[11] *Ibid.,* section 25.

[12] Originally, in 1923, there were only eleven members of the plenum, but the third congress of the Union Soviets held in May, 1925, increased it to fifteen, and by the admission of the Tadzhik Republic the number was increased to sixteen.

[13] Sup. Court Act, section 10.

preme Court shall be guided by the interests of the Union as a whole and those of the separate republics and shall defend their sovereign rights."[14] The idea that the plenum is to be in constant touch with the constituent sovereign republics permeates the provisions dealing with its organization and functions. For example, the procurator of the supreme court of any constituent republic or his assistant may participate, by an advisory vote, in all the sessions of the plenum; further, if he submits any question, he may himself report on it, though the plenum may appoint its own reporter.[15]

2. Sessions of the Plenum

The plenum holds regular and special sessions. Its regular sessions are held bi-monthly, while special sessions take place whenever deemed necessary by the president of the court, and must be held immediately upon request by the Procurator of the Union, the procurator of any constituent republic, or upon demand by three members of the plenum.[16] To constitute a quorum not less than three fifths of its membership, including three presidents of the supreme courts of the constituent republics, must be present. In exceptional cases a quorum may consist of seven judges, two of whom must be presidents of the supreme courts of the constituent republics.[17] All questions before the plenum are decided by a majority vote. In case of a tie the matter is presented to the presidium of the Union *Tzeek* for final determination.[18]

3. Function and Authority

The plenum, as the highest judicial body within the Union, exercises, theoretically speaking, an authority compatible with its position. The law provides that the Supreme Court, through its plenum, is to see that the Constitution of the Union and its laws are properly understood and executed. To this end the

[14] These words are quoted from the Instructions of 1924 which were repealed by the Act of 1929. But this latter Act is permeated with the same idea.

[15] Sup. Court Act, section 19.

[16] *Ibid.*, section 17.

[17] *Ibid.*, section 18.

[18] *Ibid.*, section 20.

plenum is to promulgate, under prescribed conditions, its authoritative instructions, or offer explanations concerning general Union legislation to the supreme courts of the constituent republics at their request, or at the suggestion of the Procurator of the Union or the procurators of the constituent republics, or of its own motion.[19] Such explanations or interpretations are also given on the initiative of the Union *Tzeek's* presidium or on request by the Soviet of People's Commissars of the Union.[20]

The plenum may of its own motion review and reverse regulations, verdicts and decisions rendered by any regular department, or special judicial session, of the Supreme Court of the Union, or it may do so on motion of the president of the Union Supreme Court or upon complaint of the Procurator of the Union. Reviews may also be taken up by the plenum on the motion of the presiding judge of the court which rendered the decision, etc., or on complaint of the procurator participating in the case.[21] The procedure and the effect of this review are similar to cassation, for if the verdict or decision is in violation of law, the plenum either returns the case for re-trial or, whenever possible, modifies the virdict or sentence itself.[22] This is practically the only instance where causes terminate in the plenum of the Supreme Court, whose opinion in such cases is ordinarily conclusive and final[23]—that is, the opinion does not require any confirmation or approval by the presidium of the Union Central Executive Committee *(Tzeek)*. But there are some situations where the superior powers of the executive authorities of the Union may be called upon even in these cases to exercise a check upon the decisions of the highest judicial institution. The law provides that: "The decisions of the plenum of the Union Supreme Court, which do not require the confirmation of the presidium of the Union *Tzeek,* shall be binding on all the courts and institutions of the Union and the constituent republics, but they may be made subject of complaint before the pres-

[19]*Ibid.*, section 3, subsection a.
[20]*Ibid.*, section 2, subsection d.
[21]*Ibid.*, section 3, subsection c.
[22]*Ibid.*, note to section 3.
[23]This statement must not, however, be taken in the sense that the court knows of no authority superior to it.

idium of the Union *Tzeek* exclusively at the instance of the procurator of the Union Supreme Court, the Soviet of People's Commissars of the Union, or the presidia of the central executive committees of the constituent republics."[24] It is worth noting that only a few of the highest authorities can demand a review of the verdicts or decisions of the Union Supreme Court.

The plenum of the Supreme Court is also vested with the power to review legislation and regulations of the central legislative and administrative authorities, which are usually concentrated in one body, both of the Union and of the constituent republics. This takes place whenever any act, decree, or regulation is attacked on the ground of its being inconsistent with the provisions of the Union Constitution or the general Union legislation. In addition, it may review legally binding verdicts, judgments and decisions of the supreme courts of the constituent republics. The plenum of the Supreme Court of the Union takes jurisdiction if the verdict, decision, etc., is either alleged to be contrary to general legislation of the Union or is prejudicial to the interests of another republic of the Union. These powers would seem to make the Union Supreme Court a high tribunal, with reviewing powers analogous to those of the Supreme Court of the United States. But such an analogy would be wholly erroneous. Unlike our own Supreme Court, the Supreme Court of the Soviet Union is not a tribunal whose word or opinion in all matters within its purview is final. On the contrary, this court, in examining the validity either of legislation or verdicts of other supreme courts, merely renders its opinion, which the presidium of the Central Executive Committee of the Union may or may not confirm. In accordance with the Soviet system of government, the Supreme Court of the Union is merely a part, the judicial branch, of the Central Union Government; it is the latter's expert legal commission whose opinion will in most cases be confirmed. But, nevertheless, the approval of the presidium may conceivably be withheld where a question of policy is involved. Whether this approval is absolutely required before the court's opinion may

[24]Sup. Court Act, section 7. The repealed Supreme Court Act of 1924, section 4, excluded the presidia of the central executive committees of the constituent republics.

have any legal force, or becomes necessary upon the demand of certain authorities objecting to the court's rulings will be discussed later. The constitutonal provision creating the Supreme Court is highly instructive. It states "* * * there shall be created a Supreme Court of the Union which shall be attached to the Union Central Executive Committee."[25] The Court is, therefore, plainly made a part, the judicial instrument, of the all-powerful *Tzeek*.

Verdicts and decisions as well as legislative and administrative acts arrive before the plenum of the Supreme Court for review through different routes according to the circumstances. Where acts and decrees are to be reviewed, the Court passes on their constitutionality only upon the request of the presidium of the Union Central Executve Commttee, if the question concerns enactments of the Soviet of Labor and Defense, the Soviet of People's Commissars of the Union, the central executive committees or the soviets of people's commissars of the constituent republics or their presidia.[26] By the Act of 1929, the Supreme Court may itself or at the suggestion of the Union Procurator petition the presidium of the Union *Tzeek* to permit deliberation on the question of the validity of acts and decrees of the central executive committees of the constituent republics and their presidia. This is done with a view to submit the legislative acts in question to the presidium of the Union *Tzeek* for annulment.[27] But if the order or decree whose constitutionality is attacked was passed by one of the commissariats of the Union, or by any Union central body except the Union *Tzeek*, its presidium or the Soviet of People's Commissars of the Union,[28] the Union Supreme Court may review it either on its own initiative or at the suggestion of the presidia of the central executive committees of the constituent republics or the

[25]Constitution, U.S.S.R., section 43.

[26]Sup. Court Act, section 2, subsection a.

[27]*Ibid.*, section 2, subsection c.

[28]*Ibid.*, section 2, subsection b. Before the passage of the Act of 1929, there was considerable discussion as to whether the enactments or decrees of the Soviet of People's Commissars of the Union could not be brought for review to the Union Supreme Court directly. See A. M. Turubiner, *Essays on Government Organization of the U.S.S.R.* (in Russian), page 62, Moscow, 1925.

Procurator of the Union. Should the court deem any act or decree inconsistent with the Union Constitution, or the general Union legislation, it submits them to the presidium for suspension or annulment.[29] In last analysis, this arrangement tends merely to facilitate the work of the presidium of the *Tzeek,* by rendering it expert legal advice, so that it may know how to decide constitutional or legal questions.

The Union Constitution specifically provides that the presidium of the Union *Tzeek,* and not the Supreme Court, "shall have power to suspend or annul enactments of the Soviet of People's Commissars and the separate commissariats of the Union, and of the central executive committee and the soviet of people's commissars of the constituent republics".[30] The question whether the Supreme Court may, on its own initiative, deliberate on the validity of certain acts and state its conclusions to the presidium, or must refrain from doing this unless requested by the latter, is a point of procedure, though an important one, rather than a fundamental matter of constitutional principle.

In reviewing verdicts, sentences and civil judgments rendered by the supreme courts of the constituent republics, a function termed judicial supervision, the Union Supreme Court is called upon to exercise its supervisory powers whenever the verdicts or sentences complained of are either inconsistent with the laws of the Union or prejudicial to the interests of another constituent republic. In the latter instance the theory that the Supreme Court of the Union shall concern itself with the interests of each republic is put into practice. The verdict or decision is then reviewed by the plenum of the Union Supreme Court either on its own motion, or that of the Procurator of the Union, or of the constituent republic whose interest is affected by the verdict or decision challenged.[31] If the plenum of the Supreme Court finds that any verdict, decision or decree is invalid because either in-

[29]Out of forty recommendations for annulment of acts or regulations of the organs of the Union, the presidium of the *Tzeek* agreed with the court in thirty instances, disagreed in four cases and transferred six to the Union Soviet of Commissars for action. See V. K. Dyablo, *The Judicial Safeguard of the Constitution,* Moscow, 1928, page 109. *(Sudebnaya Okhrana Konstitutzii.)*

[30]Constitution, U.S.S.R., section 31.

[31]Sup. Court Act, section 3, subsection b.

consistent with the laws of the Union or prejudicial to the interests of any other constituent republic, it will present such verdict, decision or decree to the presidium for annulment.[32] If, on the other hand, it dismisses the charge of invalidity, the decision would seem to be final.[33]

The verdicts, decisions or decrees of the supreme courts of the constituent republics which are annulled by the presidium, usually on the recommendation of the Union Supreme Court, are remitted to the central executive committee of the respective constituent republic for proper action; but if the protest, or what amounts to a recommendation to annul, of the Union Supreme Court is not acceptable to the presidium, the case is returned to the supreme court of the constituent republic, whence it came;[34] since the latter's decision is upheld the case stands in the same position as if it were never contested.

The various reviewing and interpreting functions of the Union Supreme Court, excercised through its plenum, may be thus briefly summarized:

(a) The Court exercises powers of review over the decisions of its own departments. The decisions reached are final unless and until steps are taken by certain of the highest executive authorities to bring them before the presidium of the Union Central Executive Committee, for final determination.

(b) The court reviews and merely renders its opinion, *which is not a decision or judgment,* with regard to the constitutional validity of legislative acts or decrees. This review may be divided into two parts:

(1) Where the contested enactment was passed or decreed by the Soviet of Labor and Defense, the Soviet of People's Commissars of the Union, or by the central executive committee

[32]This is nothing more than a recommendation which may be made to the presidium also at the initiative of the court.

[33]This is one of the instances where the court's opinion does not require the confirmation of the Union *Tzeek,* before it becomes legally binding. Therefore such an opinion of the court would be final unless the Procurator of the Union removes the matter, which he may, to the presidium of the *Tzeek.*

[34]Such procedure was explicitly provided by the Instructions, which are no longer in force since the passage of the Supreme Court Act of 1929. But it would seem that the same procedure would still be followed.

or its presidium of any constituent republic, the court presents its opinion to the presidium of the Union Central Executive Committee, only when requested by this presidium. Naturally, the question presented will revert to the presidium whence it came, regardless of the nature of the court's opinion.

(2) Where the challenged enactment was passed by the central executive committee of any constituent republic, the court may also deliberate and present its opinion to the presidium upon obtaining the permission of this presidium to do so.

(3) If the legislation or regulation attacked comes from other sources than those above enumerated, the order of procedure is reversed. The question will not reach the presidium unless the court is in favor of annulment. The Union Supreme Court may wield here indirectly a considerable power, since it may prevent a veto or annulment by the presidium with the result that the decree or regulation stands.

(c) It reviews verdicts, judgments, or decisions of the supreme courts of the constituent republics.

(1) When the challenge is based on constitutional grounds or a violation of the general legislation of the Union, or it is contended that the decision is prejudicial to the interest of another constituent republic, the Union Supreme Court may render its opinion for annulment and send the case, with the opinion or recommendation, to the presidium.

(d) It explains and interprets general Union laws to the highest authorities of the Union as well as to the supreme courts of the constituent republics. Such interpretations are ordinarily final unless they are challenged by the Procurator of the Union.

c. *Criminal Judicial Department*

The judges of the Criminal Judicial Department, like the judges of the other departments, are appointed by the presidium of the Union Central Executive Committee, which alone may dismiss them.[85] The Judicial Department is organized by the

[85] This was originally provided in the Instructions, section 2. That the Act of 1929 left this rule intact can be inferred from sections 13 and 15 of the Act.

plenum of the Union Supreme Court, and consists of a president and one regular judge, both specifically named for these offices by the presidium of the Union *Tzeek,* and three judges assigned for one year by the plenum of the Union Supreme Court from among its judges. The president of the Department is, as we know, a member of the plenum. By this arrangement the Department, through its president, is always in close contact with the plenum, as it is his duty to take part in the plenary sessions of the Union Supreme Court.[36] The president of the department not only presides at the sessions, but, with the consent of the president of the plenum, also appoints Supreme Court judges to serve at the Special Sessions of his Department held outside the capital.[37] These criminal sessions take place in each case only upon the direction of the presidium of the Union Central Executive Committee.

1. Composition and Jurisdiction

At each administrative or judicial session of the Criminal Judicial Department three judges, including the president, take part. One of the three judges may be a co-judge specifically appointed for the particular case from among the group of twenty-nine co-judges appointed by the presidium of the Union *Tzeek* for judicial duty on the Union Supreme Court. Fourteen of these co-judges are selected from a list of candidates submitted by the presidia of the central executive committees of the constituent republics, and fifteen are chosen from the candidates recommended by the Union Supreme Court.[38]

This Depatrment or court takes original jurisdiction (a) over members of the Union *Tzeek* and other high officials of the Union when charged with crime in office, political crimes and economic offenses; (b) over criminal cases of exceptional importance either to the Union or to two or more constituent republics. The latter jurisdiction, to be sure, is not absolute, for the order of the presidium of the Union *Tzeek* is a prerequisite in

[36]Sup. Court Act, sections 9 and 11.
[37]*Ibid.*, section 40, subsections a and c.
[38]*Ibid.*, section 14 as amended in 1930. See Collected Laws, U.S.S.R., No. 27, Article 30, 1930. ((*Sobranie Zakonov,* S.S.S.R., 27-30, 1930.)

each instance.[39] The Department when trying a criminal case applies the laws of the republic where the alleged crime was committed.[40] It is characteristic of the entire scheme that the Union Court maintains, in many ways, a contact with the judiciary of the separate republics. For example, the preliminary inquiry, which is rquired in all cases tried by the Criminal Judicial Department, may, at the suggestion of the Union Procurator, be conducted by the senior inquisitor attached to the procuracy of the constituent republic where the trial is held. The Union Procurator may, however, assign one of the inquisitors attached to the Union procuracy to conduct the preliminary inquiry.[41]

To facilitate the work of this Department, all the governmental organs of the Union as well as of the constituent republics are required to carry out the orders and requests made upon them by the Department in connection with its activities.[42]

By the Supreme Court Act of 1929 the jurisdiction of the Criminal Judicial Department was considerably extended by granting to it power to order a conditional release of a prisoner before his term expires, in cases where the sentence was imposed by this Department or by the Special Session.[43]

2. Special Session for Criminal Cases

The Criminal Judicial Department is not the only court through which the Union Supreme Court exercises its original criminal jurisdiction, as provided by the Union Constitution and the Supreme Court Act. There is also the Special Session of the Supreme Court. This Court, as its name indicates, is not a regularly functioning branch of the Supreme Court, but is organized to try a specific case, only upon the direction of the presidium of the Union Central Executive Committee. This Session is composed of three judges, including the presiding judge, appointed from the personnel of the Supreme Court or its reserve judges, if there are any such.[44] Each sitting of this Special Session

[39] Sup. Court Act, sections 4 and 29.
[40] *Ibid.*, section 5.
[41] *Ibid.*, sections 65 and 80.
[42] *Ibid.*, section 6.
[43] *Ibid.*, section 36.
[44] *Ibid.*, section 12.

is made up of three judges, including one co-judge appointed by the plenum of the Union Supreme Court. Such Special Session takes jurisdiction over criminal cases that touch upon the interest of one or more of the constituent republics—cases charging certain offenses against members of the Central Executive Committee and other high officials.[45] The verdicts or sentences of both the regular Criminal Judicial Department and the Special Sessions are not subject to cassational complaint but may be carried, as already described, to the plenum of the Union Supreme Court, by designated authorities, and such attack temporarily suspends the sentence.[46] The original jurisdiction of the Union Supreme Court extends also to disputes between constituent republics, but it then is presumably, a purely civil and not criminal matter.

The Special Session, as well as the Judicial Department, applies the substantive and procedural law of the constituent republic in which the court sits.[47]

d. *The Military Department of the Supreme Court*

1. Composition and Original Jurisdiction

Unlike the Criminal Judicial Department, the judges of the Military Department are directly assigned for service by the presidium of the Union Central Executive Committee. This Department is made up of a president and six judges, and functions under the direct supervision of the Union Supreme Court.[48] The Military Department has original jurisdiction over cases of exceptional importance, assigned to it by the presidium of the Union Central Executive Committee or by the plenum of the Union Supreme Court; it also takes jurisdiction over certain high military officials against whom criminal charges are made.[49] Like the Judicial Department, this Military Department has also power to grant a conditional release to a prisoner sentenced by it before his term expires.[50]

[45] *Ibid.*, sections 12 and 29.
[46] *Ibid.*, section 34.
[47] *Ibid.*, section 5.
[48] *Ibid.*, section 11, third paragraph.
[49] *Ibid.*, section 43.
[50] *Ibid.*, section 46.

2. Cassation and Supervision

Unlike the other departments of the Supreme Court, the Military Department exercises great powers of a cassational and supervisory nature, which were first developed under the Union Act on Military Tribunals[51] of August, 1926. Before this date the supervisory powers of this Department were scant. It could petition the presidium to trasfer any criminal case from local Union military tribunals to itself; it had also authority to institute proceedings before the plenum of the Union Supreme Court, through the president of the Military Department, in order to carry a decision of a supreme court of a constituent republic before the presidium of the Union Central Executive Committee, whenever such decision was cassational and concerned a verdict rendered by a local military tribunal.[52] This authority has now lost its significance, since the connection between military tribunals of the Union and the supreme courts of the constituent republics has been severed. Prior to the Military Tribunals Act of 1926, the power of cassation, i. e. annulment of verdicts and decisions of the local Union military tribunals, was vested in the supreme courts of the constituent republics.[53] But this power was first transferred by the Act of 1926 to the Military Department of the Union Supreme Court,[54] which at present has direct supervision over all the military tribunals within the Union.[55]

The Act of 1929 has greatly extended and clarified the cassational and supervisory powers of the Military Department, while it has abolished the hitherto existing Military-Transport Department.

The cassational session comprises a president and two judges, one of whom is a representative of the supreme court of the constituent republic on whose territory the crime was committed.[56] A cassational complaint must be heard in the presence of the special assistant procurator, within one month from the time it

[51]Act on Military Tribunals and Military Procuracy, Collected Laws, U.S.S.R., No. 57, Article 413, 1926. (*Polozhenie O voennykh Tribunalakh i Voennoi Prokurature Sobranie Zakonov,* S.S.S.R., 57-413, 1926.)

[52]Instruction, section 55.

[53]*Ibid.,* section 53.

[54]Act on Military Tribunals, *op. cit., supra,* note 51, section 29.

[55]Sup. Court Act, section 53.

[56]*Ibid.,* section 47.

was filed, or within one week in capital cases.[57] The power to review by way of cassation or supervision extends to all verdicts and sentences rendered by any military tribunal of the Union.

The president of the Military Department has the authority to demand that any case decided or pending before the military tribunals shall be transferred to his Department, and the latter may review it by way of supervision, with the power to suspend sentence.[58] The power to demand a transfer from a military tribunal is also vested in the president of the Supreme Court, its procurator and his assistant. In addition to this the Department may grant a stay of execution in capital cases, even when no cassational complaint has been made.[59] This power arises because of the information which must be furnished to the Department by the tribunal imposing the capital sentence.

e. *Procuracy at the Union Supreme Court*

The procuracy connected with the Supreme Court is not merely a prosecuting agency, but occupies the high position of an organ entrusted with great supervisory powers. The Constitution of the Union provides that the Procurator of the Union Supreme Court, and his deputy, shall be appointed by the presidium of the Central Executive Committee of the Union. Among his duties and powers is the rendering of opinions on all questions submitted to the Supreme Court of the Union. The law provides that whenever the Supreme Court of the Union, at its plenary session, shall render a decision in disagreement with the procurator's opinion, he shall have the right to protest the decision to the presidium of the Central Executive Committtee of the Union. By the Act of 1929, the plenum of the Supreme Court of the Union is required to explain its reasons for rejecting the opinion or conclusion of the Union Procurator.[60]

The powers of the procuracy are colossal. There is not a single important step to be taken towards reviewing a verdict or annulling a law, alleged to be contrary to the Union Constitution or prejudicial to any of its republics, in which the procuracy

[57] *Ibid.*, sections 48 and 49.
[58] Act on Military Tribunals, *op. cit., supra*, note 51, section 33.
[59] *Ibid.*, section 37.
[60] Constitution, U.S.S.R., section 46. See also Sup. Court Act, sections 22 and 67, subsection c.

can not exert its authority in one way or another. It should suffice to recall that the plenary session must take up any question submitted for its deliberation by the procurator;[61] that the latter may demand the reviewing of a decision rendered by a supreme court of a constituent republic;[62] that an extra session of the plenum must be convoked upon the demand of the procurator,[63] etc. The watchful eye of the procuracy must be everywhere. The law explicitly provides that no Supreme Court session may take place without the participation of the procurator or his assistant.[64] Furthermore, the administrative sessions of the Judicial Department and the Special Session must deliberate in the presence of a member of the procuracy.[65] A remarkable feature of the Union procurator's powers is the provision that he is to look after the lawfulness of the acts of the State Political Bureau of the Union, which is the powerful political secret service organization.[66] One of the Union senior assistant procurators is assigned to supervise this formidable Political Bureau.[67] There are two other senior assistant procurators of the Union. One is to supervise the Military Department of the Union Supreme Court and the military procuracy of the Union, and the other is designated to supervise over the judicial activities.

II. MILITARY TRIBUNALS

a. *Judges and their Appointment*

Military tribunals are instituted at the military circuits, corps and divisions.[68] The tribunals of all grades consist of a president, his deputy, and members the exact number of whom is fixed by regulations of the Military Department of the Union Supreme Court, with the consent of the Commissariat for Military and Naval Affairs. A tribunal-bench is made up of a president and two judges.[69] All the judges of the tribunals are appointed, and may be dismissed by the Military Department of the Union Su-

[61] Sup. Court Act, sections 1-3.
[62] *Ibid.*, section 59, subsection b.
[63] *Ibid.*, sections 17 and 21.
[64] *Ibid.*, section 19.
[65] *Ibid.*, section 32.
[66] *Ibid.*, section 73.
[67] *Ibid.*, section 63.
[68] Act on Military Tribunals, *op. cit.*, *supra*, note 51, section 1.
[69] *Ibid.*, section 4.

preme Court.[70] No qualifications are prescribed for a judge of a military tribunal; the question of fitness is apparently left entirely to the discretion of the higher authorities.

b. *Original Jurisdiction*

The military tribunals take original jurisdiction over military crimes,[71] which are enumerated by nineteen different sections of the Criminal Code; crimes against the Union of a counter-revolutionary nature, crimes committed by designated officials, and certain offenses against property, as stipulated in the Criminal Code of the R.S.F.S.R. or similar statutes of other republics, provided, however, such crimes are committed by persons in the military service and the acts are of such a nature as to threaten or undermine the strength of the Red army or military discipline. In addition to this, the military tribunals have jurisdiction over all crimes, regardless of who committed them, in places where owing to extraordinary circumstances the ordinary courts are not functioning.[72]

c. *Procedure in the Tribunals*

Although the tribunals are military courts, they are to be guided by the rules of procedure prescribed by the codes of criminal procedure of the constituent republics for the provincial courts.[73] The tribunals, as well as the military inquisitors and investigators, are to apply the laws of the Union (which is practically without law on the subject) and the criminal codes and codes of criminal procedure of that particular republic in any given case where the alleged crime was committed.[74]

At the local military tribunals there functions a special military procuracy which is organized upon the general plan of the Soviet procuracy with all its widely extended powers of prosecution and supervision.

The verdicts or sentences of the military tribunals are subject to cassational complaint to the Military Department of the Union Supreme Court.[75]

[70] *Ibid.*, section 6.
[71] Cr. Code, 1926, part nine.
[72] Act on Military Tribunals, *op. cit., supra*, note 51, section 8.
[73] *Ibid.*, section 28.
[74] *Ibid.*, section 19.
[75] *Ibid.*, section 29.

The Supreme Court of the Union occupies a rather precarious position. With the exception of its Military Department, which functions actively as a court of cassation for the local military tribunals, it is the most conspicuously forlorn institution of high rank in the Soviet Union. The court's high sounding name, incompatible as it is with its true character, has been sufficient to bolster up unwarranted pretensions of power and authority while it has enjoyed neither.

Unlike the supreme courts of the constituent republics, which exercise enormous control over the judicial policy of their respective republics, the Supreme Court of the Union has been practically reduced to the function of a jurisconsult to the Union Central Executive Committee. This situation has evidently been admitted as intolerable. The question, therefore, of the future of the Supreme Court had been the subject of heated discussion in the Soviet legal press for some time, prior to the passage of the Act of 1929.

There were those, chiefly among whom was the president of the court, A. M. Winokurov, who persistently purposed to widen the scope of this court by granting to it the authority to review the constitutionality of legislative acts of the constituent republics, on the court's own motion without the preliminary request of the presidium of the *Tzeek*. The same group strenuously advocated the extension of the court's power in the realm of judicial supervision by vesting in it the authority to demand the transfer to it of the record of any case pending in any court for judicial review. In line with these suggestions, it was maintained that the Supreme Court of the Union should be reorganized structurally so as to include a presidium and a disciplinary department.[76] These persistent demands for enlarging the powers of this court would apparently, the critics argue, go to the point of converting it into a court of constitutional review,[77] instead of an adviser to the *Tzeek*.

That such proposed change should have met with strenuous opposition is not at all surprising. The significant point in the

[76]The Propositions of A. U. Winokurov are discussed and criticised by Radus-Zenchenko, *The Weekly*, No. 20, 1928.

[77]*Ibid.*

controversy was the fact that the presidents of the supreme courts of the constituent republics, who are themselves members of the plenum of the Union Supreme Court, were unwilling to have the court's authority extended.[78] It seemed almost certain that some changes in the position of the Supreme Court of the Union had to take place. The president of the court consistently demanded that it should be made either a real supreme court, and not merely one in name, or be abolished. To the latter alternative the critics of the court fully agreed, though it was unlikely that so extreme a course would ever be followed.

The Supreme Court Act of 1929 seems to be the result of a compromise between the two extreme tendencies above described. While no fundamental changes in the nature of the court were effected, its friends have gained somewhat. The Union Supreme Court, to be sure, still remains the jurisconsult of the Union *Tzeek*. Nevertheless, its scope was widened to some extent and it received greater opportunity to originate a review of legislative acts and to submit them to its superior, the *Tzeek,* for annulment. In other words, it became a more effective adviser to the *Tzeek*. In this connection the Supreme Court, as well as the Union Procurator, was vested with the right of legislative initiative.[79]

[78] *Ibid.*, page 593.
[79] Sup. Act, sections 8 and 69.

Chapter IV

PROCURACY, PRELIMINARY INQUIRY, INVESTIGATION AND THE BAR

The procuracy, the organs of investigation and inquiry and the Bar function alongside the courts, and are so completely interwoven with the entire system of the Soviet judiciary as to make them an integral part of it. It is, therefore, quite natural that the outstanding characteristics and peculiarities observed in the structure of the courts proper should be embodied also in these institutions which a Russian legal writer termed "the auxiliary organs"[1] of the courts.

I. THE PROCURACY

a. *History of its Development*

The procuracy is, historically speaking, a modern institution in Russian life. It first appeared in the eighteenth century when, by an order or edict *(ukaz)* of Peter the Great, issued January, 1722, a procuracy was established. Its original purpose was to supervise the lawfulness of the acts of governmental agents, and to preserve the interests of the State. It was not yet a prosecuting agency; such functions were assigned to it by the judicial reforms of 1864.[2] After this reform the procuracy grew into a formidable factor in the judiciary. It became more than a mere prosecuting agency, but the sphere of its activity and influence did not extend beyond the judiciary. The Soviet procuracy, however, made a tremendous advance in its influence which was now extended even to matters which were, strictly speaking, non-judicial. Like other branches of the Soviet legal system, the procuracy had to undergo a metamorphosis before it fully developed into its present state.

The First Decree of 1917 completely wiped out the Tzarist procuracy, and its place was unoccupied for some time. The

[1]Temashev, page 236.
[2]Encyclopedia.

establishment of a new Soviet procuracy was, in the first years of the Bolshevist Revolution, deemed unthinkable. The old procuracy was too closely identified with the severe persecution of the revolutionists in the days of the Tzars. The picture of the feared, hated, and despised Tzarist procuracy "was so fresh in the minds of the toiling masses that the mere thought of reviving the office of procurator was deemed a reactionary move towards a return to the old order."[3]

The only substitution for the once mighty procuracy which the framers of the First Decree could offer was the provision that every "unblemished citizen" of either sex may appear as prosecutor[4] (or defender) in open court. The remarkable feature about this provision is that there was not to be any organized public prosecution at all. This provision, as a matter of fact, was so broadly applied that the presiding judge, as a rule, asked persons present at the trial if there was any one who wished to appear as a prosecutor (or as a defender) at the time when the "judicial inquiry," as the trial is called, came to a close.[5]

This "systemless system" of overdone judicial liberalism and "pure" democracy, which aimed to bring the courts "nearer to the masses" in times of a raging civil war and a tumultuous social revolution presents a picture which is strikingly contrary to the general conception of the behavior of a revolutionary mob during a social upheaval. For the courts, and even the revolutionary tribunals, which conducted their trials in direct contact with, and under the influence of, the highly excited masses in the first days immediately following the November Revolution, either acquitted monarchists and noted counter-revolutionists, or imposed upon them such "terrible" sentences as a "public rebuke".[6]

The rather vague idea of having the people at large act as public prosecutors did not last long. The instructions to the revolutionary tribunals of 1917 had provided for the institution of a college of persons *(collegium)* who were to act either as

[3]Krylenko, *The Judiciary and the Law*, 1927, page 91.

[4]First Decree, section 3.

[5]Krylenko, *op. cit.* note 3, *supra*, page 9.

[6]Such a sentence was imposed upon Parushkevich, the famous militant monarchist, counter-revolutionary, and leader of the extreme reactionaries in the Imperial Duma. Krylenko, *Fundamentals of the Judiciary*, Moscow, 1927, page 6.

prosecutors or defenders.[7] This was not yet, to be sure, an orderly, well-organized state prosecution. It was merely a body from which the court could appoint someone to act as public prosecutor in any given case.[8] But the public was still allowed to participate in the final argument at the close of a trial, by having one person speak for and one against the defendant.[9] One step, however, towards creating a semblance of an organized prosecution had been made.

The Second Decree on courts which followed the Instructions of 1917 incorporated the same idea of a *collegium* of attorneys-at-law *(pravozastupnikov)* whose members were to be elected and recalled by the local soviets.[10]

The revolutionary tribunals, which were always more aggressive and the first to evolve the doctrines of control and centralization, were soon to have their own prosecuting board. As early as May, 1918, it was decreed that each revolutionary tribunal was to have a board of three persons elected by the local soviets, either directly or on the recommendation of such tribunal or the Commissariat of Justice of the Republic.[11] About the same time there was also created a central board of state prosecutors for the revolutionary tribunals, attached to the Central Executive Committee. This central board already had a faint semblance of a procuracy, for it could delegate its representative to appear as prosecutor in any criminal case. In addition to this, it exercised the right to demand the records of the local prosecuting boards, and enjoyed some power of supervision, for the law assigned to it the duties of "uniting and regulating the activities of prosecutors attached to local revolutionary tribunals".[12] A still greater advance, though of a temporary nature, had been made in the city of Moscow, which steered its own course for a while. In April, 1918, there was created at Moscow,[13] as a local enter-

[7]Collected Laws No. 12, Article 170, 1917, section 7, subsection b. (See Chapter 1, note 96.)

[8]*Ibid.*, section 8.

[9]*Ibid.*, section 10.

[10]Second Decree, sections 24 and 25.

[11]Collected Laws No. 35, Article 471, 1918, section 5. (See Chapter 1, note 104.)

[12]Collected Laws No. 41, Article 520, 1918, section 5. (See Chapter 1, note 106.)

[13]Immediately after the Revolution, the capital of the new régime was Petrograd, but Moscow revolutionaries went their own way. The control of the Central Government began with the transfer of the capitol to Moscow.

prise, a Commissariat of Public Prosecution which also had the duty of looking after the conduct of officials, and bringing them to account. This Commissariat had developed a sort of investigating department of its own. The whole scheme existed only about a month and a half and was abolished by the abovementioned Act of May, 1918.[14] In the ordinary criminal courts, outside the revolutionary tribunals, the system of a college of attorneys, from which both prosecutors and defenders were drawn, was apparently maintained up to the end of 1920, when it was discarded.

b. *The Procuracy in 1920*

The People's Court Act of 1920 provided that the provincial departments of justice should institute subdepartments of prosecution, the number of prosecutors in each case to be fixed by the respective departments.[15] (Similar subdepartments were established for the revolutionary tribunals in 1920.) The prosecutors were to be appointed by the provincial executive committee, on the presentation of its department of justice, and were subject to dismissal by the same authority. To be eligible for appointment as a public prosecutor, a person had to have the qualifications required for a people's judge.[16]

The prosecuting apparatus was henceforth to receive more attention. Thus, the special instructions issued by the Commissariat of Justice in November, 1920, required that prosecutors should, besides answering the prescribed qualifications, be persons capable of appearing in public gatherings; and, if they were not party men (communists), they should at least be thoroughly acquainted with the Soviet system, and with the working of the trade unions.[17] Besides the public prosecutors, private persons might appear as prosecutors representing Soviet institutions and workingmen's organizations, which might institute criminal proceedings growing out of acts connected with their institution or organization.[18]

[14]Krylenko, *Jud. System*, page 83.
[15]P.C. Act, 1918, section 39.
[16]*Ibid.*, section 40.
[17]Collected Laws No. 100, Article 543, 1920, section 1.
[18]P.C. Act, 1920, section 42.

We should note that the system inaugurated by the People's Court Act of 1920 merely created public prosecutors—officials whose duty it was to represent the state in criminal cases. The procuracy of today was still in embryo.

c. *The Procuracy Act of 1922*

The growing tendency towards centralization and rigorous governmental control over the judiciary, revealed by the judicial reform of 1922, found its most illuminating expression in the Procuracy Act of May, 1922.[19] This act created the huge hierarchy of prosecutors and supervisors entrusted with tremendous powers and elaborate machinery of its own. With a few modifications the Procuracy Act of 1922 was incorporated in the Judiciary Act of 1926.[20]

d. *Theories of the Procuracy*

Before we describe the organization and functions of the procuracy, as it exists today, let us look into the various conflicting theories and controversial ideas which had to be reconciled before the erection of such an important structure in the Soviet governmental system could be finally effected. Such a discussion is imperative for a better understanding of this very peculiar institution.

About 1922 there seemed to be among Soviet leaders a general acquiescence in the idea of re-establishing a procuracy, an organ which should regulate and supervise the administration of the law on behalf of the government. But a wide and heated discussion immediately ensued as to the exact nature of the contemplated procuracy. The major problems were: (1) The relation of this procuracy to the courts and to the then existing provincial departments of justice which supervised them; (2) the relation of the provincial procuracy to the highest authority in the province—the provincial executive committee; (3) the relation of the Central Procuracy to the People's Commissariat of Justice of the Republic.[21] These major questions, together with

[19]Procuracy Act, Collected Laws No. 30, Article 424, 1922.
[20]Collected Laws No. 85, Article 624, 1926, chapter IX.
[21]Krylenko, *The Judiciary and the Law*, 1927, page 93.

other kindred problems which we cannot analyze here, were thoroughly discussed at the Fourth Conference of Soviet Judicial Workers in January, 1922, and later at the session of the highest legislative and executive body, the All-Russian Central Executive Committee (the *Vtzeek*), and in the legal press.

The Soviet government, as we know, is so constructed as to have in each territorial unit an executive body to which all governmental institutions, including the judiciary, are directly subordinate in one way or another, leaving to the central authorities the general supervision. But now a plan, astounding in theory, from the Soviet point of view, was advanced. It was proposed to create a state agency, a procuracy, not only independent of the provincial executive committee but even free from the supervision of the Commissariat of Justice at Moscow—something unknown and obviously contrary to the Soviet scheme. To clear the ground for the procuracy, the abolition of the provincial departments of justice was also insisted upon. The adherents of this extreme idea proposed that the Commissar of Justice of the Republic should be also the Procurator of the Republic, and his holding both offices should be the only connection between the procuracy of the Republic and the Commissariat of Justice. Such a scheme was said to be necessary in order that an entirely independent agency might supervise the administration of the law in all its phases—a function which was hitherto lodged with the Commissariat of Justice. The opponents of this innovation, on the other hand, went as far as to oppose even the elimination of the control of the provincial executive committee over the local procuracy, on the ground that this theory was in full accord with the very spirit of the Soviet system, as already pointed out.

While the entire dispute ended in a compromise the advocates of an independent procuracy, on the whole, got the upper hand. The provincial departments of justice were abolished; the local procuracy was made entirely independent of the provincial (regional or circuit) authorities; and the only supervision indirectly accorded to the Commissariat of Justice of the Republic over the procuracy was the fact that its chairman, the commissar, was the Procurator of the Republic.

The argument that swayed the Soviet leaders to establish the procuracy in this form was that it is intolerable to have a procuracy look after the activities of the local authorities, as it should, and at the same time be dependent on the latter. Such a reason could be effectively advanced only after the much disputed question as to the scope of the authority of the procuracy was well settled in favor of its extension far beyond a mere connection with the work of the judiciary, as was the case with the Tzarist procuracy.[22]

Thus, the procuracy, unlike any other branch of the government, emerged as a highly centralized state agency, totally independent of local authorities, created for the avowed purpose of supervising the lawfulness of the acts of all governmental organs of the R.S.F.S.R., state and social institutions, etc.[23]

The form of interrelation that exists between the procuracy and the judiciary has been indirectly touched upon in the description of the functions of the court. We might, for the present, merely quote Mr. Krylenko, who, in order to clarify, for the benefit of all institutions concerned, the theoretical and the practical question of the interrelation of the courts and the procuracy, stated: "The Procuracy is neither above the courts nor attached to them. *It occupies a place alongside the courts, as an equally important part of the judicial apparatus,* and the judicial system of the entire land; *it is on a par with the courts,* and, therefore, it has the authority to protest, [*i. e.,* take to a higher tribunal any of the court's verdicts or decisions]; *but it is subordinate to the courts from the moment it participates in the trial of a case, appearing there as a party.*"[24] In other words, the procuracy is subordinate to the courts only when it exercises the function of public prosecutor at the trial.

e. *Present Hierarchy of the Procuracy*

At the head of the procuracy is the Deputy Commissar of Justice of the R.S.F.S.R., who is, as we know, termed the Pro-

[22] One of the theories advanced by Soviet leaders was that the procuracy must not exercise any authority outside of the Judiciary. See Krylenko, *op. cit.* note 21, *supra,* pages 90-109, especially at page 100.

[23] Jud. Act, 1926, section 9. See also Basic Principles of the Judiciary, section 14, Systematic Collection of Existing Laws of the U.S.S.R., Book V, 1926.

[24] Krylenko, *op. cit.* note 21, *supra,* page 95.

curator of the Republic. It is he who is the direct supervisor of the Department of the Procuracy at the Commissariat of Justice.[25] This arrangement resembles somewhat that in Tzarist Russia where the Procurator-General was also the Minister of Justice.[26] But the present Procurator of the Republic is not a figurehead, but has a number of duties to perform, and is therefore, unlike the corresponding official in Imperial Russia, the active head of the procuracy.

The Procurator of the R.S.F.S.R. has a number of regular assistants who are appointed by the presidium of the All-Russian Central Executive Committee, on the presentation of the Procurator of the Republic. This does not yet complete the personnel of the Central Procuracy. As the supervisory duties of the procuracy are numerous, the method of specialization was adopted and further special procurators are appointed for special functions. First, there is a special procurator to supervise labor cases, appointed by the Procurator of the Republic with the consent of the Commissariat of Labor. There are also special procurators connected with the Commissariat of Justice, and a procurator and assistants attached to the various departments of the Supreme Court of the R.S.F.S.R. All these procurators and their assistants are appointed directly by the Procurator of the Republic.[27]

The next step on the procuracy ladder is occupied by the provincial, circuit or regional procurators, who are subordinate to the Procurator of the Republic and are appointed as well as dismissed by the latter.[28] The provincial, circuit, or regional procuracy consists of a procurator, his deputy and assistant procurators, whose number is fixed for each territorial division by the central authorities, and who are also appointed by the Pro-

[25] Jud. Act, 1926, section 60. But by later legislation, Collected Laws No. 46, Article 343, 1928, the Commissariat of Justice was reorganized, by providing for two deputy commissars, one of whom is to be the Procurator of the Republic. This law will have to be approved by the Central Committee of the Union, for the basic laws of the latter provide that the Commissar of Justice shall be the Procurator. This is, however, a mere formality, and it will undoubtedly be approved by the Union legislators.

[26] The Ukrainian Judiciary Act of 1925, section 95, revived the old term of Procurator-General for its Commissar of Justice, the equivalent of the Tzarist Minister of Justice.

[27] Jud. Act, 1926, section 61.

[28] *Ibid.*, section 62.

curator of the Republic on the presentation of the procurator of such division. The assistant procurators are attached either to the provincial office of the procurator, or are stationed at the different counties and districts within the province where they take charge over all the business of procuracy under the direct guidance of their immediate chief, the provincial, regional or circuit procurator.[29] In the autonomous territories, the procuracy is organized and functions on the same basis as in the province. But in the autonomous republics, the arrangement is similar to the one provided for the R.S.F.S.R. itself, with the commissar of justice of the autonomous republic at the head.[30]

1. Scope of Authority

The procuracy, thus constituted, is entrusted with the impressive authority of inquiring into the "legality of the acts of all governmental organs, economic institutions, public and private organizations and of private persons." This extensive supervision is made effective either "by means of a protest against any enactment or order which violates the law", and a request to the respective authorities for its suspension or reversal, "or by the institution of criminal, disciplinary, or administrative proceedings against the violators."[31] This right to protest furnishes the basis for the all-embracing, immense authority of the procuracy. Among the other powers granted to the procuracy are the direct control and supervision over the inquisitors and the organs of the State Political Bureau and their conduct of the preliminary inquiry, general supervision over the organs of investigation, and the organs engaged in combating crime.[32] The procuracy is, of course, to conduct the accusation at the trial, and is to state its opinion in all criminal cases which come up before the cassational court.

The function of the procuracy does not, as one might suppose, cease with the securing of a conviction. The procuracy is to see that the sentences imposed are properly carried out and

[29] *Ibid.*, section 63.
[30] *Ibid.*, sections 6 and 65.
[31] *Ibid.*, section 59, subsection a.
[32] *Ibid.*, section 59, subsections b, c and g.

that no one is unlawfully held in custody; it must also look after conditions in the places of imprisonment or detention.[33]

The extent of the procuracy's activity in looking after places of detention can be best indicated by the fact that its members visited and inspected the prisons 12,361 times in 1924, 12,739 in 1925, and 4,739 in 1926,[34] the latter figure being only for 29 provinces of the Republic. To make their visits more effective, members of the procuracy receive also complaints and petitions which the inmates may wish to present. In 1924, 94,923 of such requests and complaints were made, of which 84 per cent. were decided in favor of the complainants, 93,386 in 1925, 67 per cent. of which were well taken, and 23,229 in 1926, the latter figure covering only 22 provinces out of a total of 42 administrative units.[35]

2. Participation in Civil Actions

An interesting feature is the provision that the procuracy is "to participate in civil trials for the purpose of safeguarding the interest of the state and the toiling masses."[36] The latter provision is not entirely an innovation created by the Soviet régime. The Tzarist procurators also had to appear on certain occasions at the civil trial, though this was a rather rare occurrence, for the pre-revolutionary procuracy was, naturally, not required to safeguard the civil interests of the "toiling masses". That the latter is not an empty phrase can be seen from the fact that the number of procurators participating in civil cases has grown from year to year. In 1923, the procuracy participated in 1230 civil trials;[37] in 1924 the figure jumped to 4934, while it reached 8232 in 1925, and 25,722 in 1926.[38] In 1925 the procuracy demanded from the lower courts 19,595 civil cases to be sent to higher courts for a review by way of supervision,[39] while in 1926, the number of such demands advanced to 30,020.[40]

[33] *Ibid.*, section 59, subsection 8.
[34] Official Report of the Procuracy for 1926, Moscow, 1927, page 147.
[35] *Ibid.*
[36] Jud. Act, 1926, section 59, subsection e.
[37] N. Logovier—*The Weekly*, No. 31, 1926.
[38] Official Report of the Procuracy for 1926, page 135.
[39] *Ibid.*
[40] *Ibid.*, page 143.

The Soviet authorities have issued a pamphlet entitled "The Working-women, Peasant-women and the Soviet Procuracy."[41] In popular language and readable style the peasants and workers (though the women are addressed) are urged, after due laudation of the Soviet system, to avail themselves of the services of the procuracy for the purpose of safeguarding their civil interests. This will apparently become an important part of the procurator's task, especially in the lower courts. Out of the 1742 times when members of the procuracy appeared in trials at the people's courts during the first quarter of 1926, 737 were civil cases.[42]

3. Duties Assigned

Although the Procurator of the Republic is the actual head of the entire procuracy, and exercises authority in allotting the duties among his subordinates, the Act of 1926 defines the exact nature of the duties with which each unit of the procuracy is to be immediately and directly concerned. This is especially true in regard to its function in watching over the legality of the legislative and administrative acts. The Procurator of the Republic is in duty bound to look after the legality of all the activities of the people's commissariats and other central organs, and is to strive for the annulment or modification of any unlawful regulation or order issued by these bodies. This is accomplished by protesting the alleged unlawful order or regulation, to the Soviet of People's Commissars, or, when the protest is against an act of the latter, to the presidium of the All-Russian Central Executive Committee. To this presidium the Procurator must also submit a yearly report concerning his own activities, as well as those of his subordinates, including the procurators of the autonomous republics.[43]

The provincial, regional or circuit procurators have similar powers within their own sphere. The regional procuracy, although attached to a larger territorial unit, is organized on the same basis and has the same duties and powers as the pro-

[41] N. Logovier, (Moscow, 1927). This is one pamphlet out of a series of similar publications which bear the characteristic slogan: "Workers and peasants, get to know the law of the Soviet Republic".

[42] A. Chernyshev. *The Weekly*, No. 45, 1926.

[43] Jud. Act, 1926, section 67.

curacy of the province.[44] The procurators of these territorial units protest to their respective executive committees any unlawful or unauthorized administrative regulation or order of any governmental agency subordinate to the latter committees and request their annulment or modification; or, where necessary, the procurator may protest, through the Procurator of the Republic, to the Soviet of the People's Commissar or to the presidium of the All-Russian Central Executive Committee.[45] The latter high authorities are called upon to act when the alleged unlawful order, regulation, or ordinance emanated from the highest authorities within the administrative area, the executive committees.

The authority to supervise state agencies and insure their strict adherence to formal law vested in the mighty, independent procuracy is quite frequently resorted to by the latter, as is indicated by protests filed in 17,437 instances in 1924, 29,849 times in 1925, and 25,324 in 1926.[46] The significance of this weapon becomes apparent when we learn that 16,977 of all the protests in 1926 were well taken—that is, the unlawful or unauthorized orders or decisions were repealed or corrected. Examples of such protests occur in cases when unlawful fines are imposed, or unwarranted confiscations take place, etc. These figures embrace only objections against the activities of the provincial, regional or circuit authorities and those below them, such as the county, district, or *volost* administrations, but do not include any of the higher authorities, whose decisions and enactments may also be scrutinized by the procuracy, and if necessary submitted for annulment in the same way. That the procurator really has his fingers in every pie, to use a colloquial expression, is seen in the remarkable fact that the procuracy was called upon in 6570 instances in 1926 to adjust, intervene, or help in matters within the jurisdiction of the land commissions, which settle land disputes between peasants.[47] To what extent the people look to the procuracy for redress, whenever they think an unlawful act has

[44] *Ibid.*, section 144 and see sections 141-147.

[45] *Ibid.*, section 68, subsections a and b.

[46] Official Report of the Procuracy for 1926, page 61. The figures for 1925 and 1926 given in *The Weekly*, No. 23, 1927, page 698, vary somewhat from those stated in the official report. The discrepancy seems to be due to the fact that the latter report covers fewer administrative units.

[47] *The Weekly*, No. 5, 1927, page 125.

been done, is illustrated by the startling fact that in 1926, 341,613 written complaints[48] were submitted to the various offices of the procuracy. These do not include requests to institute criminal proceedings, which come sometimes directly to the procurator, or the oral complaints which in some provinces reach a higher figure than the written ones. This somewhat extensive discussion will, it is hoped, help us to realize the exact nature of the procuracy which is an indispensable wheel in the machinery of the administration of the criminal law.

The provincial, regional or circuit procuracy is the effective agency for carrying out the daily routine. It supervises, we recall, the preliminary inquiries and investigation, and discontinues proceedings whenever necessary; and it is the local procuracy which usually institutes a criminal proceeding. A novel feature is the requirement that the procurator affirm the accusation, called the "accusatory conclusion" drawn by the inquistor, and only when the procurator does not approve of the form of the conclusions of the inquisitor does he draw another document himself.[49] The provincial procurator must submit a semi-annual report of his own activities, as well as of the activities of his assistants, to the Procurator of the Republic.[50]

From what has been said we can easily comprehend the wide scope of the procuracy's activity as a mighty supervisory institution exerting its influence inside as well as outside the courts. The procurators and their assistants have different means, in accordance with their various positions, for exercising these powers. The Procurator of the Republic, we remember, may demand an extra session of the Union Supreme Court plenum, and may take an appeal to the plenum of the Supreme Court of the R.S.F.S.R. against verdicts and decisions of the latter's Cassational Department. He is also one of the few high authorities who may order any criminal case pending in any court for trial in the Supreme Court.

[48]Official Report of the Procuracy for 1926, page 68.

[49]Jud. Act, 1926, section 68, subsection g, and Code, 1927, section 229. The recent amendment to the Code of Criminal Procedure (Collected Laws No. 78, Article 756, 1929, sections 221 and 224) would seem to change this rule by providing that if the Procurator disagrees with accusatory document he is to return it to the inquisitor with the appropriate remarks.

[50]*Ibid.*, section 69.

The provincial procurator has similar powers within his purview. He must participate at the sessions of the plenum of the provincial court, and if he disagrees with the latter's decisions or conclusions, the entire case or question must be transmitted to the Supreme Court of the Republic; the provincial procuracy is always represented on the commission which makes up lists of co-judges for the people's court[51] and for the provincial court.[52]

To make it possible for the procuracy to perform its manifold supervisory duties outside the courts, the law provides that the procurator, or his assistant, may participate by an advisory vote in the sessions of the executive committees of all the governmental organs and institutions within the procurator's area[53]—republic, province, region or circuit, etc. For a similar purpose is the provision that the procurator may, in the performance of his duties, demand documents or information from any governmental agency, institution, or organization. Even the secret documents of the State Political Bureau (political secret service) are accessible to the procuracy,[54] the only limitation being that the Bureau may demand that the procurator examine the documents desired personally.

II. INVESTIGATION AND INQUIRY

a. *Early Development*

The clean sweep effected by the celebrated First Decree of 1917, did not spare the pre-revolutionary system of judicial inquisitors, as they were called. The act provided that the newly created people's judges were to perform, temporarily, the function of inquisitors.[55] The prevailing tendency of that time to make small boards (collegia) perform certain judicial functions which formerly were performed by one person alone was also carried out with regard to the preliminary inquiry. The Instructions to the revolutionary tribunals of December, 1917, provided for inquisitorial commissions of six persons elected by the

[51]See Chapter II, page 57.
[52]*Ibid.*, page 63.
[53]Jud. Act, 1926, section 71.
[54]*Ibid.*, section 70.
[55]First Decree, section 3.

soviets.[56] A similar commission consisting of three persons was created by the Second Decree on Courts. This commission was to conduct preliminary inquiries in criminal cases more serious than those under the jurisdiction of the people's court.[57] In the revolutionary tribunals, which proceeded in their own way, the commission arrangement was not consistently maintained. The Act on Revolutionary Tribunals of 1919 maintained the inquisitorial commission. But the Basic Act of 1920[58] provided that, in cases tried at revolutionary tribunals, the preliminary inquiry was to be conducted by various governmental organs, such as the extraordinary commission, the *cheka,* and others, under the supervision of the inquisitor-reporters attached to the revolutionary tribunals.[59] The Supreme Revolutionary Tribunal, on the other hand, created by the same act had an Inquisitorial Commission.

The commission system was elaborated in connection with the ordinary criminal courts. The People's Court Act of 1918 provided for an inquisitorial commission made up of a president and two members, to function in the counties and cities which were to be divided into inquisitorial districts. The commission was to take jurisdiction in all criminal cases which were tried at the people's court with six co-judges.[60] The latter act was the first to require certain qualifications for membership on such a commission. It provided: "The president and the members of the inquisitorial commission must satisfy the following requirements: (1) They must have the right to vote and be elected to the soviets; (2) they must have a theoretical and practical training for the office of soviet inquisitor."[61]

This commission method was continued up to the end of 1920. Apparently, it did not prove very satisfactory, for it was completely abandoned by the People's Court Act of 1920.[62] This act provided for individual inquisitors to conduct preliminary inquiries in all criminal cases tried before the bench of six co-judges of the people's court. The inquisitors were to be elected

[56]Collected Laws No. 12, Article 170, 1917, section 3.
[57]Second Decree, section 21.
[58]Collected Laws Nos. 34 and 24, Article 115, 1920, section 8.
[59]*Ibid.,* section 9.
[60]P.C. Act, 1918, sections 28, 29 and 30.
[61]*Ibid.,* section 31.
[62]Collected Laws, No. 83, Article 407, 1920.

and recalled by the provincial executive committee, and were to perform their duties under the supervision of the soviet of people's judges.[63] With some important modifications and changes necessary to suit the reorganized judiciary, this system was incorporated in later enactments, and has been maintained to this day.

b. *The System of Inquiry*

The inquisitorial system at present consists of three different groups—"(1) the people's inquisitors attached to the inquisitorial districts, (2) the senior inquisitor placed at the provincial court, (3) inquisitors for the most important cases attached to the procuracy of the Republic and the Supreme Court."[64] The people's inquisitors are now appointed, as already indicated, by the presidium of the provincial court, and may be dismissed by the order of its plenum. But both their appointment and dismissal must have the consent of the provincial procurator and the approval of the provincial, regional or circuit executive committee,[65] or of the city soviets, in certain large cities. The other two groups of inquisitors are appointed and dismissed by the respective courts to which they are attached.[66] This arrangement by which both the provincial court and the procuracy share in the control over the people's inquisitors was a compromise between two opposing factions. One group insisted that the inquisitors ought to be completely divorced from the influence and control of the procurators, for otherwise, it was argued, the former would inevitably assume the rôle of prosecutors, a result which was clearly not intended. Among the supporters of this contention we found the president of the Supreme Court, P. Stuchka. Even recently, when the trend was unquestionably drifting the other way, he firmly maintained that the organs of inquiry must be subordinate only to the courts and not to the procuracy. "The inquiry is already nine-tenths under the control of the procurators who may exercise their influence upon the inquiry. If that is to continue, the [preliminary] inquiry will, of course,

[63] *Ibid.*, sections 28 and 30.
[64] Jud. Act, 1926, section 73.
[65] *Ibid.*, section 75.
[66] *Ibid.*, section 76.

turn into an auxiliary organ of the procuracy, as the organ of the prosecution."[67] Such a situation would tend to increase the one-sided prosecuting character of the preliminary inquiry. The other group maintains the view defended by Krylenko that the procurators are to have the sole control over the people's inquisitors. This group is gaining ground at the present time.

To test the latter view the procuracy of the City of Moscow has been given complete supervision over the inquisitors and their functions. This scheme will probably soon become the law for the entire R.S.F.S.R., for all the legislation proposed in respect to criminal procedure incorporates the basic idea that the inquisitors should be assistants to the procurators so far as the preliminary inquiry is concerned.

1. Appointment of Inquisitors and Their Jurisdiction

To be eligible for the office of inquisitor a person must be a citizen with a constitutional right to vote.[68] In addition he must have served, prior to his appointment, not less than two years in a Soviet judicial office not lower than secretary of the people's court, or in lieu thereof, he must have passed an appropriate examination with the provincial court.[69]

The inquisitor must take jurisdiction and conduct a preliminary inquiry in the case of a great number of offenses covered by specific sections of the Criminal Code, without regard to what court tries the case. Prior to 1924, the question of the absolute necessity of a preliminary inquiry in a given case, and consequently the duty of the inquisitor to conduct it, depended upon the particular court which was to try the case. For example, by the first Code of Criminal Procedure of 1922, the preliminary inquiry was made obligatory in all cases tried either at the people's court with six co-judges, or at a revolutionary tribunal. After the reorganization of the judiciary in 1923, this requirement was changed to cases tried at the provincial court and the military tribunals which were, before the Union was created, a part of the judicial system of the R.S.F.S.R.[70] Since 1924 the jurisdic-

[67]*The Weekly*, No. 4, 1928, page 116.
[68]See Chapter I, note 54.
[69]Jud. Act, 1926, section 74.
[70]Code, 1922, section 110 and Code of 1923, section 108.

tion of the inquisitor is over specific offenses as we have shown above, although the particular offenses requiring a preliminary inquiry have been changed a number of times since that date.

The requirement of a preliminary inquiry no longer depends upon any particular court which has jurisdiction of the case. While most of the cases tried at the provincial court are listed among those requiring the preliminary inquiry there are a number of offenses tried at this court in which a preliminary inquiry is not mandatory. Among the latter group of cases we find some serious offenses punishable by three years' imprisonment.[71] On the other hand, a preliminary inquiry is absolutely necessary in a considerable number of the more serious cases tried at the people's court, such as larceny, robbery, white slavery, etc., and the various grades of homicide, except what we would term murder in the first degree, which is not triable at the people's court.

Besides the cases in which a preliminary inquiry must always be had, it must also be conducted in other offenses upon a special decision or order of the court in any given case or at the suggestion of the procurator.[72] The tendency, however, is to simplify the procedure by authorizing the inquisitor to take charge over cases which are plainly too difficult for the organs of investigations, whose duties will be explained later. In a recent circular issued by the Commissariat of Justice,[73] the inquisitor is given explicit authority to take over, at his discretion, cases of the latter category and conduct a preliminary inquiry on his own initiative without first waiting for a suggestion of the procurator, who must, however, be notified immediately afterwards. This regulation was prompted by the fact that certain cases, the nature of which ordinarily does not warrant the necessity of a preliminary inquiry, may, however, contain some complicated features which the police, as an organ of investigation, are not properly equipped to investigate. The criterion for the inquisitor to follow in taking the investigation out of the jurisdiction of the police is the fact

[71]Cr. Code, 1926, section 111.

[72]Code, 1927, section 108. This provision was re-enacted when the section was again amended in 1928. Collected Laws No. 9, Article 81.

[73]Circular of the Commissariat of Justice, No. 32, Feb. 22, 1928. Published in *The Weekly*, No. 8, 1928.

that a particular case is too complicated or is of peculiar public importance.[74] To make this procedure more effective, the inquisitor is held responsible if he leaves with the organs of investigation cases which they can not well handle.[75]

2. Powers and Duties

The powers and duties of the inquisitor are innumerable. In general his duty is to bring to light every possible angle of a case. The law specifically provides that the inquisitor is in duty bound to investigate and clear up all circumstances which may prove the defendant's guilt as well as those which will lead to his acquittal.[76] In order to accomplish his task, the inquisitor is to question the accused, examine witnesses and experts, order, under certain circumstances, searches and seizures, fix the necessary measure to ensure the appearance of the defendant at the investigations and trial, etc.[77] The authority of the inquisitor in all matters within his purview is not final; his acts may be modified or reversed by the procurator or by the court. Nevertheless, the inquisitor exercises great powers, for he is the official who has the immediate control of the inquiry.

The inquisitor has the authority to decide either to discontinue proceedings instituted and forward the material collected to the proper court,[78] or to hold the defendant for court. In the latter instance he must draw up a document called "the accusatory conclusion" (a kind of information) and then forward this conclusion, with the entire record of the case, to the procurator.[79]

[74] *Ibid.*, section 2.

[75] This regulation has now been enacted into law by the amendments to the Code of 1923. (Collected Laws, 1929, No. 78, Article 756, section 108.) This amendment also provides that the inquisitor may, with the permission of the procurator, transfer any case subject to an inquiry to the organs of investigation. We may note here that this section in its amended form was taken wholly from the project for a new Code approved by the Commissariat of Justice on Dec. 7, 1928.

[76] Code, 1927, section 111.

[77] *Ibid.*, sections 143 and 144. These measures are explained in Chapter VI, page 162.

[78] Code, 1927, section 203. The amendments of October, 1929, seem to have broadened the power of the inquisitor by giving him the authority to discontinue the proceedings in certain cases without sending the records to the court. Such a discontinuance is subject to an appeal within one week to the procurator.

[79] *Ibid.*, section 208 as amended in October, 1929.

All the acts, orders, and regulations of the inquisitor are subject to an appeal to the procurator.[80]

The wide scope of the inquisitor's duties and his immense powers while conducting the preliminary inquiry undoubtedly make him a very strong factor in the process of criminal investigation and prosecution. On the other hand, the complete supervision which the procuracy exercises over his activities greatly reduces the importance of his position. A well-known Russian legal writer, Professor P. I. Lyublinsky, asserted that such a scheme has changed the inquisitor, who was at one time more or less independent, to a mere assistant to the procuracy.[81] This statement was made immediately after the judicial reforms of 1922. Since that time the tendency has been to increase the powers of the inquisitor, especially in the realm of supervision over the organs of investigation, without, however, diminishing the general powers entrusted to the procuracy. A comparative study of the first and later codes of criminal procedure will clearly demonstrate the constant additions to the authority and powers of the inquisitor.[82] Even by the original edition of the present Code of Criminal Procedure (enacted in February, 1923) all the acts of the investigating organs (which will be presently discussed) were still under the immediate control and supervision of the procurator, who was to receive the results of the investigation and decide as to the further steps to be taken. The subsequent amendments to the same Code modified the procedure so as to shift the actual control and supervision over the activities of the investigating organs to the inquisitors,[83] leaving to the procuracy indirect supervision over such organs through its direct and complete supervision over the activities of the inquisitors. The latter's increased powers are by no means indicative of any growing independence. On the contrary, it would seem that the assignment of wider powers is merely to facilitate the carrying out of their duties. So far as their relations with the procuracy are concerned, the tendency to make them complete assistants to

[80] *Ibid.*, section 212. In 1922 the appeal was to the court.
[81] Quoted by Temashev, page 242.
[82] Compare sections 97-107 of the original edition of the Code of 1923.
[83] Code, 1927, section 107.

the procurators with respect to the preliminary inquiry is swiftly developing, if they have not already arrived at that point.[84]

c. *Organs of Criminal Investigation*

The organs of criminal investigation are the police *(militzia)* and the organs of criminal detection, the State Political Bureau, the organs of inspection for offenses within the purview of their duties of inspection over sanitation, labor, etc., and all governmental officials for cases of unlawful acts alleged to have been committed by their subordinates.[85]

1. The State Political Bureau

Although the State Political Bureau is explicitly classed as one of the organs of investigation, it is, nevertheless, by its very nature, an institution of quite different functions from those assigned to other organs of investigation. It was first organized by a decree issued in February, 1922, and came into being as the legal and actual heir of the abolished extraordinary commission, the dreadful *Cheka,* the mere mention of which sent a cold shiver over the spines of multitudes, and scared many a reluctant child into bed, both in Russia and abroad.

The State Political Bureau (G.P.U.) was created in the period of the new economic policy, the *nep.* Although stripped of many of the unbridled powers with which its predecessor was endowed, it still retains some of the characteristics of the old *Cheka.* The G. P. U. was made a part of the Commissariat of Internal Affairs and was entrusted with the duties of checking overt counter-revolutionary activities, including banditry; protecting the railroads and waterways; safeguarding, politically, the borders, etc.[86] For this purpose the G. P. U. has its own remarkably well organized machinery including special military divisions. By a special act,[87] the G. P. U. was permitted to punish

[84]Since these lines were written, the prophecy has become true. Although the necessary legislation is still pending, the inquisitors have been entirely transferred to the procuracy. Heretofore the courts have also shared a part of the supervision over the inquisitor.

[85]Code, 1927, section 97.

[86]Collected Laws No. 16, Article 160, 1922. (*Sobranie Uzokonenie* 16-160, 1922.)

[87]Collected Laws No. 65, Article 884, 1922. *(Sobranie Uzokonenie* 65-884, 1922.)

at its discretion in a non-judicial way, even by shooting, "all persons apprehended while participating in a banditry raid or armed robbery". The G. P. U. is now legislatively organized on a Union or federal scale under the name of the Joint State Political Bureau (O.G.P.U.).[88] The avowed purpose of this vast powerful, partly secret organization is to "unite all the revolutionary powers of the republics for the purpose of combating political and economic counter-revolution, espionage and banditry". Its activity as an organ of investigation or inquiry is restricted to the above-mentioned crimes, which are more numerous than they appear at a glance. Once an alleged criminal act comes within the jurisdiction of the Political Bureau, the scope of its power in the realm of preliminary investigation resembles in every respect that given to the inquisitor, who has no control or supervision over activities of the Political Bureau as he has over the other organs of investigation.[89]

2. Jurisdiction of the Other Organs of Investigation

The jurisdiction of the organs of investigation except the Political Bureau, is very restricted. They may conduct certain preliminary investigations with regard to any alleged criminal act, and if a case is subject to a preliminary inquiry, it must be transferred immediately to the inquisitor. In other less serious cases, the scope of their authority is much wider and more impressive. In such instances these organs have the authority to conduct investigations which with but few exceptions equal the scope of the preliminary inquiry conducted by the inquisitor in cases which are exclusively within his jurisdiction.

Only in a very few minor cases are these organs of investigation permitted to discontinue the proceedings of their own accord; in all other cases the entire record must be sent by them to the inquisitor (before 1923 it went to the procurator) for

[88]Act on the Joint State Political Bureau of the U.S.S.R. Collected Laws of the U.S.S.R. No. 19, Article 183, 1924. *(Sobranie Zakonov* S.S.S.R. 19-183, 1924.)

[89]The State Political Bureau plays a tremendous rôle in the political life of the Soviet land. But so far as its connection with the judicial system is concerned, it is merely an important investigating organ, and only as such is it of interest to us, all of its other functions and activities being of a purely administrative order.

final action. Prior to the amendments of October, 1929, the organs of investigation, unlike the inquisitor, had no authority to frame a document of accusation, but had to send the record of their investigation directly to the court, with the recommendation to hold the defendant for trial. In more serious cases, which still did not require a preliminary inquiry but which were too complicated for these organs to handle, the record had to be sent to the inquisitor.[90] These amendments provide that the organs of investigation are also to frame a document of accusation, in cases within their jurisdiction. This document is then forwarded, together with the record of the investigation, to the inquisitor if the alleged crime is punishable by more than one year's imprisonment. In less serious offenses the record with the accusatory conclusion is sent directly to the court.[91]

d. *Theory of Present System of Preliminary Investigation and Inquiry*

This entire scheme is an innovation introduced by the Soviet judicial system. In the pre-revolutionary Tzarist Russia the police were empowered to conduct certain investigations in alleged crimes, but their power did not approach a well-defined system of criminal investigation as distinguished from the system of preliminary inquiry. The present arrangement, besides its practical effect in relieving the inquisitor of the less serious and comparatively simple cases, is significant in that it involves a principle of prime importance.

In Imperial Russia there was an organization for secret criminal detection, the acts and proceedings of which could never be brought in at all at the trial as a part of a case. Their investigations were useful only in so far as they revealed certain facts or witnesses. Then, there were the acts of a formal investigation, conducted by the police or by the gendarmerie. The findings of this investigation could figure in the case only within certain limits, and could never be introduced at the trial as formal, judicial testimony. Finally, there were the acts of the preliminary inquiry conducted under certain prescribed forms by a qualified

[90]Code, 1927, sections 98-106.
[91]*Ibid.*, section 208 as amended by the Act of October, 1929.

inquisitor-judge who was a member of the bar as well as a member of the judiciary. The acts of the latter and the data obtained therefrom had a significance as testimony at the trial in so far as they were not disproved or rebutted.

The present Soviet system of pre-trial proceedings retained the difference between the investigation and the preliminary inquiry in name, scope of activities and jurisdiction, but has destroyed, what is more important, any distinction, in theory or in practice, between the two in the judicial value and trustworthiness of their results. The profound principle involved is quite obvious. The old Russian law, modeled upon Western European systems, drew a clear-cut line of demarcation between the acts of the administrative organs, on the one hand, and the judicial acts, performed by the inquisitor, on the other, the former being devoid of any weight as evidence unless and until verified by a designated officer of the judiciary. Soviet writers, however, denounced as a "bourgeois theory"[92] and a mere "dead scholastic principle"[93] the very idea of requiring any division between administrative and judicial acts prior to trial. There are now, roughly speaking, two branches of one system of criminal investigation or inquiry without the slightest distinction *in the ultimate judicial value of their proceedings.* Both are charged with the same duty of searching and digging up all relevant facts establishing the guilt or innocence of the person charged with, or suspected of, the commission of a crime. The organs of investigation are more restricted in the extent of their activities, for it is to them that the less involved cases are assigned; all their activities are directly supervised by the inquisitor. The latter, on the other hand, takes care of the more serious, more complicated offenses while acting under the direct and immediate supervision of the procuracy.[94]

[92]Krastin, I., *The Criminal Trial in R.S.F.S.R.* 1927, page 52.

[93]Krylenko, *The Judiciary and the Law*, 1928, page 112.

[94]In the proposed Projects for a new Code of Criminal Procedure, the distinction between organs of investigation and the inquisitor was abolished. One term was used for all those who investigate criminal acts. But the police were restricted in their powers and are always under the control of the inquisitor. The amendments of October, 1929, purport to abolish this distinction, by incorporating the one term for both, the inquiry and the investigation, as suggested in the above-mentioned project. But the sections of the Code which provide for the organs of investigation were left unchanged.

III. THE BAR—ADVOCACY

a. *Prior to 1922*

The pre-revolutionary institutions of sworn and private attorneys, established by the judicial reforms of the sixties of the last century, were also abolished by the First Decree,[95] which provided that any person might be an attorney and defend. The highly dignified council of sworn attorneys bitterly resented such a humiliation at the hands of the "plebeians". The sworn attorneys of Petrograd (now Leningrad) gave vent to their rage by formally expelling the sworn attorney, P. Stuchka, then acting Commissar of Justice and now president of the Supreme Court, from their council (which by the way had been already dissolved by the decree signed by the same P. Stuchka, among others).[96]

The rather vague and all inclusive idea that "everybody may be an attorney and defend" was not to continue; some form of organized bar was soon established. The Instructions to the revolutionary tribunals of 1917, as well as the Second Decree on Courts, created, we recall, a *collegium* of persons who should devote themselves to the duties of an attorney for the purpose of carrying out the functions of both prosecution and defense. Each citizen could become an attorney if recommended by the soviets of worker's, soldier's, and peasant's deputies.[97] This system prevailed for some time. The People's Court Act of 1918 merely elaborated this method by providing that the members of the college of attorneys should be officials of the Soviet Republic and should receive a remuneration equal to the salary fixed for people's judge.[98] The attorneys, members of the college, were assigned for duty either to prosecute or to defend at special gatherings of the *collegium*.[99] An interesting feature was the provision that the court should require from the defendant (or the parties in a civil suit) a fee for the advocate's services, and that the amount so collected should be entered as part of the income of the Republic.[100] Besides the members of the college,

[95]First Decree, section 3.
[96]P. Stuchka, "Five Years of Revolutionary Law." *The Weekly*, Nos. 44 and 45, 1922.
[97]Collected Laws No. 12, Article 170, 1917, section 7, subsection c.
[98]P.C. Act, 1918, section 42.
[99]*Ibid.*, section 44.
[100]*Ibid.*, section 48.

the courts were to allow the near relations of the defendants—children, spouses, brothers and sisters—to appear as defenders. This right to appear as defender was also extended to the legal advisers of Soviet institutions, appointed by the person in charge of the particular institution.[101]

The idea of having one department from which both public defenders and prosecutors were recruited was abandoned in 1920, and the People's Court Act of that year provided for a separate institution of advocates. In accordance with the doctrine of "labor conscription", which was in vogue among Soviet leaders of that period, the courts were to draft advocates from among citizens capable of exercising such a function. For this purpose the executive committees of the county or city soviets were to compile special lists of persons who would be called for service when required.[102] The persons so drafted for temporary service as advocates were to receive remuneration in equal proportion to that paid to people's co-judges.[103] Immediately following the People's Court Act of 1920, the Commissariat of Justice issued a circular of instructions in which the conscription idea was made clear. It reads: "The defense in court, in criminal cases, is a social duty of all citizens who, by reason of their profession, their education, or their party or official position, are qualified to appear as defenders at the trial."[104] No one was to be taken away from his customary occupation for more than six days in every six months.[105] The provisions of the previous Act of 1918, allowing near relations and governmental representatives to act as defenders, were also incorporated.[106]

b. *The Advocacy Act of 1922*

This doctrine of conscription of labor soon began to lose ground, and its complete discard became obviously necessary with the inauguration of the new economic policy, the *nep*. During the general reforms of the judiciary in 1922 the advocacy was

[101] *Ibid.*, section 47.
[102] P.C. Act, 1920, section 43.
[103] *Ibid.*, section 48.
[104] Collected Laws No. 100, Article 543, 1920, section 5.
[105] *Ibid.*, section 7.
[106] P.C. Act, 1920, section 46.

also not overlooked, and thus in May, 1922, the Advocacy Act was passed.[107] This act, which laid down the fundamental principles governing the Soviet Bar of today, explicitly repealed the sections of the People's Court Act of 1920 concerning the advocacy. The ideas embodied in the provisions of the Advocacy Act of 1922 were constantly elaborated and extended by the Judiciary Acts of 1923, 1924 and 1926. (The first Judiciary Act of 1922 did not have any sections on the advocacy, apparently leaving the special Advocacy Act of 1922 intact.)

c. *The Judiciary Act of 1926*

The Judiciary Act of 1926 declares: "For the purpose of rendering legal aid to the population, especially by way of carrying out the duties of judicial defense in criminal * * * cases, a college of advocates shall function, under the direct supervision and guidance of the territorial, provincial, and circuit courts."[108] The number of advocates for each province, territory, etc., must not be restricted.[109] This is an important provision, for it clearly repealed the special regulations issued by the Commissariat of Justice in 1922,[110] giving the provincial department of justice the authority to regulate—that is, to restrict—the number of advocates for each province.

1. Eligibility for Membership to the Bar

Each citizen who has a constitutional right to vote may become a member of the college of advocates provided he or she has a standing of two years' service in the Soviet judiciary in a position not lower than a people's inquisitor, or in lieu thereof, passes an appropriate examination with a special commission or examining board at the provincial court.[111] Persons who are expelled from social organizations for offenses or misconduct may not become advocates before they have been reinstated.

[107]Advocacy Act, Collected Laws No. 36, Article 425, 1922. *(Polozhenie Ob Advokature, Subranie Uzakonenii* 36-425, 1922.)

[108]Jud. Act, 1926, section 11.

[109]*Ibid.*, section 80.

[110]*The Weekly*, Nos. 24 and 25, 1922.

[111]Jud. Act, 1926, section 81.

2. Structure and Functions of the Bar

The bar is organized on the general basis of Soviet institutions. The members of each college of advocates at a general meeting elect a presidium, a small body which manages the numerous affairs of the organization. The presidium deliberates and decides on all general problems concerning the duties of the advocates; it works out the general plan for establishing special bureaus for the purpose of rendering legal aid to the population, and it determines what percentage of a member's legal fees shall go into the funds of the college.[112] These funds are used to maintain the work of the presidium, organize the legal aid bureaus, and to pay member-advocates who are assigned for service in court by the college or by the court.[113]

New members of the bar who have satisfied the requirements are admitted by the presidium, but the latter is required to inform the presidium of the provincial executive committee, through the provincial court, of any admissions. This information is not designed to serve as a mere record, for the presidium of the provincial executive committee may, within a month from the day it is informed, reject the newly admitted member. A decision of the presidium of the college of advocates refusing to admit an applicant can be appealed to the provincial executive committee, whose decision in the matter is final. The surveillance of the executive authorities over the advocacy is so complete that the provincial, regional or circuit executive committee, but not its presidium, has the power to recall a member of the college of advocates without regard, apparently, to his length of service.[114]

Besides the college at the provincial, regional or circuit courts, the presidium of the college may institute county bureaus of advocates, new members to the bureau being admitted at a general meeting of all the advocates of a given county. Such bureaus exercise in the county many of the functions of the presidium of the college of advocates at the provincial capital.[115]

The members of the college may not hold any office in a government institution or enterprise. From this rule are ex-

[112] *Ibid.*, section 86.
[113] *Ibid.*, section 90.
[114] *Ibid.*, section 82.
[115] *Ibid.*, section 87.

cepted persons occupying elective governmental offices, professors and instructors of jurisprudence (who are deemed to be holding government positions since there are only state law schools), and jurist-counsellors of government institutions or enterprises.[116]

3. Duties of the Advocates

The duties of the advocates are thus defined: (a) They must defend without any remuneration in criminal cases at the suggestion of the court or when appointed by the presidium of the college of advocates; (b) they must participate in the work of the organized bureaus to render legal aid to the population. These duties are absolutely compulsory and a failure to carry them out may result in the expulsion of the offending member from the profession.[117]

That the advocacy is now regarded as a part of the judicial system may also be seen from the fact that the Judiciary Act defines not only the functions and duties of the advocates and prescribe qualifications for membership to the profession, but the method by which the advocate's fees are fixed and collected is also provided for. The prospective clients are divided into four groups: (1) Persons recognized as poor by the people's court pay no fee for legal services in criminal or civil cases; (2) workers, clerks, peasants and artisans who are not employers of labor for profit have a right to pay (apparently in installments if necessary) for legal services rendered to them at a rate fixed by the Commissariat of Justice; (3) persons not belonging to the two above-mentioned groups for whom advocates are appointed in accordance with the requirements of the Code of Criminal Procedure pay to the fund of the college of advocates in accordance with the rate fixed by the Commissariat of Justice; (4) all persons not included in the first three groups pay for legal services in accordance with their agreement with their advocate.[118]

[116] *Ibid.*, section 83.
[117] *Ibid.*, section 84.
[118] *Ibid.*, section 89.

All the members of the bar are subject to disciplinary proceedings for any breach of professional duty. The presidium of the college of advocates serves as a disciplinary court of the first instance. Its decisions are subject to appeal, through the procurator and the president of the provincial court, to the disciplinary department of the latter court.[119]

[119] *Ibid.*, sections 86 and 88.

Chapter V

CRIMINAL PROSECUTION

I. THE PERSON WHO PROSECUTES

a. *Procuracy and Institute for Public Prosecution*

The general principle is that the state procuracy conducts the prosecution at the trial[1]—public prosecution being the rule. Certain exceptions to this rule are permitted, as we shall presently see.

Public prosecution is not always conducted by members of the thoroughly centralized procuracy. Throughout the country there is organized by, and maintained under, the control of the procuracy, the so-called institute for public prosecution. Members of this institute are recruited from among the more intelligent workers and peasants who, after some preliminary training in their own circles, appear at trials to prosecute in the name of the procuracy, usually together with members of the latter, but sometimes also without the participation or aid of the procurator.

These members of the institute for public prosecution are volunteer workers who perform occasionally public or social functions without remuneration. They are commonly to be seen at the spectacular, "exemplary" trials. This form of well-advertised trial is staged as a great public exhibition whenever a crime is a result of the uncultured life and habits of the defendant, or for the exhibition of an unhealthy state of affairs inherited from the old days. The participation of these volunteer prosecutors at criminal trials is growing steadily. In 1923 they appeared in 2420 criminal trials. Their appearance advanced to 8660 in 1924, 16,612 in 1925, and reached 17,384 in 1926.[2]

While public prosecution, either by the procurator or by the members of the institute, is generally the rule for criminal prosecution, there are a number of offenses which, though included in the Criminal Code, are apparently considered to be of a private or quasi-public nature, and are therefore not necessarily included in the sphere of the procurator's activities and duties.

[1]Code, 1927, section 8. See Chapter I, note 127.
[2]Official Report of the Procuracy for 1926, Moscow, 1927, page 31.

b. *Private Prosecution*

The law singles out a number of offenses in the Criminal Code in which criminal prosecution may not be instituted unless the injured party makes an oral or written complaint.[3] Among these offenses are premeditated, bodily injury not causing any serious impairment of health,[4] deliberate infliction of a blow, or any other act of violence causing physical pain,[5] insulting a person by word or in writing,[6] insulting a person in print or by picture distributed or exposed to view,[7] and publication of matter known to be false and injurious to the reputation of another person.[8] In the trial of all of the above-mentioned offenses, none of which is punishable by more than six months' forced labor without imprisonment or by a fine higher than five hundred rubles ($250.00), the injured party, or his attorney, may conduct the accusation at the trial—that is, by private prosecution.

In these criminal offenses, which are considered of a private nature, the law permits the parties to settle the dispute between themselves at any time before the verdict rendered in the case becomes binding. If, however, the state procuracy deems it necessary to step in for the purpose of safeguarding public interest, it may take over the prosecution once it has been instituted and consequently a settlement between the parties themselves will be of no legal effect.[9] The latter provision is apparently a mere precaution, to permit the procuracy to interfere should it become necessary. In general these cases are carried on by private prosecution.

c. *Private—Public Prosecution*

There is a second group of cases which are started also only by the complaints, written or oral, of the injured party. But in these cases once the prosecuting machinery is set in motion the parties may not settle it for themselves, for the state procuracy takes over the case completely.[10] In this group we find cases

[3]Code, 1927, section 10.
[4]Cr. Code, 1926, section 143, part 2.
[5]*Ibid.*, section 146, first part.
[6]*Ibid.*, section 159.
[7]*Ibid.*, section 160.
[8]*Ibid.*, section 161.
[9]Code, 1927, section 10.
[10]*Ibid.*, section 11.

involving deliberate utilization of another person's invention in violation of patent laws, a deliberate use of literary, musical, or other artistic or scientific creations,[11] utilization, for purposes of unfair competition, of another person's trade, factory or industrial mark,[12] sexual intercourse by physical violence, threats, putting in fear or by taking advantage through fraud of the helpless condition of the injured person.[13] Such crimes are punishable by imprisonment up to five years. The state does not institute a criminal prosecution in these cases, not that it considers them of a purely private nature, but, as the commentators of the Code of Criminal Procedure correctly point out,[14] because the very nature of these offenses demands that the injured party be willing to proceed.

All other criminal prosecutions begin either by a complaint made by a private person, not necessarily the injured party, or by some institution or organization, or at the suggestion of the procurator, or through the initiative of the organs of investigation (police, detective bureau, etc.), or by the inquisitors or the court.[15] From what has been said, we may conclude that only a small number of cases are prosecuted privately, by the injured party or his representative, while the overwhelming majority of cases in which the prosecution participates are prosecuted by the state procuracy, and sometimes also, in addition to the procuracy, by representatives of certain government institutions in cases affecting their institutions.[16] These representatives do not participate in preparing the case or in conducting the preliminary investigations, neither do they take the place of the procuracy; what they do is simply to support the accusation at the trial, representing one branch or department of the government, while the procuracy represents the state as a whole.[17] In this connection we might note that before the trial the procurator is said not to be a party to the criminal proceedings, or, strictly speaking, not to represent a party, but rather a representative of the

[11]Cr. Code, 1926, section 177.
[12]*Ibid.*, section 178.
[13]*Ibid.*, section 153.
[14]*Commentaries*, page 24.
[15]Code, 1927, section 91.
[16]*Ibid.*, section 50.
[17]*Commentaries*, page 48.

state who is to look after the correctness of the acts done in conducting the investigation and preliminary inquiry, leading to the uncovering of all possible circumstances in connection with the case. He takes a different position, however, when all these preliminaries are finished and the case is in court; at the trial the procurator is called a party to the action, conducting the accusation, just as the advocate is called the party who is attempting to defeat the accusatory charges.[18]

d. *Civil Claimant*

Another interesting feature, though not novel to Russian procedure, is the civil claim which any injured party may bring in and make a part of the criminal case.[19] This civil claimant, as he is called, becomes a participant for certain purposes in the criminal proceedings, and his participation in the trial as such indirectly helps and strengthens the prosecution, though he is not recognized as a party in the criminal, punitive aspect of the case.

II. METHODS OF PROSECUTION

Though the Soviet system does not know of the technical niceties which, to a certain degree, still cling to our forms of indictment or information, there are, nevertheless, two well-defined methods of prosecution—namely, (1) the summons, (2) the accusatory conclusion. These two methods are not concurrent. Each one depends wholly upon the nature of the case and incidentally also upon the particular route by which such case travels to the trial court.

a. *The Summons*

The summons is employed only for simple, less complicated cases in the following two instances: (1) When a case reaches the people's court by a private complaint lodged directly with it, provided the court considers the case so simple as not to need investigation or preliminary inquiry; (2) when a case reaches the court directly through the organs of investigation—that is, when the alleged crime investigated is punishable by not more

[18]*Ibid.*, page 49.
[19]Code, 1927, section 14.

than one year's imprisonment.[20] In these instances a single judge of the people's court may decide to hold the accused for court (although a decision to discontinue must be approved by a full bench consisting of one judge and two co-judges). The single judge fixes the day of the trial and the accused is served with a summons in which the essence of the accusation is pointed out.[21] We may note that while the law does not specifically correlate the question of public or private prosecution with the method of prosecution, it is clear that the summons is the method applied to cases privately prosecuted, since such cases, as we have seen,[22] are not punishable by imprisonment.

b. *The Accusatory Conclusion*

Prior to October, 1929, there was a method of prosecution which was known as the decision to hold for court. This was a formal document drawn by the people's inquisitor in cases which did not require by law any preliminary inquiry. The entire investigation in such cases was conducted only by the organs of investigation. But if the alleged offense was punishable under the Criminal Code by not less than one year's imprisonment, the organ of investigation could not send the case directly to the court, but the entire record had to be transferred to the people's inquisitor.[23] If the inquisitor determined that the data collected during the investigation warranted the framing of a criminal charge against the accused, he was to draw up the formal paper called the decision to hold the accused for court, and then forward the entire record to the court.[24] This decision had to include a brief summary of all the facts which, taken together, formed the basis for the accusation. It was also to state the name of the accused, his age, previous convictions, the class to which he belonged, his occupation, etc., and the motive which led him to his alleged acts, in so far as they were brought out by the investigation. Likewise the paper had to state briefly the testimony of the injured party, and the place and time of the commission of the

[20] *Ibid.*, section 105, subsection 2.
[21] *Ibid.*, section 233.
[22] See *supra*, page 146.
[23] Code, 1927, section 105, subsection 3.
[24] *Ibid.*, section 223.

crime. In addition, the inquisitor was required to point out the exact law under which the alleged crime was punishable. This document, when sent to the court, was to be accompanied by a list of persons to be summoned to the trial.[25] The inquisitor also was required to name in the list of witnesses the persons who would testify favorably to the accused. The people's judge who received the decision to hold for court fixed the day of the trial,[26] and a copy of this document had to be handed to the accused not later than three days before the trial.[27]

By the recent amendments to the Code the accusatory conclusion has been made the method of prosecution applicable to all cases which go through either the investigation or the preliminary inquiry.

The accusatory conclusion, unlike our indictment or information, is nothing more than a summary of all the facts, for as well as against the accused, which were brought to light by the thorough inquiry conducted by the inquisitor or the organ of investigation. It is the basis upon which the court frames its decision either to put the case on the trial list—to use our phraseology—or to discontinue it. The accusatory conclusion must not be framed one-sidedly; it must not neglect to bring out all the facts favorable to the accused. This is considered so fundamental that a failure to comply with this rule was held by the Supreme Court of the R.S.F.S.R. a ground for annulling a verdict of a provincial court.[28]

The law in effect before October, 1929, required the accusatory conclusion to consist of two parts. The first part, the descriptive, had to contain a description of the circumstances of the case as brought out by the preliminary inquiry, and the testimony upon which the inquisitor based his conclusion to hold the accused for court. The second part, the determinative, was to state, if it was possible, the name of the accused, his age, previous criminal record, if any, the class to which he belongs, his occupation, place and time of the commission of the crime, likewise the

[25] *Ibid.*, section 224.
[26] *Ibid.*, section 234.
[27] *Ibid.*, section 245.
[28] Decisions of the Cassational Department (Collegium) of the Supreme Court of the R.S.F.S.R., 1924 case No. 29774. Cited in the *Commentaries*, page 222.

motives which prompted the accused to such acts, and the testimony of the aggrieved party. In addition the determinative part had to point out by which particular penal law the alleged crime was punishable.[29] The inquisitor was to submit a list of persons for and against the accused who were to be called to the trial. The amendments of 1929 did away with the necessity for the two separate parts mentioned above but the contents of these parts are fully retained. The amendments made the accusatory conclusion more elaborate by requiring that it shall state (1) all the circumstances for and against the accused, (2) what measures were taken to ensure the satisfaction of a judgment in favor of a civil claimant if a civil claim is filed, (3) the particular page of the record on which the facts relied upon are to be found, and (4) the amount of time the accused has already been held in custody. In addition to this the authority which frames the accusatory conclusion is given the power to limit the list of witnesses to those who are absolutely necessary, and to omit the name of any witness if the facts to be proved by him are such as can be proved by other witnesses summoned or if such facts are uncontradicted.[30]

The accused is served with a copy of the document not less than three days before the trial. The rules for drawing up the accusatory conclusion are to be strictly followed. The procurator's approval, as has been already stated, is always necessary before the case may proceed further. If for any reason the procurator disapproves of the document drawn up by the inquisitor, or if the inquisitor disapproves of the document drawn up by the organs of investigation, he sends it back to the authority who drew it up with his objections and instructions.[31]

Before the amendments of 1929 the accusatory document did not automatically bring the accused to trial on the charges advanced in the conclusion. The court still in every case had the final decision, after receiving the official paper, whether drawn by the inquisitor or the procurator, with the recommendation of the latter to hold the accused for trial. The court at its administrative session examined the accusatory conclusion and delib-

[29]Code, 1927, section 210.
[30]*Ibid.*, section 207, as amended in 1929.
[31]*Ibid.*, section 224, as amended in 1929.

erated on the following questions: (a) whether the charge was sufficiently supported by the facts stated in the first, or descriptive, part of the accusatory conclusion; (b) whether the conclusion was correctly formulated; (c) whether the charge was covered by the Criminal Code and by what particular section; (d) whether any change should be made in the list of persons to be summoned to the trial.[32] These amendments of 1929 empower the procurator or the inquisitor, as the case may be, in a proper case to affirm an accusatory conclusion sent to him, by a short resolution which in effect holds the accused for court.[33] The judge who receives the record may, before putting the case on the trial list, refer it to the preparatory session of the court, formerly called the administrative session, under circumstances which will be discussed later.[34]

[32] *Ibid.*, section 236.
[33] *Ibid.*, section 221, as amended in 1929.
[34] *Ibid.*, section 236, as amended in 1929.

Chapter VI
PROCEEDINGS PRIOR TO THE TRIAL

In the long, involved process of administering the criminal law, the preliminary inquiry or investigation occupies a significant and unique place within the Soviet system of criminal procedure as it does, generally speaking, in other systems on the Continent. This inquiry passes through different stages of development which vary according to the exigencies of a particular case. We shall now proceed to analyze separately the various steps of the preliminary proceedings.

I. INSTITUTING A CRIMINAL PROCEEDING

a. *How Instituted*

Criminal proceedings may be instituted in the following ways: First, it may begin at the suggestion of the procurator, the organs of investigation or the inquisitor or the court, in all of which cases it is necessary to carry the proceedings to completion; second, a criminal case may be started by a written or oral complaint or statement submitted to any one of the above mentioned authorities by a citizen, an organization, a government institution, an official, or by the confession of the alleged criminal himself.[1] In this second group of instances the authorities may proceed if the complaint or confession presents a *prima facie* criminal case;[2] otherwise, in the absence of criminal elements appearing in such complaint or statement, the organs of investigation, the inquisitor, or the procurator are not to proceed. The complaining person or institution, however, must be notified of the decision not to proceed and this decision is subject to appeal to the proper court within seven days.[3] We observe that there are a number of authorities who, upon proper grounds, may set in motion a criminal proceeding. The particular manner in which a given case is then to proceed, and the question as to which of the authorites are to have jurisdiction will depend entirely on

[1]Code, 1927, section 91. See also *Commentaries*, page 81.
[2]*Ibid.*, section 96.
[3]*Ibid.*, section 95.

the nature and seriousness of the case. Though the people's court may, when the complaint is made directly to it, put a case on the trial list without first sending it for a preliminary inquiry or investigation,[4] this, we may assume, occurs rarely, and only in absolutely clear and simple cases. The usual method of procedure is to have a case undergo either an investigation or an inquiry, or both.

b. *Arrest Not a Prerequisite*

Before we discuss the procedure of the investigation and the preliminary inquiry, let us note the significant fact that, unlike our own system in which a criminal proceeding usually starts with the arrest of the person charged with the commission of crime, the Soviet system does not make the arrest a necessary step in the long chain of criminal proceedings. To be sure, there is a very definite body of law concerning arrest. But, as pointed out, the arrest bears no direct relation to the institution of a criminal action; nor must it absolutely be made at any stage of the criminal proceedings. A case may be instituted and prosecuted to the very end without any actual or formal arrest though as a practical matter in most cases this is unlikely to happen. We shall return to this subject more fully in another connection.

II. CRIMINAL INVESTIGATION

The Soviet criminal system, we recall,[5] provides two methods of pre-trial proceedings, the investigation and the preliminary inquiry. Though both have similar functions and are, in the last analysis, parts of one system designed to investigate what appears to be a crime, the spheres of their activities are quite distinct. We shall, therefore, describe and discuss their activities separately, observing first the functions of the investigation in its particular field.

While the organs of investigation are not the only agencies which institute a criminal proceeding, we can readily perceive that the usual case would have its starting point with these organs, or, to be more specific, with the police *(militzia)*, since the latter

[4] *Ibid.*, section 96, subsection 4.
[5] See *ante*, pages 130, 135, 137-138.

would naturally be the first to learn of the fact that an apparent crime had taken place.

The course which the police or any other organ of investigation are to follow depends wholly on the nature of the alleged criminal act.

There are two distinct main lines to be followed—one where the alleged crime is by law subject to a preliminary inquiry, and the other where it does not have to undergo such an inquiry.

a. *Cases Subject to Preliminary Inquiry*

In cases requiring an inquiry, the authority of the police, or any other organ of investigation, is quite circumscribed. Its functions are limited to a preliminary questioning of the suspect and the eye-witnesses, as well as other persons who may offer some testimony of assistance in the immediate clearing up of the case. The investigators are also to adopt measures necessary to prevent the suspect from evading the inquiry and the trial or destroying any evidence. Whenever it is feared that evidence will be destroyed the police have the power to conduct searches and seizures, make inspections, etc.[6] All the proceedings are normally conducted within a short time, since the organs of investigation must notify the inquisitor and the procurator within twenty-four hours that the proceedings have been instituted,[7] and immediately thereafter forward the case to the inquisitor.

One might wonder what the investigator can really accomplish in twenty-four hours. We have before us a reprinted official record of a murder case,[8] which illustrates most strikingly the speedy moving of the machinery of investigation before the case is transferred to the inquisitor. On March 14, 1923, at 8 o'clock in the morning a citizen informed the police that upon entering the house of a neighbor she discovered the dead body of one of its occupants. During the twenty-four hours that followed the police had performed innumerable acts, as evidenced by the official protocols on record. It examined three persons, with the

[6]Code, 1927, section 99.

[7]*Ibid.*, section 96, subsection 1.

[8]Case No. 596, 1923, tried in the Odessa Provincial Court, archive No. 694. Reprinted in the *Criminal Process in Motion (Ugolovnyi Protzess v evo Dvizhenii)* by M. K. Rudnev & G. L. Kandel, 1927.

result that valuable information was obtained, conducted a search and seized certain articles of evidence, interrogated and arrested two persons, one of whom was later convicted of the crime, and had the district physician examine the corpse (not an autopsy). The same day notification was sent to the procurator and the inquisitor, since it was a case where a preliminary inquiry had to be conducted. We might add in passing, that all the official papers, the protocols, must always be read to the witness or the suspect, who then signs them, stating that he has read them or that they have been read to him. It is quite reasonable to assume that the above illustration of the activity of the police represents an extreme case. But nevertheless it indicates what can be accomplished by way of preliminary investigation in a short time.

After the case is transferred to the inquisitor, the latter assumes complete jurisdiction, and immediately notifies the procurator of this fact.[9] The organs of investigation have no further jurisdiction over the case, and they may thereafter act only upon the instructions of the people's inquisitor.[10]

b. *When a Preliminary Inquiry Is Not Required*

1. Scope of the Investigation

We are now to concern ourselves with the second situation, where a preliminary inquiry is not mandatory. In these cases the investigation of the police takes the place, roughly speaking, of the preliminary inquiry. The inquisitor, however, may at any time examine the record of the case conducted by the police, and suggest the course to be followed by it,[11] since the police, we may recall, are under the direct supervision of the people's inquisitor in whose district they operate. Notwithstanding the supervision of the inquisitor, however, it is the organ of criminal investigation (usually the chief of police) which in these cases takes all the steps necessary in the preparation of the case. The law authorizes it to examine witnesses and experts, conduct searches and seizures, look over places and things, decide the

[9]See *supra*, note 7.
[10]Code, 1927, section 110.
[11]*Ibid.*, section 107.

exact scope of the investigation, etc. In all these actions the investigators are to follow the rules prescribed for the procedure of the preliminary inquiry conducted by the inquisitors. Usually the investigation is performed by the organs of investigation directly and on their own initiative. But there still remain a number of acts which they may not perform without first obtaining permission of the inquisitor or the procurator. They may not take proceedings to determine the mental condition of the accused or take any steps concerning the filing of a civil claim in conjunction with the criminal case, or ensuring the satisfaction of a money judgment which may be rendered at the trial; they may not make any suggestions for the suspension of the suspect from office.[12] These limitations upon the authority of the organs of investigation are deemed necessary owing to the inherent complexity of such tasks, and because the fundamental theory on which the system of criminal investigation is based, as distinguished from the preliminary inquiry, permits the former to handle only problems of comparative simplicity.[13] Should it appear, however, that it is advisable for the organs of investigation to perform such difficult tasks in any given case, the inquisitor may, in his discretion, give his consent.

2. Proceedings After the Investigation

The organs of criminal investigation, after completing all the necessary proceedings of searching and investigating, which may not be prolonged beyond the period of one month,[14] must decide whether to suspend or discontinue the proceedings, or to hold the accused for court. A case is suspended whenever a suspect is suffering from a temporary mental disease, or whenever there is a failure to discover the guilty person. A case is discontinued if the suspect is afflicted with an incurable mental disease, or the statute of limitation has run, or if there is a lack of criminal element in the case, etc.[15] The distinction between suspension and discontinuance was for the first time drawn by the amendments to

[12] *Ibid.*, section 101. See also the *Commentaries*, page 100.

[13] *Commentaries*, page 101.

[14] Code, 1927, section 105, as amended in October, 1929. The investigation, including the holding for court must be completed in one month. An extension may be permitted by the procurator.

[15] *Ibid.*, sections 202 and 204.

the Code of October, 1929. The authorities which suspend the proceeding may reopen the case.[16] Should the investigating authorities, on the other hand, consider that the data collected by them are sufficient to hold the suspect for trial, they are required to draw up the accusatory conclusion and then send the record directly to the people's court, whenever the alleged crime is punishable by not more than one year's imprisonment. When it is punishable by imprisonment for more than one year, they forward it to the people's inquisitor in whose district the investigation has been conducted.[17] The inquisitor may, irrespective of the opinion of the investigating organs, suspend or discontinue the proceedings upon proper grounds, return the case for further investigation, or affirm the accusatory conclusion by a brief resolution which in effect amounts to a holding of the accused for court.[18]

Before we leave the subject of criminal investigation let us dispose of the problems of arrest and bail; questions with which the organs of investigation are constantly confronted.

c. *Apprehension and Holding in Custody*

1. Constitutional Guaranties

The legal and highly involved law of arrest, as it exists in our own system of law, is totally unknown in Soviet Russia, just as it was in Imperial Russia. Since there has never been any deeply rooted and cherished tradition of personal liberty, it is not at all surprising to note the utter lack of any required formality, in the form of affidavit, warrant, etc., before a person may be arrested or held in custody. It would, however, be an error to assume that one may be arbitrarily arrested without any legal cause. The law states: "No person shall be deprived of his liberty and taken into custody otherwise than in the instances and in the manner provided by law".[19]

It is rather interesting to note that this pretentious, high-sounding provision, which may be erroneously taken for an

[16] *Ibid.*, section 205.
[17] *Ibid.*, sections 206, 207.
[18] *Ibid.*, section 221.
[19] Code, 1927, section 5.

important, far-reaching constitutional guaranty of personal liberty, was wholly borrowed from the so-called Tzarist Constitution of 1906,[20] and was, almost verbatim, inserted in the first Soviet Code of Criminal Procedure of 1922, whence it was taken over into the "Basic Principles of Criminal Procedure" adopted by the Union in 1924,[21] and, therefore, must be followed by all the soviet republics. The famous Soviet Procurator and legal writer, N. V. Krylenko,[22] ridicules the insertion of an obviously constitutional declamation in a code of criminal procedure. He frankly charges his comrades with trying to make the Soviet Code "reflect constitutional norms, borrowed from the bourgeois conception of right." He correctly points out that the legislators did not achieve their purpose, since the constitution states that the "Russian Socialist Federative Soviet Republic is granted the power to deprive certain individuals or groups of individuals of rights which they enjoy in opposition to the interest of the Social Revolution".[23] But while this provision of the Code is not a constitutional safeguard against possible legislative encroachment upon the personal liberty of the individual citizen, it is at least a protection against arrest without the color of legislative sanction.

2. Reasons for Taking Into and Holding in Custody

The Soviet law knows of two distinct general situations where incarceration may take place. A person may be held in custody as "a measure of social protection", as the phrase runs, and this occurs always as the result of a decision reached by a court—a sentence. The other form of holding in custody occurs either before the trial, or before the verdict becomes legally binding, that is, when an appeal to a higher jurisdiction is pending, and is applied only as an extreme measure, to ensure the presence of the accused at the investigation, inquiry, or trial, as the case may be. The latter form is naturally the one which is of imme-

[20] Collected Laws 1906, Article 603, section 331. See *Fundamental Laws of the Russian Empire*, 1911, Volume 1, section 73.

[21] Systematic Collection of the Existing Laws of the U.S.S.R. Book V, 1926. *Basic Principles of Criminal Procedure*, section 9.

[22] Krylenko, *The Judiciary and the Law*, 1928, pages 52 and 53.

[23] Constitution of the R.S.F.S.R., 1925, section 14.

diate moment to us in connection with our discussion of the preliminary proceedings.

3. Authority of the Organs of Investigation to Arrest

The authority of the organs of investigation to effect an arrest depend upon the nature of a given case. They may arrest a person suspected of the commission of a crime which is subject to a preliminary inquiry only as a means of preventing the suspect from evading the inquiry and the trial. But even then the right of the investigators to take a person into custody is restricted to the following cases: (a) When a person is apprehended while making direct preparation to commit an alleged crime, or while actually engaged in its commission or immediately afterwards; (b) when the victim or an eye witness points to a specific person as the one who committed a crime; (c) when articles of evidence connected with a crime are found on the person of a suspect or in his dwelling; (d) when a suspect attempts to flee or is in flight; (e) when a suspect has no permanent place of abode or a permanent occupation; (f) when a suspect cannot identify himself.[24] These rules are the same as those which existed in Tzarist Russia with respect to the right of the police to effect an arrest.[25] It is well to observe that all these conditions do not make the taking into custody obligatory. The police or any similar investigating authority, are merely given the power to arrest in those six instances should they deem it necessary or advisable.

In the case of an offense which is not subject to a preliminary inquiry, provided the crime is punishable by one year's imprisonment or less, one of the six conditions above mentioned must also be present in order to supply a legal ground for effecting an arrest of a person charged with the crime. In the absence of these conditions the investigating authorities may not arrest or hold the suspect, but merely ask him to sign a declaration that he will appear when summoned.[26] There is still another situation in cases which, while not subject to a preliminary

[24]Code, 1927, section 100.

[25]*Fundamental Laws of the Russian Empire,* 1911, Vol. XVI, section 257. (This law was enacted in 1864.)

[26]Code, 1927, section 103.

inquiry, and therefore entirely in the hands of the organs of investigation, are of such a serious nature that conviction would carry a sentence of more than one year's imprisonment. In this case the investigating authorities, after examining the suspected individual, may select one of the established measures to prevent his absconding, one of which measures is holding in custody.[27] This may be applied only under certain carefully prescribed conditions, which taken as a whole restrict this power to a considerable extent.

All arrests effected by the organs of investigation must be reported, within twenty-four hours, irrespective of the nature and seriousness of the case, either to the inquisitor in whose district the investigating organ operates, or to the nearest people's judge. These two authorities, upon notification, must either affirm or reverse the decision of the investigator.[28] By a special instruction to the police, the latter are required to state in connection with the notification of the arrest the following: (a) who made the arrest; (b) the place, date and hour of arrest; (c) the information obtained regarding the person held; (d) the essence of the crime with which he is charged; (e) the reason which prompted the arrest; (f) the name of the official who signed the order or the decision to effect the arrest.[29] The rules regulating arrests made by the State Political Bureau as an organ of investigation are prescribed by special enactments[30] which are usually not made public.

We are now ready to turn our discussion to the second, higher and more important branch which conducts the proceedings prior to the trial.

III. PRELIMINARY INQUIRY *(sledstvie)*

a. *General Purpose*

The preliminary inquiry is the most important factor in unearthing all the facts and circumstances of any serious criminal case and the motive actuating the person who committed the

[27] *Ibid.*, section 102.
[28] *Ibid.*, section 104.
[29] *Commentaries*, page 107.
[30] Code, 1927, note to section 104.

offense. This proceeding, the purpose of which is to dig into the mass of complicated and contradictory facts and, in theory at least, without bias, prejudice or preconceived aims to uncover, explain, and check up every detail, really serves as an effective instrument in the hands of the courts in their administration of the criminal law.

b. *Two Stages of the Inquiry*

The procedure before the trial undergoes two distinct stages of development. Though the Codes do not draw any clear-cut line of demarkation, such a division may, nevertheless, be inferred from the way the subject is treated. First, there is a stage of general inquiry which occurs before any person is charged with the commission of the unlawful act. Should the inquisitor or the organ of investigation be informed of a certain occurrence which indicates on its face the commission of a crime, whether or not any particular person is implicated, he must inquire into the nature of the act. If a crime was really committed, he must then direct his search towards discovering the person who committed the crime. During this stage of the proceedings, there is no person who may legally be considered as "the accused". At most there may be someone who is under suspicion. It not infrequently happens that the proceedings do not pass beyond the limits of the first stage, either because no crime has been committed, or the inquiry can not fasten the charge on any particular person or persons.

The second stage, on the other hand, concerns itself with inquiring into all the relevant circumstances of the case, the person or persons formally accused of the commission of the offense being the central figure or figures of the proceedings. It is well to bear in mind the distinction between these two stages when discussing the question of the proper measure to be adopted in order to prevent a possible absconding.

c. *Measures To Ensure Attendance*

There are five measures to ensure the attendance of the accused. One is a signed promise by the accused not to leave the town or place designated by the inquisitor or by the accused himself, without the permission either of the inquisitor or the court. The accused is at this time also informed that in case he fails to live up to his promise he will be subjected to a more severe measure.[31]

The second is a personal parole or property parole. Property parole is the term used when a financially responsible person or organization signs a written pledge to pay a certain sum of money should the accused fail to appear at the inquiry, investigation or trial as the case may be, when summoned to do so. The personal parole is a guaranty given by trustworthy persons, not less than two, for the appearance of the accused whenever wanted, and also a direct promise to hand him over to the inquisitor or the court upon demand. For a failure of the accused to appear in this case, the guarantor is subject to a fine or forced labor up to three months as in the case of a witness who fails to appear or refuses to testify.[32]

The third is cash bail, that is, money or property put up either by the accused himself, or by other persons or by an organization in his behalf, in order to secure his appearance. The exact amount of bail or personal property is determined by the inquisitor in accordance with the seriousness of the case, the weight of the testimony against the accused, the financial dependability of the bondsmen, and all other relevant circumstances.[33] Cash bail and property parole are criticised by Soviet legal writers as affording the more well-to-do people an advantage in securing freedom for themselves during the preliminary proceedings. The Fifth Congress of the Soviet Judicial Workers in 1924, accordingly, adopted a resolution against such measures to ensure attendance.[34] This has, however, not been altered up to this date. It is interesting that even in the rather drastic draft of a new Code of Criminal Procedure which is being discussed in the Soviet legal circles the measures of cash bail and property parole have been retained.[35]

[31]*Ibid.*, section 144, subsection 1, and section 149.

[32]*Ibid.*, section 144, subsection 2, and sections 150, 151 and 152. (See also Cr. Code, 1926, section 92.)

[33]*Ibid.*, section 144, subsection 3 and sections 153 and 154.

[34]*The Weekly*, 1924, Nos. 12 and 13.

[35]*Ibid.*, 1928, No. 28.

The fourth is home arrest. This means that the accused person is isolated in his own home, with or without a guard.[36] This method is usually restricted to cases where the accused cannot be taken into custody owing to illness, or, if a woman, pregnancy, infant nursing, etc.[37] As in all similar cases, the inquisitor enjoys wide discriminatory power and may settle the details in accordance with the needs of each case.

The last method is holding in custody. This is obviously an extreme measure and the law is specific as to when it should be applied. The provisions of the Code dealing with this subject have been modified over and over again, the tendency apparently being to narrow down the scope of the inquisitor's diccretionary power by further limiting the number of cases where this harsh measure may be applied. The particular section, as finally amended,[38] is divided into three parts, and provides:

"Holding in custody as a means of cutting off the possibility of absconding is permissible only in crimes in which [upon conviction] the court may impose a sentence of imprisonment for a period of over one year."[39] In addition to this, there must also be present a well-grounded reason to fear that the accused, if at large, will hinder the process of discovering the truth. Furthermore, the organ which selects this extreme measure must take into consideration the seriousness of the evidence against the accused, his occupation, age, health and family.

Holding in custody is allowable also in cases where a person is accused of a crime covered by a specific section of the Criminal Code, such as failure to report knowledge of either preparation for or the accomplishment of acts of mass disorder, cases involving bribery and counterfeiting, stealing or destroying of secret government documents; the secret manufacturing or selling of narcotics, certain types of what we call larceny, robbery and forgery. All these crimes are punishable by im-

[36]Code, 1927, section 143, subsection 4 and section 157.

[37]*Commentaries*, page 188.

[38]Collected Laws No. 50, Article 331, 1927, amending the section 158 of the Code, 1923.

[39]In the original Code of 1923, and even in its edition of 1927, the test was whether the case could result in any sentence of imprisonment, but by the amendment of May, 1927, it was provided that only when the sentence may be over one year, may the measure of holding in custody be applied.

prisonment not exceeding one year, and, therefore, holding in custody would not apply to them, without this specific provision. Holding in custody however, as a means of securing attendance in these cases is restricted to instances where it has been proved that the accused has connections with criminal, underworld circles, or that he has no permanent place of abode or has once evaded the inquiry or the trial.

The third part of the section provides for holding in custody in cases involving very grave offenses, including banditry, organized mass disorder, etc. Holding in custody before the trial in the latter cases is permissible only on the ground that the alleged crime is of a socially dangerous nature. Such a provision is rather remarkable, for it is clearly contrary to the general theory of the Soviet system of procedure which maintains that holding in custody before trial should take place only as a measure to prevent the absconding of the accused. Here the Code speaks of an entirely different reason, namely, social protection or security, which is the underlying reason for imprisonment after one is found guilty at the trial, but not before.

To sum up the entire question of holding in custody before the trial, or, to use our term holding without bail, the fundamental grounds which may justify such a measure are (a) the danger that the accused, if at large, will hinder the uncovering of the truth, (b) the possibility that the accused will evade the inquiry or the trial, (c) the peculiar, socially dangerous nature of the crime with which the accused is charged, (d) the fact that the accused is a professional criminal or has connections with the underworld, while being charged with one of a number of specified crimes, even though these are not punishable by over one year of imprisonment. In the first three instances there is the additional requirement that the alleged crime shall carry a sentence of not less than one year's imprisonment. The fourth instance is an exception to the general rule and is typical of the Soviet attitude towards the professional criminal. Such a person is *a priori* deemed to be socially dangerous irrespective of the nature of the crime he has committed.

We may note in passing that these rules merely describe the situations under which the proper authorities may, should they deem it necessary, select this extreme measure. The authorities, usually the inquisitor, when deciding to take this step must state in writing the exact circumstances which have led them to their decision.

One of the five measures to secure attendance is selected only after the person has been formally accused. It will generally, therefore, not be applied by the organs of investigation in cases in which a preliminary inquiry is required, for in those cases the extent of their authority never goes beyond the first stage, the general investigation. The police, on the other hand, may take a person into custody even at the beginning of the criminal action, before such person has been formally accused, but only under certain conditions, as we have seen.[40] From this discussion it would seem that the inquisitor does not have any authority to order the arrest and holding of a person before he is put in the legal position of an accused and in the ordinary, normal case that is true. But the law grants to him powers sufficient to meet the exigencies of a particular case where an immediate arrest would be indispensable. The Code provides: "Means of cutting off the possibility of absconding shall be selected only after the suspected person has been formally accused * * * In exceptional cases these means may also be applied to mere suspects who have not yet been declared accused."[41] By this provision the inquisitor is vested with discretionary powers to consider a given case within the definition of exceptional and, therefore, to order the immediate arrest of a person suspected, if the nature of the case warrants the application of this extreme measure. But within fourteen days the inquisitor must have gathered data against the suspect sufficient, in the eye of the law, to declare him the accused, otherwise the measure must be set aside and the individual freed.[42] At this point we may note that the writ of habeas corpus is a thing totally unknown to the Soviet system. Any person unlawfully incarcerated would have to seek redress from the supervisory authorities, who have the power to order the release of the prisoner.

[40]See *ante*, page 160.
[41]Code, 1927, section 145.
[42]*Ibid.*

d. *Formal Accusation*

The proceeding of designating a person as the accused is an important feature in the Soviet system of criminal procedure; it signifies the entering of the case upon a new, a second, stage in the preliminary inquiry, and is quite naturally looked upon as a landmark in the criminal prosecution. The status of a person as a mere suspect and as the accused differs considerably. In the former stage one might not even know that he is suspected of the commission of a crime. But the decision of the inquisitor, based upon proper grounds, to attach to the suspect the stigma of an accused puts him directly under the supervision of the inquisitorial officials.

In addition to any measure which is selected, the accused is required to sign a promise that he will appear when summoned to the inquiry or the court, and that he will notify the authorities of any change of residence.[43] This promise is not the same as that which serves as one of the five measures to ensure attendance. In many ways the legal position of the accused resembles the status of the individual against whom an indictment has been found under our system.

1. Framing the Decision

Since the act of designating a person as the accused affects him gravely, the law is explicit in demanding that the inquisitor must have sufficient grounds upon which to act.

The inquisitor frames a document called the decision when he has gathered sufficient information to justify the accusation.[44] This document must contain the name of the accused, the time, place and all surrounding circumstances of the alleged crime, in so far as they are known to the inquisitor, and the exact facts upon which the decision was based.[45]

The accused is then summoned, by mail, telegram, or telephone, to appear before the inquisitor, or is brought to him if upon being summoned he fails to appear without cause. The decision designating him as the accused is formally made known

[43] *Ibid.*, section 143.
[44] *Ibid.*, section 128.
[45] *Ibid.*, section 129.

to him. Although the law does not stipulate any exact procedure by which the accused is notified of his new status, the practice is well established and is strictly followed. The inquisitor reads to him the decision which briefly states the reasons upon which he is designated as the accused. Whereupon the accused, and the inquisitor sign the document.[46] The signature of the former has not the effect of an admission of guilt or even a recognition that certain facts as stated therein are correct. It merely signifies that he has read the document, or that he has been informed of the charges against him. The accused, after signing the paper, has a right to appeal from the decision of the inquisitor to the procurator,[47] whose decision in this matter may be appealed to the provincial court.[48]

As the status of an accused, with all the disadvantages it carries, begins to operate from the moment the inquisitor has reached his decision, and not, as one would suppose, from the time of formal notification, the law provides that the fact of the accusation must be communicated to the accused not later than forty-eight hours from the time of the decision.[49] With this procedure completed, the inquisitorial machinery is set in full motion. The way the inquisitor is now to proceed is carefully and elaborately set forth in the provisions of the Code.

e. *Interrogating the Accused*

This is one of the first important functions to be performed by the inquisitor. It takes place simultaneously with the formal notification to the accused. Usually it immediately follows the official reading of the decision but sometimes occurs before that; it must take place not later than twenty-four hours from the time the accused appears.[50] The inquisitor must, to start with, make sure of the identity of the person, and then explain to him the essence of the accusation. This is necessary because the inquisitor may wish to question the accused before reading to him the formal notification. But even when the notification precedes the

[46] *Commentaries*, page 149.
[47] Code, 1927, section 212.
[48] *Ibid.*, section 220.
[49] *Ibid.*, section 128.
[50] Code, 1927, section 134.

interrogation, the inquisitor, nevertheless, is to repeat the essence of the charge, for the accused may not have clearly understood the contents of the official, and in a sense formal document.[51] That he should be well aware of the charges against him is evidently a basic requirement of the Soviet law of criminal procedure.

The inquisitor starts the examination of the accused by suggesting to him to tell all he knows about the case. Afterwards the accused is questioned on all relevant matters. The entire proceeding, the story of the accused and the questions and answers are entered into the official protocol, as far as possible verbatim. The protocol is then read to the accused, who may demand that corrections, modifications or additions be made to correspond with his testimony. The accused has also a right, if he wishes, to reduce to writing his own version of the case. The protocol, thus corrected, is then signed by both the inquisitor and the accused.[52] The practical result of the signing of this document is to prevent the raising of objections, or casting of doubts as to the bare fact that the writing represents the true version as once given by the accused himself. Naturally, there is always room to object to the protocol on grounds of forgery or the use of force or threats.

The inquisitor has great latitude in selecting the exact method of conducting the inquiry, framing his questions, etc. The law, however, specifies that the accused be interrogated, as a rule, in the absence of other accused, if there are such, in the same criminal action. But the inquisitor may, when the exigencies of the case warrant, confront several persons accused in the same charge with each other or with the witness. Although the law apparently considers the accused as the most important witness in the case, he is, nevertheless, not bound to answer questions or give any testimony at all. This right is not explicitly given to him, but it is beyond doubt the law, though this important privilege is granted by way of inference. First, the Code does not provide for any punishment for the refusal of the accused to testify, as in the case of other witnesses. Furthermore, it is specifically stated that the inquisitor shall not obtain testimony, or confes-

[51]*Commentaries*, page 157.
[52]Code, 1927, sections 138, 139.

sions, from the accused by means of violence, threats, or similar methods.[53] While such a rule is in line with the best traditions of enlightened methods of criminal prosecution, it is rather inexplicable why it is not carried to its logical conclusion by a provision that the inquisitor must explain to the accused his legal right not to testify, just as the defendant at the trial is told of his specific rights.[54]

After the first interrogation of the accused, the inquisitor decides whether the measure previously selected to secure attendance, if any one was employed, should be changed to another.[55] The inquisitor enjoys here, as in other instances, great discretionary power in selecting the measure. But each decision must be accompanied by a written opinion stating the reasons for the selection. This decision, with the opinion, must be forwarded immediately to the procurator and to the accused.[56] The extent of the inquisitor's power in fixing the measure to prevent the accused from absconding is best illustrated by the fact that while the procurator is entrusted with the direct supervision over the activities of the inquisitor, the latter's decision with regard to the security may not be finally changed or modified by the procurator. The latter may, however, suggest a change, but if the inquisitor disagrees with his suggestion the question is forwarded to the proper court for final determination. If, however, the procurator's suggestion is favorable to the accused the inquisitor must carry it out immediately, having the right to appeal to the court.[57] In general, we may note that the measure selected is not of a permanent nature, but may be changed and modified repeatedly, in accordance with the shifting situation of a case. Such changes are usually effected by the inquisitor himself except that where a particular measure is selected by the procurator, only the latter may modify or change it.[58]

[53]*Ibid.*, section 136.
[54]*Ibid.*, section 377.
[55]*Ibid.*, section 145.
[56]*Ibid.*, section 146.
[57]*Ibid.*, section 148.
[58]*Ibid.*, section 161. (By the Code, 1922 this power was vested only in the court.)

f. *Examining Witnesses and Experts*

1. Scope of Examination

The examination of witnesses is logically the next step in the preliminary proceedings. All the rules and regulations with regard to summoning, interrogating, signing the protocol, etc., prescribed for the examination of the accused are applicable to the procedure of examining all other witnesses. The only real difference between the two is found in the fact that the witness must, willingly or otherwise, testify. He is obliged, under a penalty for refusing, to answer all questions put to him by the inquisitor. Furthermore, he is liable to punishment if he does not tell the truth. While the oath has been abolished as a solemn procedure which automatically adds weight to the veracity of testimony, the law against those falsely testifying has not been relaxed. The inquisitor before examining the witness warns him regarding the penalty he may incur by refusing to testify or by testifying falsely.[59] Self-incrimination is, as one would expect, no excuse. The only exception to this rule is when the witness is asked irrelevant questions. The law stipulates that "the witness may be interrogated only about facts which have to be ascertained in the particular case, or concerning the personal characteristics of the accused."[60] We may safely conjecture that this modification of the otherwise rigid rule has little practical significance. The witness will have to be absolutely certain that the question put to him is outside the authority of the inquisitor before daring to refuse to testify; for, should his interpretation as to the relevancy of the question be wrong, he assumes the risk of punishment.

Unlike pre-revolutionary procedure, Soviet law does not seem to exempt the near relations of the accused from the requirement to testify, for the Code provides that only the following persons may not be called or examined as witnesses: (1). The advocate of the accused; (2) persons who by reason of physical or mental deficiencies are incapable of realizing the import of the case and of giving correct testimony.[61] To determine the question of capacity experts may be consulted.

[59] *Ibid.*, section 164.
[60] *Ibid.*, section 166.
[61] *Ibid.*, section 61.

As the inquisitor is to conduct an inquiry which is a complete and many-sided hearing of the case, the law provides that "The inquisitor shall not have the right to refuse the request of the accused or of the complainant to summon additional witnesses or examine experts if the facts or circumstances sought to be established may have any bearing on the case".[62]

2. Relevancy of Testimony

Facts or circumstances are considered as having a bearing on the case, not only if they help to establish the fundamental question of guilt or innocence, but also if they serve as a factor in determining the exact measure of the social protection (punishment) to be applied, if the accused is found guilty. Among the latter we find the following questions: Was the alleged crime committed for the purpose of restoring the bourgeoisie to power; was it done from base, venal motives; was the accused being charged with a crime for the first time; did the commission of the crime take place under coercion, threat, or by reason of economic strain; was the alleged offender at that moment in a state of hunger, destitution, or influenced by the extremity of personal or family conditions; was he in a state of strong excitement, etc.[63] We observe that the inquisitor, in order to establish all relevant facts, must delve into every detail surrounding the commission of the crime. It is, therefore his duty to summon all the witnesses and experts available, irrespective of whether their testimony will help or harm the cause of the accused. The ultimate goal of the inquiry is not only to determine the question of guilt or innocence but to establish all the circumstances under which the accused lived, the physical, economic and mental conditions which influenced him to commit a crime, either directly or by merely reducing his moral power of resistance. Unlike our system of administration of criminal law, the Soviet system considers that circumstances, environment, and motives are extremely relevant for the proper disposition of a criminal case. It is not only the act itself, but, however foreign it may seem to us, the

[62] *Ibid.*, section 112.
[63] *Ibid.*, section 113. (See also Cr. Code, 1926, sections 45, 47 and 58.)

history of the accused which is often to a greater or lesser degree the determining factor.

Should the inquisitor or the organs of investigation deem it advisable to refuse the request of the accused to conduct a certain line of inquiry the reasons for such refusal must be stated in writing.[64] This matter is not, as it might seem, within the discretion of the inquisitor. The Supreme Court of the R.S.F.S.R., in one of its reports, has emphasized the fact that the inquisitor cannot explain his refusal to allow the request of the accused in this matter merely by stating that it was not essential for the determination of the desired fact.[65]

3. Expert Testimony

The use of expert testimony seems to have gained vogue in Soviet Russia. The law provides that expert testimony shall be used whenever it is necessary to establish a fact requiring special knowledge of science, art, or trade.[66] Furthermore, expert testimony in pre-trial proceedings is made obligatory for the purpose of determining the cause of a death, the nature of bodily injuries, the determination of the mental condition of the accused or of a witness, whenever the inquisitor or the court has a doubt on such points.

Experts, like other witnesses, must appear when summoned to testify and must give their conclusions. A refusal to comply may carry a punishment of a fine of fifty rubles, while a punishment of three months' forced labor or a fine of one hundred rubles ($50.00) may be imposed upon other, non-expert witnesses.[67] All witnesses are entitled to recover expenses incurred by them in connection with their appearance as witnesses, and are to be remunerated for being taken away from their usual occupation. The number of experts to be summoned is determined by the inquisitor. The latter *may*, upon the request of the accused, invite additional experts. This rule seems to modify the rule previously mentioned that the inquisitor has no right to refuse the request of the accused to summon certain wit-

[64] *Ibid.*, section 114.
[65] *The Weekly*, 1925, No. 7.
[66] Code, 1927, section 63.
[67] *Ibid.*, section 64. (See also Cr. Code, 1926, section 92, second part.)

nesses or experts.[68] The inquisitor, however, cannot arbitrarily refuse a request made. The law provides that a refusal "may follow if the inquisitor finds that it is impossible to get the desired expert, or when the granting of the request of the accused would tend to delay the preliminary proceedings, beyond the time limit set by law for completing the inquiry.[69]" The modification permitting the inquisitor to disregard the petition of the accused to have additional expert testimony at the preliminary proceedings is probably based on the theory that the inquisitor, who is, in contemplation of law, not in opposition to the accused, will obtain reliable, disinterested, expert testimony.

The inquisitor must warn the experts, as in the case of ordinary witnesses, of their liability before the law should they furnish false conclusions. He must submit to them points upon which the conclusions are to be given, and the accused has a similar right. To facilitate his work the expert has the right, upon the permission of the inquisitor, to familiarize himself with those circumstances of the case which may assist him in reaching a conclusion.[70] As his testimony is designed to assist the inquiry, and later the court, to arrive at a proper disposition of the case, such testimony, or conclusion, must be fully and clearly stated. If it is not clear or complete, the inquisitor, on his own initiative or at the request of the accused, must appoint other experts to investigate and render conclusions on the points in doubt.[71]

g. *Question Of Insanity During The Preliminary Inquiry*

Whenever the question of insanity is raised during the preliminary inquiry the services of experts are always engaged. Insanity is not a mere defense which has to be pleaded but, "whenever there is evidence in the case concerning the irresponsibility of the accused at the time he committed the alleged crime, or of a deranged mental condition which developed afterwards, the inquisitor must collect all the data indispensable for a determination of the mental condition of the accused by means of expert medi-

[68] *Ibid.*, sections 61, 65.
[69] *Ibid.*, section 169.
[70] *Ibid.*, sections 170, 171.
[71] *Ibid.*, section 173.

cal testimony through examination of the accused himself as well as through questioning of his nearest relations and others".[72]

Although the amendments of 1929 excluded the sections of the Code dealing with the method of determining the question of insanity before trial, other sections, nevertheless, provide that the organs of investigation, the inquisitor or the court shall suspend or discontinue a case on grounds of insanity during the pre-trial proceedings. It would seem that the purpose of the amendments was to give the authorities more latitude in working out the details of procedure formerly provided by the Code. These details will probably be provided for by the procuracy or the Commissariat of Justice.

The medical expert is relied upon to determine the question of insanity of the accused, but the inquisitor is to prepare the basis for the experts' work. In a special instruction issued by the Commissariat of Justice, which instruction is not repealed by the amendments,[73] the inquisitor is required to submit a number of questions, prepared by the Commissariat of Public Health, upon which the expert is to base his conclusions. Briefly stated, those questions touch upon the mental life history of the accused and his ancestry. Thus, it is pertinent to the issue whether or not the accused or his near relations have ever suffered from syphilis, alcoholism, or narcotism, whether there were any instances of insanity among his ancestors, in what kind of social atmosphere the accused lived, whether the accused showed abnormal tendencies in his childhood or adolescence, etc. The findings of this thorough investigation are then forwarded to the court which has jurisdiction of the case for a determination of the issues involved.

The question of insanity investigated in the preliminary proceedings was, prior to the amendments of 1929, presented to the administrative session of the court after the inquisitor has obtained all the necessary testimony, expert or otherwise. The court at once decided the question upon the basis of the record before it, or ordered the accused to be placed in an appropriate

[72] *Ibid.*, section 196.

[73] Circular No. 76, 1924, Collected Circulars of the Commissariat of Justice, Moscow, 1927, page 313.

medical institution for observation. In the latter event the question of insanity was again considered at a later administrative session of the court, after the results of this medical observation were obtained. All of this was a part of the preliminary proceedings and did not settle the question of insanity permanently, especially if the court held the accused sane, for the same question might come up again at the trial of the case. But should the court be of the opinion that the accused was insane when he committed the crime, the proceedings were discontinued. On the other hand, if the court was of opinion that the insanity developed after the time of the commission of the crime, the case was merely continued, provided the disease was curable.[74] This important proceeding at the administrative session, unlike similar proceedings at the trial, was based entirely upon the record, as neither the accused nor the experts nor the witnesses were to appear before the court.[75] By the above mentioned amendments the inquisitor or the organs of investigation may themselves suspend a case on the grounds of temporary insanity. But if they consider the insanity incurable the record is forwarded to the court which may either discontinue the case[76] or adopt measures of social protection of a medical nature, such as a "forced cure", or committing the accused to an appropriate medical institution.[77]

h. *Search and Seizure*

The purpose of the preliminary inquiry, as we have observed, is to unearth every possible fact or piece of evidence which will lead to the ultimate aim—a just and speedy disposition of the case. The inquisitor, to this end, is endowed with broad powers of taking possession of documents, articles, mail, etc.

Without any restrictions from legislative enactments or constitutional guaranties, the road to unrestricted searches and seizures lies open before the penetrating eye of the inquisitor. The law states that whenever the inquisitor has sufficient grounds to

[74] Code, 1927, sections 199-201.
[75] *Commentaries*, pages 209-211.
[76] Code, 1927, section 202, as amended in 1929.
[77] Cr. Code, 1926, section 24.

believe that objects having a relation to the case may be found in a certain dwelling, or in the possession of a person, he is to demand that the object be turned over to him. In the event of a refusal, he may conduct a search and seize the articles if found.[78] "The searches and seizures are to be conducted during the day time (except in cases which can not be postponed), in the presence of invited witnesses or watchers and the person occupying the dwelling, or a member of his family, or his neighbors."[79] No party[80] to the case, or any relation, may be invited as a watcher at the search and seizure.[81] Before starting this proceeding the inquisitor must formally announce the decision to search made either by himself or by the court. In performing this function he may break open any closed building or object if the owner refuses to open it voluntarily.[82] The inquisitor is, however, not permitted to overstep the bounds necessary for his purpose. (The same rule applies to organs of investigation.) For example, he is required to avoid unnecessary damaging of locks, doors, etc., though a forced entry may be warranted; likewise "he is to see that the private life of the dwellers who have no connection with the case shall not be made public".[83]

The results obtained in the search and the nature of the articles or documents seized, which must have a bearing on the case, are to be written down in a protocol to which a list of everything seized is attached. The articles seized must be counted in the presence of the watchers, and any pertinent remark, statement or claim made at the time of these proceedings is to be entered in the protocol, a copy of which is left with the person whose property was so searched or with the members of his family. Finally, all the articles or documents to be later carried

[78]Code, 1927, section 175.

[79]*Ibid.*, section 177.

[80]*Ibid.*, section 23, subsection 6, defines the word "party" in a criminal action to mean: The procurator who *conducts* the prosecution at the trial, the civil claimant or his representative, the defendant, his legal representative and his advocate, and the injured person, when he has a right to conduct the prosecution.

[81]Code, 1927, section 74.

[82]*Ibid.*, sections 179, 198.

[83]*Ibid.*, section 181.

away must be sealed at the place where the search was conducted.[84]

An interesting feature is found in the rules provided for the interception of mail. Should it be deemed necessary for the inquiry that postal or telegraphic correspondence of the accused be seized, the inquisitor must notify the proper authorities to that effect. In order to seize the correspondence thus intercepted, the inquisitor must first obtain the permission of the procurator or his assistant. Once such permission is obtained, the procedure becomes very simple. The seizure must, however, take place in the presence of a representative of the postal-telegraph institution.[85]

At the time of a search and seizure, the inquisitor is merely to see whether the object found has any relation to the case, as required by law, but the detailed examination is conducted usually at the office of the inquisitor, where experts are invited to help accomplish the task. The results of this examination are also entered in a protocol, which is signed by the watchers and experts.[86] Whenever a protocol of an autopsy is made, the results must be recorded by the physician and signed by the inquisitor.[87] All medical experts used in connection with the preliminary proceedings, such as those needed in making autopsies, examining the person injured, etc., are obtained by the inquisitor through the provincial branch of public health; when this is impossible the nearest physician is invited.[88]

It is rather noteworthy that the law permits not only the inquisitor, but also the watchers, or any other person invited to be present when medical examination is performed, to enter, or cause to be entered, into the protocol any remark or opinion in reference to any act of the physician which seems questionable to them.[89]

i. *The Civil Claimant*

Among the various functions and duties of the inquisitor we particularly note his duties and powers concerning the rights of

[84] *Ibid.*, sections 183, 184 and 185.
[85] *Ibid.*, sections 186—188.
[86] *Ibid.*, sections 189, 192.
[87] *Ibid.*, section 195.
[88] *Ibid.*, section 193.
[89] *Ibid.*, section 194.

the civil claimant, whose connection with the case furnishes a noteworthy feature in Russian jurisprudence. The civil claimant, as we know, is the person who has suffered any property damage or personal injury as a direct result of the crime, and who files a civil claim against the accused or against those who are legally responsible for his acts. Such claim is disposed of in conjunction with the criminal proceedings of the case.[90] In this connection the inquisitor must inform the injured party of his right to file the civil claim.[91] But the mere filing does not automatically bring the question before the court. The inquisitor examines this question preliminarily and decides either to recognize the claim as valid on its face or to disallow it on the ground that there was no direct damage, or for any other proper reason. In either case the inquisitor enters the reasons for his decision in a protocol.[92] The powers of the inquisitor extend even further than the mere allowing of the claim. He may, on his own initiative or upon the petition of the injured party, take the necessary steps to ensure the payment of a possible money judgment, if otherwise the injured party runs the risk of being deprived of its recovery.[93]

Before we close the discussion of the preliminary inquiry, let us note that all the different steps in the proceedings described above are not necessarily required of the inquisitor himself. It may happen that the records of a case received from the organs of investigations, in cases where preliminary inquiry is obligatory, are sufficiently clear for an immediate termination of the preliminaries. Under such circumstances, the inquisitor is only required to notify the accused of his formal designation as such,

[90] *Ibid.*, section 14. (It seems to the writer that while this rule is apparently of a theoretical significance, it is not of great practical value. In the many cases which he has heard tried, when he visited Soviet Russia in 1928, there were no civil claims except in cases of embezzlement, where the government or the co-operatives prosecuted the civil claim. This would, presumably, be so because usually the defendants in criminal cases are not financially responsible persons.)

[91] *Ibid.*, section 119.

[92] *Ibid.*, section 120. (See also *Commentaries*, pages 132-134.)

[93] *Ibid.*, section 121. (The civil claim, brought in conjunction with the criminal case, is not the same as a civil suit which may be brought separately for the same injury.)

to interrogate the accused, and to draw up the accusatory conclusion.[94]

j. *Completion of the Inquiry*

1. Recommendations of the Inquisitor

The inquisitor having completed all the necessary search and examination is now ready to decide upon the further proceedings. He may reach the conclusion that the case should be dropped because the data collected, taken as a whole, are insufficient to justify holding the accused for trial, or that there is some other reason in the case which requires, according to law, a discontinuance.[95] In the latter event the inquisitor suspends or discontinues the case. The inquisitor's decision to discontinue the proceedings may be appealed to the procurator within one week, and from the procurator's decision to the court having jurisdiction of the case within one month. The ruling of the court in this matter is final.[96]

The provision that the inquisitor may himself discontinue the case—and such a power is also given to the investigating organs—is a striking innovation introduced by the amendments of October, 1929. Since the People's Court acts of 1918 and 1920, the Soviet criminal procedure has permitted the inquisitor only to recommend a discontinuance of a criminal case to the court which alone had the authority to discontinue. This principle was embodied in the first Code of Criminal Procedure of 1922, and was fully maintained in the Code of 1923 and in all the amendments up to October, 1929. Thus, the law required that if the inquisitor was of the opinion that the case should be discontinued, he was to transfer the entire record of the case to the proper court stating the reasons for his action. A notice was simultaneously sent by the inquisitor to the procurator, for the latter had to participate at the administrative session of the

[94] *Ibid.*, section 109.

[95] *Ibid.*, section 4. This section enumerates the following grounds: the death of the accused; where the acts with which the accused is being charged do not constitute a crime; a settlement of the parties in certain cases; the absence of a complaint filed by the injured party, in cases where such a complaint is a condition precedent to the starting of the criminal action; where the statute of limitation has run; in cases of amnesty.

[96] *Ibid.*, sections 202 and 204, as amended in 1929.

court where the question was to be finally decided. The court had the authority either to affirm the recommendation of the inquisitor to discontinue the case, or to disregard such recommendation and return the record to the inquisitor for a further inquiry, in the manner directed.[97] The pocurator had the power to appeal to a higher court from a decision to drop the prosecution. By a special interpretation given to the Code by the plenum of the Supreme Court, the administrative session of the lower court had the power to decide that the record presented by the inquisitor warranted holding the accused for trial, notwithstanding the recommendation of the inquisitor to the contrary, in which case the accusatory conclusion was not to be drawn up by the inquisitor, as it was in the usual case, but by a member of the court appointed for that purpose.[98] This rule pointedly showed the attitude of the law which aimed to prevent the preliminary proceedings from being carried out independently of the courts. While this was the law it became a highly debatable point among the Soviet legal writers, some of whom were demanding that the preliminary proceedings should be completed independently of the influence of the court.[99] That the tendency was drifting towards such a course was quite evident.[100] The amendments of 1929 fully incorporated this change in principle.[101]

The amendments provide that the authorities which order the *suspension* of a case have the power to re-open it.[102] So far as the re-opening of a case *discontinued* is concerned, the question is open to conjecture. Prior to the amendments the Code provided that after a case had been discontinued, with the approval of the court, it could never be reopened except by the order of the court having jurisdiction. The court decided the question of reopening a case at its administrative session, after

[97] *Ibid.*, sections 202, 203 and 204, prior to October, 1929.

[98] *The Weekly*, 1926, No. 3.

[99] A Idkowsky, *The Weekly*, 1926, No. 10.

[100] The project for a new criminal code of procedure drafted by a special commission, adopted by the Commissariat of Justice in December, 1928, and published in *The Weekly*, 1928, Nos. 46-47, divorced the preliminary inquiry from the court, for the procurator or the inquisitor was to decide the question of holding for court, leaving to the courts only certain powers of review.

[101] Code, as amended in 1929, sections 202, 221 and 225.

[102] *Ibid.*, section 205.

listening to the conclusion of the procurator.[103] These provisions do not appear in the amended Code.

We have been heretofore dealing with a discontinuance or suspension by the inquisitor at the close of the inquiry. Let us now examine the situation where he decides to hold for trial.

If the inquisitor after completing his task has established the occurrence of a crime, obtained all the necessary information about the person accused, such as his social position, the class to which he belongs, his connections with the crime, the motives which prompted him to commit it, as well as all the circumstances which supply the grounds for holding him for trial, the case proceeds to the next stage.[104] But before it completely leaves the jurisdiction of the inquisitor, he must make sure that the accused has presented his side as fully and favorably as possible. The law therefore stipulates that if the inquisitor considers the preliminary inquiry completed, he must notify the accused of this fact. The latter is now, for the first time, allowed access to the entire record of the proceedings. The inquisitor must always inform the accused of his right to examine the record and ask him whether there is anything he desires to add to the investigation or inquiry.[105] Should he point out some relevant fact or circumstance which was not inquired into before, the inquisitor must add it to the preliminary inquiry.[106]

The provision to allow the accused access to the records of the entire proceedings and thus acquaint himself with all the facts and testimony against him is undoubtedly a very interesting and a fundamental feature in Soviet criminal procedure. There is no game to be played as we have it in our system; the accused cannot, and should not, be surprised at the trial. He is to know beforehand all the testimony and the nature of the evidence to be presented against him, and it is for him to be ready to refute this evidence, if he can, and establish his innocence.

[103]Code, 1927, sections 204 and 205.

[104]*Ibid.*, section 206.

[105]*Ibid.*, section 207. (The amendment of 1929, section 206, made practically no change.)

[106]*Ibid.*, section 208.

After the inquiry has been completed, the inquisitor draws up the accusatory conclusion which is forwarded to the procurator.[107]

2. Time for Completion

In accordance with the tendency to speed up criminal proceedings, it is provided that the preliminary inquiry must be completed within two months from the time the defendant is formally declared the accused in the case. This significant rule is indicative of an earnest desire on the part of Soviet legislators to speed up proceedings—a characteristic which permeates all their legislation. Such a desire encounters, however, an uphill fight against traditional slowness and apathy. Experience, so far, has proved that only a little more than one-half of all preliminary inquiries are completed within the time set by law. The very section which laid down the drastic requirement of a time limit provided for deviations from the strict adherence to it, by stating that if the completion of the inquiry within such time is absolutely impossible, the inquisitor must state to the procurator the reasons for the delay.[108] In this connection we might note that no newspaper publicity or other outside influence may check the plans or hinder the proceedings of the inquiry, for the facts obtained or discovered during the preliminary proceedings may be made public only to the extent deemed advisable by the inquisitor. It is a criminal offense to publish any data collected by the inquiry without its permission.[109] This discretionary power in the inquisi-

[107] *Ibid.*, section 211.

[108] Code, 1927, section 116. The amendments of 1929 provide that if an extension of more than one month is desired the procurator of the Republic must consent. (From the number of cases completed by the people's inquisitor in the first half of 1926 only 22.8% were completed not later than within two months, while 24.8% were in progress over three months. In the second half of 1926 there was an improvement since only 21.7% of all the cases in the hands of the inquisitors were not completed within three months, while 64% were finished before two months. See Official Report of the Procuracy of the R.S.F.S.R. for 1926, Moscow, 1927, p. 115. For the second half of 1927 the number of cases completed by the inquisitors within the two months period again advanced from 64% a year ago to 66.3%, while 14.2% of all the cases still dragged on for over four months. A. Rodnyanskii, *The Weekly*, 1928, No. 33, p. 906.)

[109] Code, 1927, section 115.

tor would seem, according to the Code, to apply equally to the heads of the organs of investigation.[110]

k. *Inquiry Subject to Appeal*

Every act or decision of the inquisitor, during the preliminary is subject to an appeal, or complaint, to the procurator. (In 1922 such appeals were made to the court.)[111] The appeal may be taken not only by the immediate parties—the accused and the injured person—but also by witnesses, experts, interpreters, watchers, bondsmen,[112] or by any other person whose rights are affected by any act of the inquisitor.

It is interesting to note that this appeal may also be presented orally, either through the inquisitor or directly to the procurator. The oral complaint is immediately reduced to writing by the inquisitor or the procurator to whom it was brought, and the complaining party must sign it. The general rule is that appeals from an action or decision of the inquisitor must be taken within seven days from the time the aggrieved party learns of such adverse action or decision; but seven days' limitation does not, however, apply to appeals from any measure to ensure attendance, or complaints against the slowness of the proceedings conducted by the inquisitor, or any illegal proceeding, none of which is subject to any time limitation.[113] If the complaint is made through the inquisitor himself, he must within twenty-four hours forward it together with his explanation to the procurator who is required to review the question within three days from the

[110]This rule is a bit complicated. The section which covers this rule with regard to the inquisitor is one of the many sections of the Code which are to apply to the organs of investigation, whenever the latter are to conduct the investigation. But by a circular issued by the Commissariat of Justice, No. 8, 1922, the organs of investigation were forbidden to give out information concerning the preliminary investigation unless permitted by the procurator. This circular is still quoted in the *Commentaries,* page 128. But the circular just cited was clearly repealed by the Commissariat of Justice. (See Collected Circulars, 1927, page 330.) At the same time section 96 of the Criminal Code makes it a crime to publish such information unless permitted by the head of the investigation, which would naturally include any head of the police, etc.

[111]Thus, against the people's inquisitor the appeal is taken to the district procurator, against the senior inquisitor to the provincial procurator, while an appeal from the acts of the inquisitor for the most significant cases will go to the procurator of the Republic.

[112]Code, 1927, section 212.

[113]*Ibid.,* sections 113-115.

time he receives it.[114] He may demand of the inquisitor additional information or explanations and may, furthermore, ask that the entire record of the proceedings be transferred to him, unless he can properly dispose of the question raised by the appeal without it. The decision of the procurator is, however, not final, for "either the complainant or the inquisitor may appeal from the procurator's decision to the provincial court."[115] The court which has jurisdiction of the case decides any dispute between the procurator and the inquisitor when the latter disagrees with the rulings of the procurator concerning the measure to ensure the appearance of the accused.[116] Unlike appeals from verdicts and decisions of a court, appeals from the acts or decisions of the inquisitor do not, before the question of the complaint is decided, "suspend the execution of the act or order of the inquisitor complained of."[117]

1. *Character of the Inquiry*

In this preliminary inquiry, the proceedings are not a mere search for relevant data on the case, detached from all other essential issues to be determined later at the trial; on the contrary, the inquiry is an organic inseparable part of the entire criminal proceedings. Any basic error committed during the stages of the preliminary proceedings may be a ground for a reversal even after a verdict is obtained. This possibility of reversal is not based upon any strict adherence to mere technicalities, which is repugnant to the very spirit of the Soviet system, but is rather predicated on the theory that the preliminary inquiry is preparing the groundwork upon which the court is to base its final and just decision. In an official report of the Criminal Department of the Supreme Court,[118] which report serves as an instruction to, and a guide for the entire judiciary, the significance of the preliminary inquiry is stressed. The highest Court

[114]*Ibid.*, sections 217-218.

[115]*Ibid.*, sections 219 and 220. To permit the inquisitor to appeal from the decision of the procurator—except in cases of selecting a measure to ensure attendance—would seem utterly to contradict the spirit of the Code, especially the marked tendency to reduce the inquisitor to the position of an assistant to the procurator.

[116]*Ibid.*, section 148.

[117]*Ibid.*, section 216.

[118]*The Weekly*, 1926, No. 7.

of Cassation within the R.S.F.S.R. states that forty per cent of all the verdicts reversed by this court up to 1925 have met such fate on grounds of lack of a thorough, correct preliminary inquiry or investigation, such as the failure to summon and examine witnesses who should have been called in order to establish for the accused an alibi, or the refusal to do certain things requested by the accused, etc. In the same document the court outspokenly rebukes the marked and quite comprehensible propensity of some inquisitors to take the rôle of prosecutor. The court sounds a warning against such a "highly dangerous, absolutely intolerable" accusatory approach to a case under inquiry.[119]

Such an attitude of the court is naturally in full accord with the spirit as well as the letter of the law which says that "the inquisitor [and the investigators] must inquire into both the circumstances which are adverse to the accused as well as those which favor him".[120] The inquisitor is, therefore, in the eye of the law, not antagonistic to the interests of the accused. A conviction is not necessarily his goal; he is a special investigating official who, theoretically speaking, knows no bias or passion and no desire except to reveal the material truth of a case. The utter impartiality required by law of the inquisitor is best demonstrated by the fact that the accused may challenge him for cause on the same grounds as are provided for the challenge of a judge, and one of the fundamental grounds for challenge is the presence of some circumstance which may cast a doubt as to the absolute impartiality or the unprejudiced attitude of the officer.[121]

IV. HOLDING FOR TRIAL

Although the criminal investigation or preliminary inquiry is usually considered and spoken of as the only preliminary proceeding, there is still another formal step to be taken before the case is ready for trial— that of holding for trial, which, we may observe, always occurs at the end of the preliminary inquiry or investigation.

[119]In the writer's personal contact with both judges and inquisitors, he was assured that the inquisitors are doing their utmost not to appear or act as prosecutors. Whether this is possible from the very nature of things, is another question.

[120]Code, 1927, section 111.

[121]*Ibid.*, sections 122, 43 and 44.

Holding for trial takes place, according to the particular nature of a given case, in three different and distinct ways: (a) by a single people's judge, (b) by the inquisitor, and (c) by the procurator.

a. *By the People's Judge*

The people's judge, sitting alone, possesses the authority to hold a person for trial in the following instances: (a) In cases which come directly to the people's court and which are so simple as not to require any investigation or inquiry;[122] (b) in cases which reach the people's court through the police or any organ of investigation. We may recall that the organs of investigation perform all investigatory acts and forward the record with the accusatory conclusion directly to the people's court, whenever the alleged crime is subject to a sentence of less than one year's imprisonment.[123] The requirement of a formal holding for trial on the part of the people's judge in this second group of cases is not explicitly provided by the Code, but it is generally agreed that such is the law, and a failure to comply with it is considered a direct violation of the law of procedure.[124]

b. *By the Inquisitor*

The inquisitor is the one to hold the accused for trial in all cases which have been investigated and sent to him by the organs of investigation. These are cases which, though not subject to a preliminary inquiry, are punishable by not less than one year's imprisonment. As we have already seen,[125] the entire record in these cases is forwarded by the organs of investigation with their accusatory conclusion to the inquisitor; if he approves of such conclusion, he is to affirm it by a formal resolution holding the accused for trial. The record then is forwarded to the presiding judge of the provincial, circuit or regional court, or to the people's judge, according to the nature of the case. The judge receiving it puts the case on the trial list. If, however, the inquisitor disagrees

[122]*Ibid.*, section 247, subsection 3, and also section 233, after the amendment of 1929.

[123]Code, as amended in 1929, section 208.

[124]See official Report of the People's Commissariat of Justice for 1925, Moscow, 1926, page 87.

[125]See *ante*, page 158.

with the accusatory conclusion to hold for trial on the ground that the record does not justify it, or that it does not properly designate the crime, or that an improper measure to ensure attendance was adopted, etc., he may place the record before the administrative session of the court. This session which consists in the people's court of one judge and two co-judges, and of the presiding judge and two additional judges in all other courts, has the power to discontinue the case, return it for further investigation, or redraft the accusatory conclusion.

c. *By the Procurator*

The inquisitor is required in all cases subject to a preliminary inquiry by him to forward the record with his accusatory conclusion to the procurator in charge of the particular district. The procurator, if the conclusion of the inquisitor meets his approval, affirms it by a resolution holding the accused for trial. The proceedings that follow are identical with those described in the case where the inquisitor approves the accusatory conclusion drawn by the investigating organs.

The procedure and method of holding for trial by the inquisitor or the procurator is one of the outstanding features of the amendments of October, 1929. Prior to these amendments the organs of investigation were in no case to draw up any document of accusation. This was left either to the inquisitor or the court. In cases in which the organs of investigation upon completion of their duties had to send the record to the inquisitor, the latter was required to "draw up within two weeks from the time he received the case the decision to hold the accused for trial",[126] which act put the accused on trial. This, however, was true only in cases tried at the people's court. In those cases which came under the jurisdiction of the provincial, regional or circuit court, if a preliminary inquiry was not mandatory, the "decision of the inquisitor to hold for court" did not automatically put the case on the trial list. The law provided that in all cases tried at the provincial court, the question of holding for

[126]Code, 1927, section 105, subsection 3 and sections 222, 223 and 224.

trial had to be first considered at the administrative session of the court, with the participation of the procurator.[127]

It is also true that prior to the amendments, the administrative session of the court consisting of one permanent judge and two co-judges, deliberated on the question of holding for trial in all cases which went through the stages of a preliminary inquiry. The accusatory conclusion, which the inquisitor drew and sent to the procurator, together with the entire proceedings of the case, was then forwarded by the latter to the proper court—people's, provincial, regional, as the case might be—with his suggestion attached to affirm the document and hold the defendant for trial. But the suggestion of the procurator was, of course, not binding upon the court. It was only the formal decision of the latter that placed the accused on trial.[128] The court in deliberating on the question of holding a person for trial had before it the entire record of the preliminary proceedings, and not merely the official document, the accusatory conclusion, drawn by the inquisitor or the procurator, as provided by the first codes of 1922 and 1923.[129] This method was known as holding for trial by the administrative session of the court. The amendments of 1929 have basically changed the policy of the Soviet law concerning the functions of the court on the one hand and the procuracy with its subordinate organs of inquiry and investigation on the other, so far as the pre-trial proceedings are concerned. From the very beginning of the Soviet régime the doctrine that the courts were to supervise and direct all that happens in a criminal case before trial has prevailed. It was the province of the procuracy to look after the activities of the inquisitors and the organs of investigation, but the courts were to check up every significant step made during the pre-trial proceedings. No case could be discontinued and no accused was to be held for trial, except in minor cases, without the direct

[127]*Ibid.*, section 390. It is interesting to note that this section is not affected by the important amendments of 1929, although it would seem that the administrative session was abolished, or its powers diminished at least as far as the power of holding for court is concerned.

[128]*Ibid.*, section 240.

[129]Code, 1922, note to section 240. The latter section was incorporated in the present Code under section 236, but the note to this section was later repealed. See Collected Laws, No. 78, Article 784, 1924.

approval of the court. We recall that every case subject to a preliminary inquiry had to be submitted to the administrative session of the court before the accused could be held for trial.

The amendments for the first time in Soviet legal history uphold those in Soviet Russia who have contended that the powers of the procuracy with regard to the pre-trial proceedings should be enlarged. Now the organs of investigation, the inquisitor and the procurator are made part of a unified system of investigation or inquiry.[130] The organ which investigated may discontinue the case, subject to an appeal to its immediate superior. The organs of investigation complete a case under its jurisdiction by drawing up the accusatory conclusion in which case the inquisitor has the authority to approve the conclusion and formally hold the accused for trial. A case subject to a preliminary inquiry if completed by the inquisitor with an accusatory conclusion has to be approved and the accused held for trial by the procurator. The administrative session of the court deliberates on the fate of a case before trial only in exceptional instances. Another important feature of the amendments of 1929 is the fact that the administrative session of all the courts except the people's court consists of three judges, without the participation of co-judges.

At the present time, as before the amendments, after a copy of the accusatory conclusion, or other document which serves the same purpose, is delivered or submitted to the accused[131] he becomes the defendant *(podsudimii)* awaiting trial, and the case is completely out of the jurisdiction of the inquisitor.

V. HISTORY AND THEORY OF SOVIET PRELIMINARY PROCEEDINGS

By this time a fact of fundamental importance must have been observed that at no time during the numerous stages of the preliminary inquiry or the holding for trial has there been any open and public hearing; nor have we noticed the appearance of an attorney, an advocate, accompanying the person who passes through the metamorphosis from suspect to accused, and finally evolves into the defendant. The question is: Why was the

[130] M. Strogovich, *The Weekly*, No. 50, 1929, page 1176.
[131] Code, 1927, section 245.

entire process of pre-trial inquiry so arranged as to exclude both defense counsel and an open or public hearing? To answer this we shall have to approach the problem not only from the angle of the practical ends sought to be attained; we shall have to go beyond mere technicalities in order to examine the problem from the point of view of those principles upon which the complete system of criminal procedure is developed; furthermore, we must comprehend the principles which go to the very root of the system of Soviet jurisprudence, and which touch upon the most profound ideas of right and conceptions of justice affecting the status of society, or the state, and its individual citizens.

Before we attempt to analyze the principles upon which the present Soviet system of preliminary proceedings is based, let us briefly review the history of its development.

a. *Two Systems of Inquiry*

There are, generally speaking, two diametrically opposed systems of pre-trial, or preliminary, proceedings. One is the so-called "detection-process", a system which prevailed in Tzarist Russia before the judicial reforms of 1864. This system is characterized by a procedure which is neither open nor public, and in which the participation of defense counsel is not allowed, its ultimate aim being the detection of a criminal act without the slightest regard for the personal rights of the accused. Such a method is quite natural in a political state ruled by an absolute monarch. The other system is the Western, or Anglo-Saxon, based upon the liberal idea which builds its forms of procedure on the theory of a contest between the state and its citizens who must have an equal opportunity in the contest. The permission to have counsel as well as an open and public hearing follows as a necessary corollary, just as other single problems in the long process are solved in compliance with this basic idea.

b. *Soviet Inquiry Prior to 1920*

It is rather remarkable that the first period of the volcanic Bolshevik Revolution, which bluntly proclaimed the complete up-rooting of the previously existing political, economic, and social system, adopted, nevertheless, a very liberal form of preliminary procedure. The First Decree on Courts of 1917 proclaimed the broad principle that the "participation of prosecution and defense is permitted also during the stages of the preliminary inquiry."[132] The Second Decree of 1918 incorporated the same principles, leaving to the Inquisitorial Commission the power to restrict this right under certain conditions, subject to appeal.[133] Later enactments either repeated this particular provision explicitly or affirmed it inferentially by incorporating all the rules on procedure stipulated in the Second Decree.[134] Furthermore, even the People's Court Act, of 1918, which, we recall, was a turning point in the Soviet judicial policy in that it rejected many prevailing liberal methods, re-enacted the provision of the Second Decree permitting, with some exceptions, the participation of defense counsel in the preliminary proceedings.[135]

The same situation we find with regard to cases tried at the revolutionary tribunals, which were created for the express purpose of combating counter-revolution and other activities affecting directly the existence or the stability of the newly established political order. The Act on Revolutionary Tribunals of May, 1918, inferentially allowed the participation of defense counsel, for it stipulated that the fact of the completion of the preliminary inquiry should be disclosed either to the accused or to his attorney.[136] That this was the prevailing idea among Soviet judicial leaders at that period can best be seen from the fact that the Conference of the Revolutionary Tribunal Judges held at Moscow, at the end of 1918, incorporated the idea of permitting defense counsel at the preliminary inquiry in the resolutions[137] they adopted, which were to serve as a model for a new act on the revolutionary tribunals. Following the special instruction to the inquisitorial commissions attached to the revolutionary tribunals of Moscow in 1918, this commission was to decide all questions of taking into custody or holding for trial, after an open and public hearing in which the accused, the prosecutor, and defense

[132]First Decree, section 3.

[133]Second Decree, section 21.

[134]Third Decree, and the Instructions to the People's Courts, Collected Laws, No. 53, Article 597, 1918.

[135]P. C. Act, 1918, section 34.

[136]Collected Laws, No. 35, Article 471, 1918, section 9.

[137]This important conference was held at Moscow between October 29 and November 3, 1918.

counsel participated and argued. At this open hearing the question was to be determined whether the inquiry conducted was complete enough and whether the data collected were sufficient to hold the accused for court.[138] This liberal system established at Moscow was apparently not an innovation, for we are told[139] that in the period between 1917 and 1920, the principle of a public hearing, as well as the theory of contest by permitting the participation of counsel during the preliminary inquiry prevailed if not by explicit legislation at least by general acquiescence. By the enactment of the Revolutionary Tribunals Act of 1919,[140] which transferred the preliminary inquiry to the *Cheka,* and the People's Court Act of 1920,[141] which instituted a single people's inquisitor, a new era was heralded, an era which frankly threw aside all the liberal enlightened principles and methods which the Soviets term "bourgeois", which aim not only to strengthen the state in its attempt to combat crime but also to protect the rights of the individual citizen against over-zealous officials.

c. *Since 1920*

Since 1920 the tendency has been to diminish and minimize the rights of the accused before the time of the completion of the preliminary inquiry. Even his right to participate at the examination of the witnesses by the inquisitor, which was provided by the first Code of Criminal Procedure of 1922,[142] was abridged by the re-enacted Code of 1923. Thus we come to the present Soviet system of criminal preliminary inquiry which, as we have seen, is conducted by a single inquisitor who is not an independent judge, but an agent of the procurator, the entire procedure being conducted in complete secrecy both as regards the public and the accused himself. The latter is, however, to be formally notified, at a certain stage of the proceedings, of the exact charges to be preferred against him, and he is also to get full access to the entire record of the inquiry—a very important

[138]Krylenko, *The Judiciary and the Law,* 1927, pages 113, 114.
[139]*Ibid.,* page 113.
[140]Collected Laws, No. 13, Article 132, 1919.
[141]P. C. Act, 1920, sections 28-38.
[142]Code, 1922, section 117.

right—but not before all the preliminary proceedings are completed.

Thus, while such an arrangement undoubtedly represents a compromise between the two antagonistic points of view and is sometimes referred to as the "mixed system", it is frankly admitted that the present system leans more towards the theories prevailing in Russia before 1864, and that in respect to secrecy it bears all the signs of the inquisitorial detection process without the application, of course, of torture or violence. All these proceedings are, however, later reviewed by an open and public court.[143] Such a sharp change of attitude is explained and justified by the dire necessity of safeguarding the proletarian dictatorship in the midst of a class war during a transitory period which must be passed through before the building up of a communistic society. Such an explanation can hardly be satisfactory, even from the point of view of the Soviet system, for a glance at the data available reveals that the overwhelming majority of all the defendants in criminal cases are workers and peasants,[144] whom the soviets regard as being inherently friendly to their system.

In searching for a more rational and more plausible explanation than that stated above, we must turn to the principles which are embedded in the Soviet system.

d. *The Interests of Society Paramount*

It is clear, we presume, that during the proceedings of the preliminary inquiry, as indeed during all other stages of the criminal prosecution, there frequently occurs what seems to be a collision between the rights and interests of the individual citizen, the accused, and those of society. What is then to happen? Whose rights and interest must give way? The solution of this question is admittedly a fundamental problem, the weighing and balancing of which is the profound concern of any system of criminal procedure. The Soviet system, flatly repudiating any

[143]Krylenko, *The Judiciary and the Law,* 1927, page 113.

[144]Thus of all the persons convicted for crimes 87.1% were workers and peasants in the first half of 1924, while in the second half of 1924, their number was about the same, 87.8%, the corresponding figures for 1926 were 87.2% and 86.3% respectively. See official Report of the Commissariat of Justice for 1925, Moscow, 1926, page 141.

theory based on inherent, and therefore inalienable, rights of the individual, maintains that the system of preliminary inquiry must be built upon the fundamental principle that *"The interest of the whole and the necessity to safeguard the social order* should be the deciding factors in building up the judicial procedure."[145] Such a point of view is in full accord with the political philosophy of the Soviet government, which regards society—or the ruling class, the proletariat, which personifies society—as the all important, supreme entity; it is the interest of the whole, and not of the individual, which is considered first, last and above everything else. We may note in passing that this view is to be distinguished from the German-Hegelian conception of the State as the permanent entity, for in the Soviet system it is Society which represents the enduring entity, the state being a mere instrument for the accomplishment of a certain purpose.

It is from this point of view that the entire structure of the Soviet procedure has been erected. Society, while being of paramount importance, does not desire to convict or cause unnecessary inconvenience to its members, if its interests as a whole are not jeopardized. How is this to be done?

It is to be noted that, like our own system of criminal procedure, the Soviet system fully accepts the broad, fundamental doctrine of presumption of innocence until a verdict of guilt is duly rendered by a court of justice.[146] The unavoidable conclusion should follow that the defendant, being deemed innocent, must be given all the opportunities to disprove any strong contentions to the contrary, even in the preliminary stages of the trial. Such a right or opportunity is in theory not denied to the accused, since he may produce all the testimony he wishes, and

[145]Krylenko, *The Judiciary and the Law,* 1928, page 152.

[146]*Ibid.,* page 150. It is interesting to note that during the famous Mine-Shakhta trial, the correspondent for the *New York Times,* Mr. Walter Duranty, wrote: "According to the Russian conception a trial merely serves to establish the degree of guilt. But that a man is presumed to be innocent until he is found guilty is an alien folly. Unless he is guilty he would not be brought to trial." *New York Times,* June 17, 1928. This statement is entirely erroneous, as Krylenko, who was prosecuting the Shakhta conspirarcy case, takes it as a matter of course that a person is *innocent* until a verdict is rendered. The writer has also discussed this statement of Mr. Duranty with P. Alimov, a member of the Commissariat of Justice, who was formerly the Procurator of the Siberian Region. He too denied that there is any such theory embodied in the Soviet criminal law.

the inquisitor must not only examine it but must, furthermore, look for any testimony favorable to the accused. Here the legal fiction of objectivity reaches its summit. The inquisitor, we are told, is not merely an investigator bent upon the task of finding that the accused has really committed the alleged crime, but he must also attempt, so the theory goes, to establish if possible the innocence of the accused. In other words, it is presumed that the inquisitor can take such an absolute objective attitude that he will display equal zeal searching for or against the accused. The procurator, or prosecutor, who supervises the inquiry is said to be, by the same legal fiction, not an interested party in the case but a mere state representative to supervise the lawfulness of the proceedings. As a logical sequence, we find the Soviet system unequivocally and unqualifiedly repudiating the "contest theory" at the pre-trial proceedings for there are no two antagonistic, fighting parties, and therefore there is no need for an attorney to represent the accused. The Soviet theory as to the trial will be discussed in another chapter.[147]

With all this in mind we are ready to discuss the proceedings at the trial.

[147]See page 247.

Chapter VII

THE TRIAL

The trial, or "the judicial inquiry", as it is called, as distinguished from the preliminary inquiry, represents the second important stage in the criminal proceedings. It is the proceeding where the material obtained through the elaborate preliminary investigation or inquiry is examined, verified and analyzed. The fundamental importance of this proceeding is that it culminates in a final judicial decision, a verdict for or against the defendant. Furthermore, since a case cannot be reconsidered on its merits by a higher tribunal, as was allowable in Imperial Russia, the trial is the first and only judicial hearing of the substance of the criminal case.

The nature and general character as well as the ultimate aim of the trial in the provincial, regional or circuit court is analogous to the trial in the people's court. But so far as the right of the defendant is concerned, the difference between the two types of courts is quite considerable, and, therefore, our discussion will be confined to one at a time. We shall first analyze the proceedings with regard to the trial at the people's court.

From the moment the question of holding the accused for trial is determined by the proper authorities, he assumes a new status and becomes the defendant in the case.[1] This status in many ways alters the legal position of the erstwhile accused, just as his being declared the accused at an earlier stage of the proceedings created a marked difference from the legal position he occupied as a mere suspect. From the time he is held for trial until the opening of the trial session some time may elapse during which all the legally necessary preparations for the trial are being made.

[1]Though the Code does not definitely draw a clear line between the accused *(obvinyaemii)* and the defendant, *(podsoodimii,* or the one on trial) such a division clearly exists. Thus, to cite one example, the moment the individual becomes a defendant he may have the services of an advocate and have the opportunity to confer with him privately, whenever he is committed to jail before the trial.

A. Trial at the People's Court

I. PREPARATION FOR TRIAL

By preparation we mean not only the required arrangements for holding the court sessions, but certain performances pertinent to the proceedings at the trial. These are conducted either by the permanent people's judge, individually, or by the administrative session of the court consisting of one judge and two co-judges.

a. *By the Individual Judge*

The people's judge fixes the day for trial, orders the summoning of witnesses and experts, and, in cases where the participation of counsel for the defendant is required, appoints defense counsel, usually through the college of advocates, whenever the defendant has failed to arrange for his own attorney.[2] The judge must also see that the accusatory conclusion is served upon the defendant within the time fixed by law, which is not less than three days before the trial. This requirement is deemed so fundamental that a failure to comply with it is reversible error, though the defendant expressly offers to waive his right to receive the document within the proper time.[3] In the comparatively few cases where no accusatory conclusion is required, as in cases which are brought directly to the court by the complainants, the people's judge issues a summons which must contain the basis for the accusation. The judge must see that this summons which is a substitute for the more formal accusatory conclusion is served upon the defendant. In addition he may, before placing the case on the trial list, ask the defendant to appear for the purpose of explaining to him personally the essence of the accusation and of inquiring of him whether he desires that any additional witnesses, or experts be called or any other testimony obtained. The questions asked the defendant as well as his statements or requests are entered into the protocol.[4] Although the law provides merely that the judge *may* summon the defendant, without making this procedure obligatory,

[2] Code, 1927, section 250.
[3] Supreme Court case reports for 1925. Case No. 31394.
[4] Code, 1927, section 256.

such a practice is strongly recommended by legal writers, and apparently it has become generally accepted.[5] Any requests made by the defendant at this time are not passed upon by the people's judge, but are submitted by him to the administrative session of the people's court for action. By the amendments of 1929 the individual judge was also given the authority to settle all matters with regard to summoning experts or witnesses for the trial, a function previously exercised by the administrative session of the court which, we recall, consists of one judge and two co-judges.

b. *By the Administrative Session of the Court*

All the acts performed by the individual people's judge do not always complete the preparations for the trial; numerous significant matters may still be brought up before the administrative session of the court. Although the functions of this session have been greatly diminished by the Amendments of 1929, it may still be called upon to discuss various features of the case before it is put on the trial list, such as the completeness of the preliminary investigation, the justification for the holding for trial or the question of reversing, changing, or modifying the measure to secure the attendance of the defendant.[6] This session may change the list of witnesses and experts to be summoned to the trial which has been prepared. The administrative session must also hear and determine petitions of the parties concerning the summoning of additional witnesses or experts; every petition must indicate what particular facts or circumstances are to be established by such witnesses or experts. The court must not refuse any request if the desired testimony may have any bearing on the case.[7]

1. Defense Counsel

Another important matter to be disposed of by the administrative session of the court is the question of defense counsel. We know that the accused did not have the aid of any counsel

[5]*Commentaries*, pages 262, 263.
[6]Code, 1927, section 236, as amended in 1929, Collected Laws No. 78, Article 756.
[7]Code, 1927, sections 54 and 253.

during the preliminary proceedings. But he may have counsel immediately after the decision to hold him for trial is reached. The law provides that when the accusatory conclusion is served upon the defendant, he is to be advised of his right to select an advocate, or that he may have one by the appointment of the court.[8] But it would seem that the question of defense counsel may be settled even before that. The Code of Criminal Procedure provides that "Simultaneously with the deliberation on the question of holding the accused for trial, the court, at its administrative session, shall act on the petition of the party for approval of the particular counsel selected by him or shall appoint counsel if the defendant has not yet chosen one for himself."[9]

As the matter of defense counsel is one of the features which distinguish the trial at the people's court from that in the other courts, let us attempt to clear up this point. While there are a number of sections in the Code dealing with, or touching upon, the question of defense counsel, the important question of the right to such counsel is not stated with absolute clearness and precision. But a careful study of all the sections involved, together with the interpretation and explanation given by Soviet legal writers,[10] will inevitably lead us to the following conclusions.[11]

First, the defendant in the people's court may always avail himself of his absolute right to select an advocate from among the persons who have a right to act as such—namely, members of the college of advocates, close relations of the defendant, or duly appointed representatives of the government institution or trade union of which the defendant is a member.[12] Second, should the defendant desire to have as his advocate any person not included in these categories, the approval of the people's judge is required.[13] Third, the judge itself must appoint defense counsel from among the members of the college of advocates, if

[8] *Ibid.*, section 246.
[9] *Ibid.*, section 243.
[10] *Commentaries*, page 247.
[11] People's judges, with whom the writer had discussed this point, took it for granted that the defendant may as of right engage counsel in all cases heard at the people's courts.
[12] Code, 1927, section 53.
[13] *Ibid.*

the defendant fails to select counsel himself, in all cases which may not be tried without the participation of an advocate. Such cases are as follows: (a) When the defendant is dumb, deaf, or in general when he suffers from such physical impairment as renders him incapable of correctly understanding the proceedings at the trial; (b) cases in which the prosecution participates,[14] if the defendant himself does not refuse to have an advocate.[15] The latter provision is very strictly and literally interpreted. The Supreme Court reversed a verdict in a case which was tried in the absence of defense counsel, but with the participation of a representative of the civil claimant, "whose functions", the court said, "are similar to those of the prosecutor".[16] The civil claimant is, of course, in no real sense a criminal prosecutor, but the Supreme Court by its interpretation very definitely set up an important bulwark in support of the defendant's right not to be placed at a disadvantage at the trial. The civil claimant who may not touch upon the case from its purely criminal aspect nevertheless does so indirectly by helping to establish the occurrence of certain events which incidentally are detrimental to the cause of the defendant. It is important to note in this connection that many cases in the people's courts, and sometimes even in the provincial courts, are tried by the court itself in the absence of any representative of the procuracy, or any person conducting the case against the defendant, who is called the private prosecutor. In such an event the court itself directs both sides of the case.

Let us note here that while the defendant, in the people's court, may always avail himself of the services of counsel at the trial, the court's duty to appoint an advocate applies only in certain specified instances. We can, therefore, easily conceive of a case in which th prosecutor does not participate, which happens quite frequently, and where the defendant does not suffer from the physical defects specified, and, therefore, the court does not have to appoint counsel.

While discussing the question of defense counsel, we note that in cases in which several defendants are jointly tried, the

[14]See *ante*, Ch. I, note 127.
[15]Code, 1927, section 55.
[16]Decisions of the Supreme Court, 1925. Case No. 27103.

court may appoint one counsel for all defendants only when the defense of one does not contradict the defense of any other; otherwise, separate advocates must be named.[17]

The moment the advocate is selected or appointed he is vested with important privileges. He has a right to interview the defendant if the latter is held in custody; he, as well as the defendant himself, is permitted to have full access to the entire record of the case, and is allowed to transcribe any part of it deemed necessary for his preparation for trial.[18]

In connection with this discussion of the proceedings in preparation for the trial, let us note that, theoretically speaking, for the first time during this stage we may have the appearance of adverse parties; prior to this there has been no one, we are assured, to emphasize the guilt or innocence of the accused, for there was no person who had to strive for particular results. The inquisitor, or the organ of investigation, was said to be a mere unbiased collector of data, while the procurator acted solely as a supervisor whose duty was to see that the inquisitor performed his functions according to law. But after the accused is formally held for trial, the procurator becomes the public prosecutor and the advocate the defender. There are now two adverse parties, each of whom strives to direct the case in a particular way, although the law emphatically asserts that the procurator's duty is not necessarily to convict, nor must the advocate set himself, at all events, to have the defendant acquitted, but that the function of both is to help the court reach the ultimate goal—a just verdict.

With all the preparations taken care of the case is ready for trial.

II. QUESTIONS INCIDENT TO THE TRIAL

Before discussing the procedure at the trial, let us digress for a moment to dwell upon a few questions incidental to the trial itself, which may have to be decided before the trial of the case actually begins.

[17]Code, 1927, section 251.
[18]*Ibid.*, section 252.

THE TRIAL

a. *Jurisdiction*

The Code of Criminal Procedure which deals in detail with problems of venue has nothing to say on questions of jurisdiction —that is, when and under what circumstances a criminal court of the R.S.F.S.R. has jurisdiction over an offense and may proceed with the trial of the case. The Criminal Code, however, sets forth the principles of jurisdiction as follows:

> 1. "The provisions of this Criminal Code shall apply to all citizens of the R.S.F.S.R. who have committed socially-dangerous acts within the boundaries of the R.S.F.S.R., as well as outside the boundaries of the U.S.S.R., whenever they shall be apprehended on the territory of the R.S.F.S.R.
>
> 2. "The citizens of other constituent republics shall be held responsible in accordance with the laws of the R.S.F.S.R. for crimes they commit on the territory of the R.S.F.S.R. as well as outside the boundaries of the U.S.S.R. whenever they shall be apprehended and shall be held for trial or inquiry on the territory of the R.S.F.S.R.
>
> "For the crimes committed on the territory of the Union, the citizens of the constituent republics shall be held responsible in accordance with the laws of the place where the crime shall have been committed.
>
> 3. "Foreigners who commit crimes on the territory of the U.S.S.R. shall be held responsible in accordance with the laws of the place where the crime has been committed.
>
> 4. "The question as to the criminal responsibility of citizens of foreign countries who enjoy the right of extra-territoriality shall be decided each time by diplomacy."[19]

Paragraph 1 omits the question of jurisdiction over offenses committed by citizens of the R.S.F.S.R. outside the territory of the R.S.F.S.R. but within the Union. Whether this omission is intended to be supplied by the second subsection of paragraph 2, is open to question. From the position of this subsection alone, it would seem to apply only to citizens of the other constituent republics, and not those of the R.S.F.S.R. At least it is clear

[19]Cr. Code, 1926, sections 2, 3, 4 and 5.

that foreigners and the group intended to be covered by subsection two are in the same category. They are subject to the criminal law of the particular constituent republic where the crime was perpetrated. We may infer that it is the intention that the courts of the R.S.F.S.R. are to take jurisdiction and try the case if the offender is apprehended within its boundaries. Otherwise, the provision as to which criminal law should be applied would be meaningless. The next question which presents itself is that of venue.

b. *Venue*

We have already discussed the question of jurisdiction of each type of court with regard to the nature of the particular offense.[20] The problem of venue is which people's court, or which judicial district, as there is one court for each district, is to try a given case. From the general character of Soviet jurisprudence one would expect a rather simple method of dealing with such problems. The Code provides: "Each case shall be tried in that court which sits in the district where the alleged crime was committed. If this is impossible to determine, the case shall be tried in the court which is situated in the district where the criminal proceedings were first instituted."[21] The normal rule of venue was apparently adopted for mere reasons of practicability, for in the ordinary case all the necessary evidence will be found in the district where the crime was committed. But the rule is flexible enough to be modified in accordance with the exigencies of a particular case. The law adopting the locus of the crime as the basis of venue is not grounded on any theory of protecting the defendant's right, but was enacted simply for reasons of expediency; neither is there any rigidity in this rule as it will be disregarded for the purpose of obtaining just results. The law states that "Any case may be transferred from one [people's] court to another if a more unprejudiced, speedy and thorough judicial hearing of the case will be achieved thereby."[22] In accordance with the structure of Soviet judiciary, the provincial, regional or circuit court has absolute authority to transfer any

[20]Code, 1927, sections 24-27. See, *ante,* pages 54, 69, 70, 79, 86 and 88.
[21]*Ibid.*, section 29.
[22]*Ibid.*, sections 30, 32 and 34.

case from one people's court to another, within the same province, region or circuit, as the case may be. But only the Supreme Court has the power to change the venue from one province (region, etc.) to another.[23] Furthermore, the rule of venue can also be waived by the parties. The Code provides that although a court trying a case finds that the case is within the jurisdiction of another court of similar jurisdiction—an error of venue—the court may nevertheless continue to dispose of the case, provided, however, the trial has already begun and the parties have not presented any objections.[24] But if objections are raised the case is transferred to another court, which must assume jurisdiction although it may have been sent there erroneously, for disputes between courts on such questions are absolutely forbidden. If a court thinks that a case has been improperly sent to it by a court of equal jurisdiction it may appeal to the proper higher court by way of supervision, not, however, before a verdict is rendered.[25]

c. *Parties at the Trial*

Besides the bench which is made up of one judge and two co-judges, there must be present a court secretary and parties to the action. The Code of Criminal Procedure defines the term "parties" in a criminal case to mean the procurator who conducts the accusation at the trial, the civil claimant or his attorney, the defendant and his advocate, the injured party or his attorney whenever he may conduct the accusation (in cases of a private prosecution). The Code names the civil claimant and the injured party as different parties, though they may conceivably be one person.

d. *Absence of Parties*

1. The Defendant

The presence of the defendant at the trial may be required by the court in each case. But unless his presence is so required, which must be stipulated in the summons, it is not obligatory in cases which do not carry a prison sentence. On the other hand,

[23] *Ibid.*, section 31.
[24] *Ibid.*, section 39.
[25] *Ibid.*, section 40.

the defendant must be present at the trial in cases where the offense is punishable by imprisonment. To the latter rule there are, however, the following exceptions: (a) When the defendant directly expresses his consent to be tried in his absence, which, of course, must be an absolutely voluntary waiver; (b) when it is proved that the defendant has evaded the service of the summons, or has absconded.[26] These exceptions to the general rule have been so strictly interpreted by the Supreme Court that it is clear that the policy of Soviet law is to have the defendant present at the trial as the best means of ensuring a comprehensive judicial inquiry, with a possibility of obtaining evidence of the motives which prompted the commission of the alleged offense. A number of verdicts have been reversed by the Supreme Court on the ground that the trial court did not thoroughly investigate the reasons for the defendant's failure to receive the summons or the cause of his absence.[27]

Much confusion at one time arose as to what stage of the pre-trial proceedings must be reached before the absconding of the defendant will justify a verdict in his absence. It is settled now by the plenum of the Supreme Court[28] that a defendant may be tried in his absence, on the ground that he has absconded, if he disappeared either after he was formally held for trial—that is, following the completion of the preliminary inquiry—or after he was notified that the preliminary inquiry was completed, which really means just before he could formally be held for trial. The disappearance of the accused, therefore, at any earlier stage of the pre-trial proceedings will prevent his being placed on trial.

We have been heretofore dealing with the situation where the defendant has failed to appear. But there also may be an exceptional case which will be tried in the absence of the defendant, though the latter presents himself. The law permits the court to expel the defendant from the court room without interrupting the proceedings if he disobeys the order of the presiding judge or if he creates disturbances. But this extreme measure

[26] *Ibid.*, section 265.

[27] Supreme Court decisions, 1924, cases Nos. 28017, 28862, 210041.

[28] Explanation given by the Plenum of the Supreme Court on November 27, 1924, quoted from the *commentaries*, page 271.

may be applied by the court only if his disobedience or misbehavior continues[29] after he has been warned that he will be removed from the court room.

2. Prosecution

(a) Public Prosecutor

A public prosecutor must participate in the trial at the people's court if either the court, or the procurator so orders. In the latter case, the procurator must notify the court of his order simultaneously with his recommendation to approve the accusatory conclusion.[30] In these instances the trial may not proceed in the absence of a member of the procuracy.[31] If the one appointed is absent without good reason he is subject to disciplinary proceedings provided by law.

In this connection we may observe that the presence of public prosecutors at the trials in the people's court is the exception rather than the rule. Out of 202,970 cases tried in the people's courts of twelve provinces in 1926, members of the procuracy participated in only 2,843 instances (1.4%).[32] Sometimes, as we recall, members of the "institute of public prosecution" act alone, not merely as assistants to the member of the state procuracy, but as public prosecutors at the trial.

(b) Private Prosecutor

The failure of the private prosecutor or his attorney to appear at the trial in cases tried with a private prosecutor generally results in the discontinuance of the case. This is in line with the theory on which private prosecution is based. The state is ready to help the injured party to obtain redress; but as he must take the initiative, his failure to appear will signify his unwillingness to proceed, and nothing is left for the court to do but to drop the case. But, if the defendant for some reason wishes to have a judicial disposition of the case, the court must

[29] Code, 1927, section 259.
[30] *Ibid.*, section 225, as amended in 1929.
[31] *Ibid.*, section 268.
[32] Official report of the Procurator of the R.S.F.S.R. for 1926 submitted to the Pesidium of the All-Russian Central Executive Committee, Moscow, 1927, page 127.

proceed with the trial, though the private prosecutor or his attorney is absent.[83]

3. Advocates

Cases in which defense counsel must participate, or cases where the defendant in pursuance of his right has selected one may not be tried without such counsel. The latter's failure to appear will invariably cause the postponement of the trial. The court may not substitute another attorney without the consent of the defendant,[84] as it may do in a case where the public prosecutor appointed is absent.

4. The Civil Claimant

The civil claimant, or his attorney, must be at the trial to present his side of the case. His failure to be present will automatically eliminate his civil claim as far as the criminal trial is concerned, unless the case is continued for some other reason, in which event he will have a right to present his claim again at the postponed trial.[85] We may note in passing that even when the civil claim is dropped because of the claimant's failure to appear, it will in no way prevent the injured party from bringing a separate civil action. Should the defendant be convicted, the verdict will be legally binding upon the civil courts in so far as the happening of the events out of which the civil claim grew is concerned.[86]

e. *Language in which Trial is Conducted*

As the doctrine of national self-expression and the equality of national minorities is one of the basic principles of the Soviet régime,[87] the Russian language is not necessarily the one in which

[83]Code, 1927, section 270.
[84]*Ibid.*, section 268.
[85]*Ibid.*, section 269.
[86]*Ibid.*, section 13.
[87]The constitution of the R.S.F.S.R., section 13, speaks of the equality of all nationalities and declares that "it is absolutely incompatible with the basic laws of the Republic to oppress even to any small degree the national minorities, or to limit their equality or to tolerate any privileges, directly or indirectly, bestowed upon any nationality." This section goes as far as to permit the secession of any national group, upon the decision of its Congress of Soviets. Similiar provisions are inserted in the respective Constitutions of the Ukraine, (section 32) White Russia, (sections 20, 21) Uzbek, (section 16) Turkman, (section 15) and in the Constitutions of the three Republics which comprise the Transcaucasion Federated Soviet Republic.

the courts, even in the R.S.F.S.R., conduct their business. Already at the beginning of 1918 the Second Decree on Courts proclaimed the general doctrine that "in courts of all instances proceedings shall be allowed to be conducted in all local languages."[38] The same provision was incorporated completely in the important act on the people's court, at the end of 1918.[39] This principle was, with some elaboration, made a part of the first Code of Criminal Procedure, and has unfailingly been maintained in the later enactments or modifications of the Code. The law provides that "Proceedings in a criminal case shall be conducted in the Russian language or in the language of the majority of the population in the locality in which the court sits."[40] If the defendant, the injured person, the witnesses, or the experts do not speak the language of the official proceedings, interpreters are employed. The defendant's right goes much farther, for he is to be furnished with a copy of the accusatory conclusion and other official documents in his native language, and these documents are also to be read at the trial in that language, if demanded by the defendant. A striking provision is that persons who have a legal interest in the case may file any paper or statement in their native tongue if it has been proved that they do not employ the language in which the court proceedings are conducted.[41] Such a rigid application of the doctrine of equality of national minorities is deemed to serve as a "real guarantee for bringing the masses nearer to the court."[42] In this connection a Soviet legal writer points out that in Tzarist Russia where cases were always tried in Russian a case was often in fact tried by interpreters and not by the court, as the judges frequently did not understand the language of the defendant or the witnesses.[43]

f. *Publicity of the Trial*

The general principle is that all criminal trials are open and public, and only children under fourteen are to be excluded from

[38]Second Decree, section 7.
[39]P. C. Act, 1918, section 21.
[40]Code, 1927, section 22, Part 1.
[41]*Ibid.*, Part 2.
[42]I. A. Krostin, *The Criminal Process, Moscow,* 1927, page 14.
[43]*Ibid.*

the court room.[44] But the court may decide to close the trial, or parts of it, to the public whenever a military, diplomatic or state secret is involved, or whenever the case charges certain forms of rape or abnormal sexual relations with minors.[45] But even under these circumstances the verdict must be read in open court.[46]

III. PROCEEDINGS AT THE TRIAL

a. *Opening of the Session—Rôle of the Presiding Judge and the Court*

The permanent people's judge, who always presides, is naturally the person vested with the authority to conduct every step of the trial. He opens and closes the sessions, maintains order, announces decisions, etc. Though the permanent judge enjoys no greater rights and wields no greater powers than the two temporary co-judges who sit with him he is, nevertheless, the spokesman of the court, speaking for and in the name of the full bench. He is, therefore, merely by virtue of his position, apt to impress his personality upon the proceedings of the trial, and thus exert a far greater influence than the comparatively passive co-judges. This is especially true when we think of the very nature and character of the Soviet bench and the active part it takes in conducting the judicial inquiry.

It is well to bear in mind that, unlike our own system of criminal procedure, at least in many of our states, the Soviet system does not conceive of the court as a mere impartial, unbiased umpire who must see that the legal game played by the two parties shall conform to all the established rules and regulations of the combat. The Soviet court, on the contrary, is considered an active governmental agency which investigates, tests and decides in accordance with the policies of its government; the parties, defense as well as the prosecution, are there merely to assist the court in establishing the truth. But it is the *court,* and *not the parties,* that carries on the judicial inquiry. This is

[44] Code, 1927, sections 19 and 20.
[45] *Ibid.,* section 19.
[46] *Ibid.,* section 21.

one of the basic theories upon which Soviet criminal procedure is constructed.[47]

The Code of Criminal Procedure in prescribing the rules for the procedure at the trial speaks in terms either of the "presiding judge" or "the court". Whatever term is used it is the former who makes orders, announces decisions, etc., but it is the entire court which acts and decides upon the matter of any order or decision. The distinction between the two terms used is interpreted to be that whenever a certain right is given by the Code to the presiding judge, it is meant that he should proceed to act without first consulting the co-judges, but with a tacit concurrence of the latter. If they should disagree with the act of the permanent judge, they may reverse it.[48] On the other hand, whenever the Code employs the term "court" it signifies that the presiding judge must first consult the co-judges before speaking in the name of the court, as he always does.

In accordance with what has just been said, the presiding judge opens the session of the court, announces the case to be tried and orders that the defendant be brought in.[49] The latter, though he has been at large up to this moment, may now conceivably be taken into custody, if the court, in a stated opinion, declares it necessary as a means to ensure his presence at the trial.[50]

The presiding judge asks the defendant, after the latter is identified, whether he has received the accusatory conclusion or its equivalent;[51] the judge must likewise make sure of the presence of the parties without whom the trial may not proceed. He is also to check up on the presence of the witnesses who have been summoned, and in case some of them are absent, he must after listening to the arguments of the parties as to the advisability of proceeding without them decide whether or not to

[47]*Commentaries*, page 265.

[48]*Ibid.*, page 264.

[49]Code, 1927, section 262. (It is apparently a rule requiring the bringing in of the defendant at this stage of the trial, if he was not there already. For as a matter of practice, as the writer has observed, the defendants who were under guard had always been brought in before the opening of the proceedings.)

[50]*Ibid.*, section 263.

[51]*Ibid.*, section 264.

postpone the trial.[52] The court must also inquire of the parties whether they desire additional witnesses summoned, or any other testimony obtained which has a bearing on the case.[53] At this stage of the proceedings the court takes the initiative and inquires concerning possible additional testimony, but the parties may petition the court to that effect at any stage of the proceedings.[54]

Among the more important features of the proceedings during the so-called "opening session" are the presiding judge's explanations to the injured party that he has a right to file a civil claim, if he has not already done so,[55] and to the defendant that he has a right to interrogate or cross-examine witnesses and experts, as well as other defendants in the case, if they testify, and to make statements concerning the case as a whole, or any particular circumstance, at any stage of the trial.[56] These undoubtedly valuable rights the defendant possesses irrespective of the participation of defense counsel. It is noteworthy that these significant privileges accorded to the defendant are not based upon any theory of rights for the defendant as a person, but are grounded on the avowed assumption that it is to the interest of the state, whose mere humble agent the court is, to create such conditions in the criminal proceedings as will tend to ensure the conviction only of the guilty.[57] The defendant is only an incidental "party beneficiary", and gains advantageous rights simply because they happen to coincide with the interest of the state.

b. *Challenging for Cause*

After the presiding judge explains to the parties[58] their respective rights, he announces the composition of the court, telling the parties of their rights to challenge any of the judges for cause.[59] This procedure is obligatory, and compliance with this rule must be entered in the protocol. Challenges may be made

[52] *Ibid.*, section 271.
[53] *Ibid.*, section 272.
[54] *Commentaries*, pages 276, 277.
[55] Code, 1927, section 276.
[56] *Ibid.*, section 277.
[57] *Commentaries*, page 280.
[58] As a matter of practice only the defendant is asked if he has any reasons why this court may not sit in his case.
[59] Code, 1927, section 278.

on the ground that the judge or any co-judge is a party to the action or is related to one of the parties, or that his relatives are interested in the outcome of the case; that any judge sitting has participated in the case—either in the preliminaries or in a former trial—as a witness, expert, investigator, prosecutor, advocate, or representative of the interests of the injured person, or as civil claimant, or that there are circumstances which create a doubt as to the impartiality of the judge or judges; finally, that the sitting judges are related to each other.[60] While the latter ground would not seem to have any real merit, the Supreme Court reversed a verdict in a case where a brother and sister sat as co-judges.[61] The validity of the challenge is to be decided by the unchallenged judges, in the absence of the one whose fitness is questioned. In case of a tie the challenge is sustained.[62]

All the formalities described above complete the proceeding known as the opening of the judicial session.

c. *The Judicial Inquiry (Trial)*

1. Reading the Document of Accusation

The trial proper begins with the reading, by the judge or the court secretary, of the document upon which the defendant is being prosecuted.[63] The contents of this official document are very similar to the opening address of the district attorney in our courts, supplemented by a statement of what the defendant has attempted to prove in his defense. Though it is not written in any formal language so as to make it unintelligible to the average person, the president judge is, nevertheless, required, after the document has been read, to explain to the defendant in a manner and form understandable to the latter[64] the substance of the accusation made against him, asking him whether or not

[60] *Ibid.*, sections 41, 43 and 45.

[61] Supreme Court Decisions for 1925, case No. 212001.

[62] Code, 1927, section 47.

[63] *Ibid.*, section 279.

[64] Without such requirement the defendant would often remain uninformed at the trial as to the contents of the accusatory document. Though the latter is always read, it is frequently done in such a way as to merely comply with a formality. The writer, who attended many trials, could seldom follow the exact wording of the document.

he admits the charges.[65] This is a kind of arraignment. The immediate course to be taken will naturally depend upon the answer or plea of the defendant. Should he admit the charges as stated, he is then given an opportunity, if he so desires, to testify or make any statement or give any explanation with regard to the crime. If the defendant then makes any statement the court may, if it is of the opinion that the case has already been made clear, drop any further judicial inquiry and proceed to listen to the final arguments of the parties, the prosecution and the defense.[66] But in case the defendant, though he admits his guilt, refuses to testify, his admission alone is not sufficient to consider the judicial inquiry completed. More light must be thrown upon the case. A mere confession out of court is never deemed sufficient ground to sustain a conviction;[67] the court must inquire into and verify the admission of guilt. Even when the defendant has testified, after his admission, the court may, if it so chooses, examine other witnesses, documents, etc.

Should the defendant deny the accusatory statements, as a whole, or in part, the judicial inquiry must proceed in the regular manner.[68]

The order in which parties or witnesses are to testify is not laid down by the Code. This is to be decided in each case separately by the court, after obtaining the opinion of the parties.[69] With all this done, the court is ready to enter upon the essential feature of the trial—the hearing of testimony.

2. Rules of Evidence

Unlike our own system with its elaborate body of law of evidence, Soviet jurisprudence knows of no rules, worth the name, on evidence; the court is, therefore, not hampered in its attempt to elicit everything the witness may know. The Code provides: "The court shall not be bound by any formality of the testimony,

[65]Code. 1927, section 280.
[66]*Ibid.*, section 282.
[67]By the project for a new Code of Criminal Procedure, (*The Weekly*, Nos. 28 and 29, 1928) section 115, the court is given a discretionary power to proceed to a conclusion by listening to the final word of the defendant whenever the latter pleaded guilty at the trial. In other words, the present rule (section 282) that the court's authority to do so is conditioned upon the willingness of the defendant to testify, is excluded.
[68]Code, 1927, section 282, second part.
[69]*Ibid.*, section 281.

and it shall be utterly within the discretion of the court to decide, under the circumstances of the case, whether it should admit any given testimony, or demand such from third persons [not parties to the action], which demand shall be complied with."[70] This section deals with two important problems. In the first place it deprives any evidence of a binding, formal significance. The court is not to be bound by any "formality"—that is, by any rules of law laid down beforehand as to the extent, weight and veracity of any testimony.[71] For example, there is not to be any rule which would compel the court to believe the testimony of X rather than of Y, though the latter has been previously convicted of a crime, or stands in some peculiar relations to the defendant, etc. Naturally, the court will take into consideration all such circumstances, but it is free to pass on the weight of the testimony or the veracity of the witness in accordance with its own "inner conviction". All this goes to the question of weighing the credibility of the testimony already admitted. In the second place the court is given an absolutely free hand in admitting, or demanding, any testimony whatsoever. Thus, no one could object to the admission of evidence which might seem irrelevant to the issue before the court. On the other hand, it is to be noted that the law which gives such sweeping powers to the court *to admit* all the testimony it desires, for what it is worth, does not invest it with a free rein *in rejecting* certain evidence, for any evidence submitted by the parties *must* be admitted if it has any bearing on the case.[72] (The amazingly broad meaning of the latter term we have already discussed in connection with pre-trial proceedings.)

No oath is administered to witnesses. The president, however, makes clear to the persons testifying their duty to tell all they know of the case, and warns them of the criminal liability they may incur by testifying falsely. This warning is put in writing, and each witness must sign his name thereto.[73]

[70] *Ibid.*, section 57.

[71] *Commentaries*, pages 55, 56. This point is illustrated by the following examples: There is no such rule that a confession under given circumstances must be believed; or that when two witnesses contradict each other, the testimony of the one who has never been convicted of a crime should be believed, etc.

[72] Code, 1927, sections 253, 254, 272 and 273.

[73] *Ibid.*, section 274.

As each witness is ordinarily examined in the absence of any witnesses who have not yet testified, except in cases where one witness is to confront another, the president judge must see that the witnesses not yet examined are kept out of the court room in a room designated for the purpose and prevented from communicating with each other about the case. In complicated and lengthy cases, however, the practice is to permit them to depart, fixing the time for the appearance in court of each witness.[74] All these rules are applicable only to ordinary witnesses; experts are permitted to remain in the court room during the trial even before they have taken the stand, except when the court, on its own motion or at the request of one of the parties, deems it absolutely necessary to deprive the expert of his usual right to be present in the court room.[75]

3. Examination of Witnesses

(a) *Examination by the Court*

Before the witness is to tell his own story with regard to the substance of the case, he is interrogated by the court concerning his name, occupation, education, party affiliation, etc. He is also questioned for the purpose of determining his relations to the case and to the parties interested therein.[76] This latter requirement is apparently of great importance, for not only is the civil claimant, or the private prosecutor eligible to testify in the case,[77] but even near relations of the defendant are not excluded or excused as witnesses. As the court is to take the testimony of each witness for what it is worth, it should be a matter of great concern to it to discover what interest a particular witness may have in the outcome of the trial.

The examination of the witness begins by the court's asking him to tell all he knows about the case, avoiding any information the source of which cannot be proven.[78] The witness is thus given an opportunity to tell his version of the case in his own way. This method would seem to serve as a preliminary step to

[74] I. A. Krastin, *The Criminal Process,* Moscow, 1927, page 105.
[75] Code, 1927, section 275.
[76] *Ibid.,* section 284.
[77] *Ibid.,* note to section 284.
[78] *Ibid.,* section 285.

the actual examination. The Code specifies that after the witness is through with his narrative, the presiding judge must invite the parties, in the proper order, to interrogate the witness on each point, as they may think necessary.[79] Though the law does not specifically provide that the court shall examine the witnesses before they are interrogated by the prosecution and defense, such is, as a matter of practice, the ordinary procedure. The presiding judge and sometimes also the co-judges hurl questions at the witness freely, in order to help him to clarify his own story, before he is turned over for examination by the prosecution and the defense.

(b) *Direct and Cross Examination*

The beginning of the interrogation is conceived of, at least in theory, as something similar to the direct examination in our own courts, for the witness is first questioned by the party upon whose request he was summoned, then the adverse party takes up the cross-examination.[80] In this connection it is interesting to note that while the court is not deemed to be leaning on the side of the prosecution, any witness summoned on the motion of the court itself is first to be examined by the prosecution. The order of examination provided by the Code is apparently not strictly adhered to, for, as the writer has observed, the prosecutor is usually the first to interrogate all witnesses and the advocate has his turn afterwards. The defendant himself is always asked by the court at the completion of the examination whether he desires to present some questions to the witness.[81] It is also to be noted that the terms direct and cross-examination, as employed here, are not to be taken in the sense used in our courts, for so far as the nature and scope of the examination are concerned, there is no distinction between them. Our elaborate rules against leading or incriminating questions, as well as other technicalities which provide a shelter for a reluctant witness (especially if he is also the defendant), and which frequently hamper the uncovering of very relevant information, are unknown in Soviet juris-

[79] *Ibid.*, section 286.
[80] *Ibid.*, section 287.
[81] The writer has observed such order in all the trials he has witnessed.

prudence. (The merit of such rules from the broader point of view is a different question.)

(c) *Wide Latitude of the Examination*

The witness, provided he is not the defendant, must under pains of punishment answer any question put to him by those having the right to examine, if such question tends to establish any material fact necessary for the determination of the case, including matters touching upon the character of the defendant.[82] Irrelevancy is the only ground upon which the presiding judge, whose duty it is to direct the trial in the proper manner, may exclude certain evidence.[83] Even this requirement must not be taken in the same sense as under our definition of relevancy.[84]

From what has been said, it seems obvious that there should be no strict rules as to the interrogation of a witness. Each party may again and again present questions in order to have any point explained or completed which was brought out by the adversary during his examination of the witness.[85] The presiding judge and the co-judges may ask questions during the interrogation conducted by the parties or afterwards, at any stage of the proceedings.[86] In general, every advisable means is to be utilized for the sole purpose of eliciting all the information desired which is obtainable. In line with such an attitude, a witness may be examined in the presence of another witness, or may be confronted by him; likewise, if deemed necessary, the entire interrogatory procedure, as described above, may be repeated.[87] In other words, the latitude in examining witnesses is so great as to permit anything which may help to reach the ultimate goal—a proper verdict.

Though there is no expressly stated general rule as to the method of testifying, the law provides that the "Witnesses, when

[82] Code, 1927, sections 166 and 286.

[83] *Ibid.*, sections 257 and 286.

[84] In one of the trials which the writer attended where a person was charged with rape, a number of girls had testified without any objection, as to the fact that the present defendant once attempted to rape them, or had done so, though those acts were not charged against him at this particular trial.

[85] Code, 1927, section 288.

[86] *Ibid.*, section 289.

[87] *Ibid.*, section 290.

testifying, may have with them written notes in instances where the testimony concerns some data which are difficult to remember."[88] The witness is also permitted to read any document which has a bearing upon his testimony. But it is for the court to decide whether the document itself shall be incorporated and made a part of the record of the case.[89]

The testimony of the witnesses or the defendant during the preliminary inquiry or investigation is usually not to be read at the trial, for the accusatory conclusion, directly or indirectly, had already incorporated the testimony of all the witnesses. But when a witness at the trial contradicts the testimony previously given by him at the pre-trial proceedings, or fails to appear at the trial, though summoned, his testimony at the preliminary hearing may be read at the trial, on the motion of the court, or at the request of one of the parties. When one of the defendants dies before the trial his testimony may be read in favor of or against the other defendants.[90] The reading of the pre-trial testimony of a witness who has not been summoned to the trial is permissible only upon a special decision of the court.[91] The testimony of the defendant obtained during the preliminary inquiry must be read at the trial if he refuses to testify at the trial,[92] which he may do.

4. Expert Testimony

As in the proceedings at the preliminary inquiry, the expert at the trial is furnished beforehand with specific questions upon which he is to base his answers. Such questions put in writing may also be submitted by the defendant or his counsel. Unlike the ordinary witness, the experts may consult among themselves, if they so desire.[93] They testify orally by stating their conclusions which, however, are later to be reduced to writing, and become a part of the record.[94] These conclusions are not absolutely binding upon the court. Whenever the court does not follow any

[88] *Ibid.*, section 292.
[89] *Ibid.*, section 293.
[90] *Ibid.*, sections 294, 295, 296, 297.
[91] *Ibid.*, note to section 297.
[92] *Ibid.*, note to section 294.
[93] *Ibid.*, sections 172 and 173.
[94] *Ibid.*, section 298.

expert opinion, it must state in detail the reasons for such departure either in the verdict (which is a verdict and sentence combined), or in a separate opinion. A failure to give in writing a detailed explanation is reversible error.[95] We may note here that the spectacle, not infrequently witnessed in our courts, of medical experts defending opposite views is unimaginable in Soviet Russia, though in theory this is possible. Owing to the fact that the entire medical profession is controlled by the state, and every physician is a government employee, though he may also practice privately, it is unlikely that the lure of compensation, if such should be offered, would bias the opinion of a medical expert. The state prosecutor is not expected to search for a medical expert who will necessarily support the accusation. He simply invites a state medical institution to assign one of its staff for the required examination or the defendant is placed in such an institution for observation.

5. Court's Power in Conducting the Inquiry

The scope of the court's authority in all matters relating to the judicial inquiry is almost unlimited. Should it be necessary to review a place or examine bulky objects, the court may either commission one of its members for such purpose, or the entire session of the court may be transferred for a time to the place concerned. In the latter event the presiding judge opens the session there, and conducts regular proceedings, the parties having a right to call to the attention of the court anything which may seem significant to them. The information obtained from these proceedings, together with any relevant remarks made by the parties, must be entered upon the official protocol.[96]

We have already had occasion to point out the singularity of the Soviet system in making the trial court an investigating body which authenticates the information obtained during the proceedings prior to the trial. In accordance with this basic theory, the court is not, in every instance, required to render a verdict. As the judicial inquiry nears its completion the investigators—that is, the court—may, on their own motion or on the

[95] *Commentaries*, page 293.
[96] Code, 1927, section 301.

petition of one of the parties, conclude that the case has not been made sufficiently clear, and that new information may still be obtained by a further inquiry outside the court. The court may then either continue the case and itself seek to obtain the additional facts, or turn the case over to the inquisitor or the organs of investigation.[97] If the case is turned over to these officials, it will have to go through the regular stages of pre-trial proceedings—namely, the process of completing the inquiry, framing the accusatory conclusion and the formal holding of the defendant for trial. In other words, the case will revert to the stage of the preliminary inquiry as if the trial had never started.

But should the court, after examining all the witnesses and other testimony, decide to proceed to a conclusion, the people's judge must, in analogy to the proceedings during the preliminary inquiry, ask the parties whether or not they have anything to add to the judicial inquiry. After any such new evidence is presented and admitted, or refused on proper grounds, the judicial inquiry is declared completed. The parties, who are deemed to be assistants to the court, are now called upon to interpret and analyze the mass of evidence usually piled up during the trial. This is known as the final argument of the parties.

Before we proceed to a discussion of the final arguments, and thus leave the subject of judicial inquiry, we may touch upon a few matters which may occur during the judicial inquiry.

d. *Additional Charges Developed at the Trial*

The general rule is that the judicial inquiry may concern itself only with persons who, being charged with a specific crime, have been, prior to the opening of the trial, formally held for court; and the proceedings of the trial must be restricted to the subject matter stated in the accusatory document.[98] This is in line with the fundamental principle of Soviet criminal procedure. The court is deemed well equipped properly to perform the function of a final judicial inquiry only after a preliminary investigation has been held. The defendant is to have the right to be informed of the subject matter and nature as well as the extent

[97] *Ibid.*, section 302.
[98] *Ibid.*, section 311.

of the charges against him. Furthermore, the defendant, we recall, must be informed of all the evidence obtained against him during the preliminary inquiry, for he is given full access to the records of the case, after the completion of the pre-trial inquiry. The defendant is, therefore, in a position to prepare himself to meet the charges as well as to rebut the evidence upon which they are based.

This general rule is not without exception. If, during the trial, a new accusation is brought out whether or not it is *closely connected* with the charges upon which the defendant has been held for trial, the court may proceed with the trial on the old and the new accusation, if the newly brought-out charges are so clear as not to require a preliminary inquiry, and do not carry a more severe measure for social safety—that is, punishment. In other words, the defendant is not to be put in a worse position while the additional charges are being disposed of. In the absence of either of these two conditions the case must be continued and return to the stage of the preliminary inquiry.[99] The words "closely connected", as explained by the commentators to the Code, are to be understood in the following way: If the fact of the commission of one offense by the defendant will help to establish the commission of another offense or will aggravate it, they are deemed to be closely connected. For example, if a defendant is charged with the offense of forgery as a public official, under section 120 of the Criminal Code, and at the trial it develops that he was bribed to commit this forgery, which is a more serious offense under section 117, part 2, the two offenses are said to be so connected that they must be tried together, and as the new charge carries a more severe punishment the case must be returned for a new preliminary inquiry.[100] A case must also

[99]*Ibid.*, section 312. This rule is clearly stated only with regard to situations where the new charges were not connected with the charges on which the defendant was brought to trial. The second part of this section (312) which deals with new charges closely connected with the acts of the defendant mentioned in the formal accusation, states that the trial should be continued only if the new charges must be preliminarily investigated, but *does not* provide for a similar procedure if the new charge may carry a severer punishment. However, it is asserted that in either case, the trial will be continued, if by adding the new charge the defendant may be put in a worse position. See *Commentaries*, pages 302 and 305.

[100]*Commentaries*, page 303.

be sent back for a new preliminary inquiry whenever additional persons, other than the defendant, are implicated in the same offense while the trial is going on, if the court does not deem it proper to allow separate trials.[101]

We have heretofore discussed cases where new charges or new defendants are to be added. But the court may be confronted with a similar situation whenever it becomes necessary, as a result of the testimony at the trial, to change the form of the accusation. (For example, if the defendant is charged with premeditated killing under section 137 of the Criminal Code, and at the trial it is brought out that the crime was committed out of greedy motives, which aggravates the offense, according to section 136 of the Criminal Code, or vice versa.) The court may proceed with the trial without any interruption if the modified accusation will not place the defendant at a disadvantage. But should it be of such a nature as to aggravate the crime, the court, upon the request of either party, prosecutor or defense, must continue the trial and send the case for a new preliminary inquiry and holding for trial.[102]

e. *Final Arguments and Rebuttal*

The final argument, when there are parties to argue, begins with a speech of the public prosecutor; the speech of the civil claimant or his attorney follows, and finally that of the counsel for the defense, or of the defendant himself if he has no advocate.[103] These arguments are not limited as to time, and the speakers may, true to Russian tradition, talk to their heart's desire. (A speech of two or three hours is not deemed too long in Russia.) But the presiding judge is to see that the arguers do not go beyond the issues involved in the case.[104] Another limitation placed upon the

[101]Code, 1927, section 316. A verdict was reversed on cassation because X, the defendant, was found guilty and sentenced to imprisonment for stealing a horse, though at the trial it was testified that Y also participated in the criminal act. The trial court, therefore, violated section 316 for not transferring the case back to the inquisitor for a new preliminary inquiry. (Supreme Court Decisions for 1925, Case No. 213809.)

[102]*Ibid.*, section 313. The *commentaries* maintain that it is obligatory on the presiding judge to explain to the parties their right to ask for a discontinuance.

[103]*Ibid.*, section 304.

[104]*Ibid.*, section 308.

speakers, when making the final arguments, is that they are not to present new matters or raise questions which were not brought out during the trial.[105] The latter provision does not absolutely preclude the parties from raising new points or presenting new data after the close of the judicial inquiry. They may merely request the court to reopen the inquiry for such purpose and the proceedings then move on in the ordinary way as if the final argument had not yet begun. Carrying the procedure back and restoring it to an early stage, wiping out all that has taken place since that stage, is a practice permitted throughout Soviet criminal proceedings.

The final speeches may be followed by a rebuttal, the parties speaking in the same order as in the arguments.[106] After the rebuttal the president declares the arguments closed, and then the defendant himself, irrespective of whether or not he has had counsel, is to have what is known as the final word. The fact that he has already argued on his own behalf during the final speeches and rebuttal does not deprive him of his right to be heard just before the judges retire to deliberate on the verdict. In his final word, the defendant may speak his mind with complete freedom and he may not be interrogated or interrupted either by the parties or by the court.[107]

There can be no further proceedings after the defendant has spoken his final word; this must complete the trial. Should the defendant, however, bring out new facts or touch upon new circumstances which were not disclosed during the trial proceedings, the court may, on its own motion or at the request of either party, reopen the proceedings and have the new fact inquired into in the regular manner of the judicial inquiry. The latter will have to be followed again by final arguments and rebuttals of the parties and the final word of the defendant.[108] A failure to repeat all these is clearly reversible error.[109]

[105]*Ibid.*, section 305.
[106]*Ibid.*, section 307.
[107]*Ibid.*, section 309.
[108]*Ibid.*, note to section 309.
[109]Supreme Court Decisions, 1925, Case No. 212063.

f. *Right of Counsel to Withdraw*

We have so far discussed the question and methods of the final arguments and rebuttal of the parties. The question may arise whether the public prosecutor or counsel for the defense must carry on the case to completion. With respect to the former, the answer is clear. He has the right to drop the accusation and withdraw from his rôle as prosecutor, whenever he becomes convinced that the testimony presented at the trial fails to support the charges made against the defendant. Strange as it may seem, however, the withdrawal of the prosecutor will in no wise affect the further proceedings, though we may easily conceive that it may influence the result. The Code provides that the fact that the procurator gives up the prosecution shall not "relieve the court of its duty to proceed with the inquiry of the case, and to determine in the ordinary course the question of the correctness of the accusation made against the defendant."[110]

Has the advocate a right to withdraw from the trial? This highly important question agitated the minds of Soviet legal writers and judicial workers for quite a time. Here, as in other legal problems, where profound principles are involved, the difference of opinion is marked. There are the "weak", the "unpardonably liberal-minded", who still cling to their inherited "bourgeois prejudice", no matter in what newly-coined phrases they wrap it, and do not approve of allowing an advocate to withdraw. On the other hand, there are the "stalwarts", those who are eager to convince themselves that they have burned behind them all the bridges which connected them with the follies of the liberals.

Heated discussions are going on constantly as to the right of the advocate to give up his client's case in the midst of the trial, if he becomes convinced of his client's guilt, just as the prosecutor may do if he is convinced of the weakness of the prosecution. Says one side: "A court is not a theatre" where the actor must perform, play his part to the bitter end; instead of trying to becloud the issues, "the advocate, as the court's assistant, should honestly state his opinion * * * ",[111] and thus refuse to defend. Not at all, argues the other side, the advocate

[110]Code, 1927, section 306.

[111]Yul. Elkin and Wl. Kaufman, *The Weekly,* No. 23, 1925, page 845.

must remain as a defender. While he must not try to falsify, he must give his conclusions, in other words, point to what the defense has brought out.[112] The tendency is, however, clearly drifting towards the novel and unheard-of doctrine, which permits defense counsel to desert his client, and thus openly admit his guilt, in the midst of the trial. A recent regulation made by the Commissariat of Justice aims "to legalize the right of the advocate to refuse to defend his client at the trial."[113] While a decision of the Commissariat which is in the nature of new legislation must go through the regular legislative channels, the All-Russian Central Executive Committee or its presidium, or sometimes only the Soviet of the People's Commissars, before it becomes law, this decision is convincingly indicative of the trend of opinion in the matter.

As we have already learned, immediately after the defendant has had his final word, the court retires to the consulting chamber to deliberate on a verdict.

IV. THE VERDICT

a. *Deliberation*

The minute and painstaking judicial inquiry into the various phases and circumstances of the case is, after all, a mere prelude to the ultimate goal, the disposition of the case in accordance with its intrinsic merits—rendering a verdict or a judgment.

The three judges composing the court are the only persons to deliberate on the outcome of the case. The law specifically provides that no one except the judges who tried the case may be present in the consulting chamber.[114] The court, in analyzing the testimony of the case, must base its verdict exclusively upon the data obtained and examined during the judicial inquiry[115] in open court. But in weighing the force and truthfulness of each piece of evidence presented, as well as in judging the facts of the case, looking at all the circumstances as a whole, the court is guided by its own "inner convictions". As the three judges

[112] Al. Levin, *The Weekly*, No. 35, 1925, page 1163.
[113] *The Weekly*, No. 26, 1928, page 749.
[114] Code, 1927, section 317.
[115] *Ibid.*, section 319.

perform the functions of our judge and jury combined, they are also to take up and determine the question of insanity, if it was raised either at the preliminary inquiry or at the trial itself, even though such question may have been decided previously at the administrative session of the court;[116] provided, of course, such session has declared the accused sane, for otherwise the case would not have come up for trial. Should the court decide that the defendant was insane when he committed the alleged criminal act, or that he has become incurably insane afterwards, any further deliberation as to guilt or innocence becomes unnecessary. But the court may still proceed to deliberate and to determine whether any measure of social protection, such as placing the defendant in an institution, etc., should be adopted.[117] If no question of insanity has been raised, or, if raised, is resolved against the defendant, the court must deliberate on the merits of the case.

b. *Method of arriving at Verdict*

The Code is very specific in describing the procedure by which the court reaches its decision. The judges have to determine the following questions: (1) Did the acts with which the defendant is charged take place? (2) Do these acts contain the elements of a crime? (3) Were they committed by the defendant? (4) Should the defendant be subjected to a measure of social protection—punishment—for such an action?[118] There may frequently occur instances where, though the first three questions are answered in the affirmative, the defendant would still not be subject to any punishment, as when he acted neither intentionally nor negligently, or where the rule of remoteness (statute of limitation) applies,[119] etc.[120]

[116] *Ibid.*, section 321.

[117] *Ibid.*, section 322.

[118] *Ibid.*, section 320, subsections 1, 2, 3 and 4.

[119] Cr. Code, 1926, section 14.

[120] *Commentaries*, page 315. It would seem an obvious inconsistency to say that an act has all the elements of a crime and yet is not subject to punishment because it was not committed wilfully or negligently. Apparently by an element of a crime is meant certain acts forbidden by a specific section of the Criminal Code. On the other hand the same Code, section 10, provides that no "measure of social protection" is to be applied unless the person "acted wilfully, *i. e.*, he has foreseen the socially dangerous nature

After all the four questions are answered in the affirmative, the next questions for deliberation are: (5) The exact nature of the punishment to be meted out to the defendant, and whether he has still to serve it, for a decree of amnesty may perhaps apply to the case, or the sentence may not perhaps be for a longer period than that which the defendant has already served in jail during the preliminary inquiry. (6) Is the civil claim to be granted, or, if such claim has not been filed, is the court to adopt any measure to ensure the satisfaction of a possible subsequent civil judgment? (7) What is to be done with the articles of evidence obtained during the inquiry? (8) Who is to pay the legal costs?[121] The question of legal costs, including the compensation paid to witnesses, experts, interpreters, as well as expenses incurred in storing, transporting and examining articles of evidence,[122] is settled in the verdict in a general way, by a mere statement as to the person who is to pay them, and the details are worked out later at the administrative session of the court.[123] Whenever the defendant is found guilty he must, as a general rule, pay the legal costs,[124] unless he is financially unable to do so, in which case the state will pay all the expenses incurred.[125]

The questions enumerated above are, after due deliberation, presented by the presiding judge in the order described, and they are framed so that a simple answer of yes or no will be possible.[126] Each of the three judges must participate and vote; the majority decides in the name of the court, while the dissenting judge has a right to attach to the verdict his written opinion.[127] This serves not only the purpose of allowing the dissenting judge to express his personal view, but it may carry great weight should the case be taken to the court of cassation.

of the result of his acts, desired these results or consciously permitted their realization". A somewhat similar definition we find with regard to criminal negligence.

[121]Code, 1927, section 320, subsections 5, 6, 7 and 8.

[122]*Ibid.*, section 88.

[123]*Ibid.*, section 332.

[124]*Ibid.*, section 89.

[125]*Ibid.*, section 90.

[126]*Ibid.*, section 323.

[127]*Ibid.*, sections 324 and 325.

c. *Contents of the Verdict*

After all these questions are voted on and settled the court must draw up its formal verdict which consists of two parts—one, the descriptive, the other the determinative.[128] Immediately following the latter part the verdict must state he time and manner for filing a cassational complaint.[129] As the result of all the proceedings are, in the last analysis, reflected in the verdict, the law is very specific as to its form and contents.

The Code provides: "The descriptive part of the verdict shall consist of a formulation of the accusatory charges of which the defendant was either exonerated or convicted. It must also state the christian name, surname, or nickname of the defendant, his age, social position and the class to which he belongs [that is, worker, peasant, clerk, professional man, etc.], the name and description of the injured party, the place and time of the offense, and the means by which it was accomplished, likewise, other outstanding characteristics or circumstances of the case."

"The determinative part of the verdict must consist of a statement as to the name and description of the defendant, the fact of his acquittal or conviction, and the particular punishment imposed by the court.[130]

As the language of the Code clearly indicates, the verdict is not a mere pronouncement of guilt or innocence. The first part, the descriptive, presents the factual aspect of the case. The court is required to describe in a clear, concrete form the happening of certain events which show precisely and accurately the nature of the crime, and the circumstances under which it was committed. No general legal terms will satisfy these requirements, which are rigidly enforced by the cassational courts. Thus, a mere statement in the descriptive part of the verdict that A killed B out of venal motives, or that X was bribed, etc. are considered mere legal conclusions and will not suffice. Such a verdict will be considered defective, and reversible on cassa-

[128] *Ibid.*, section 333. Before the amendments of 1929, the accusatory conclusion was also divided in two such parts, but this was abolished by the amendments. With regard to the verdict, however, the division was left.

[129] *Ibid.*, section 336.

[130] *Ibid.*, section 334.

tion.[131] This descriptive part corresponds, roughly speaking, to the finding of a special verdict by our jury,[132] though the Soviet system does not draw any line between the authority to find facts and to pass on the law.

The determinative part of the verdict, on the other hand, is the decision of the court based upon what was brought out in the first part of the verdict, and resembles somewhat, at least in character, the sentence imposed by judges in our criminal courts. "The determinative part * * * is a continuation of the descriptive part in the language of the appropriate section of the criminal law."[133] The sentence must be stated with clearness and precision in order that no doubt as to its exact meaning can possibly arise when it will have to be executed.

d. *Discretion of the court*

In imposing the sentence, the court exercises great discretionary powers and may effectively reduce their own sentence. If it does so, it must state the grounds for its leniency.[134] This requirement is of great importance since the prosecutor may file a protest in the court of cassation against what he regards as an insufficient sentence. The record of the case should, therefore, indicate on its face the reasons of the trial court for taking a generous attitude towards the defendant. But the trial court has no power, as it once had at an earlier period of the Soviet régime, to suspend the sentence completely. Should the court be convinced, from the circumstances of the particular case, that justice requires that the defendant should not serve his sentence, it may petition the presidium of the All-Russian Central Executive Committee to suspend the sentence.[135]

[131] *Commentaries,* page 325.

[132] *Ibid.*, page 326.

[133] Supreme Court Letters of Instruction, No. 1, 1926, *The Weekly,* No. 8, 1926.

[134] Code, 1927, section 335. In one of the trials the writer had attended, a woman was sentenced to six months' imprisonment for insulting a police officer when the latter attempted to perform his duty. But the verdict or sentence stated: "Taking into consideration that she, the defendant, was never before on trial, and that her four small children are dependent upon her for their support, etc., the court has found it possible to reduce the sentence to a fine of five rubles" ($2.50).

[135] *Ibid.*, section 326, subsection 3.

The verdict reached by the judges, or at least by a majority of them, is, without any interruption or recess, reduced to writing by one of the judges, signed by all of them, and immediately taken into open court where the permanent, or presiding, judge reads the entire, often very lengthy, writing in the name of the R.S.F.S.R. During the reading all persons present in the courtroom, not excluding the judges, must rise and remain standing.[136] (This ceremony takes place whenever the court enters or retires.)

e. *The Defendant's Status after Verdict*

1. In Case of Acquittal

Whenever there is an acquittal, or when the defendant is released from serving the sentence, the presiding judge after reading the verdict immediately declares him free, and any measure which might have been previously adopted to assure his attendance must be forthwith lifted.[137] This is a rather remarkable provision in favor of the defendant, since he thus gains his liberty before the verdict becomes legally binding. (The legal meaning of this term will be discussed presently.) The favorable verdict may yet be upset by the procurator's cassational protest.

2. In Case of Conviction

Should a verdict of guilty be brought in, the court determines the necessary measure to secure the defendant's appearance in accordance with the general rule. The defendant does not begin to serve his sentence before the verdict becomes legally effective, which takes place only after the expiration of the fixed period in which cassation may be taken and no complaint (appeal) is made; in cases in which a cassational complaint or protest is brought, the verdict becomes legally binding on the date when the cassational court sustains or dismisses the complaint or protest.[138]

f. *Verdict Rendered in the Absence of the Defendant*

We have been dealing here with the usual case where the verdict is rendered in the presence of the defendant, or where,

[136] *Ibid.*, sections 337, 338, 339.
[137] *Ibid.*, section 340.
[138] *Ibid.*, sections 341 and 342.

though the latter's presence was required, he had failed to appear by evading the service of the summons or by absconding, or where he had so misbehaved at the trial that he was expelled. But we encounter quite a different situation in those cases where the presence of the defendant is not obligatory. It is the latter situation which results in what is known as the "verdict in the absence of the defendant" *(Zaochni Prigovor)*. Such verdicts are naturally rendered in minor cases which, as we know, involve a sentence of either a fine or forced labor without imprisonment.

A copy of a verdict rendered in the absence of the defendant must be served on him not later than three days after its rendition. To this paper must also be attached all the necessary information with regard to the time and manner of filing either a complaint against the verdict or a petition for a rehearing of the case.[139] Though the court was permitted to try the case in the absence of the defendant, the latter may, within seven days from the date he receives the official transcript of the verdict, petition the same court for a new trial, stating the reasons for his absence. (We may note that this is the only ground on which the trial court may be asked to grant a new trial.) The court must act on the petition within three days. If it finds the reasons for the defendant's absence well taken, a new trial will be granted, or, if the contrary is true, the petition will be dismissed. In the latter instance, the defendant may appeal from the dismissal only in conjunction with the filing of a cassational complaint against the verdict itself. The complaint may be taken by the defendant within seven days from the time he is notified that his petition has been refused. The right to bring a cassational complaint against the verdict itself is, naturally, in no way affected by the defendant's failure to petition for a retrial.[140]

V. SUMMARY PROCEEDINGS AT THE PEOPLE'S COURT

In our discussion of the trial proceedings at the people's court, we have seen that the power to render a verdict and impose a sentence may be exercised only after an elaborate and exhaustive judicial inquiry. But while this is the general rule,

[139] *Ibid.*, section 352.
[140] *Ibid.*, sections 353-357 and 359.

there are a number of exceptions in which the people's court imposes valid sentences without the prior investigations which give to Soviet criminal procedure its characteristic inquisitorial tinge. These exceptional cases are disposed of, and verdicts rendered, either by the court, consisting of three judges, or by the people's judge himself.

a. *By the Court*

The court may impose a punishment without any prior proceedings whatsoever upon a witness or expert[141] who either fails to appear in court, without good reasons, when subpoenaed by the latter, or refuses to answer questions put to him by the court or by any one who has a right to interrogate.[142] A similar authority is given to the court to impose a fine, or imprisonment for a term not exceeding two weeks, upon any person—except the defendant, the procurator or the advocate—who violates the orders of the court during the trial.[143] Neither the fine nor the short term of imprisonment is subject to any cassational complaint, though it may be reversed by way of supervision.[144]

In this connection we might mention the proceedings which take place at the specific branch of the people's court, known as the "waiting court". This court, the functions of which we have discussed elsewhere,[145] has not become widespread, and in some sections of the country it is a thing unknown. The peculiarities of this court are that it disposes of simple, clear cases which do not require any investigation soon after the criminal act has occurred. Among the particular offenses to be tried at such courts, according to a circular issued jointly by the Commissariat of Justice and the Commissariat of the Interior,[146] are those involving street hooliganism and bootlegging (which consists of selling legitimate *vodka* above the fixed price), assigned to this

[141]The Code, sections 60 and 64, speaks of punishment. But section 92 of the Cr. Code, 1926, provides a sentence of either forced labor up to 3 months or a fine not to exceed 100 rubles. Section 93 of the Cr. Code provides a fine of 500 rubles in the case of expert witnesses.

[142]Code, 1927, sections 60, 62 and 64.

[143]*Ibid.*, section 261.

[144]*Ibid.*, section 347.

[145]See *supra*, page 59.

[146]Collected Circulars of the People's Commissariat of Justice, No. 252, page 277, 1925.

court as a means of speedily and effectively stamping out the apparent increase of such offenses. By another circular the Commissariat of Justice instructed the court, or the permanent people's judge, to proceed with holding the accused for trial in these cases, as they may do in any case which comes directly before them, and immediately thereafter proceed to try the defendant, providing they have all the necessary data.[147]

b. *By the Individual Judge*

The people's judge, individually, has the power to dispose of certain cases by way of judicial order. The law singles out a number of offenses in specific sections of the Criminal Code, which, from their very nature, may be quickly disposed of by the people's judge sitting alone. These are simple violations of rules and regulations, such as using radio service without a subscription or in violation of its terms, violating the rules with regard to putting out printed matter, or acting contrary to the regulations of the cinematographic censors, keeping of certain books and documents without paying the stamp tax, knowingly giving false information to officials when registering certain commercial, tenant, or other societies, and a few more violations of a similar nature. But to justify a judicial order it is absolutely required that the "violation be clearly indisputable".[148] None of these violations or offenses, as we may recall, is punishable by more than three months' forced labor without imprisonment or a fine exceeding three hundred rubles ($150).

There is, however, a marked tendency in Soviet Russia today to extend the jurisdiction of the single people's judge to a greater variety of simple cases, especially to those of a private nature.[149] The Ukrainian Code of Criminal Procedure of 1927 made quite a headway in that direction.[150]

c. *The Judicial Orders*

The summary nature of the judicial orders, as they are called, is obvious. They are handed down even without the sum-

[147]*Ibid.*, Circular No. 11, 1926, page 194.

[148]Code, 1927, section 366.

[149]The project for a new Code of Criminal Procedure, section 71 enumerates eight different crimes and violations subject to the jurisdiction of a single people's judge sitting alone.

[150]Ukrainian Code of Criminal Procedure, 1927, section 26.

moning of the parties, but the prosecutor and the defendant may appear and explain their positions, if they wish to do so. It is correctly pointed out[151] that a judicial order is conceivable only in the form of a conviction, because if the violation for which the defendant was brought before the judge could be disputed or doubted, the case could not be disposed of in this summary manner.

As explained in a special circular issued by the Commissariat of Justice, these judicial orders or sentences may not be made later than two weeks from the date the case was forwarded to the court and not later than one month from the day the alleged offense took place.[152] Other characteristics of such an order are that it must not be issued in any case to which a civil claim is attached, and, unlike verdicts issued in the regular manner, it becomes legally binding immediately, though it is subject to an appeal within fourteen days to the provincial, regional or circuit court, as the case may be. Where such an appeal is filed, the people's judge may, on petition of the defendant, stay the execution of the order until a higher court renders its decision. But before such a stay is granted, the judge in his own discretion may demand of the defendant security to ensure his carrying out of the order if the appeal should be dismissed.[153]

The rights of the defendant in these cases have been narrowed by amendments. By the earlier codes the defendant, after the order was issued, had three days in which to petition the same people's court for a regular trial. The judge who received such a request within the period of time fixed was to place the case on the regular trial list.[154]

As the order may be carried by way of cassation to a higher court, it must contain the name of the defendant, his age, the exact offense charged against him, the time and manner of its

[151]*Commentaries*, page 342.

[152]The Circular of the Commissariat of Justice, No. 51 for 1922 is quoted in part in the *Commentaries*, page 344, which state that only those parts of the Circular which have not lost their value are given. However, in the Collected Circulars for 1926, page 332, the above mentioned Circular of 1922 is noted among those which were either repealed or had lost their significance.

[153]Code, 1927, sections 370 and 371.

[154]Code, 1922, sections 410 and 411, and the original Code of 1923, sections 370 and 371.

commission, the particular section of the Criminal Code applicable, and the nature of the punishment inflicted.[155]

B. Trial at the Provincial Court[156]

1. General Characteristics

The provincial court (or the regional and circuit court when they take the place of the provincial)[157] as a court of original jurisdiction is, as we know, the direct heir of the defunct revolutionary tribunal. It is, therefore, not at all surprising to find the characteristics of the latter, such as rigidity and the extensive discretionary powers vested in the judges, reflected in the provincial court.

Although the judicial division of the provincial court, which is generally called the provincial court, handles less than ten per cent of all the criminal cases, and the tendency to narrow the scope of its original jurisdiction is steadily growing, the fact remains that most of the important, complicated criminal cases are tried at the provincial, regional or circuit courts.

We shall not have to discuss here every step in the trial proceedings at the provincial court, for the law provides that "The procedure in the provincial court shall be governed by the rules laid down for the procedure in the people's court, with the exceptions hereinafter mentioned.[158]

To be sure, the exceptions which will be presently discussed are not numerous, but they contain such strikingly significant features as sufficiently to change some of the fundamental principles governing the procedure at the people's court. What then, is the nature of those exceptions which differentiate the proceedings at the provincial court from those of the people's court described above? Let us now analyze each stage at the trial separately.

155 Code, 1927, section 368.

156 The term provincial court is used here to cover a certain *type* of a court. Therefore whenever the word provincial court is used, it necessarily includes the circuit, regional and similiar courts wherever these operate instead of the provincial court. In fact as the new rearrangement of the administrative units in continuing to spread, the provinces as units are being gradually abolished, and the smaller unit of the circuit take their place.

157 The Jud. Act, 1926, section 2.

158 Code, 1927, section 380.

II. PREPARATION FOR TRIAL

a. *Powers of the Administrative Session*

Unlike the procedure at the people's court, all cases tried at the provincial court had to, before the amendments of 1929, be taken up preliminarily at the administrative session of the court, where the question of dismissing the case or holding the accused for trial was decided. Thus, even those cases which, though subject to the jurisdiction of the provincial, regional or circuit court, did not require a preliminary inquiry, and therefore reached the court on the inquisitor's decision to hold for trial, could, nevertheless, not be placed on trial before the administrative session had decided their fate even though the formal holding for trial by the inquisitor had already taken place. Where a preliminary inquiry had been held, before reaching any decision to affirm the charge and hold the accused for trial, the court had to listen to the conclusion reached by the procurator[159] who had to be present at each administrative session of the provincial court. The administrative session of the people's court, on the other hand, had to deliberate on the case as a whole after the procurator had confirmed the inquisitor's accusatory conclusion—in other words, when the case had gone through a preliminary inquiry, which but few of the cases tried at the people's court do, and also before the defendant had been formally held for trial. To what extent the Amendments of 1929 have modified this procedure is a matter of conjecture. The section of the Code providing that every case under the jurisdiction of the provincial court must, before being put on the trial list, be deliberated upon at the administrative session of the court was left unchanged. But the sections of the Code affected by the Amendments would by inference seem to indicate that the administrative session will deliberate on a case in certain circumstances only.

1. Preparing List of Witnesses

At the administrative session of the provincial court the question of preparing the list of witnesses and experts who are to appear at the trial is determined. The discretionary power given to the court in this connection is startling. It may decide

[159] *Ibid.*, section 390.

not to subpoena witnesses examined at the preliminary inquiry, if the truthfulness of their testimony does not raise any doubt, although all persons examined at the preliminary inquiry must be summoned to the trial whenever their testimony which has a bearing on the cases is incomplete, or was contradicted by the testimony of other witnesses.[160] Notwithstanding the stipulations tending somewhat to temper this harsh rule, the fact remains that the administrative session may (even assuming that this will rarely happen) take for granted certain testimony adduced by the inquisitor without verifying it at the judicial inquiry in open court, and without subjecting the witnesses to cross-examination by the defendant or by anyone else. It is one of the rules adopted in order to speed up and simplify the procedure at the provincial court which are deemed necessary in fighting dangerous crimes. The Supreme Court in one of its letters of instruction[161] to the courts pointed out that while methods are provided for cutting short certain formalities in a given case, they should, however, be applied only where they will not interfere with the proper disposition of the case and the possibility of eliciting the truth. The courts are, therefore, urged to pay careful and thoughtful attention in appraising the circumstances of each case before they may determine to make use of their power to limit the number of witnesses and other powers of a similar nature. Any abuse by the court of its own discretionary powers will result in a reversal of the verdict.[162]

2. Participation of Prosecution and Defense

Another matter of great importance to be decided at the administrative session is the question of the participation of the procuracy and defense counsel at the trial. While in the people's court the defendant may engage counsel as a matter of right, in cases tried at the provincial court, the defendant is deprived of such an absolute right. The law states that "The participation of prosecution and defense in cases tried at the provincial court shall not be obligatory; the administrative ses-

[160] *Ibid.*, section 391.

[161] Letter of Instruction of the Supreme Court of the R.S.F.S.R., No. 2, *The Weekly*, 1925, Nos. 31 and 32.

[162] Supreme Court Decisions for 1925, Case No. 27304, Moscow, 1926.

sion of the court shall decide this for each case separately, taking into consideration the complexity of the case, the quantum of evidence tending to prove guilt, or the peculiar political or social nature of the case. The court, however, must permit or appoint an advocate whenever the prosecution is allowed to participate."[163]

Here again the court is vested with a dangerously sweeping, almost unbridled discretionary power in a matter touching gravely upon the interest of the defendant. The extent to which the courts are to avail themselves of this tremendous power is a matter of speculation. It is said that the courts are not to exercise this power too freely, and should not deprive themselves of the valuable assistance of the prosecutor and the advocate except in extraordinary cases.[164] A similar interpretation is given by the Supreme Court in its above-cited letter of instructions which bids the courts to be very cautious in trying a case without defense and prosecution, especially where the defendant "is illiterate, or timid, or is clearly incapable of coping with the circumstances of the case and defending his interest."[165] While the attitude taken by the higher court may lessen the apparent evil of the rule, nevertheless, the inherent danger of such power is too obvious to require any elaboration.

In line with the provision just discussed, the provincial court may reject any person as counsel, though such person is qualified to act, as for example, when he is a member of the college of advocates, whenever the court "recognizes" that the particular person is not fit to appear in the case[166] (usually for political reasons). We must remember that this rule is applicable where the defendant has a right to have counsel, as when the prosecution is participating in the case, or whenever the court has permitted the defendant to have an advocate.

These are the important features which distinguish the proceedings preparatory to the trial at the provincial court from those

[163]Code, 1927, section 381. There can be no private prosecution at the provincial court. The citation, therefore, must refer only to the procuracy.

[164]*Commentaries*, page 352.

[165]See *supra*, note 161.

[166]Code, 1927, section 382.

at the people's court. We might also point out that while the permanent people's judge has a number of functions to perform during the stage of the proceedings under discussion, the provincial judge, acting alone, has none. All other matters, such as jurisdiction, venue, publicity of the trial, civil claims, etc., discussed in connection with the trial at the people's court, are applicable here with one additional exception. In the provincial court the trial may proceed without the presence of the defendant whenever the defendant is out of the territory of the R.S.F.S.R.[167] The application of this rule is, however, of very rare occurrence.[168]

III. PROCEDURE AT THE TRIAL

While the various rules of procedure prescribed for the trial at the people's court are applicable here, there are four important, outstanding exceptions which profoundly distinguish the trial at the provincial court.

a. *Discontinuance of the Examination*

The law provides that "The court shall have the power to discontinue the examination of a witness or witnesses at any moment during their interrogation, provided it recognizes that the testimony of the witnesses already examined has fully brought out the circumstances which the other witnesses summoned were to establish."[169] This harsh rule has been interpreted by the commentators on the Code,[170] in the light of their activities at the Cassational Department of the Supreme Court, to mean that the court, exercising its discretionary power, may discontinue the further examination of witnesses only in a very clear, indisputable case, and even then, only with regard to witnesses who have not yet taken the witness stand, and that once a witness has been called to testify, he must be fully and completely interrogated by all parties concerned. The explicit language of the section stating that the rights to discontinue the examina-

[167] *Ibid.*, section 393.
[168] *Commentaries*, page 359.
[169] Code, 1927, section 394.
[170] *Commentaries*, page 362.

tion of a witness may take place "at any given moment" is declared to be merely an unhappy phrasing, an oversight on the part of the editors.[171] There is also no doubt that any failure of the court to exercise its discretion within the proper bounds will result in a reversal of the verdict by the Cassational Department of the Supreme Court. This may happen in a case where five witnesses were thoroughly examined.[172]

b. *Completion of the Case*

As the aim of the legislators in creating the provincial court was to accomplish a "speedy repression of crime"[173] the court must endeavor to clear up the matter before it during the judicial inquiry. Unlike the people's court, which may, without any restrictions, send back the case for a preliminary inquiry or investigation, the provincial court is forbidden to send the case on trial back to the inquisitor, except in those instances "when the provincial court shall establish such an incompleteness of the testimony as can in no way be remedied during this judicial session."[174] In the latter instance the court must render a decision to that effect, stating its reasons for so doing.

c. *Introducing Evidence of Pre-Trial Proceedings*

The court may, on its own motion or at the request of the parties, read documents that have already been attached to the case or may attach new ones presented, and may "make public"—that is, read at the trial session—the testimony of the witnesses at the preliminary inquiry or investigation, whether or not they have been summoned to the trial. In the same way the testimony of the defendant at the preliminary inquiry or investigation may be made public at the trial.[175] Here the court is vested with great discretionary power without being bound by any prerequisite condition as is the case in the people's court.

In line with the above rule the Code states that "The parties shall have a right during their final arguments to rely upon all

[171] *Ibid.*, page 360.
[172] Supreme Court Reports for 1926 (January-April) Case No. 22419, and Supreme Court Reports for 1925, Case No. 212954.
[173] *Commentaries*, page 364.
[174] Code, 1927, section 398.
[175] *Ibid.*, section 395.

the testimony and documents in the case, irrespective of whether or not they were made public during the trial."[176] This rule is necessary since the court may decide not to summon certain witnesses who testified at the preliminary inquiry. Nevertheless, such testimony being a matter of record, the parties may well avail themselves of it to the advantage of their cause.

d. *Final Arguments*

The parties do not have an absolute right to make final arguments in a trial at the provincial court, for the Code stipulates that "The provincial court shall have the power to disallow the final arguments of the parties if it thinks the case has been made sufficiently clear during the judicial inquiry, irrespective of the fact that the court has previously decided to permit the parties [the prosecutor and the advocate] to participate in the proceedings of the trial."[177] Here the theory, or the fiction, that the prosecutor and the advocate are nothing more than assistants to the court is brought to its logical, even if absurd, conclusion. Since the final arguments are, according to this theory, a mere device by which the court may be assisted in straightening out some complicated matters they become utterly unnecessary, and therefore are to be discarded, whenever the court deems everything so clear as not to require the gratuitous service of its "assistants". It is quite in line with this rule for the court to allow the final arguments and then disallow the rebuttals, which apparently happens more often than the doing away with the arguments themselves.[178]

Let us note in passing that whatever the difference in *raison d'être* of these final arguments in Soviet procedure and in our own, the final speeches of the prosecutor and the advocate are similar to those heard in our own courts. The prosecutor

[176]*Ibid.*, section 396. It is interesting to note that at the revolutionary tribunals, which functioned before 1923, the same rule had existed. See Collected Laws, Nos. 22 and 23, Article 115, 1920, section 20.

[177]Code, 1927, section 397. (See also for a comparison, Collected Laws, Nos. 22 and 23, Article 115, 1920, section 20.)

[178]In the considerable number of trials which the writer had attended, while living in Soviet Russia, he had not observed that the court should discard the final arguments. But in one important case, rebuttals were not permitted, though the procurator privately told the writer that he thought he could rebut an important point at issue.

or counsel for the defense, however, in a Soviet court will rarely embark upon a vain attempt to appeal to the passions or prejudices of the three judges, as our own lawyers frequently appeal to the jury. But impassioned appeals on the one hand "to teach a lesson" to the defendant who by his act has undermined the discipline and shattered the stability of his co-workers, or, on the other hand, not to be too hard on the occasional sinner whose pedigree is worthy of consideration, his father, or even his grandfather, having been proletarian or peasant, are not unheard of.[179]

The right of the court to exclude final argument presents a very interesting question. Is the court also authorized to exclude, at its discretion, the final word of the defendant, who is always present even when the prosecutor and the advocate are barred. It would seem quite certain that though the rule speaks of *parties*, thus including also the defendant, it does not deprive the latter of his right to make a statement before the court retires to deliberate on a verdict. For, as we have observed, the final word of the defendant is not, strictly speaking, considered a part of the final arguments of the parties, but a separate and distinct proceeding which must always take place, if the defendant wishes. True, we have learned of this law with respect to the trial at the people's court. But it is applicable also to the proceedings at the provincial court, unless a different rule has been specifically provided. That such a conclusion is sound may be inferred from an analogy to the proceedings at the abolished revolutionary tribunals, where the judges, while possessing the power to eliminate the final argument of the parties, could not bar the final word of the defendant, according to the specific provisions of the law.[180]

IV. VERDICT AND JUDGMENT

There is only one possible instance where the regulations providing for the deliberation and rendition of the verdict by the people's court differ from those of the provincial court. The law provides that "The provincial court when rendering a verdict shall

[179]The writer had frequently heard such appeals made by the procurators and advocates, in their final arguments.

[180]Collected Laws, No. 13, Article 132, 1919, section 21, and Nos. 22 and 23, Article 115, 1920, section 21.

have the authority to take into consideration * * * documents and testimony irrespective of whether they have been made public at the judicial session."[181]

Here it is clear that the judges, when deliberating in the consulting chamber, rely on the *entire official record of the case,* while with regard to the people's court the question is still doubtful. The section of the Code which explicitly forbade the people's court to take cognizance of anything but the testimony made public at the trial was repealed. Enough was left, however, in other sections to warrant the conclusion that the rule expressed by the section repealed is still in force, especially since the different rule for the provincial court was inserted among the exceptions which distinguish the proceedings at the provincial, regional or circut courts from those at the people's court.

C. The Trial at the Supreme Court

I. JUDICIAL DEPARTMENT

The Supreme Court as a tribunal of original jurisdiction occupies a very insignificant place. As we have seen, its jurisdiction is of very restricted nature. This court, which began to function at the beginning of 1923, has decreased in significance as a trial court from year to year. Thus, while in 1923 it tried 411 cases out of a total of 12,820 criminal cases which reached the Supreme Court for all purposes, the number of cases of original jurisdiction dwindled during 1926 to only 36 out of a total of 19,731 criminal cases, thus giving its Judicial Department only 0.1/16% of the criminal cases that reached the Cassational Department.[182] During 1927 it tried only 7 cases.[183]

At present there is only one judge who is assigned to the Criminal Judicial Department, the only branch of the Supreme Court to figure as the highest court of original jurisdiction as against seventeen judges in the Cassational Department. This judge is a lonely figure in his "Department", without even a

[181] Code, 1927, section 396.

[182] Supreme Court—Department of Cassation—Decisions for 1926, Jud. Practice, No. 4, 1927, page 1.

[183] *Ibid.*, page 4.

regularly assigned staff at his disposal.[184] But whenever the Supreme Court does act as a court of original jurisdiction, all the rules and regulations that govern the proceedings at the provincial court are applicable.[185]

[184]This fact was told to the writer by the Deputy President of the Supreme Court.

[185]Code, 1927, section 448.

Chapter VIII

SOME OUTSTANDING CHARACTERISTICS OF THE SOVIET TRIAL

After the detailed discussion of the proceedings at the trial, we may indulge in a more scrutinizing analysis of the outstanding features and peculiarities that are characteristic of the Soviet criminal trial.

To begin with, let us examine the general fundamental theory, or theories, upon which the trial is founded, as this should help us in our endeavor to appreciate its peculiar traits. What, then, are those basic principles, and in what respect do they differ from the basic ideas behind the modern western criminal trial?

I. FUNDAMENTAL PRINCIPLES GOVERING THE SOVIET TRIAL

a. *The Contest Theory*

The Anglo-American theory of the criminal trial, as well as that prevalent in Europe, is termed the "contest theory" by Soviet, as well as Russian non-Soviet, legal writers. By this is meant "a form of trial proceedings in which the government takes on itself the burden of proving to the court or the jury, as the case may be, the fact of the commission of the crime by the defendant on trial. The defendant is given an opportunity to disprove the accusation openly and publicly, the presumption being that he did not commit the crime charged until the prosecution has proved the contrary. This is the basic principle of the trial. In addition the defendant has equal rights with the prosecution."[1] As a legal consequence of such a theory the rule of participation of defense counsel on equal terms with the prosecution follows.[2] As this is, roughly speaking, a fair statement of the principles upon which our own criminal trial rests, the question is: Does the Soviet system repudiate this basic idea, and if so, to what extent?

[1]Krylenko, *The Judiciary and the Law*, 1928, page 93.
[2]*Ibid.*, page 93.

This undoubtedly interesting problem has been discussed by Soviet legal writers innumerable times, but neither with harmonious approach nor with unanimity of conclusion. While here and there words are spoken or written which would indicate a complete rejection of the "theory of contest" with all its connotations,[3] as something reared in the "bourgeois world," a conclusion that such is the general attitude would be wholly erroneous. One would rather be led to believe, after examining what has been said and written on the subject as a whole, that the fundamental theories of trial by contest have been incorporated into the Soviet system, not, however, without important modifications, as we shall presently see.

During an unusually interesting discussion on the merits of a proposed draft for a new code of criminal procedure,[4] arranged by the department of law and government at the Communist Academy (a university), one of the outstanding Soviet legal writers, A. Ya. Estrin, speaking for the faculty said: "Such fundamentals as personal liberty, and the directness, publicity and the oral method of the trial, and the right [of the defendant] to have an advocate are in their essence democratic and cultural attainments which we have to recognize, among a number of other cultural achievements, even in a class government of the proletariat, *i. e.*, in a proletarian democracy as a democracy of a higher order, rejecting, however, all which is unnecessary, harmful, and contrary to the interest of the toiling masses."[5] This statement is highly illuminating, for it reveals with amazing clearness the difficulties under which the Soviet legal theorists are laboring. Here A. Ya. Estrin starts out with a clear-cut proposition pointing to the acceptability to the Soviet legal system of a certain set of fundamental principles. But before we have finished his statement, we find that it winds up with "rejecting, however, etc.", and thus we are left to grope in the darkness of

[3]The deputy president of the Moscow Provincial Court said to the writer in an interview: "We reject the theory of a trial by contest because it is grounded in bartering, in market morals and tactics. We want the court and not the parties to try the case."

[4]This project which was based upon the thesis of Krylenko, published in *The Weekly*, No. 47, 1927, was later dropped. A new project was drafted by a special commission and published in the above mentioned journal, Nos. 28 and 29, 1928.

[5]*The Weekly*, No. 4, 1928, page 115.

the Soviet legal labyrinth, without any light as to where the speaker for the academy really stands. For to reconcile both parts of the statement is not an easy task. To begin with a straight adherence to certain fundamental principles and then provide for sweeping exceptions to them is repugnant in its very terms as well as inconceivable in theory. Fundamentals are accepted in order that they may serve as guides under all circumstances. The moment we may deviate from them under the guise of vaguely phrased conditions, which we ourselves are to designate at any time in order to determine what constitutes uselessness, harmfulness, etc., we are no longer guided by those fundamental principles; at least they cease to be fundamental or basic.

Such inconsistencies on the part of Soviet legal writers are to be found again and again. For example, we read: "The attempt to shorten and simplify our [criminal] procedure at the price of removing from it the basic ideas of a contest, must be recognized as rooted in a fallacy." This is unequivocal. But only a few lines below, in the same report, the speaker is quoted as saying: "The trial at the people's court, as a rule, and the trial at the provincial court to a *considerable extent* ought to be built on the basis of a 'contest' ".[6] (Italics are added.) If even in the name of the most cherished desire "to speed up and simplify the trial" these principles are not to be discarded, why, one may ask, are reservations made with regard to the provincial court; is not the same charge of a fallacy applicable when referring to the trial at the latter court? But here we are approaching another problem—namely, the different attitude taken toward the two separate types of courts, a problem to which we shall soon return.

Similar contradictions are encountered in studying the utterances and writings of other Soviet legal theorists. Even N. V. Krylenko, who always makes the most unrelenting attacks upon the weaklings who still cling to legal theories and doctrines steeped in the bourgeois point of view, has been accused by a colleague of flirting with this bourgeois theory, for while he has rejected the theory of a "contest he is nevertheless still in the thralls of that theory."[7] This accusation has undoubtedly more

[6]*Ibid.*

[7]Prushitzkii, *The Weekly,* No. 4, 1928, page 118. It is a quotation from his speech at the debate mentioned.

than a grain of truth in it. For Krylenko really adopts the contest doctrine, though he laboriously tries to explain away all that is repugnant to him. Thus he finds that "The essence of the doctrine of a trial by contest is not grounded in the fact that there is a prosecutor and an advocate who are unavoidably to argue against each other. The defendant appears as a party at the trial and states that you, the state, must prove the accusation. Inasmuch as trial technique has established that the best methods for bringing out the material truth, independent of the general political significance of the case, are the directness of the process, the publicity and the oral method of the trial, as well as the extension to the defendant of certain rights, these may be accepted as the embodiment of the essence of the contest."[8]

To have defense counsel as of right, however, is, Krylenko contends, not necessarily a part of the contest, for the party to the conflict is the defendant himself. "The right to have an advocate, as a right to have a specific representative who would replace the defendant himself * * * is not a part of that cultural achievement which we have to safeguard absolutely at the present moment."[9] Thus Krylenko while adopting some of the fundamental features of the contest doctrine in the same breath rejects this important, integral element of the same doctrine, as well as others. He, moreover, maintains that "the basic theory of the [Soviet criminal] trial must be a rejection of the principles of contest as taken in its pure form".[10] His ardent ire against the "pure form" is mainly directed against the doctrine requiring the compulsory participation of defense counsel, which leads inevitably to the "assumption beforehand that one of the parties [usually the advocate for the defense] will necessarily have to lie, *i. e., hide from the court the material truth,* and thus diminish the power of self-defense of society."[11] Such a situation is deemed plainly anti-social. While the defendant is permitted indirectly to lie to the court, since he is not subject to any punishment therefor, it is a personal privilege which he cannot delegate to his counsel who is—so the argument runs—a stranger

[8]*The Weekly,* No. 4, 1928, page 119.
[9]*Ibid.*
[10]Krylenko, *The Judiciary and the Law,* 1928, page 93.
[11]*Ibid.*

to the contest, and therefore should be jailed if he attempts to do likewise, for "he [the advocate] is to assist the court and not figure as its opponent; wherefore he cannot have the right knowingly to conceal the truth from the court."[12]

There is, to be sure, no specific law which clearly rejects the principle of representation by counsel or, to be more exact, the right of the defendant to have counsel who, in a sense, is a substitute for the defendant at the trial and enjoys the latter's rights. Nevertheless, the expressions of the writers above quoted as to what the law should be are significant as well as helpful in explaining some features of the trial proceedings. Even Soviet legal writers who maintain and, we think, correctly that the contest theory of the criminal trial is to be retained not only for its technical usefulness "but as a matter of principle and of policy"[13] arguing that "the trial by contest is a judicial conception",[14] concede, however, that under certain conditions the court may eliminate the participation of defense counsel.[15] This is in full harmony with the views held by Mr. Krylenko, who is the exponent of the doctrine that the court must have the power to say to the defendant: "I must under certain conditions deprive you of this right [to have an advocate] without, however, disturbing the basic rules as to the publicity and the oral process of the trial."[16]

b. *Rights of the Defendant*

Behind all the discussions in respect to the theory upon which the trial is based lies the unavoidable question of the extent of the rights of the defendant—a problem clearly interwoven with the very functions of a trial court.

As the Soviet political system unequivocally repudiates any theory of government based upon a division of powers for purposes of checking and balancing each other, the judiciary is naturally converted into merely one inseparable part of the entire governmental machinery. The court, therefore, functions not as an impartial arbiter between the state and its individual citizen;

[12]*Ibid.*, page 94.
[13]A. Ya. Estrin, *The Weekly*, No. 2, 1928, page 46.
[14]*The Weekly*, No. 4, 1928, page 115.
[15]*Ibid.*, page 118.
[16]*Ibid.*, page 119.

on the contrary, being an integral part of the functioning apparatus of the state, it is charged with the duty of carrying out the latter's general policies. The trial court must consequently have in view not "only the judicial purposes, but also the general aims of the collective and the state, the working class as a whole, and must have the power to sacrifice the interest of the individual."[17] The trial, to be sure, must be organized so as to secure a maximum of efficaciousness in establishing the true facts, but there is always "the presumption that in all instances *the interests of the whole,* the duty *to safeguard* the social order, are to be the decisive criterion * * * ."[18]

While the above quotations are the expressed opinions of only one conspicuous figure within the Soviet judiciary, they are undoubtedly a correct exposition of the spirit which permeates the entire Soviet legal system. This anti-individualistic point of view, the conscious rejection of any doctrine of inalienable rights of the individual citizen, must be borne in mind as we discuss the problem of the two different forms of trials, one for the people's court and the other for the provincial (regional or circuit) courts.

II. TWO DISTINCT FORMS OF TRIAL PROCEEDINGS

a. *Novelty of the Arrangement*

A characteristic feature of the Soviet criminal trial is the marked distinction between the proceedings affecting the trial in the two separate types of courts of original jurisdiction.

The novel and striking point of the arrangement lies not in the bare fact that a separate set of rules is provided for the proceedings at the provincial court, but in the unusual attitude taken by Soviet legislators in circumscribing the rights and privileges of the defendant on trial in a court having jurisdiction over the more important and serious criminal cases. The line of demarcation as to the rights of the defendant at the trial is not drawn between different types of cases—though in the last analysis it comes to that[19]—but between the separate types of courts.

[17] *Ibid.*

[18] Krylenko, *The Judiciary and the Law,* 1928, page 95.

[19] Usually the provincial, regional and circuit courts have a fixed jurisdiction. But according to Soviet law, certain authorities may transfer a case

When we analyze the rules that govern the trial procedure at the people's court, we do not find them peculiarly different, to any extent, from those generally prevailing in the western systems of criminal procedure. The defendant enjoys an undeniable right to have at the trial all his witnesses who must be examined with practically no restrictions; he may as of right have the services of an advocate who cannot be prevented by the court from making the final argument and rebuttal. In addition to that there is the personal privilege of the defendant to make statements, to interrogate all the witnesses and have his final word, which closes the trial. As a non-Soviet Russian legal writer correctly remarked, "The principles of a trial by contest run through the entire proceedings [at the people's court] in about the same proportion as they were embodied in the rules adopted by the great judicial reform of 1864."[20]

b. *Principles Involved*

The singularity of the principles upon which the Soviet system of criminal procedure has been built, as discussed above, is not to any great extent reflected in the proceedings at the people's court. For the latter court in dealing with crime is not looked upon as the agency created for the purpose of combating the enemies of the state—that is, the present political and social order, and consequently a conflict or a collision between the interest of the state and the rights of its individual citizen is not likely to occur. But an entirely different situation is encountered when we turn to the trial proceedings at the provincial, regional or circuit, etc., court where, as we have seen, the court in exercising its vast discretionary powers may well deprive the defendant of some of his most precious rights and privileges, though it is, quite unjustifiably, contended that in spite of all the restrictions "these courts [provincial, etc.] are so constituted as to safe-

normally tried at the people's court to the provincial, etc., court. Thus the harsher rules of procedure will be applicable to cases which normally come under the jurisdiction of the people's court. A reverse situation by a similar process is also conceivable. In the latter instance a provincial court case will be tried at the people's court with all the rules applicable to that court.

[20]Temashev, page 268.

guard the fundamental guarantees of the defendant no less than the people's court."[21]

What really is the position which the provincial court occupies within the Soviet legal system? Is it considered merely another higher type of ordinary court, or must it be regarded as an exceptional and temporary tribunal to be retained only during the transitory period in the development of the new political, socio-economic order? That these important questions are not entirely clear and settled even to Soviet judicial workers is quite apparent. For we are told that "With regard to determining the rôle and importance of our [Soviet] provincial courts, as a court of original jurisdiction, within our general judicial system, hazy and partly incorrect ideas are still prevalent * * * ."[22]

The problem narrows down to this: Is the provincial court, as a trial court, to be taken as "an ordinary and general court", such terms being applied to the ordinary Russian courts before 1917, or does the fact that it maintains in a striking manner exceptional characteristics which distinguish it from the people's court place it in the category of an exceptional court? Upon the way we answer this question will depend the solution of another problem—namely: Is the provincial court to be looked upon as a *permanent court,* like any other court having jurisdiction over a certain type of criminal cases, or, being an exceptional court, is it merely temporary in character?"[23]

N. V. Krylenko maintains that it would be incorrect to put the question in such a clear-cut form, for, he contends, it would not correspond to the Soviet point of view on the nature of courts. "From the fact that the pre-revolutionary military courts, courts martial and similar tribunals, which bore the characteristics of exceptional courts, existed as temporary courts", Krylenko argues, "it does not follow that our [Soviet] exceptional courts have to be 'temporary' in nature; and from the fact that according to liberal ideas of jurisprudence all courts must be of the ordinary type, we [the Soviet authorities] must not necessarily con-

[21]I. A. Krastin, *The Criminal Process in R.S.F.S.R.*, Moscow, 1927, page 124.

[22]Krylenko, *The Judiciary and the Law*, 1927, page 66.

[23]*Ibid.*

sider extraordinary a situation whereby ordinary and exceptional courts function side by side."[24]

Mr. Krylenko, while asserting that it is altogether idle to attempt to answer the question under consideration because it would not solve any matter of principle, indulges, nevertheless, in a lengthy discussion on this very topic, criticising his Soviet legal opponents who deem the provincial court *"so far a part of the general system of our judicial hierarchy that they cannot imagine any other system,* and hence they consider the provincial court just as ordinary a branch of the judicial system as any people's court."[25] In his vigorous and fiery manner he points to the various features which determine the exceptional nature of the provincial court. In the realm of procedural rights there are general rules for all the courts, with exceptions applicable only to the trial at the provincial court. In the latter court "the rights of the defendant are more limited * * * which is but another indication of its exceptional character, and the fact that the provincial court is the direct descendant of the undoubtedly exceptional revolutionary tribunals is an additional proof of its nature." Thus we have in the provincial court not merely a higher bench, but a court which "bears all the earmarks of an extraordinary court";[26] hence the specific harsh rules of trial procedure, which tend to broaden the discretionary powers of the court while making inroads on the rights of the defendant in order to achieve a maximum of speed, simplicity and resoluteness during the trial.

c. *Justification Advanced*

It is constantly maintained that such a policy was unavoidable in order to achieve two definite objectives. In the first place the aim was to secure a rigid and outspoken class policy, a policy which may be seen in the fact that even a member of the organized legal profession may be rejected by the court as an advocate in any given case for political reasons. Secondly, there was the aim to shorten the period of time that elapses between the commission of the criminal act and the final determination

[24] *Ibid.*, pages 66 and 67.
[25] *Ibid.*, page 68.
[26] I. A. Krastin, *The Criminal Process*, Moscow, 1927, page 124.

of the case by the provincial court. These aims are imperative—it is further argued—because the type of crimes tried at the latter court are such as either "directly aim at the destruction of the very foundation of the Soviet state, or threaten to hinder seriously, or to make impossible or difficult, the maintenance of the administrative machinery of the Soviet Union."[27] In other words, the provincial court tries criminal cases growing out of acts which directly or indirectly threaten the very existence of the Bolshevik political state, which is engaged in a bitter class warfare in order to wrest from the bourgeois classes any vestige of power which they may still possess. Therefore this court must be endowed with discretionary powers which will make its proceedings flexible to such a degree that a speedy and determined counter attack against class enemies may be effective. As the rights of the individual citizens are to be brushed aside as soon as they come in conflict with the interests of society, or the state, there is little wonder that the privileges of the defendant on trial at the provincial court are narrowed.

The next question that presents itself is whether the existence of the provincial court, so far as its original jurisdiction is concerned, with all its ear-marks of an exceptional though judicial tribunal as shown in its trial proceedings, is to be deemed a permanent arrangement. The commentators on the Code of Criminal Procedure assert that "To the extent of the stabilization of the domestic and international situation of the Soviet Union, the jurisdiction of the provincial court, as a court of the first instance, will undoubtedly diminish and finally be abolished."[28] Even Mr. Krylenko who resents the term "temporary" as applied to the criminal judicial division of the provincial court is willing to prophesy that "upon the disappearance of the sharp form of the class struggle, the provincial court will disappear sooner than the other courts."[29]

All this is of course a mere expression of wishes which may be realized on some bright far-off future day. But what is of immediate interest is the question whether the two distinct forms of trial proceedings are to be maintained during the near future?

[27] *Commentaries*, page 350.
[28] *Ibid.*, page 351.
[29] Krylenko, *The Judiciary and the Law*, 1927, page 68.

As an answer we have two indications flatly contradictory to each other. Krylenko, who undeniably has exerted a tremendous influence on the development and shaping of the Soviet legal system, thinks that "We shall have not one but two [separate] forms of procedure definitely distinguishable from one another—one form of trial for the people's court, and the other for the provincial court." The latter court, we are reminded again and again, has a specific aim—"to serve as an instrument of vengeance,[30] upon its class enemies, while the people's court is to pursue the purpose of organizing the working class and the intermediate elements, and to uphold within their ranks the social-labor discipline."[31] On the other hand, there is a strong tendency to repudiate the present distinction between the trial procedure of the two types of courts. The latter idea has been incorporated in the proposed project for a new code of criminal procedure,[32] drafted by a special commission appointed for that purpose by the Commissariat of Justice.[33]

III. SUMMARY OF THE OUTSTANDING CHARACTERISTICS

The outstanding characteristics of the Soviet criminal trial, so far discussed, may be thus briefly summarized:

(1) The doctrine of a trial by contest is, with some important modifications, adopted as the ruling principle upon which the trial in all courts is based. This finds its expression in the

[30]In his little book, *The Basis of the Judiciary in U.S.S.R. and the Constituent Republics,* Krylenko writes that not a uniform law of procedure for all courts is necessary but separate, specific rules should govern the trial at the provincial court, for the latter court must realize its specific function to serve as a "weapon of class vengeance upon the more dangerous enemies of our social order." (p. 24). The assumption that the courts, especially the provincial courts, are in truth merely organs of judicial *rasprava, i. e.,* getting even, or vengeance, is very often repeated by Mr. Krylenko and by him alone. As far as the writer knows, no Soviet legal writer has gone that far.

[31]Krylenko, *The Weekly,* No. 4, 1928, page 119.

[32]*The Weekly,* Nos. 28 and 29, 1928.

[33]The project for a new Code is based upon the idea that one set of rules should govern the trial at all the courts. Thus with regard to the participation of defense counsel a compromise is made. On the one hand the court, as a rule, decides whether or not an advocate should take a part in the trial. But, on the other hand, the number of conditions which make the participation of defense counsel obligatory was greatly extended. Naturally the project is not yet the law, nor is there any positive indication that it will be ratified in its present form.

fact that (a) the trial is always open and public;[34] (b) the defendant is permitted to participate actively in the proceedings, enjoying absolutely equal rights with the prosecutor; (c) whenever the latter participates in the trial,[35] the defendant, irrespective of the type of court, may as of right engage the aid of an advocate whose privileges are in no way less than those extended to the prosecutor. Furthermore, the presence of the advocate is not to affect the status of the defendant who may still cross-examine witnesses, make statements and have the final word.

(2) The principle of a trial by contest is modified to the extent that (a) the court does not sit as an independent arbiter between the parties, the state and its citizen, impartially and unconcernedly observing that the rules of the contest be fairly and correctly applied; (b) the judges, even in the people's court, actively participate in the case, thus eliminating any free play of the two opposing sides; (c) the rule prevalent almost everywhere permitting participation of defense counsel under all circumstances and in all cases is rejected, and (d) the widely recognized right, not to say duty, of the defense counsel to present his client's defense, even where the counsel knows that his client is guilty, or, to be more accurate, that he has committed the act, is seriously questioned.[36]

(3) A separate set of harsh, exceptional rules of procedure for the trial of criminal cases at the provincial, circuit, regional, etc.,[37] courts has been created. Thus the chances of the defendant's successfully meeting the charges against him in the most serious cases and gaining his freedom is greatly curtailed by

[34]The exceptions to the rule, namely, that the public is excluded when certain sexual crimes are tried or where state secrets are involved, are not of such a nature as to change the general principle of an open and public trial.

[35]See *ante*, pages 201 and 239.

[36]At a general meeting of the members of the Moscow Provincial Bar (collegium of advocates) held in November, 1926, the President of the Moscow Provincial Court, Stelmakhovitch, was asked how should an attorney proceed after he has learned that his client was guilty. It is rather interesting that the answer was evasive. He maintained that usually the defendant lies also to his attorney, and then that one must act according to the dictates of one's conscience in certain cases, etc. See *Legal Aid to the Population* for 1926, official publications of the Moscow Bar, Moscow, 1927, page 134.

[37]These courts do not function simultaneously. It is either the provincial or the circuit, etc.

granting the court the power, in its own discretion, to deprive the defendant of the services of an advocate, to eliminate the final arguments of the advocate and the prosecutor wherever they take part in the trial, to refuse the summoning of certain witnesses who have testified at the preliminary inquiry while making such testimony a part of the record of the case, to limit, under certain conditions, the number of witnesses to be examined at the trial, etc. The avowed purpose in establishing such powers, as already indicated, is to create a flexible form of criminal procedure capable of moving swiftly and effectively when combating what are considered socially dangerous crimes. The fact that such an achievement—laudable from the point of view of the state—is achieved at the expense of a citizen's rights is of little concern to Soviet anti-individualistic political thought. It is said, however, that even in the somewhat exceptional provincial court the defendant always enjoys certain rights as a party, for he may at least examine and cross-examine witnesses, make statements at any stage of the trial, and have his final word.

All we have learned about the peculiarities of the Soviet trial procedure cannot be fully visualized, and its true nature and value determined, until we consider the most striking feature of the Soviet legal system—the complete abolition of trial by jury. While superficially the composition of the agencies which carry on the trial bears no direct relation to rules of procedure at the trial, yet the intrinsic value of certain rights of the parties can be fully estimated only in conjunction with a knowledge of how these agencies are made up. Let us now proceed to examine this important characteristic.

IV. A SUBSTITUTE FOR TRIAL BY JURY

The outstanding problem with which we are now concerned is the total elimination of the jury as a factor in the Soviet criminal trial.

We may recall that the institution of co-judges as a substitute for the jury was effected at the very beginning of the Soviet régime, and such juryless system has been continuously maintained up to this time. What were the basic theories and ideas which caused such an innovation?

a. *Co-judges Prior to November 1917*

Before we attempt to answer this question, it is worth noting that the idea of people's co-judges was introduced into the Russian legal system by P. Kerensky who became Minister of Justice in the first Provisional government established immediately after the Revolution of February, 1917. To be sure, the system of co-judges was inaugurated only in a few cities and with the explicit intention of having it function temporarily. Immediately after taking over the office of Minister of Justice on March 7, 1917, P. Kerensky issued a temporary decree to the effect that "in order to dissolve the misunderstanding between the soldiers, the populace and the workers, it is recommended to all justices of the peace [who tried cases without juries] to organize provisional courts for the clearing up of such misunderstanding, which courts shall consist of one judge, one representative of the army and one of the workers."[38] This was to affect only a few districts in the City of Petrograd. But by subseqent decrees many other cities were included in the scheme.[39]

A special instruction as to these new courts was later issued.[40] This instruction provided, among other things, for the jurisdiction of these courts which was to include cases involving attempts to overthrow the new order. But no punishment exceeding imprisonment for one year and six months could be inflicted by the new tribunals.[41] These new courts merely added co-judges to the former bench of a single justice of the peace or a municipal judge, without displacing the jury trial, which, in the higher courts, was in no sense disturbed. On the contrary, trial by jury was given a wider scope by the abolition of the special sessions of the circuit court and the judicial *palata* (chamber), which tried cases only with representatives of the castes, and the substitution of jury trials therefore.[42] But after the Bolshevik Revolution of November 7, 1917, the system of co-judges came to displace the jury system entirely. We turn back to our problem as to the theories and reasons which brought about such a change.

[38] *The Bulletin of the Provincial Government No. 1,* March 3, 1917.
[39] *Ibid.,* Nos. 7 and 19.
[40] *Ibid.,* No. 19, March 22, 1917.
[41] *Ibid.,* No. 3, 1917.
[42] *Ibid.,* No. 21, March 30, 1917.

b. *Co-judges after the Bolshevik Revolution*

The Revolution of November 7, 1917, unlike other great Revolutions in history, was carried out for the avowed purpose of benefiting only the soviets, that is, the workers and the peasants. The slogan of "all the power to the soviets" was heard everywhere, while the turmoil which culminated in the November *coup d'état* was brewing. The Revolution was, therefore, not to sweep the people at large into power, but only the workers and the peasants. In other words, the class character of the new political state was outspokenly proclaimed. All the institutions of government, including the courts, were henceforth to be dominated exclusively by representatives of the new ruling class. This must be borne in mind when discussing the institution of co-judges effected by the First Decree on Courts promulgated by the new class régime.

As the co-judges were, in one way or another, to be elected and recalled by the soviets or councils of workers and peasants, they would naturally represent the views of the socio-economic groups in whose name the Revolution was wrought and accomplished, and therefore they were intended to be a body of more importance, entrusted with greater powers, than those hitherto possessed by the juries. "They [the co-judges] are given equal powers with the permanent judges by participating in the case from beginning to end * * * This is the fundamental difference between the people's co-judges in our [Soviet] courts and the former trial by juries."[43] This distinction between the two methods of trial is constantly emphasized in Soviet legal writings. In an unsigned article published in the official journal of the Commissariat of Justice, we read: "We summon the people's co-judges to participate in the court without the limitations which existed in the old order when the jurors decided only questions of fact but not of law. Our co-judges have been made full-fledged judges."[44]

There are still other important differences which may affect the rights and interests of the defendant to a considerable degree. A significant feature of the jury system is the fact that jurors

[43]Krylenko, *The Jud. System*, page 41.
[44]*The Weekly*, No. 38, 1923.

are selected by a general method, uncontrolled and unhampered by any person or group, that the names of the jurors who are to sit in a particular case are unknown in advance to either the judge or the parties, and that the latter have something to say in selecting a particular jury by means of their peremptory challenges which reach, in some jurisdictions, as high as thirty in capital cases.[45] The co-judges, on the other hand, are not picked at random, but are very carefully selected, and the defendant has to accept them unless they can be challenged for cause, no peremptory challenges being allowed. Thus, not the people at large, without discrimination, are called in to act as impartial jurors who impose their laymen's point of view in giving a verdict, but a few representatives of those social and occupational groups which the government considers as inherently friendly to its socio-economic and political system are to act as temporary judges.

We may recall that the framers of the First Decree on Courts intended that co-judges should be elected on a democratic basis, and only temporarily were to be appointed by the soviets. At that time the number of the co-judges sitting in a case was so great as to make it impossible for the permanent judge to exert any great influence on them. Furthermore, at the circuit court, which was to become for a time the important criminal court, the permanent judge was to sit in the consulting chamber merely as an adviser. But all this was soon given up. As the true nature of the new order began to chrystalize, the courts began to shape themselves accordingly. The number of co-judges for each case was reduced to six in very serious cases, while two co-judges were to sit in ordinary cases at the people's court. This system remained in force until 1923, when the number of two cojudges was made to apply to all the courts.

c. *The Soviet Point of View*

These changes are undoubtedly consistent with the general Soviet point of view concerning the functions of the judiciary. Is the court to be "an independent branch of the government responsible only before the Iaw?" This quotation from the

[45]Gil. Cr. Code, 1929, Code of Cr. Pr., section 373 (N. Y.).

new German constitution is cited by a leading Soviet jurist, P. Stuchka,[46] who contends that such a thing is absolutely impossible. "The court", another Soviet legal writer boldly asserts, "has always been and still remains as it ought to be according to its nature—namely, one of the organs of governmental power, a weapon in the hands of the ruling class for the purpose of safeguarding its interests."[47] The courts are, therefore, nothing more than an instrument of domination in the hands of a given class. Hence it follows that the judiciary in Soviet Russia ought to be not only one of the institutions of the dictatorship of the proletariat, but the great power whose ultimate aim is to defend the given political system, and "at the same time the organ which carries out the *politik* of the governing class."[48]

Mr. Krylenko in carrying his theories of government to their logical extreme maintains that "In principle there is no real difference between a court of justice and any other non-judicial organ of vengeance."[49] The only real distinction between those two is that the former, the "judicial vengeance, offers a greater guarantee that there will be no error,"[50] in the finding of the true facts.

These declarations of principle, though they are far from being consistently carried out when applied to the everyday practice in Soviet courts, as we shall see later, lead us to the answer to our inquiry as to why the present system of co-judges was substituted for the trial by jury. Notwithstanding the vigorous insistence on the part of N. V. Krylenko, that courts are nowhere an independent, impartial, judicial institution as "bourgeois writers" claim, but are in fact a weapon in the hands of the ruling classes, he is nevertheless bound to admit that a jury may entirely upset all the calculations of the rulers and decide contrary to the wishes and interests of the governing class which, according to him, should have full control of the

[46]P. Stuchka, (now President of the Supreme Court and Deputy Commissar of Justice) *Political (state) Science and the Constitution of R.S.F.S.R.*, 1923, page 255.

[47]Krylenko, *Jud. System*, page 10.

[48]Krylenko, *The Judiciary and the Law*, 1927, page 16.

[49]Krylenko, *Jud. System*, page 15.

[50]Krylenko, *The Basis of the Judiciary of the U.S.S.R. and the Constituent Republics*, Moscow, 1927, page 8.

judicial branch. That such things happen is not unknown to Krylenko. With a sort of brutal frankness characteristic of Russians, he discusses the famous Russian cases of Vera Zasulich[51] and M. Beilis[52] and the William Z. Foster case[53] in America. While the government did not have the same interest in all these cases in securing a conviction, they were all cases of a political nature, in which the jury's verdict was directly contrary to the wishes of the party in power in the government. (In the Foster case the jury could not agree on a verdict, and the case was dropped.)

The mere possibility of such an unnatural outcome is anathema to Mr. Krylenko. He therefore flatly rejects any system of criminal trial which may sometimes work contrary to the general policies of the government, which is, according to Soviet political ideas, a mighty apparatus by which one governing class can successfully suppress the other opposing classes.

One might say that the fact that a jury decides contrary to the political wishes of the government is convincing proof that a jury is capable of a genuine expression of justice, irrespective of the political desires and manipulations even of the government itself, and is the very thing which makes the institution so valuable and so desirable. But no: "We don't need your justice", Krylenko determinedly exclaims. Mindful and fearful of the political enemies which are still in hiding, he wants to *"avoid forms of courts which might, in a critical moment for the proletariat, offer a counter-attack and thus betray the latter by adher-*

[51]Vera Zosulich, a famous Russian revolutionary was a young girl when she shot and wounded the chief of the St. Petersburg (now Leningrad) police, Trepov, in the eighties of the last century. Zasulich fired at Trepov in order to avenge a revolutionary by the name of Bogolyubov who was flogged by the order of the Chief of Police for not removing his hat when the mighty personage visited the jail where Bogolyukov was held as a political prisoner. The girl revolutionary admitted the shooting, but justified her act by a desire to arouse public opinion to the mistreatment of political prisoners. The jury acquitted her stating, strangely enough, that she did not do the shooting.

[52]Beilis was arrested, in 1912, in the City of Kiev on a charge that he committed a murder of a Christian child for ritual purposes. The whole ugly frame-up engineered from above aroused the indignation of intellectual and liberal Russia. Beilis was acquitted by a jury after a sensational trial in 1913 and "the government was discredited in the clumsily manipulated Beilis trial". (Karnilov, *Modern Russian History*, Vol. II, page 337.)

[53]Foster was arrested charged with the participation in a secret communist gathering in Michigan.

ing to its own class interest."[54] As the terms "workers", "state" and "government" are used synonymously, the interests of the one are completely identified with the interests of the other. "For us, the government of the workers and the peasants, ***there cannot be applicable any other form of courts except such as will, under all circumstances, secure and defend the interests of the workers***"[55] (the state).

As the court system is said to reflect the general political philosophy of the ruling class it becomes obvious that trial by jury is not the appropriate judicial method. The unknown mysterious unit named "The People" is not to be relied upon. If we are to entrust our cases to the people in general, a jury, "there will be all kinds of shiftings and deviations, * * * and to depend on their judicial decisions would mean to give up all judicial *politik*."[56] Although the government speaks of itself as the representative of both workers and peasants, as a matter of fact the latter are not to be trusted. By having trial by jury "we would stand the risk, in a peasant country, of receiving decisions fundamentally contradictory to the aims of the judicial *politik* maintained by the vanguard of the proletariat."[57] Such a course is plainly unthinkable to those who adhere to the political philosophy of the Soviet system, which unhesitatingly looks upon itself as a working class government, a body politic whose present aim is to annihilate the bourgeois class, and whose ultimate aim is the creation of a classless community. During such class warfare, which is the period of dictatorship, the court is conceived of as one important branch of the entire government and inseparable from it. It is an organ called upon to carry into effect the state's general purpose, and, therefore, the maintenance of a definite judicial *politik* is necessary.

Here we have the answer to the question as to why the system of co-judges came into being. The same reasons should suffice

[54]Krylenko, *Jud. System*, page 13.

[55]*Ibid.*, page 15.

[56]*Ibid.*, page 55. To illustrate his point, Mr. Krylenko tells us that he had once tried a homicide case as prosecutor in a circuit court (1918) where, as we know, twelve co-judges were sitting, and the defendant was acquitted because he killed out of jealousy. The judicial *politik* of the government is naturally not to have the jealousy motive serve as any justification, or excuse.

[57]Krylenko, *The Judiciary and the Law*, 1927, page 55.

to explain why even the number of six co-judges which, as we know, prevailed for the trial of more serious casses up to 1923 was cut down to two. It is asserted that this change rested on grounds of mere practicability. "The institution of a bench of six co-judges was abolished exclusively because it proved unnecessary, since the number of [six] co-judges did not show any reason for preferring it in the sense of a better trial."[58] Krylenko, however, is nearer the truth when he remarks, speaking of the court with six co-judges, that "Such a body was already a complete imitation of a jury system."[59] True, it lacked some of the fundamental characteristics of a jury, as pointed out above; nevertheless, it could still bring in the non-political attitude of the layman, a point of view which might, in spite of all the political precautions taken, cause havoc within the entire "judicial *politik*."

It is highly interesting to note that when the proposal to abolish the bench of six co-judges was being discussed, a legal circle of workingmen[60] after "listening to the opinions of former and present people's judges", made public a resolution which was adopted by that body, to the effect that the bench with six co-judges should be continued. There were two reasons for favoring that system. "First, verdicts rendered with the participation of only two co-judges are reached, in the overwhelming number of cases, under the influence of the people's judge who may without much effort on his part succeed in winning over to his side at least one of the two judges * * * and a majority decides. Second, the greater number of co-judges adds to the solemnity of the proceedings, is more in accord with the popular character of the courts and more fully guarantees an unprejudiced and profound deliberation."[61]

The truth of this interesting resolution can hardly be disputed. For though it is earnestly contended by members of the

[58] *The Weekly*, No. 50, 1923, page 115.

[59] Krylenko, *Jud. System*, pages 40 and 41.

[60] In many factories and mills the workers are organized into different circles, as literary, dramatic, etc. They have also legal circles where the interest of the members is concentrated upon legal problems. Members of those circles are often recruited into the various short law courses and even to the universities. Many of the present day judicial office holders have started their career from those "circles".

[61] *The Weekly*, Nos. 46 and 48, December 30, 1922.

Soviet judiciary[62] that the co-judges as a whole act independently, and that there are instances where the co-judges have rendered the verdict, with the permanent judge writing a minority opinion, nevertheless it is almost unthinkable that the permanent, more experienced judge will not exert a tremendous influence on the casual co-judge in most cases. The people's judge who in an article criticized the attitude of the co-judges who say to the judge "Just as you say, you ought to know better",[63] is apparently not talking of an exceptional case. It is not at all unreasonable to assume that the number of co-judges was reduced because a bench of two co-judges is politically safer, and can be depended upon not to deviate from the straight red line of the judicial *politik* adopted. It is of interest to note that Soltz, a conspicuous legal writer, and others have proposed that the bench should be composed of three permanent judges and two co-judges, in order that the government could be sure of a majority.[64]

d. *The Necessity for Co-judges*

The next question which presents itself is why it is necessary to have any co-judges at all. Would it not be still more compatible with the political ideas of the present Soviet régime, conceiving of the judiciary as a mere agent of the government, to dispense with co-judges altogether? Instead of the fundamental and historic reason behind our jury system that a man should be tried by his peers, the co-judge is not invited for the protection of the individual citizen defendant but in order that the masses may participate in the working of the judiciary for the benefit of the toiling masses themselves. The programme adopted by the Communist Congress in 1919 stated that a bench of co-judges was established "* * * in order to induce the masses of the proletariat and the peasantry to take part in the administration of justice"; and the party, the real source of power in Soviet Russia,

[62]All the Soviet judges with whom the writer has had an opportunity to converse firmly maintained that co-judges are not influenced by the permanent judges. Whether this is possible from the very nature of things may be seriously doubted.

[63]*The Weekly,* No. 47, 1923, page 1089.

[64]Krylenko, *The Judiciary and the Law,* 1927, page 57.

pledged itself to do its utmost "to induce all workmen without exception to perform judicial duties."[65]

A special decree on the people's co-judges was issued in December, 1920, stating in its preamble that "Without inducing the toiling masses to participate in the trial of cases which usually occur among the laboring people, it will be impossible to disseminate any real understanding of proletarian justice among the politically backward masses, or to make them familiar with the new Soviet law."[66] The same preamble goes on to say that the system of co-judges is designed as a means of heightening the authority of the court, as well as the political development of the masses. The idea to "induce all the workmen without exception" has been repudiated long ago, and a method of careful selection, especially for those sitting at the provincial court, has been substituted. But the educational and political value of the co-judges' participation is still insisted upon. It is persistently suggested that the court could not *"decide in harmony with the general principles of the Soviet government, as the government of the toiling masses, otherwise than with the direct participation of the representative of the laboring people* [the co-judges] *in the deliberations of the court"*,[67] and that "the defense of the interest of the workmen and the peasants [as a whole, not as individuals] is conditioned upon the fact that the laboring classes in conjunction with the judge will take an active part in the work of the courts."[68]

The writer confesses that he entertains a profound doubt as to the soundness of all these explanations concerning the necessity of any co-judges. Since the court is nothing more than an integral part of the government, just as any other administrative branch, why, one may wonder, is a system of temporary representatives of the workers and peasants so imperative in the courts, and unnecessary in any other department which is equally called upon to defend the interest of the workers and peasants?

[65]Programme of the Communist Party, adopted at the VIII Conference held in Moscow, in 1919.

[66]Collected Laws, No. 100, Article 542, 1922.

[67]Krylenko, *Jud. System*, page 41.

[68]P. Alimov, "To the Election of People's Co-judges", *The Weekly*, No. 34, 1927, page 1042.

Are we not perhaps confronted here with a faint imitation of the condemned "bourgeois" jury? Furthermore, is not Soviet law still enslaved, to a degree at least, to the consciously rejected western systems of jurisprudence? We shall return to these questions more fully later.

Chapter IX

JUDICIAL REVIEW OF CRIMINAL CASES

The important function of the criminal appeal, as a method by which a verdict or a sentence of one court may be reviewed by another higher tribunal, assumes an aspect even more than usually significant in Soviet Russia. This will be realized if we remember that owing to the peculiar socio-political conditions created by the Revolution of November, 1917, the judges of the Soviet trial courts are on the whole slightly trained, and are less experienced jurists than trial judges elsewhere on the continent.

The present Soviet judicial system has two methods by which the record of a criminal case may come to a higher court for review—namely, cassation and supervision or control. These two separate forms of review, while they have something in common so far as the ultimate objective is concerned, strikingly vary both in the scope of the review itself and in the principle and ideas underlying the corrective powers granted to the higher court. These two modes of criminal review, therefore, must be considered separately in any general discussion of the problems and proceedings connected with the review of criminal cases in Soviet Russia.

I. DEVELOPMENT OF CRIMINAL REVIEW IN RUSSIA

Before we proceed to describe and discuss the functions and powers of the courts of cassation and supervision and the procedure therein, it is well to digress for a moment in order to get a brief survey of the modern development of criminal review in Russia, since this should prove of assistance to us when we come to analyze the changes and innovations wrought by the present régime.

The great Judicial Reforms of 1864, which took the French judicial system as a model, adapting it to peculiar Russian ways and needs, had established two methods of criminal review. One was known as appeal *(apelyatziya)* and the other as cassation *(kasatziya)*. The court of appeals was either the conference of the judges of the peace of a certain district (somewhat similar to the English quarter sessions of the county) for cases originally tried at the justice of the peace court[1] *(mirovoi sud)*, or the judicial chamber *(palata)* for those tried at the important circuit court *(okruzhnoi sud)* without a jury.

The basic idea underlying the method of appeal as distinguished from cassation was that the party aggrieved by the verdict or judgment—the defendant, the injured or wronged person, or the state procurator under certain conditions—could as of right have an appeal, which was a retrial in a higher, more competent court with a greater number of judges sitting. The proceedings at the appellate court were in effect very similar to, if not identical with, those in the court below. For the law unequivocally provided that "The parties may present testimony and bring the witnesses [to the appellate court] who testified at the trial below, as well as those who for some good reason could not appear at the justice of the peace court."[2] Similar rules applied to the proceedings at the judicial chamber when it sat as a court of appeals. This court could either leave the verdict and sentence of the court below undisturbed or render an entirely different verdict or sentence. The punishment, however, could not be more severe than the one originally inflicted, unless the private prosecutor or the state procurator appealed the case.[3] The judgment thus pronounced was said to be final, but could be carried farther on proper grounds to the court of cassation.

The court of cassation, on the other hand, was the cassational department of the highly dignified Governing Senate. The latter took up complaints against final judgments, that is, judgments rendered by appellate courts, or by circuit courts with the participation of a jury. When a jury participated in a case the original verdict was considered non-appealable,[4] but could be reversed by a court of cassation.[5] In order to obtain a reversal in the latter court the complainant had to prove that in the pro-

[1]In large cities there were municipal (or city) courts, the judges of the latter court participated in the district conference of the justices of the peace or had a conference of their own. But both, the justice of the peace and the judges of the municipal court, belonged to the same type.

[2]*Fundamental Laws of the Russian Empire*, 1911 edition, vol. XVI, chapter 8, section 159 (Law of November, 1864, No. 41476, section 158).

[3]*Ibid.*, sections 168 and 914.

[4]*Ibid.*, section 854.

[5]*Ibid.*, section 855.

ceedings below there occurred a violation of the law, an incorrect interpretation, a fundamental error in the rules of procedure, or that the "judicial bounds were overstepped."[6] Neither the parties nor the witnesses were summoned, but the former were permitted to attend the session of the court[7] and to make a statement or offer an explanation of the particular position they were seeking to maintain.[8] The court was to examine only the errors assigned, and only such errors as were included among the few legal grounds for cassation. Such, briefly, was the system of criminal review which prevailed in Russia up to 1917.

The new régime set up by the Revolution of November, 1917, was quick to decree the complete destruction of the entire judicial system, root and branch, and substituted a system of its own. The First Decree on Courts promulgated by the Soviet Government laid down a fundamental principle of criminal review when it declared that "In cases which result in a fine of over one hundred rubles [fifty dollars] or a sentence exceeding seven days' imprisonment, a complaint by way of cassation shall be permitted."[9] Thus, inferentially, the institution of appeal as distinguished from cassation was not to be re-established. This inference was strengthened by the fact that the above-mentioned decree stated that "The county conference of the people's judges, or the city conference in the capital cities, shall function as a court of cassation."[10] In pre-revolutionary Russia, the equivalent of this conference of people's judges, the conference of the justices of the peace, represented the typical form of a court of appeal. The Second Decree on Courts which was issued in March, 1918, clarified the entire matter by providing that "A complaint * * * shall be taken only by way of cassation."[11] The same idea was later, in 1924, embodied in the Basic Rules of Criminal Procedure, adopted by the newly created Union of Soviet Socialist Republics, and in that way was made binding

[6] *Ibid.*, section 912.
[7] *Ibid.*, section 918.
[8] *Ibid.*, section 920.
[9] First Decree, section 2. The idea to have small fines or light sentences excluded from the possibility of a review was soon afterwards discarded. But in the proposed project for a new code of criminal procedure a similar provision is inserted.
[10] *Ibid.*
[11] Second Decree, section 4.

on all the constituent Soviet republics. These basic rules stipulate that "All cases tried on their merits in one court [*instantzia*] shall not be subject to appeal, but may be reversed by way of cassation or supervision."[12]

The reason for abolishing the *apelyatziya* was said to grow out of purely practical considerations. Why, it was asked, should one court, the court of appeals, be more trusted to judge the facts than a court of original jurisdiction?[13] In addition, it was argued, it tends to undermine the authority of the trial courts in the eyes of the people. But later a more profound explanation was given, together with the admission that the bourgeois ideas made themselves felt in the guise of practical arguments—namely, that "The appeal was abolished because of the liberal principle that what the jury has decided should be reviewed only by way of cassation."[14] This is a straight confession of sin on the part of a stalwart communist. It is well established on the continent of Europe that "the conception of appeal [as distinguished from cassation] is foreign to the idea of justice done by the peers of the accused."[15] As the people's co-judges are substitutes for the former jurors, their findings of facts should not be disturbed. It would, however, be erroneous to assume that the new order rejected completely one method, the appeal, while re-enacting fully the other form of review, cassation. For while the entire institution of courts of appeal, in which there might be a second hearing on the merits of the case in a higher court, was really discarded, some of its features nevertheless soon crept in in another form as we shall see later. On the other hand, the cassational method instituted by the Soviet régime inherited the name of its predecessor but was never restricted to the functions or to the scope of power associated with the true conception of cassational jurisdiction.

We are now to proceed with a discussion of the different aspects of cassation and supervision, as they have finally evolved

[12]Basic Principles of Criminal Procedure. Collected Laws of the U.S.S.R., Article 206, 1924, section 25.

[13]Krylenko, *Judicial System,* page 57.

[14]Krylenko, *The Judiciary and the Law,* 1927, page 61.

[15]Esmein, A., *History of Continental Criminal Procedure,* Boston, 1913, page 10.

in the development of the present Soviet system of criminal jurisprudence.

II. COURTS OF CRIMINAL REVIEW

a. *Courts of Cassation*

The cassational division of the provincial or circuit court has cassational jurisdiction over all cases tried at the people's courts within the particular province or circuit.

The division of cassation, as we know, consists of a number of permanent judges, three of whom are to sit as a bench of cassation in each case.[16] The plenum of the provincial court, with the permission of the Commissariat of Justice, may appoint a people's judge to sit as one of the three cassational judges.[17] (The Ukrainian Code of 1927 provides that each cassational bench shall be composed of two circuit judges, since there are no provincial units in Ukraine, and one people's court judge.) To be eligible for appointment as judge of the provincial court a person must have served not less than two years in a judicial capacity not lower than a people's judge and the president judge and his deputy must have served three years.[18] The people's judge, we may recall, must also have certain prescribed qualifications and experience before he can be appointed.

The Department of Cassation of the Supreme Court has the power to review by way of cassation all cases originally heard at the judicial divisions of the provincial, circuit, or regional courts.

This Department of the Supreme Court, we may recall, is composed of a president and six or more regular judges, not less than three of whom constitute a cassational tribunal. The qualifications for a judgeship in this Department are the same as required for a president judge of the provincial court.[19]

b. *Courts of Supervision*

The courts of supervision are the cassational divisions and plena of the provincial or circuit courts, and the Cassational Department and plenum of the Supreme Court of the Republic.

[16] Jud. Act, 1926, section 51.
[17] *Ibid.*, note to section 51.
[18] *Ibid.*, section 40.
[19] *Ibid.*, note to section 177.

The cassational division of the provincial or circuit court, while primarily exercising the functions of a court of cassation, may act also, under certain designated instances, as a court of supervision. The plenum, that is, the full session, of the provincial or circuit court is constituted as a court of supervision whenever a case which has already been heard and disposed of by the cassational division of the same court has been brought up by way of supervision, or in case the procurator remains dissatisfied with the decision of the cassational division, sitting either as a court of cassation or of supervision.

The Department of Cassation of the Supreme Court of the Republic has the power of supervisory review of criminal cases that have passed through any court of the Republic, either of original jurisdiction or cassational, except the Supreme Court. As a bench of supervision it is usually made up of three judges, but whenever the case comes from the plenum of the provincial or circuit court, all the judges of the Cassational Department, of whom there were seventeen in 1927,[20] must sit.[21]

The Plenum of the Supreme Court functions as a court of supervision in all cases that have been originally tried at the Judicial Department of the Supreme Court, from which a cassational complaint never lies, and in cases which have been once determined by the Cassational Department of this highest court.

The records of a contested criminal case will necessarily come up for review through one of the two methods mentioned above to a reviewing court, or even conceivably to all of them. We are now to discuss these methods, separately, with regard to the proceedings and the jurisdiction of the courts.

III. COMPLAINTS BY WAY OF CASSATION

a. *Who May Appeal*[22]

One of the fundamental principles of cassational correction, as modified by the Soviet conception, lies in the doctrine that

[20]Jud. Practice, No. 4, 1927, page 2.
[21]Code, 1927, section 443.
[22]The term appeal is here used in the general broad sense, and not as a specific method of appeal as distinguished from cassation.

every act of the court at the trial and elsewhere, as well as the regulations and orders of any judge, acting individually, are always subject to review by a higher tribunal. It is in full accord with this that the law provides that any of the interested parties—that is, the defendant, his legal representative or advocate, the injured party whenever he is permitted to support the accusation, or the procurator who prosecuted the case—may appeal from the verdict and sentence of the court on the ground that his rights were violated during the trial proceedings.[23] Therefore the appeal of one defendant does not automatically affect the status and interests of other co-defendants in the same cause, though this rule has some important exceptions. Likewise the injured or wronged party is deprived of the right to appeal unless he is by law permitted to appear as a prosecutor, that is, to conduct the prosecution.[24] The civil claimant is allowed to appeal only on grounds affecting the civil judgment, but on no point touching upon the criminal phase of the case. But to this general rule there is this significant exception, that the procurator, though he is considered as one of the parties to the trial, may protest by way of cassation the violation of the right and interest of any of the parties in the case. This is unquestionably compatible with the theory that the procurator is essentially "the guardian of the revolutionary law", and his functions and duties extend far above and beyond those of a mere state prosecutor.[25]

In this connection we may note the striking fact that the procurator may protest—the latter term is applied when the procurator is the appellant—any verdict and sentence, including a sentence of acquittal. While such a procedure may seem abhorrent to those reared in legal principles which prohibit double jeopardy, it is neither startling nor novel to the mind of the continental jurist. The Soviet law permitting the prosecutor to contest an

[23]Code, 1927, section 349.

[24]Thus the mother of a girl who was raped could not appeal as she was not a party to the case. She was neither a private prosecutor nor did she present a civil claim. Supreme Court decision reported in Jud. Practice, No. 3, 1928, page 15.

[25]It is interesting to note that at the beginning of the present régime every unblamable citizen could complain against verdicts of the revolutionary tribunals. A little later such rights were given to organizations. But with the development of the system, only parties or the procurator have the right to appeal (complain).

adverse verdict, and thus raise the possibility of a new trial which may conceivably result in a conviction or a severer sentence, is merely a restatement of pre-revolutionary Russian law which is not uncommon law on the continent of Europe.

We have so far referred only to complaints or protests against verdicts and sentences, that is, when cases have been completed. But an appeal will also lie against any single regulation or order of the judge or court not immediately connected with the verdict or sentence. This is called a special complaint,[26] or special protest when the procurator is the appealing party. Any person who is aggrieved by the regulation or order of the court, irrespective of whether or not he occupies the status of a party, as described above, has the right to file a special complaint. This would include a witness, a bondsman, a watcher, etc. The difference between the cassational complaint and the special complaint is not only a difference in terms, but the entire method and scope of the review are widely distinct, as we shall see later.

b. *Method of Complaint*

The idea of doing away with unnecessary technicalities and complications in matters judicial, ardently and consistently advocated by Soviet legal writers, has found its utmost expression in the remarkable simplicity and ease with which a cassational complaint may be set in motion. To begin with, the verdict and sentence rendered by the trial court, which are embodied in one document, a copy of which is given to the defendant, stipulate the method and time for appeal.[27] The next step must be taken by the dissatisfied party himself. As there are two distinct types of trial courts, the people's court and the second and higher type, the provincial (circuit, regional,[28] etc.) court, we shall examine the methods of appeal (complaint) with reference to the particular type of court which had original jurisdiction of the case.

[26] I. A. Krastin, *Criminal Trial in R.S.F.S.R. (Ugolovnyii Protzes)*, Moscow, 1927, page 128.

[27] Code, 1927, section 336.

[28] It is the provincial court which functions, as the name indicates, within a province, *(Guberniya)* the old Russian administrative units. But where the province as a unit has been abolished and the region and circuit substituted, we have the circuit court which takes almost all the original jurisdiction of the provincial court. The regional court standing above the former court exercises some original jurisdiction. Thus it is either the provincial court or its equivalents, the regional and circuit courts.

1. Complaints in Cases Tried at the People's Court

Cassational complaints and protests against the verdicts of the people's court, as well as special complaints and protests against orders and decisions of the single people's judge, are taken to the cassational division of the provincial or circuit court in the judicial district of which the people's court has sat. The complaint is submitted to the people's court within fourteen days[29] from the time the verdict is rendered, or the judicial order or decision announced by the people's judge and a copy thereof handed to the defendant.[30] But these fixed rules are endowed with considerable flexibility. First, as to the exact method of presenting the complaint. The general rule is that it should be brought in the trial court for the obvious reason that the latter has the records of the case which are to be transferred to the higher court as a matter of course. The law, however, provides that the filing or submitting "of a complaint directly to the cassational division of the provincial court, if filed on time, shall not serve as any objection to the review of the case by the latter court."[31] Second, as to the time limitation. In the ordinary case the people's court must dismiss the complaint if it is not filed within the period of fourteen days fixed by law; but whenever the failure to complain within the proper time is due to some good reason, a petition may be filed requesting the trial court to extend the period.[32] It seems that the court must grant such a request if there is good cause for failure to file the complaint, for should the court dismiss the petition after deliberating on the question at its administrative session, this is in turn subject to appeal (special complaint) to the provincial court.

Thus every party to the case who has a grievance against the verdict or sentence, or order or decision of the people's court, may appeal as a matter of absolute right, and such an appeal—or cassational complaint, as it is termed—will automatically serve as a supersedeas,[33] and, if the appeal is from the verdict, the sentence will not be carried out until the appeal is heard. (In case

[29]Code, 1927, section 346, part 1.
[30]*Ibid.*, section 370.
[31]*Ibid.*, section 344, part 3.
[32]*Ibid.*, section 345.
[33]*Ibid.*, section 346, part 2.

of an acquittal, however, the defendant is released immediately.) But a special complaint stays the order or regulation appealed from only if the judge or the court deems it necessary, according to the circumstances of the particular case.[34]

The simplicity of the method of the appeal will become apparent when we learn that there are no prescribed rules for the form of the appeal (complaint) or for its contents; neither, of course, are any requirements for briefs, paper books or any formal writings whatsoever. It is sufficient for the appealing party to state, "I wish to complain" against the verdict or sentence of the court, or against the particular regulation or order if it is a special complaint. The Code expressly provides that the fact that "complaints are made against the merits of the verdict [which is not an appealable matter] and in addition point out errors of law committed at the trial, or even that complaints are made against the merits of the verdict *without pointing out any legal errors at all* does not free the provincial [or the Supreme] court from its obligation to examine the complaint and the *entire proceedings of the case by the method of a review.*"[35] (The italics are ours.) The singularity of this provision is that the record will come up for a thorough re-examination by the cassational court, even though the complainant states only grounds *which are not subject* to a review by the higher court. In theory, at least, the cassational court may not consider questions touching the merits of a case. To what extent this theory is really carried out is a question which we shall attempt to answer in another connection.

The people's court which receives the complaint within the proper time must within three days transfer the entire record of the case to the cassational division of the provincial or circuit court.[36]

2. Complaints in Cases Tried at the Provincial, Circuit or Regional Courts

Complaints against the verdict or sentence of the criminal-judicial division of the provincial or similar courts, as courts of original jurisdiction, are taken to the Cassational Department of

[34] *Ibid.*
[35] *Ibid.*, section 350.
[36] *Ibid.*, section 344, part 2.

the Supreme Court.[37] The latter upon receiving the complaint must forward the record of the case, which naturally contains also the records of the preliminary inquiry, to the Criminal-Cassational Department of the Supreme Court within twenty-four hours. The provincial court which sends the record may present its own explanations concerning the complaint or protest.[38] Unlike appeals (complaints) from the people's court, appeals from the provincial courts must be filed within seventy-two hours from the time the verdict is rendered if the procurator is the protesting party, or from the time the defendant is served with a copy of the verdict, if the appeal is made by him.[39] Under the Code of 1922, the time was forty-eight hours.[40] The court will accept an appeal after the expiration of the time fixed on a petition showing good cause for failure to act promptly, as in the case of appeals from the people's court. The simplicity of starting the appeal and its immediate effect in staying execution, as described with regard to the latter court, are fully applicable to appeals from the provincial court.

A marked distinction, however, between complaints from the two types of courts is found in the method of presenting special complaints. While such complaints from the people's judge or court are submitted to the same higher tribunal which has jurisdiction of cassational complaints, special complaints from the provincial or circuit courts are taken to the cassational division of the same courts[41] and not to the Supreme Court, as by analogy one would expect.

An appeal (complaint) from verdicts and judgments of the provincial court is, under normal circumstances, a matter of right as it is from the people's court. But as the provincial court takes original jurisdiction of what the government considers the most

[37]Until 1928, appeals from all the courts of the so-called second group —provincial, circuit and regional trial courts—were to be taken to the Supreme Court. But the tendency is directed toward granting to the regional courts cassational authority. Thus in the redistricted parts of the country, cases from the people's court will be appealed to the circuit court, and cases tried originally at the latter court will be taken on cassation to the regional court. In such an event the cassational jurisdiction of the Supreme Court will be greatly reduced. The entire question is being widely discussed in the Soviet legal press.

[38]Code, 1927, section 401.

[39]*Ibid.*, section 400.

[40]Code, 1922, section 433.

[41]Code, 1927, section 405.

dangerous criminal acts aimed against the new political and social order, a characteristic emergency clause is inserted. This provides that the provincial court in regions put under martial law may request the provincial executive committee, which is the highest executive authority in the province, to block an appeal from a sentence of death. The latter body is to decide within twenty-four hours whether a complaint in any given case shall go up for review. The executive committee may, however, exercise this general power to block appeals in capital cases only upon a specific ruling of the All-Russian Central Executive Committee, the highest authority of the Republic, which must state the exact period of time during which this power may operate.[42] This extraordinary proceeding is, however, not to interfere with the general rule requiring the court of original jurisdiction to telegraph to the Supreme Court in the case of every sentence of death, so that the highest judicial authorities may, if they wish, order a stay of execution and demand that the case be removed for a review by way of supervision.[43]

c. *Hearing of Cassational Complaints and Protests*

1. At the Criminal-Cassational Division of the Provincial or Circuit Court

The hearing of a complaint in the provincial or circuit court takes place in open court at a judicial session of the cassational division to which the parties are summoned. The failure of the parties to appear, however, though they have received the summons on time, will not necessarily prevent the court from reviewing the case and disposing of the complaint at the time set.[44] It is interesting to note that in pre-revolutionary Russia such were the rules in the *apelyatziya* courts, both for the conference of the justices of the peace and at the judicial chamber,[45] while in the case of the court of cassation, the Cassational Department of the Senate, the parties were neither summoned nor notified of the hearing.

[42] *Ibid.*, section 406, first and third parts.
[43] *Ibid.*, section 406, part 2 and section 440.
[44] *Ibid.*, section 409.
[45] *Fundamental Laws of the Russian Empire*, 1911, Vol. XVI, section 159.

The judicial session of the cassational division must follow the rules of procedure applicable to the trial of the case at the people's court, in so far as they are applicable to these proceedings, such as the rules providing for an open and public hearing, the right to challenge a judge for cause, etc. The presiding judge declares the session open, after announcing the particular case to be heard, and then checks up the parties present and absent.

The proceedings begin with the reading of a report by one of the judges who has made a study of the record of the case. Usually he reads the verdict and sentence of the trial court which, as we know, contains a short history of the case, the evidence presented at the trial for and against the defendant, the conclusion reached by the trial court, and the sentence imposed, or the fact of acquittal. The reporting judge states, of course, the exact source and nature of the complaint or protest, if these are mentioned, and may briefly tell what he found when studying the case, restricting himself only to a statement of facts; he must refrain from commenting on the merits of the complaint, for argument on the merits is left to the parties and the procurator in the open session of the court, and to the court when it retires to the consulting chamber.[46] This important and undoubtedly useful method of having one judge report the case is a re-enactment of the procedure in force in both the appellate and the cassational courts in Russia before 1917.

After the report of the judge the parties may have something to comment on. The law provides that "The parties, if they participate in the session, shall offer explanations; the party complaining shall have the first word. After that the court shall hear the conclusion of the procurator and then the final word shall be given to the defendant or his advocate."[47]

The question of the participation of defense counsel, as a matter of right, is not mentioned in the Code. It is, however, pointed out[48] that all the parties who participated in the original trial may appear at the cassational hearing as of right. Thus the advocate who represented the defendant in the court below and

[46]*Commentaries*, page 372.
[47]Code, 1927, section 410.
[48]*Commentaries*, pages 367-368.

who is considered a party has an absolute right to appear and support the complaint, unless the defendant does not wish him to do so. But whether the court must permit the participation of defense counsel when the defendant has had no advocate at the trial is not quite clear, and because of the unfriendly attitude of Soviet law towards advocates in general,[49] we should venture to answer in the negative. We must, however, remember that cases heard on appeal in the provincial court are usually simple and not of a serious nature, for they all come from the people's court, which has no wide jurisdiction over grave offenses. At any rate, the participation of advocates at the cassational division seems to be the exception rather than the rule, as the writer observed while attending a great number of cassational hearings at Moscow and elsewhere. We may note in passing that at the beginning of the Soviet régime under the Instructions to the People's Court of June, 1918, the participation of advocates at the cassational hearings was explicitly and unqualifiedly permitted.[50]

The requirement that the procurator be present and give his conclusion, which was taken over from the former Russian system, is not strictly followed in practice. In 1926, the cases in which the procurator participated at the provincial cassational division for fourteen provinces amounted to 44.1% of all the cases heard there.[51] A similar percentage was given for the whole Federated Republic.[52] But the tendency seems to be towards an increase in the number of cases in which the procurator appears at the cassational court. During 1927 the average for all provinces was 49.8%, while for all the autonomous territories it amounted to 67%. The only parts of the Federated Republic where the participation of the procuracy at the provincial, and circuit cassational divisions has decreased are the reorganized administrative units, the regions, which embrace several former provinces, where the average participation in 1927 was only 35.7%.[53]

[49]In a conversation with a deputy president of a cassational division of an important provincial court, the writer was told by the judge: "I consistently and consciously chase them (the advocates) out of here."

[50]Collected Laws, No. 53, Article 597, 1918, section 56.

[51]Official Report of the Procuracy for 1926, Moscow, 1927, page 128.

[52]*The Weekly*, No. 31, 1928, page 854.

[53]B. Briskin, *The Weekly*, Nos. 40 and 41, 1928, page 1080.

An important feature in the procedure at the cassational hearing is the rule that though the presiding judge is not to allow the parties to argue on anything except the questions raised on the cassational grounds set forth in the original complaint or in the supplementary complaint which may be presented at any time before the procurator gives his conclusion,[54] this rule is not applicable to the defendant. The latter, whether he is the appellant or appellee, is not bound by any restrictions, and he may speak even as to the merits of the case, though in theory the court has no jurisdiction to review the case from this angle.

This is the procedure, usually very brief, which takes place in open court, immediately after which the court without any recess retires to deliberate on its decision. The cassational hearing is merely for the purpose of giving the parties an opportunity to add some statement or to clarify certain points at issue, the important source for the court's deliberation being the record of the case.

2. At the Criminal-Cassational Department of the Supreme Court

The high position of the Supreme Court as a reviewing and supervisory tribunal over the entire judiciary of the vast Federated Republic of over one hundred million population becomes apparent from a study of the tremendous power it exercises in directing the judicial policy of all the courts, including those of the autonomous republics. While the general control of the Supreme Court embraces even the activities of the people's courts, its direct and immediate supervision is exercised over courts of higher standing. During 1926, the Supreme Court of the R.S.F.S.R. had under its immediate supervision nine superior courts, which are the highest courts in the autonomous republics, three regional and fifteen territorial courts (both of the same standing) forty-one provincial and twenty-six circuit courts.[55]

The cassational proceedings at the Supreme Court on the whole resemble those in the provincial court, but there are a number of important differences which we are to note.

[54]Code, 1927, section 410.

[55]Report of the Supreme Court, by its President, P. Stuchka. Jud. Practice, No. 4, 1927.

First, as to the rôle of the procurator attached to the Supreme Court, who is an assistant procurator of the Republic. He, or his assistant, must not only attend every hearing and render his conclusion as to the merits of the complaint, but he is also charged with the duty of supervising the arrangement of the cases to be heard, and the method of their preparation.[56] Complaints are usually listed for hearing in the order in which they are received, except capital cases, which are listed first and must be heard not later than within one week from the day the record reaches the court.[57]

Unlike the proceedings at the cassational division of the provincial court, the parties are not summoned, but are permitted to participate in the session if they appear. The lists of cases assigned for hearing are to be made public twenty-four hours before the hearing.[58] As a matter of practice, the writer has observed that the lists of cases are always posted on the bulletin board outside the court building at least three days prior to the hearing of the complaint.[59]

The law provides that "The hearing shall take place in open court, and shall begin with a report of one of the judges, after which the court shall hear the conclusion of the procurator and the statements of the parties, if the latter are permitted to participate in the case. The defendant, however, if he is present, must be given at his request an opportunity to make a statement."[60] From this it would seem that the procurator is to speak first. The practice, however, is otherwise. The procurator is there not to oppose or contest the appeal (complaint) of the defendant, but to fulfill his duty as the guardian and supervisor of the revolutionary law and order. The writer, who attended a hearing at the Supreme Court on August 25, 1928, made the following notes at that time:

> "The presiding judge read the report, which was a verdict and sentence from the Yaroslav Provincial Court

[56]Code, 1927, section 434, part 2.

[57]*Ibid.*, part 1.

[58]*Ibid.*, section 435, part 2.

[59]While there are no rules of court, in the sense that we have them in our courts, the practice of announcing the cases to be heard three days prior to the hearing is strictly adhered to.

[60]Code, 1927, section 435, part 1.

and which in itself covered the entire history of the case, the facts presented prior to and at the trial, a description of the personalities of the defendants, their former convictions of specified crimes, and the sentence of the court—death. The president made several remarks about the case and read the appeal asking for mitigation of the sentence. The advocate for the condemned then spoke. He made a strong appeal on the grounds that the defendants were still corrigible and that the sentence was out of proportion to the nature and seriousness of the crime. (It was the second offense of both defendants. The first time they had been sentenced to death but the Supreme Court reduced the sentence to ten years' imprisonment, which is the maximum prison term that may be imposed.) The presiding judge made a few remarks concerning the points touched upon by the advocate, to which the advocate replied at some length. This exchange of remarks was conducted in a simple and informal fashion. The procurator, who was sitting at a separate table and taking notes, was then asked by the court to give his 'conclusion'. He spoke like a prosecutor opposing the advocate's plea. There was, however, no bitterness or impassioned utterances in his talk; he spoke rather coldly, in a businesslike manner. After his speech the judges immediately withdrew to the consulting chamber, from which they later emerged to announce their decision to dismiss the appeal."

As the law stipulates that the parties to the appeal are to participate if permitted by the court, this question is decided in each case by the administrative session of the court. Usually the entire problem narrows itself down to whether or not the advocate is to appear and argue. The latter must petition the court for permission to argue, but not infrequently the petition is refused. The writer has on many occasions heard the secretary of the court announce before the opening of the session the refusal in a list of cases read of requests to permit the participation of counsel. In the event of such refusal, the requirement that the court sit in open judicial session is not strictly observed. This is explained on practical grounds, in that as there is no public, it is ridiculous for the court to hold session in the spacious but empty court-room.

The presence of advocates at the Supreme Court sessions is seemingly not the ordinary practice. In 1924 defense counsel appeared at the Supreme Court in only 534 cases, affecting 1,299 persons, or only 4.6% of all the complaints heard; while in 1925 the advocates argued in 715 cases, or 4.8% of all the cassational cases reviewed by this court.[61] It is unlikely that the proportion has increased in later years, because of the marked animosity towards advocates as a class. In a resolution adopted by the Commissariat of Justice, as a basis for a project for a new Code of Criminal Procedure, it is frankly proposed that no advocates shall be permitted in cases heard upon review.[62]

The privileged position in which the law places the defendant by providing that if present he must be given an opportunity to make a statement is also of little practical value, unless the defendant has been acquitted in the court below and the appeal is taken by the procurator, or though convicted has been let out on bail, which happens but rarely. In the ordinary case, if the defendant appealing is in jail, he will have no opportunity to be present, for the court is not to summon him.

d. *Scope of Cassational Review*

The fundamental conception of the true cassational method, as we have already mentioned, is rooted in the principle that the merits of the case have already been finally settled at the trial and that the cassational tribunal is only to examine the case to determine whether the trial court has violated substantive or procedural law, *as charged by the appellant.* Any other consideration of the case or of the sentence would be utterly outside the province of the cassational courts. It is sometimes said that at the cassational hearing the trial court is the defendant, for it is charged with violating the law of the land, and the ultimate aim of the court of cassation is not so much to protect the rights of the individual citizen—though that may result indirectly—as it is to enforce the correct interpretation and application of the

[61] *The Weekly,* No. 3, 1927, page 73. Report of the Cassational Department of the Supreme Court.

[62] *The Weekly,* No. 26, 1928, page 748.

law. To what extent these fundamental features have been preserved or rejected in the present Soviet system, we shall see as we proceed.

A striking characteristic of the nature of cassation as modified by the Soviet system is the fact that the court, not being restricted in its review to errors assigned in the complaint, as was already provided by the acts on the people's courts of 1918[63] and 1920,[64] "must, irrespective of the particular complaints, examine the entire record of each case by way of a review and if any errors of law are found which may serve as a ground for reversal or modification, the verdict shall be reversed and the case sent for a new trial."[65] In other words, the court is bound to search the record for such errors as will justify a reversal. What is really necessary in order to throw open the entire record of a case for a scrutinizing examination is the bare presence of a complaint, in any form or shape whatsoever, without which the cassational court will have no jurisdiction. "The provincial court [as well as the circuit or Supreme Court] shall deliberate on the question of reversing or modifying the verdict or sentence only when there has been a cassational complaint or protest."[66] The aggrieved party need only take the initiative and express a desire to have the case reviewed, and the proceedings are fully and effectively set in motion. The pointing out of particular grounds for the appeal apparently serves only the purpose of calling the court's attention to the explicit reason for granting the relief sought. Therefore, any assignment of errors on the part of the appellant will, in the last analysis, have the effect of helping the court to detect errors and reversible grounds which it would otherwise itself have to search for. But even should the complaint state only such reason as is clearly not ground for reversal in a court of cassation, the latter must, as we know, open the record and search for other valid grounds. This liberality, an obvious departure from the usual idea of cassation, is explained on the basis of exigency. "The majority

[63] P. C. Act, 1918, section 90.

[64] P. C. Act, 1920, section 92.

[65] Code, 1927, section 412. (See also the Ukrainian Code of 1927, section 346, and the White Russian Code, section 412.)

[66] *Ibid.*, section 411.

of convicted persons," write the commentators on the Code, "do not know how to write complaints, and do not know how to point out the actual cassational grounds. To point out correctly cassational errors one would have to possess some legal training, which the average person clearly does not have. To get an attorney requires some money, as the legal aid organization cannot yet take care of everybody."[67] To this we may add that the institution of any proceeding which would necessitate the participation of counsel would be utterly repugnant to the system which looks askance at the very existence of advocates, and tolerates them as an unavoidable evil.

How the present day appeals are written is told by the Supreme Court: "The overwhelming majority of cassational complaints are written by defendants who are almost completely ignorant in general matters and especially in matters judicial. A great number of the complaints are narrowed down to either a protest of innocence [which is, in theory, not to be taken up by the cassational court], to a plea to mitigate the sentence, or to a request for a pardon,"[68] none of which is a true cassational ground.

While the situation described undoubtedly seems a valid practical reason for permitting cassational courts to go beyond the complaint itself, there is, it seems, another and more profound reason which is rooted in the theory of the structure and functions of the Soviet judiciary. For this wide scope of review is the logical outcome of the notion that cassational courts shall supervise not merely particular decisions, but all the judicial activities of the lower, subordinate courts. It is the fundamental idea of a judicial hierarchy. Outside of other aims the cassation is "to serve as a means by which the cassational court exercises its control over the activities of courts of original jurisdiction."[69]

e. *Grounds for Cassation*

Ground for cassation are:

(1) The insufficiency or incorrectness of the inquiry proceedings both prior to and at the trial;

[67] *Commentaries*, page 374.

[68] Report by the Cassational Department of the Supreme Court for 1926, Jud. Practice, No. 22, 1927, page 2.

[69] *Commentaries*, page 374.

(2) Material violations of the rules of procedure;

(3) A violation or an incorrect interpretation of the substantive law;

(4) A plainly unjust verdict or sentence.[70]

One of these must be present in the record of the case to justify a disturbance of the verdict reached at the trial. We shall now proceed to examine the nature of these four grounds separately.

"An inquiry shall be considered insufficient or incorrect if it was so conducted either preliminarily or at the trial that it failed to clear up any circumstance the investigation of which might have influenced the verdict or sentence."[71] Here we have another abandonment of one of the basic principles of the cassational method, namely, that the court is not to go beyond the realm of errors of substantive or procedural law. To require the court to search for possible insufficiency or incorrectness of the investigation must inevitably lead to an examination of the particular questions which should have been inquired into or investigated, and consequently digging into the factual side of the case must follow. Furthermore, the cassational court is to review not only the proceedings at the trial, or the judicial inquiry, but also at the minute preliminary inquiry, the insufficiency or incorrectness of which was not cured at the trial.

This ground for reversal in cassational proceedings is, as one would expect, an innovation introduced by the Soviet régime. It was first brought within the scope of cassational review at the end of 1918,[72] and it has survived all the innumerable changes and modifications which have taken place in the law since. By introducing such a ground for a cassational reversal of a verdict, the pure method of cassation was polluted with some traits of the *apelyatziya*, whose function was to re-examine the merits of the case. N. V. Krylenko, Procurator of the Republic and Deputy Commissar of Justice, admits that the "examination of the question of whether there was a lack of preliminary investigation which might have influenced the verdict is nothing other than the

[70]Code, 1927, section 413.
[71]*Ibid.*, section 414.
[72]P. C. Act, 1918, section 89.

entry into the merits of the case."[73] A distinction is, however, drawn between the former *apelyatziya* and the present cassation in that the latter "may not [as the court of *apelyatziya* did] evaluate the testimony, *i. e.,* * * * it may not decide which testimony should have been believed and which rejected; testimoney once weighed by the trial judges in accordance with their inner conviction may not be re-examined at the second [cassational] instance."[74]

"By a material error in the forms of procedure is meant such violations of the Code of Criminal Procedure as have deprived the parties of their rights guaranteed by law during the trial, and have influenced or might have influenced the nature of the verdict rendered."[75] Error in procedure is not necessarily prejudicial; the mere violation of rules of procedure does not necessarily result in a reversal unless it is of such a nature that it probably influenced the decision of the trial court. Obviously, it is within the discretion of the court of cassation to classify the nature of a given error. An illuminating example of the attitude taken by the Soviet legislature towards violations of the rules of procedure is shown by the law concerning the improper assumption of jurisdiction by the court over a particular crime. Though the trial court had no jurisdiction of the crime, the cassational court may leave the verdict undisturbed, provided (a) the justness of the verdict is beyond question; and (b) the trial court did not overstep the bounds of its competency.[76] Under this vague phrase, the plenum of the Supreme Court decided that the trial of a case at the people's court, when it should have been tried at the provincial court, is not necessarily reversible error.[77] Thus, not the mere violation of a rule is the test, but the harmful consequences which ensue therefrom. On the other hand, the law provides that certain violations of procedure must carry a reversal. These are an improper composition of the trial court, a failure of the court to dismiss the proceedings as required by law (as, for example, where the statute of limitations has run in

[73]Krylenko, *The Judiciary and the Law,* 1928, page 129.
[74]*Ibid.*
[75]Code, 1927, section 415, first part.
[76]*Ibid.,* section 419.
[77]*Commentaries,* page 394.

favor of the defendant, or a settlement was effected in cases where this is permitted, etc.), where the case was tried in the absence of the defendant if his presence is required, and where no defense counsel appeared though his participation was obligatory.[78] All these are deemed so fundamental that their violation must have influenced the outcome, and therefore they are reversible errors *per se*.

The incorrect application or violation of the substantive law means: (1) "The failure to apply a law which should have been applied; (2) the application of a law which should not have been applied; (3) the incorrect interpretation of the law so as to contradict its exact meaning or its general nature; (4) the application of laws and orders not promulgated by proper authorities, or which are contrary to decisions of the central organs."[79] The cassational court is, however, not compelled to annul the verdict unless "the errors by the court below resulted in a different verdict or sentence from that which would have been pronounced if the appropriate law had been applied."[80] Here again we see that it is not the merely technical violation of the law but the detrimental consequences of such violation that are the determining factors.

We may note in passing that the last two grounds for reversal, namely, the violation of either substantive or procedural law—are the only grounds for true cassational review. They can be properly considered by a court of cassation without any trespass into the realm of the factual side, the merits of the case, which is, in theory, the exclusive province of courts of original jurisdiction. The grounds for cassational reversal of a verdict at the Cassational Department of the Governing Senate in Tzarist Russia was, as we know, of a similar nature. The latter tribunal reviewed only alleged "obvious departures from the direct reason of the law and alleged incorrect interpretations of the law; violations of the rules of procedure so fundamental that if not applied it would be impossible to recognize the judgment as a legal decision."[81] Such practice was in full accord with the basic

[78] *Ibid.*, page 384 and Code, 1927, section 415, subsections 1-4.
[79] Code, 1927, section 416, subsections 1-4.
[80] *Ibid.*, Part 5.
[81] *Fundamental Laws of the Russian Empire*, Vol. XVI, section 912.

ideas of cassation as it has developed in the French *cour de cassation,* the prototype of the Russian court by the same name established in 1864. But, as already pointed out, the Soviet system has so widened the scope of the cassational authority as to wipe out the well-defined border lines between cassation and *apelyatzia.* A striking illustration of this is the last, fourth, ground for reversing or modifying the verdict.

What is a plainly unjust verdict or sentence? The Code states that "A sentence shall be regarded plainly unjust when the punishment fixed by the court, though within the limits of the law, is sharply out of proportion to the particular crime."[82] This explanatory section does not throw any light in defining when a sentence is to be deemed plainly unjust, and therefore it is necessarily left to the discretion of the court to analyze and weigh all the circumstances of every case.

The question which immediately presents itself is: Was this provision intended purely as a protection to the defendant or was it meant to work against his interest at times? The commentators on the Code argue that the term "unjust" could not mean anything but unjust to the defendant, and, therefore, under this provision a verdict may be reversed or modified for its severity but not for its mildness.[83] Whatever merits there may be in such strict legal reasoning, the interpretation is clearly otherwise. The numerous cases where verdicts have been reversed by the Supreme Court because of their mildness,[84] upon the

[82]Code, 1927, section 417. (The Ukrainian revised Code of 1927, section 327, thus defines the term "plainly unjust". Whenever the punishment is out of proportion to the social danger of the criminal act or to the person who committed the act.)

[83]*Commentaries,* pages 389-390.

[84]Jud. Practice, No. 11, 1928, page 11, Case No. 23545. X killed Y, a girl, for refusing to marry him. The sentence of three years' imprisonment was reversed on the protest of the procurator.

X, a member of the police exceeded his authority and appropriated 13 rubles found on a person he searched at the station house. His sentence was reduced by the trial court to one year of forced labor (without imprisonment). Reversed on the protest of the procurator. Jud. Practice, No. 20, 1928, Case No. 215060.

A representative of the provincial court together with an assistant procurator and a chief of police were given a conditional sentence of one year (parol) for misconduct in office; held too mild and a new trial was ordered on the legal ground that it was plainly unjust. Jud. Practice, No. 22, 1928, page 11, Case No. 210030.

These are but few of the numerous decisions of the Supreme Court, reversing sentences because they are too mild, and therefore out of proportion with the nature and seriousness of the crime.

protest of the procurator, are sufficient to dispel any doubts as to the meaning of the law, though the decisions of the Cassational Department of the Supreme Court are not binding as expressions of general law.[85] There is, however, this important difference. When the case is reversed on the complaint of the procurator for its excessive mildness, the cassational court cannot increase the punishment, it can only order a new trial; while on the complaint of the defendant, the court may reduce the sentence then and there. On the whole, we may safely assume that the provision for a modification of the sentence will more often inure to the benefit of the defendant than to his disadvantage.

This significant power of the cassational court appeared in Soviet law at an early stage of its development. The Second Decree on Courts of March, 1918, granted to the conference of the people's judges, then the only court of cassation, the power to reverse a verdict if it was plainly unjust.[86] Such a provision has been continuously maintained not only in the ordinary courts but even in the revolutionary tribunals during the period of their existence.[87] It came into being at a time when the new régime did not yet have any criminal code of its own making, while the courts were explicitly forbidden to apply the pre-revolutionary code.[88] The purpose of entrusting the higher, controlling court with the power to reverse or modify a sentence which was out of proportion to the nature of the alleged criminal act was necessary in order to enable the court to create and maintain a general

[85]In one of its circulars of instructions, the plenum of the Supreme Court stated that "the published decisions of the Cassational Department of the Supreme Court are only binding with regard to the cases decided, and therefore have not the force of a law, nor is its interpretation generally binding. It has merely a significance as an exemplary decision for similar cases." Only the Plenum of the Supreme Court is to interpret the law on judicial practice—Jud. Act of 1926, section 180, Part a.

[86]Second Decree, section 5.

[87]Collected Laws, No. 45, Article 545, 1918, section 4; Collected Laws, Nos. 22 and 23, Article 115, 1920, section 23. Both of these were important Acts on the Revolutionary Tribunals.

[88]The "First Decree" explicitly allowed the Tzarist criminal law to apply, as far as it was adaptable to the new situation. But by the People's Court Act of 1918, the application of the pre-revolutionary criminal law was explicitly forbidden. From that time up to 1922 there was no definite criminal law, save a general outline of penal policy adopted in 1919, under the title, "Guiding Principles of Penal Law", Collected Laws, No. 66, Article 590, 1919. *(Rukovodyaschie Nachala Po Ugolovnomu Pravu R.S.F.S.R.)*

standard for fixing penalties. Nevertheless, this provision survived even after 1922, when the Soviet government had enacted a well-defined criminal code of its own. It is now contended that "This section has become an anachronism",[89] but its application is so widely resorted to by the Supreme Court as undoubtedly to prove its value and to justify its existence.

As we have indicated, two of the four basic grounds for reversing a verdict—defects or incompleteness in the inquiry and unjustness of the sentence—will necessarily carry the reviewing courts beyond the ordinary cassational line of dealing with legal defects, and will place them directly in the position of considering the merits of the case as revealed by the record. Soviet legal writers are conscious of the necessity of establishing some standards for cassation, for to fail to do so would invite the destruction of every vestige of the cassational system to which they still adhere. They have, therefore, attempted to build up some definite lines behind which the cassational powers may not penetrate. "The cassational court," we are told, "is to see whether the court of original jurisdiction has done all it could in order to establish the material truth, and if so, whether it was correctly done, but what was truth and what falsity is the sole province of the court of the first instance."[90] For example, a verdict was reversed because contradictory testimony of a witness was not verified.[91] As another writer puts it, the cassational courts are not to weigh the testimony which the trial judges have recognized as true, but are only "to test the *formal* [legal] *correctness of the verdict and the inner logic of the conclusions arrived at by the judges of the first instance.*"[92] In other words, the reviewing courts are to refrain from disturbing the factual findings, but are to examine *"the correct legal conclusions* based upon those facts, but nothing more."[93]

These niceties may be sound legal differentiations, but it would require greater legal refinement and astuteness of mind than common among Soviet judges for them to be unerringly

[89]Krylenko, *The Judiciary and the the Law,* 1928, page 131.
[90]*Commentaries,* page 378.
[91]Case No. 2660. Reported in Jud. Practice, No. 6, 1928, page 23.
[92]Krylenko, *op. cit.,* note 89, *supra,* page 129.
[93]*Ibid.,* page 130.

guided by such a flimsy standard. It is therefore safe to assume that the scope of reviewing is even broader than it would seem at first glance.

f. *Powers of the Court of Cassation*

We are now to analyze the powers of the cassational court when, in reviewing the entire record, it has discovered one of the grounds for disturbing the verdict as described above. Unlike any court of *apelyatzia,* the court of cassation cannot, as a rule, substitute its own judgment for that rendered by the trial court. The ordinary remedy is to reverse the judgment and send the case for a new trial to another court of the same standing or to the same court with different judges sitting.[94] But the scope of the cassational authority is often broader than that. The Code specifically singles out a number of instances where the court is empowered either to reduce the sentence or to annul it altogether without remanding the case for a new trial, and thus practically to substitute a verdict of acquittal for that of conviction. These are cases where the act of which the defendant was convicted does not contain the elements of a crime, or where the court has failed to dismiss a case when it should have done so for reasons specifically enumerated by law, as where the statute of limitations has run, etc. In these cases, "the provincial court as well as the Supreme Court, reversing the verdict [and sentence] of the trial court [people's, circut or provincial, respectively] shall discontinue the proceedings of the case without sending it * * * for a new trial."[95] These are practically the only instances in which an entirely different verdict can be substituted. There are in addition certain conditions which will justify a modification of the sentence. This takes place where the cassational tribunal finds that the court below incorrectly applied the law to the facts as established by the inquiry and stated in the verdict, which, as we know, sets forth all the material facts of the case. In other words, if the facts established in the first part of the verdict (the descriptive) would require that the second part of the same document (the determinative) be based upon a differ-

[94]Code, 1927, section 420, part 1.
[95]*Ibid.*, section 418.

ent section of the Criminal Code, or "where the sentence does not correspond to the seriousness of the alleged criminal act, the provincial [or the Supreme] court may without directing the case for a new trial effect the necessary modifications of the sentence of the * * * trial court, provided, however, that the punishment fixed by the cassational court [provincial as well as Supreme Court] must not be more severe than the one originally imposed, and not lower than the minimum fixed by the appropriate section of the Criminal Code."[96]

The power of the cassational court to modify a sentence, under given circumstances, for the benefit of the defendant was first vested in the cassational division of the provincial court in 1924,[97] but previous to that, even by the Code of 1923, this power was granted to the Supreme Court, while the cassational division of the provincial court could either reverse the judgment and order a new trial, or discontinue the case completely under the specific conditions described above. By the Amendment of 1924, as stated, the scope of the provincial cassational court was so enlarged as to equal that possessed previously only by the Supreme Court.

With regard to cases tried at the people's court, the power of the provincial cassational division in the realm of corrective jurisdiction was thus enhanced to an extent unknown since the very first period of Soviet rule, when the cassational court was empowered to reduce the punishment or even pardon the defendant in its own discretion.[98] Such broad powers vested at that time in a reviewing court were obviously contrary to the basic idea of a court of cassation as distinguished from a court of appeals. Soon afterwards, by the Instruction to the people's courts, it was stated that the high court could reduce the punishment but only in exceptional cases should it suspend sentence.[99] But the first act on the people's court, the Act of 1918, which served both as a judiciary act and a rudimentary code of procedure, completely abandoned this indiscriminately wide authority

[96] *Ibid.*, section 419a.

[97] Collected Laws, No. 78, Article 784, 1924.

[98] Second Decree, section 5.

[99] Collected Laws, No. 53, Article 597, 1918, section 54.

of the cassational court, and narrowed its scope nearer to the true sphere of cassational power.

The decision reached by the cassational division of the provincial court, on the basis mentioned above, must not only contain its exact terms, but also the specific reasons which have led the court so to decide. The law requires that "Whenever the verdict is reversed, the court [of cassation] shall point out the particular sections of the law which were violated by the lower court, the precise thing which constitutes the violation thereof, as well as the reasons for considering it a material breach [and therefore reversible error]. Whenever the verdict shall be reversed because it is plainly unjust, the court shall stipulate the reasons for deeming it unjust. It must also state in its decision to which stage of the proceeding the case is to be remanded."[100] The latter requirement is important, for the verdict may be reversed for material errors which occurred during the preliminary inquiry. It may revert to the proceeding of holding for trial, or the framing of the accusatoy conclusions, or any other definite step in the long process of the proceedings prior to the trial.

Though neither the cassational division of the provincial or circuit court, nor the Cassational Department of the Supreme Court, is vested with authority to lay down general rules of law, or even interpret the exact meaning of certain sections of the Code, things which only the plenum of the Supreme Court may do, the errors found and the corrections to be made as pointed out with regard to the specific case which the court remands for a new trial are absolutely binding upon the court re-trying the case.[101] Thus the grounds which necessitated a reversal will be eliminated and corrected. The court may, and often does, make very practical suggestions—for example, that certain witnesses be examined, that a specified circumstance be made clear, that experts be called for a purpose indicated, etc.

All our discussion and analysis concerning the scope of the review and the powers of the cassational courts are the same with regard to both branches of judicial cassation—the cassational division of the provincial or circuit courts and the Cassational

[100]Code, 1927, section 421.
[101]*Ibid.*, section 423.

Department of the Supreme Court. But there is this exception. The latter tribunal, when it thinks a sentence is excessive, may not only reverse and order a new trial or reduce it within the limits of the law applicable, but it may go still farther. Whenever it is of the opinion that the merits of the case make it advisable to reduce the sentence beyond the lowest norm fixed by law, or suspend it altogether, it may petition the All-Russian Executive Committee, the highest authority in the Republic, for such a reduction or suspension,[102] which petition, we may safely presume, will be granted, as the many reported instances clearly indicate. Thus while strictly speaking the Supreme Court may not reduce the punishment beyond the limits set by law, and therefore even the highest cassational court is deprived of the power to pardon as an incident of judicial corrective method, an effective means is provided whereby the desired end may be realized. This has been deemed important in order to enable the highest court to regulate and direct the general policy of repression or punishment. During 1926 alone the Supreme Court filed such petitions in 1552 cases, which made up 9 per cent. of all the cassational cases, capital ones excepted, reviewed by the court.[103]

The decisions rendered by the cassational division of the provincial court, or by the Supreme Court, are judicially final so far as the parties are concerned, and any chance of obtaining further relief as a matter of right is eliminated. This is known in Russian criminal procedure, the new as well as the old, as the time when a judgment becomes legally binding. But this does not prevent certain authorities from opening the case and having it reviewed by way of supervision or control. The Code provides that "Cassational decisions of the provincial court are to be considered final and may be protested exclusively by the method of supervision through the plenum of the provincial court to the Supreme Court of the Republic."[104] A similar method is provided for protesting the decisions of the Cassational Division of the Supreme Court to the plenum of the same court.[105]

[102] *Ibid.*, section 437.
[103] Jud. Practice, No. 23, 1927, page 7.
[104] Code, 1927, section 426.
[105] *Ibid.*, section 438.

g. *Special Complaints*

As we have seen, special complaints are appeals or protests against decisions or orders of the court or a judge, not affecting the verdict or judgment. The cassational division of the provincial court decides such appeals whether they are taken from the people's court or the judicial division of the provincial court. When taken from the latter court, "The complaint is determined at the administrative session of the court without the participation of the parties."[106] But when such special complaints are filed against the decisions or orders of the people's court the procedure is entirely different. Though the parties are neither summoned nor directly notified, the time and place of the hearing are posted at least one week in advance in the court building, and this serves as a general notice to all parties concerned. The complaint is heard at a judicial session in open court and if the parties appear they must be given an opportunity to make a statement.[107]

The hearing begins with a report presented by one of the judges, after which the parties, if present, have a right to make their statements, the complaining party opening the argument.[108] Unlike the procedure at the hearing of the cassational complaint, the procurator is not required to participate at the hearing of a special complaint, nor is the defendant given the privilege of having the final word. This procedure resembles somewhat the cassational proceedings at the Governing Senate before 1917, where the parties were not summoned but, if they appeared, were permitted to make a statement.[109]

The scope of the review is quite limited. The court is not to examine the entire record of the case but only the particular point complained of, and only with regard to the individuals claiming to be aggrieved. When deciding the question, the court has two alternatives, either to dismiss the complaint or annul the order or regulation of the court below.[110]

[106] *Ibid.*, section 405.
[107] *Ibid.*, section 431.
[108] *Ibid.*, section 432.
[109] *Fundamental Laws of the Russian Empire*, edition 1911, Vol. XVI, section 920.
[110] Code, 1927, section 432.

h. *The True Nature of the Present Cassation*

The method of criminal review as developed by the Soviet system is neither one of *apelyatziya,* for there is no re-trial at the higher court, nor one of true cassation as known and practiced on the continent outside of Russia. The present Soviet cassation essentially differs from that of the pre-revolutionary period in that (a) it may review the entire case and not only the errors assigned; (b) it permits the filing of a supplementary complaint even at the hearing; (c) the scope of the review goes far beyond strictly legal errors; (d) its decisions, though final, may still be reviewed by way of supervision.

The present cassational review is admittedly not one of true cassation but one of *revision*—a sort of "quasi-cassation" and "quasi-*apelyatziya*". This arrangement is considered by Soviet legal writers a happy solution to the problems of criminal appeal, the ultimate aim of which is and must always be to secure correct and just verdicts. "The manner of complaint where the entire record must be reviewed guarantees a maximum of certainty of the correctness of the verdict, while it makes it possible to forego the *apelyatziya* method."[111] Thus it is maintained that "our [Soviet] cassational method of reviewing verdicts appears as one of the most significant achievements of our procedure."[112]

IV. CRIMINAL REVIEW BY WAY OF SUPERVISION

One of the most striking and interesting features in the Soviet system of criminal review is the possibility of having the record of a criminal case re-examined and corrected by a higher court through the so-called method of supervision. By this is meant that certain specifically designated authorities of the judiciary and of the procuracy may on their own motion institute proceedings to have a higher court open the record of a case at any time and have the verdict or decision reversed or modified upon the proper grounds, as if it had been brought up on cassation.

Who are the authorities who may start proceedings, and in what manner is the case re-examined?

[111] I. A. Krastin, *The Criminal Process (trial),* Moscow, 1927, page 128.
[112] *Ibid.,* page 128.

The Code specifies that "The president of the provincial court or the provincial procurator shall have the power to demand the record of any case at any stage of the proceedings from the courts of the province [or other territorial unit such as the circuit, region, etc.]; the district procurators shall have such powers only with regard to cases in the people's courts within their respective districts."[113] To this broad statement there are a few limitations. First, only the procuracy may demand the record of a case still in the stage of the preliminary inquiry; second, if the record is demanded while the case is on trial, the latter is not to be interrupted and the record is not to be sent up by the court until after the verdict is reached.[114]

Thus we see that the highest officials of the provincial or similar court and procuracy are vested with the power to demand a case for a review from any court within their administrative unit. In accordance with the same idea "The president of the Supreme Court or his deputy, the Procurator of the Republic or his assistant who is attached to the Supreme Court[115] shall have the power to demand any case from any court of the Republic for the purpose of a review by way of supervision, and to order the sentence suspended until the review is completed. The court receiving such a demand must forward the record immediately except when the case is on trial, in which case the record is not to be sent until after the rendering of the verdict."[116] Here there is no distinction made between judicial and procuracy authorities, for the president of the Supreme Court as well as the central procuracy may call for the record irrespective of the stage of the proceedings, including the preliminary inquiry.

From what has been said, the sweeping nature of this method is quite evident. "Any case at any stage" is a succinct expression of the magnitude of this reviewing method which knows almost no limitations. For, irrespective of whether the case has not yet been tried or has already been disposed of by cassation, or whether it was a case which has gone through all the numerous

[113]Code, 1927, section 427, part 1.

[114]*Ibid.*, section 427, part 2.

[115]The Procurator of the Republic has a number of assistants, one of them is specifically attached to the Supreme Court for the purpose of carrying out the functions of the procuracy in connection with its court activities.

[116]Code, 1927, section 440.

stages of a preliminary inquiry, or has come to an end by a mere summary judgment which cannot be complained against,[117] the strong, far-reaching arm of the supervising authorities may reach it effectively.

Thus far we have discussed only the very first step, the sending up of the record. What is then to happen? There are a number of possibilities which are quite thoroughly described by the Code of Criminal Procedure.

a. *Preliminary Examination of the Record*

1. When No Errors or Defects are Discovered

The particular provincial authority which receives the case demanded examines the record preliminarily, and if no substantial errors are found he returns it whence it came—to the people's court or the investigating officials—and the proceedings are considered closed.[118] When, however, the higher central authorities, the president of the Supreme Court or the Procurator of the Republic and his assistants, ask for the record, the procedure is slightly different. The record is always sent directly to the procurator attached to the Supreme Court, who examines the material and if he fails to discover defects he must secure the consent of the president of the Supreme Court before he may discontinue the proceedings.[119] Thus the concurrent approval of both branches, the procuracy and the court, must be obtained before such a case may be dismissed. In this rule the much-debated idea of vesting the courts and the procuracy with concurrent powers reaches its high peak. The actual practice, however, has been simplified to this extent, that the procurator drops the proceedings in his own discretion, without consulting the president of the court, unless the case was transferred by the order of the latter.[120]

[117]There are a number of summary orders of the court or the individual judge which are not subject to a cassation. Among these are the fines imposed by the presiding judge at the trial for misbehavior in the court room, and the fixing of bail for one convicted who wishes not to be under guard during the pending of his appeal at the cassational instance.

[118]Code, 1927, section 428, part 1. The word "provincial" is used here to denote the type of court, and the described rules equally apply to the circuit courts.

[119]*Ibid.*, section 441.

[120]*Commentaries*, page 425.

2. When Reasons for Review are Found

Should the authority who orders the transfer of the record find thereon any apparent violations, the case must be forwarded to a court for review. The exact method by which that is achieved, as well as the determination of the court having authority to review it, depend upon the circumstances of each case.

We shall now consider the situation where the provincial or circuit court authorities have instituted the proceedings.

If the president of the court or the provincial procurator receives the case and determines that the record should be reviewed he must assign the case directly to the proper court, while the district procurator, who receives a case from the people's court, must assign it through his immediate chief, the provincial procurator. Which is the proper court to re-examine the record? This will depend upon whether the verdict in the case to be reviewed has already become legally binding. A verdict becomes legally binding, as we know, only after the court of cassation has rendered its decision on a complaint or protest, or after the expiration of the time allowed to file a complaint or protest if the parties have failed to avail themselves of their right to appeal.

Whenever the verdict is not yet legally binding—for the authorities may institute supervisory proceedings before the time to file a complaint has expired or even when such a complaint has been filed[121]—the authorities setting the proceedings in motion forward the case (a) to the cassational division of the provincial court, if the case has been or is to be tried at the people's court; (b) to the plenum[122] of the provincial court if the subject-matter of the case is within the jurisdiction of the criminal judicial division of the provincial court.[123] These courts, upon examining the

[121]The procurator, or the president of the court, may sometimes remove a case for review by way of supervision, though the defendant also files a cassational complaint. Not infrequently we read in the reports that the court dismissed the cassational complaint, but agreed with the procurator's protest. In the latter event, the punishment inflicted at the second trial may be more severe than the one imposed upon by the court at the first trial.

[122]The plenum is a joint session of the judges of all the divisions, including the disciplinary division and the courts of original jurisdiction and that of cassation. The latter two in turn, consists of civil and criminal branches. The plenum thus constituted is neither a trial court nor one of cassation, but it has important supervisory functions, one of which is the reviewing of cases by way of supervision or control.

[123]Code, 1927, section 428, part 2.

record and listening to the conclusions of the procurator, determine the further steps to be taken and the instructions, if any, which are to be given to the court below.[124]

But the procedure becomes considerably more involved when the case sought to be reviewed has already reached a legally binding verdict, and therefore can in no way be brought up by cassation. Here is where the entire system of supervisory review reaches its real significance both for the state and the defendant, but usually for the latter. The provincial authorities after obtaining the record and deciding that they have a proper case for supervisory review forward the record in the following manner: (a) If the case is originally tried at the people's court, and no complaint or protest is made, the case goes to the cassational division of the provincial court, which is the same court that would have listened to a complaint if filed, and this court has the power to reverse the verdict by way of supervision; (b) if a case is tried at the people's court and is either decided once by the cassational division on a cassational complaint, or by way of supervision as stated in (a) and the cassational division disagrees with the procurator who instituted the supervisory proceeding, the record is sent to the plenum of the provincial court. If the latter agrees with the opinion of the procurator and if the president of the provincial court is in accord, it renders its decision, which is final, and a copy of this decision is sent to the Supreme Court. But should the provincial procurator or the president of the provincial court[125] dissent from the decision reached by the plenum, the record of the case, including the decision of the plenum and the dissenting opinion of the president judge or the procurator, must be transferred to the Supreme Court of the Republic for a review by way of supervision and a final disposition of the matter.[126] We observe that a legally binding verdict of a people's court may not be disturbed either by the cassational division, when no cassational proceedings were previously had, or by the plenum of the provincial court, except when there is

[124] *Ibid.*, section 428, part 3.

[125] The Code grants such authority only to the procurator, but the plenum of the Supreme Court had interpreted it to cover also the president of the court, for such an arrangement is made by the Code with regard to all similar matters. *The Weekly*, No. 47, 1925.

[126] Code, 1927, section 429, subsections a and b.

full accord between the court, its president and the procurator. If there is not such accord the authority of the Supreme Court will have to be invoked.

We have so far dealt with cases tried at the people's court. With regard to cases originally tried at the judicial divisions of the provincial (or equivalent) courts, the supervisory proceedings are more simple.

A case which has reached a legally binding verdict is transferred through the president of the provincial court to the Cassational Department of the Supreme Court, to be reviewed by way of supervision. But the president of the provincial court may first submit the case for a preliminary discussion to the plenum of his court. The latter's opinion, which is of no legal force, is annexed to the case forwarded to the Supreme Court.[127]

We are still to consider the situation when the central authorities at Moscow take the initiative in having a case reviewed by way of supervision. Whether a case has been or is to be tried at the people's, provincial, or any other court within the Republic, if the president of the Supreme Court or the Procurator of the Republic or his assistants find any reason for having the case reviewed, no matter at what stage of the proceedings, even where there is a legally binding verdict, the record is sent to the Cassational Department of the Supreme Court. But if a case was tried originally at the Judicial Department of the Supreme Court, a rare occurrence, in which instance no cassation is permitted, or if a case has once been disposed of by the Cassational Department either by cassation or supervision, the record to be reviewed by way of supervision is directed to the plenum of the Supreme Court. During 1927 the highest judicial tribunal of the Republic reviewed eighty-nine criminal verdicts,[128] forty-one of which were brought on protests by the procurator against decisions of the Cassational Department of the same court,[129] while in 1926 the procurator protested against thirty-seven of such decisions.[130]

[127]*Ibid.*, section 429, subsection c.
[128]Jud. Practice, No. 7, 1928, page 28.
[129]*Ibid.*, No. 16, 1928, page 1.
[130]*Ibid.*, No. 23, 1927, page 6.

b. *Scope of Supervisory Review*

The scope of the supervisory review, as the name of such proceedings would suggest, is much broader even than that of cassation. The latter, in theory, still prohibits any attempt to decide a case on the merits, while the supervisory tribunal knows of no such limitations and may well indulge in partaking of the forbidden fruit of weighing the evidence presented at the trial. "The judicial supervision", Krylenko declared when addressing the Fifth Congress of Judicial Workers, "is not bound by any forms, and the case may be sent for a new trial not only on a finding of a legal incorrectness in the verdict but also when the supervisory organ does not agree with the merits of the verdict."[131] Thus this supervisory method "very much approaches the *apelyatziya* proceedings, and differs from it only in the fact that the court of supervision may not render its own substituted verdict, and that its proceedings are conducted without the participation of the parties."[132]

So far as the provincial court, sitting in a supervisory capacity, is concerned, the Code speaks only of its power to reverse the verdict, which will naturally, by analogy to its power as a cassational court, result in a new trial, or to reduce the sentence within the limits of the criminal law. But, as would be expected, the power of the Supreme Court as a supervisory tribunal is wider. The Code specifically provides that the Supreme Court, in cases where no trial has yet taken place, must decide the next step in the proceedings and instruct the proper organs accordingly. Where a verdict has already been rendered, the court may reverse or modify it,[133] and is in no way bound by the opinion or conclusion of the procurator even when the case is to be sent back to the preliminary inquiry.[134] The Supreme Court may even change the form of the accusation in the second part of the verdict (the determinative), although this has been based upon the testimony taken by the court of original jurisdiction.[135] In other words, the court of supervision may disregard the "inner convictions"

[131] *Commentaries*, page 408.
[132] *Ibid.*
[133] Code, 1927, section 441.
[134] *Ibid.*, section 444.
[135] *Commentaries*, page 425.

of the trial judges and thus overthrow their findings of facts, as well as their opinion as to trustworthiness of the testimony brought out at the trial.

We may note here in passing that while the opening of the record by the method of supervision "is not hindered by any time limitation",[136] the absolute application of this rule is restricted only to verdicts of guilt, but not to legally binding verdicts of acquittal, for the latter are barred from any review after the expiration of five years from the time they assume the status of a legally binding vedict.[137]

c. *Uniqueness of the Method*

This unique method of criminal review is the logical outgrowth of the Soviet conception of the rôle of the judiciary, and the interrelation of its various divisions. As the judiciary is viewed as an integral part of the government as a whole, designed to carry out the latter's general policies in the realm of judicial matters, the structure of a judicial hierarchy seems inevitable. The higher court is not only to review decisions of the lower court when brought on cassation by one of the aggrieved parties, but it is really held responsible for all the activities of the judicial tribunals below it on the ladder of the hierarchy. Each court, from the provincial and circuit court up, is deemed a supervisory and controlling agency for all the courts within its territory, whether it be a province, a region or the republic.

At this point it is highly interesting to note the resemblance of this supervisory method of criminal review to the old English writ of *certiorari* which the King issued by virtue of his position as the fountain of justice and supreme head of the whole judicial administration.[138] As the judicial prerogative of the King was exercised by the King's Bench the latter "was regarded as the highest court in the land with a superintendence over all other courts."[139] The king was to have control over the policies promulgated by the local justices and therefore cases from the justices of the peace were later to be "transferred to the Star Chamber

[136]Code, 1927, section 430.
[137]*Ibid.*, sections 3 and 374.
[138]Frank J. Goodnow, "The Writ of Certiorari," *Political Science Quarterly*, Vol. VI, page 493 (1891).
[139]*Ibid.*, page 497.

which was to correct not merely decisions of law but also questions of fact and of expediency."[140]

We shall not, however, attempt to carry too far the analogy between the Soviet supervisory method of review and the English writ of the fourteenth century. But there is this important point of similarity. The executive branch directs the activities of the judiciary. It must, therefore, have a high court which is to be instrumental in carrying out the functions of control. As a necessary corollary this high court is to be furnished with the means and endowed with the powers to check up and correct all errors and unjust decisions of courts below it, no matter when and where they have occurred.

This method of supervisory review is, in the last analysis, merely a means to facilitate the carrying out of the functions of judicial control. The aggrieved parties cannot set the proceedings in motion, as in the case of cassational review, though their complaint to the proper authorities can be, and often is, responsible for a demand for the record and its consequent review by way of supervision. But in this latter instance the parties merely assist the controlling authorities by calling their attention to an improper or unjust verdict or decision. Such information may with the same effect come from any other source,[141] or by the examination of finished cases on record without any information or complaint.

In a circular of instruction issued by the Commissariat of Justice in 1926, it is pointed out that the number of verdicts of the people's courts complained against to the court of cassation are comparatively small, and therefore "It is indispensable for the provincial and regional courts to undertake a systematic study of all the verdicts and decisions of the people's courts subordinate

[140] *Ibid.*, page 499.

[141] The writer while discussing with the Deputy President of the Supreme Court questions of cassation and supervision, and criminal procedure in general, remarked about the absence of defense counsel in a certain murder case which he attended. In that case the defendant, who made the impression of one physically and mentally ill, while sane according to testimony of a medical expert, was convicted and sentenced to five years imprisonment. The Deputy President of the Court in the presence of the writer telephoned to the Provincial Court and ordered that the record of that case be removed to the Supreme Court by way of supervision.

to them."[142] After the circular prescribes the exact method for such study, it emphasizes that such a revision is important in order to bring out and eliminate the defects in the work of the courts.

This manner of reviewing and reversing a verdict was early established in the Soviet system. But up to the judicial reform and codification era of 1922, such supervisory power lay with the Commissariat of Justice, and not with the courts. Even by the first Code of Criminal Procedure of 1922, it was provided that decisions of the courts of cassation, at that time the soviets of people's judges, could be taken by way of supervision to the Commissariat of Justice of the R.S.F.S.R.[143] With the further development and stabilization of the judicial system this power has been given over entirely to the courts, and is now an inseparable part of the complete system of judicial control.[144]

d. *Newly Discovered Evidence as Ground for Review*

Before we leave our discussion of this review by supervision we should note still another type of review known as "The proceedings to open the record upon newly discovered circumstances." Such proceedings fundamentally differ from what we have discussed heretofore, in that the reasons for the opening of the record and reviewing the case are not to be found in the record itself, but outside of it and that there is always a legally binding verdict.

There are several grounds for instituting such proceedings: (1) When it is proved that the verdict was based on perjured testimony; (2) when the judges who rendered the verdict criminally abused their authority[145] (both of which become valid grounds for opening the record only after the perjury or the abuse of authority, as the case may be, has been established by a legally binding verdict rendered by another court);[146] (3) when any other new circumstance is discovered which was

[142]Circular of the Commissar of Justice, No. 62, Collected Circulars for 1926, Moscow, 1927, page 6.

[143]Code, 1922, section 372.

[144]It is interesting to note that the Revolutionary Tribunals were the first to exercise the power of judicial supervision.

[145]Code, 1927, section 373.

[146]*Ibid.*, section 375.

unknown to the trial court if it tends to prove the innocence of the defendant or to prove his participation in a less or in a more serious crime than the one he was charged with.[147]

Proceedings in favor of the defendant may be started on his own request or on the request of his attorney, his relatives, or on a petition of the professional or social organization of which the defendant is a member, or by the procurator. Only the latter may request the opening of the case in which a verdict of acquittal has been rendered,[148] but such a step may be taken not later than one year from the time the new facts become known and not later than five years after the verdict of acquittal became legally binding.[149]

The provincial procurator on his own motion, or at the request of one of the persons enumerated above, must make all the necessary inquiries by himself or through the staff of the organs of inquiry or investigation. After such an investigation is completed, the entire record is transferred to the Cassational Department of the Supreme Court.[150] The question as to whether new proceedings should be instituted—that is, a new trial had—is decided by the latter court by way of supervision,[151] which means no parties will be permitted to participate. We observe that this form of supervision is vested only in the Supreme Court; the provincial and other courts may supervise the decisions and verdicts only on grounds which appear on the record of the case.

V. RESULTS OF THE CRIMINAL REVIEW

The system of criminal review which we have discussed and analyzed has a few quite definite singularities reflecting the attitude of the present régime. We shall now attempt to stress the direct effect of those peculiarities upon the results obtained, illustrating it by official data obtainable.

First, there is the method of appealing which is singular for its unusual ease and simplicity. The defendant who wishes to complain has not only a clear path, but he cannot be put in any

[147] *Ibid.*, section 373, subsection 3.
[148] *Ibid.*, section 376, part 1.
[149] *Ibid.*, section 374.
[150] *Ibid.*, sections 378, 445 and 446.
[151] *Ibid.*, section 447.

disadvantageous position on account of his appeal. For while Soviet law knows of no doctrine of double jeopardy, nevertheless, "If the verdict was reversed on the complaint of the defendant, the second trial may not result in a heavier sentence than the one imposed at the first trial."[152] This significant rule is not based on any abstract theory of inherent right, but is grounded on the principle that the filing of complaints should be encouraged rather than hampered. In the proposed project for a new Code of Criminal Procedure the drafters tried to deprive the defendant of his present security against a possible severer sentence, but that proposed innovation was defeated, the writer was informed, during a discussion at the Commissariat of Justice.[153] To what extent, then do parties avail themselves of the right to appeal or complain? A glance at Table No. 1 will show that in spite of

Table No. 1[154]

COMPLAINTS AGAINST CASES TRIED IN THE PEOPLE'S COURT

Year	Aggregate number of appeals filed	The % of complaints filed to total number of verdicts rendered	The % of complaints filed to total number of cases disposed of with or without a verdict
1924	160,278	12.7	6.9
1925	139,527	15.7	8.1
1926	180,648	21.1	..

the elimination of any difficulties or expense in making complaints their number is not so great as one would expect. The ratio of appeals from verdicts rendered at the provincial and similar courts, which try only serious offenses, is somewhat higher. Thus during 1924, 22% of all the verdicts rendered at the latter courts were

[152] *Ibid.*, section 424. While this section refers only to cases tried at the people's court, it was interpreted to cover also cases tried at the provincial and similar courts.

[153] This project for a new Code of Criminal Procedure was first submitted for a discussion to the Commissariat of Justice. The latter approves it, with a number of modifications.

[154] For the data covering 1924 and 1925, see the Official Report on Courts for 1925, Moscow, 1926, pages 84, 85 and 112. Those figures dealing with 1926 were taken from the Report on the Procuracy for 1926, Moscow, 1927, page 132.

appealed to the Supreme Court, while in 1925 it reached 28%.[155] All these figures of course include also the cassational protests brought by the procurators. The number of the latter is negligible as it amounts to about 2% of all the complaints and protests filed. The cassational complaint is, on the whole, a very useful instrument in the hands of the aggrieved defendant.

The comparatively small number of complaints may be due either to the ignorance of the masses of their right to complain, especially of the peasants (though it is unlikely that even the most ignorant person would not attempt to have another person write for him some kind of complaint) or to a general satisfaction with the results reached by the trial courts.

The next question that presents itself is to what extent do the complaining parties obtain the relief sought? An examination of the following Tables, No. 2 and No. 3 will answer this question.

Table No. 2

REVIEW BY THE CASSATIONAL DIVISION OF THE PROVINCIAL COURTS OF CASES TRIED AT THE PEOPLE'S COURTS

Year	Result		
	Reversed	Affirmed	Modified
[156]1923	33%	67%	.....
[157]1924	28.5%	71.5%	.....
1925	25.5%	74.5%	.....
[158]1926	42.7%	57.3%	.....
[159]1927	.....	.....	21.1%

[155]The Official Report for 1925, pages 109 and 110, states that in 1924 the percentage of appealed verdicts was 6% less than in 1925, giving the exact data for the latter year.

[156]E. Tarnovsky, *The Weekly*, No. 35, 1926. At the beginning the percentage of reversals was greater. In the first six months of 1923, 35% were reversed. See *The Weekly*, Nos. 3 and 4, 1924.

[157]Report for 1925, page 112. Here we find the datas for both 1924 and 1925. It is interesting to note that while for the whole year of 1924 the percentage of reversals was 28.5%, it was 31% for the first six months of the same year. See Official Report for 1924, page 661.

[158]Report of the Procuracy for 1926, Moscow, 1927, pages 131 and 132. The great increase of the cases reversed is due to the fact that the provincial court began to exercise the power of modifications, which is also included under the heading "reversed".

[159]*The Weekly*, No. 4, 1928, page 103. Here we have information only of the percentage of modifications. In some provinces the reversals are comparatively few. Thus the Cassational Division of the Moscow Provincial Court reversed only 21.8% for the first half of 1927 and 15.3% for the first six months of 1928. *The Weekly*, Nos. 38 and 39, 1928, page 1019.

Table No. 3

REVIEW ON CASSATIONAL COMPLAINTS BY THE SUPREME COURT

	Offenses Less Than Capital			Capital Cases		
Year	Affirmed %	Modified %	Reversed %	Affirmed %	Modified %	Reversed %
[160]1923	60	30	9	...	...	...
[161]1924	77.6	11.5	10.9	...	...	...
[162]1925	69.1	14.1	16.8	44.7	44.6	10.7
[163]1926	71.8	13.2	14.9	60.2	31.9	7.9
[164]1927	55.3	31.2	13.5	63.2	25.4	11.4

The data does not reveal any fixed, steady average for reversals and modifications, but presents rather unstable, fluctuating tendency. There are, however, a few things to be noted. We observe that in 1926 the percentage of reversals at the provincial court rose considerably, though the latter figure includes also modification, a power vested in that court only recently. On the other hand we notice that the number of verdicts in capital cases affirmed at the Supreme Court has increased steadily since 1925. This is explained by the fact that trial courts are now more careful and considerate in imposing capital punishment.[165] A third important feature, as shown by Table No. 3, is the wide application of the power of the Supreme Court to modify the sentence—that is, to decrease its severity, especially in capital cases, which ranges from 44.6% in capital cases in 1925 to 25% in 1927.

From an analysis of all the statistical data available we learn that of all the verdicts rendered at the people's courts in 1925, 4.7% were reversed by higher tribunals; while of all the verdicts reached at the provincial courts in the same year the Supreme

[160]*The Weekly*, No. 11, 1924. Report by P. Stuchka.

[161]Jud. Practice, No. 4, 1927, page 2.

[162]*Ibid.*, No. 23, 1927, page 6. See also *The Weekly*, No. 3, 1927.

[163]*Ibid.*, No. 23, 1927, page 6. There seems to be a slight error in the official report for the total makes up only 99.9%.

[164]*Ibid.*, No. 16, 1928.

[165]In 1924, 879 death sentences were actually carried out. In 1925, 1086 persons were sentenced to death, but only 440 were executed; in 1926, 880 death sentences were imposed with 431 carried into execution; while in 1927, 863 persons were sentenced to the highest penalty, 451 of whom were executed. See *The Weekly*, No. 3, 1927, and the Jud. Practice, No. 16, 1928.

Court reversed 4.6% and modified 5.3%.[166] A comparison with the situation in the pre-revolutionary days should be of interest. During 1914, of all the verdicts rendered at the justice of the peace courts and at the circuit courts without a jury, 1% were reversed by the Cassational Department of the Governing Senate, while 8% were annulled by the proper courts of *apelyatziya*.[167] At the same time, of all the verdicts rendered by juries at the circuit court, which verdicts were not subject to appeal, only 1% were reversed by the Senate. From all the cases taken to the judicial chamber, as a court of appeal, 68% were affirmed and 32% were reversed; while from all the cassational complaints that reached the Senate from all courts, outside the justices of the peace, 82% were affirmed and 18% reversed.[168] Thus Soviet cassational courts in general reverse many more cases than did the courts of cassation in Tzarist Russia. But we must bear in mind the important fact that the present cassational jurisdiction carries within itself also many of

Table No. 4[169]

PERCENTAGE OF THE VARIOUS CASSATIONAL GROUNDS IN ALL CASES REVERSED AT THE CASSATIONAL DIVISION OF THE PROVINCIAL COURTS

	1923 %	1924 %	1925 %
For insufficient inquiry	24	26.2	34.9
Sentence plainly unjust	7	7.9	3.7
Total	31	34.1	38.6
Errors of substantive law	34	36.1	30.6
Errors of procedural law	35	29.8	30.8
Total	69	65.9	61.4

[166] Official Report for the Courts for 1925, pages 81, 83, 108 and 109. The percentages stated were arrived at by the writer by figuring out the number of verdicts rendered and those reversed.

[167] E. Tarnovski, *The Weekly*, No. 28, 1928.

[168] *Ibid.*

[169] E. Tarnovski, *The Weekly*, No. 36, 1926, brings the figures for 1923; the datas for 1924 and 1925 are found in the Official Report on Courts for

Table No. 5

PERCENTAGE OF THE VARIOUS CASSATIONAL GROUNDS IN ALL CASES REVERSED AT THE CASSATIONAL DEPARTMENT OF THE SUPREME COURT

In offenses less than capital	1924[170] %	1925[171] %	1926[172] %	1927[173] %
For insufficient inquiry........	26	34.1	36.4	38.4
For sentence plainly unjust.....	2	10.5	1.7	5.2
For absence of crime..........	37.3	34.5	40.	40.
Total	65.3	79.1	78.1	83.6
Errors of substantive law......	16.1	8.4	6.2	5.3
Errors of procedural law.......	18.6	12.5	15.1	10.3
Total	34.7	20.9	21.3	15.6

the elements and characteristics of the pre-revolutionary *apelyatziya.* This brings us to another striking feature of the present system of criminal review, that of the unusually broad scope of the re-examination, and the nature of the grounds for reversing or modifying the verdict or sentence.

As we look at Tables 4 and 5 we can fully realize the effect of the grounds for disturbing the verdict which are emphatically out of the realm of real cassation, as we have already seen. We have grouped them so as to distinguish at a glance the typical cassational grounds, based on errors of law, from the others. We observe that over one-third of all the reversals at the provincial cassational courts were directly due to non-cassational reasons, the insufficiency of the inquiry or the unjustness of the verdict.

1925, page 113. In 1927, between 31.7% in one province and 29.7% in another province of all the verdicts were reversed for the insufficiency of the Inquiry. *The Weekly,* No. 31, 1928, Article by V. Rodus-Zenkevich.

[170] *The Weekly,* No. 3, 1927. There is no data available for capital cases.

[171] Jud. Practice, No. 23, 1927, page 7.

[172] *Ibid.* Other cases amounting to 0.6% were reversed for other reasons, not classified.

[173] *Ibid.,* No. 16, 1928, page 2. For other, unclassified, reasons 0.8% was reversed.

The amazing result obtained by these grounds for annulling decisions of the trial courts is demonstrated even with greater effect in the decisions of the Cassational Department of the Supreme Court, as shown by Table No. 5. True, some reversals based on the absence of the criminal elements in the case may occur because of errors of law which are strictly cassational grounds, but very often a reversal for this reason is obtained only after a revaluation of the factual conclusions of the court of original jurisdiction. For the Supreme Court is not to "close hypocritically its eyes to the merits of the case".[174] This is the gist of the entire cassational policy of the Supreme Court.

We may safely conclude, as the foregoing tables plainly illustrate, that if complaints were restricted to purely cassational grounds, the impressive extent of redress now obtained by dissatisfied defendants would be materially reduced.

We have thus far pointed out the singularities with regard to cassation. But what is the effect of the innovation introduced by the method of supervision? Though the parties themselves cannot set such proceedings in motion, the authorities are apparently very liberal in considering such complaints. While we have no authenticated figures for the whole Republic as to the number of reviews originated through complaints of the aggrieved parties, we find that the data obtainable for some provinces point to an impressive percentage of instances where proceedings were started because of the complaint of the parties. Naturally, not all the cases demanded by the authorities are then directed for a review. For example, the procuracy in starting supervisory proceedings examined 212,618 cases preliminarily during 1927.[175] But from this mass of cases it forwarded—or protested, as the phrase goes—only 10,453 cases to the various courts for a supervisory review. The procuracy is, however, as we know, not the sole agency of effecting a review by way of supervision.

A glance at Table No. 6 will at once present to us vividly the significance and the magnitude of this unique method as compared with the ordinary and fundamental remedy in the hands of the parties, the right of cassation. That approximately two-

[174] *Ibid.*, The Report of the Cassational Department of the Supreme Court for 1927.

[175] *The Weekly*, Nos. 40 and 41, 1928, page 1081.

thirds of all the cases re-examined at the Supreme Court by way of supervision were either reversed or modified, is shown by Table No. 7. It is a telling tribute to this method of review which, not being hampered by any technicalities or time limitations whatsoever, always affords adequate redress.

Table No. 6

CASES REVIEWED AT THE SUPREME COURT (CASSATIONAL DEPARTMENT)

	1923[176]	1924[177]	1925[178]	1926[179]	1927[180]	1928[181]
By way of cassation....	9,359	11,423	14,436	17,755	17,355	14,396
By way of supervision..	3,461	1,786	1,593	1,940	2,204	2,486

Table No. 7

RESULT OF ALL THE CASES REVIEWED BY WAY OF SUPERVISION AT THE SUPREME COURT

Year	Affirmed %	Modified %	Reversed %	Discontinued %
1923[182]..............	30	30	40	...
1924................	..	..	..	...
1925................	..	..	..	...
1926[183]..............	31.5	9.2	27.9	31.4
1927................	24.9	14.8	27.8	32.5

In conclusion we may observe that, unlike the preliminary and trial proceedings, where the wide discretionary powers of the trial court often works against the defendant, the latter is the ultimate beneficiary in the cassational and supervisory tribunals by the application of the very same wide discretion. Whatever the merits or demerits of such methods of review as we have dis-

[176]*The Weekly,* No. 11, 1924, page 264. The figures are thus stated: The Supreme Court received 12,820 cases, 73% of which were brought on cassation and 23% by way of supervision. From this statement the writer arrived at the figures given in the table.

[177]*Ibid.,* No. 3, 1927.

[178]*Ibid.*

[179]Jud. Practice, No. 23, 1927, page 5.

[180]*Ibid.,* No. 16, 1928.

[181]*The Weekly,* No. 29, 1929, pages 670 and 671.

[182]*Ibid.,* No. 11, 1924, page 264.

[183]Jud. Practice, No. 7, 1928.

cussed here may be, the ultimate aim of the system is directed towards an unbridled attempt to correct judicial errors.

In a resolution unanimously adopted by the plenum of the Supreme Court concerning the functions of a cassational court, in connection with a discussion of the project for a new code, it was said: "The Soviet court must not reverse even a single clearly correct verdict, nor leave undisturbed one clearly incorrect verdict, on mere formal grounds."[184]

[184] *The Weekly,* No. 8, 1928, page 241.

Chapter X

EXECUTION OF CRIMINAL SENTENCES

We now approach the final stage in the administration of the criminal law—the carrying into effect of the sentences of the criminal courts.

A complete study of this subject would inevitably include a study of prison conditions and an inquiry into the principles underlying Soviet penal policy as well as an examination of the rather complicated form of the administrative machinery set up to carry out those principles and policies. While such a study might prove interesting, as it is perhaps a part of the administration of the criminal law in a broader sense, we shall, however, limit the scope of our discussion to the procedure more immediately connected with the authority exercised by the judiciary in the process of carrying out of its own sentences.

The carrying of the sentence into effect is not to begin until the sentence becomes legally binding. The mere pronouncement of the verdict or the imposition of the sentence does not convey the necessary legal force for execution of the sentence; the judgment is still lacking in legal finality, and therefore there is no sentence to be executed. It ripens into a legally binding judgment, as we know, either after the expiration of the time for cassational complaint or, if an appeal is taken, on the day the court of cassation renders its decision. All this applies only to sentences of conviction, for "verdicts of acquittal shall be carried out at once";[1] though they are not yet legally binding, as they are subject to reversal on the protest of the procurator. This very important exception to the usual rule is somewhat out of line with the general trend of Soviet criminal procedure, and it may conceivably create some complicated situations. The apparent inconsistency, however, of carrying out a verdict of acquittal before it assumes the necessary legal qualities has undoubtedly gained a permanent foothold in the Soviet system. All the projects for a new code of criminal procedure fully restate this principle.[2]

[1]Code, 1927, section 340.

[2]See section 145 of the Project for a New Code of Criminal Procedure as drafted by a special commission, and published in *The Weekly*, Nos. 28 and 29, 1928; also section 141 of the same project after it was revised by the Commissariat and published in Nos. 46 and 47 of the above mentioned Journal.

Even the consistently unsentimental procurator, Krylenko, adopted a rather serene attitude towards the acquitted defendant, when he said, "Such a rule is perhaps inadvisable but may be justified by the desire of the legislators to emphasize the tender attitude of the law towards the question of depriving an individual of his personal liberty when he secures an acquittal, and the desire to give him the opportunity to enjoy that liberty."[3] A consideration of the question of carrying out the verdicts and sentences of the court will, therefore, concern itself only with those of conviction.

The general rule is that a legally binding sentence must be executed without delay. "The judicial sentence shall be executed immediately upon its assuming the force of law."[4] But there are some noteworthy exceptions to this rule. The Code specifically provides that the carrying out of the sentence may be deferred in the following instances: "(1) If the illness of the person convicted prevents the carrying out of the sentence; (2) in the event of the pregnancy of a convicted woman, in which case the serving of the sentence shall be deferred until two months after the birth of her child; (3) whenever the immediate serving of the sentence may result in unusual hardship for the person convicted or his family, on account of peculiar circumstances, or peculiar conditions, to wit: a fire or other sudden misfortune, serious sickness or death of the only able-bodied person in the household, etc."[5]

The power to grant a postponement of the execution of the sentence, based upon grounds mentioned, which according to Krylenko "discloses the humanitarian spirit with which our Code of Criminal Procedure is permeated",[6] is vested in the court which renders the verdict. The question will be taken up by the court on the petition of the defendant, his attorney, at the suggestion of the procurator, or on the court's own initiative.[7] As the court is empowered to defer the serving of the sentence of imprisonment it may also postpone the payment of any fine imposed by it for a period of six months, or may allow payment to be

[3]Krylenko, *The Judiciary and the Law*, 1928, page 145.
[4]Code, 1927, section 454.
[5]*Ibid.*, section 456.
[6]Krylenko, *op. cit.*, note 3, *supra*, p. 144.
[7]*Commentaries*, page 434.

made in parts, whenever paying at once may prove too burdensome to the persons fined.[8]

What we have discussed heretofore relates to the authority of the courts to postpone the carrying out of the sentence before the defendant actually has begun to serve his term. But even afterwards the authority of the court may under certain circumstances be invoked for the purpose of interfering with the normal process in carrying out the legally binding sentence. The powers of the court to halt the serving of the sentence after it has begun is, of course, the exception rather than the rule. While at an earlier stage in the development of Soviet criminal law, the courts were to supervise the correct execution of its sentences, now the functions of the courts ordinarily ceases when they turn the matter over to the proper executive authorities by forwarding "a copy of the sentence to the house of detention, the police or other organs to whom is entrusted the actual execution of the sentence."[9] Though recently an opinion was voiced in favor of having the people's judge look after the proper execution of sentences,[10] the tendency, however, is not towards a return to the previous law in this respect.

Generally speaking, the duty to carry out the terms of the sentences imposed by the criminal courts is wholly transferred to the administrative branch of the government—the Commissariat of the Interior. The procuracy, however, as the acknowledged guardian of the law is to supervise the correctness of the execution.[11] To facilitate the proper discharge of these functions the procurator, or his assistant, always participates in the sessions of the provincial administrative prison commission, and of the supervisory board which functions at each prison. We may note in passing that a judge of the provincial court must sit as a member of the administrative provincial commission, while a judge of the people's court is one of the members of the local prison board.[12]

[8]Code, 1927, section 460.

[9]*Ibid.*, section 455, part 1.

[10]Such an opinion was recently advanced, in an article which is cited and criticised by S. Finblit, *The Weekly*, No. 31, 1928, page 67.

[11]Code, 1927, section 455, part 2.

[12]Corrective Labor Code, Collected Laws, No. 86, Article 870, 1926, sections 13 and 19. *(Ispravitelno—trudovoi kodex, R.S.F.S.R.)*

We turn back to the question of the judge's interposition during the serving of the sentence.

The court may be asked to order the prisoner released before his term expires. Grounds for petitioning the court to this effect occur whenever the prisoner becomes afflicted with an incurable disease, mental or otherwise. Upon proper request made, the court will proceed to obtain expert medical testimony from the special governmental medical commission. A decree may then issue to free the prisoner conditionally or place him in a hospital, or insane asylum, as the exigencies of the particular case may demand.[13] The power to release a prisoner conditionally prior to his serving the full sentence is also vested in the provincial or regional administrative prison commission. But such commission may act, for any good reason, only after the prisoner has served at least one-half of his sentence.[14]

After sentence has been imposed, the court may be urged to exercise its authority to postpone the serving of a sentence of imprisonment, or the paying of a fine; to substitute compulsory labor, without imprisonment, in lieu of a fine; to order a release from prison before the expiration of one-half of the term provided in the sentence, and decide any other question which may appear in connection with the carrying out of the terms of the sentence as pronounced by the trial court. The latter is to have jurisdiction over all those matters provided the prisoner is serving within its judicial district. If he is serving outside such district the provincial court in whose territory the prisoner is assigned to serve takes jurisdiction.[15]

The court, consisting of one judge and two co-judges, deliberates on all such questions at a judicial session—that is, in open court. To such session the prisoner and the procurator are always summoned. The civil claimant at the original trial is summoned only if the question to be decided may affect the civil judgment. The failure of any of these parties to appear will not prevent the court from determining the questions involved.[16] Whenever the court is to deliberate on the question of a condi-

[13]Code, 1927, section 457.
[14]*Ibid.*, section 458.
[15]*Ibid.*, section 461.
[16]*Ibid.*, section 462, part 1.

tional release, which must be taken up within one month after the petition is filed, the representatives of the organization which petitioned the court are also summoned. Their failure to appear, as in the case of the prisoner or the procurator, will not delay the proceeding. But a decree to release the prisoner before he has served one-half of the term may not issue without the participation of a representative of the provincial or regional administrative prison commission, who is required to be present and give his conclusion.

The decision reached by the court in such matters is final and is not subject to any complaint.[17]

[17] *Ibid.*, section 463.

Chapter XI

PERSONNEL OF THE SOVIET JUDICIARY AND ITS ACTIVITIES

We have heretofore attempted to study Soviet criminal procedure, or the administration of its criminal law, as an objective legal system. But no theoretical study of any judicial system is complete or even adequate without reckoning with the human element which is directly instrumental in giving vitality to the system. To analyze, therefore, the essential elements which compose the system of the administration of Soviet criminal law, we must necessarily know something of the personality of the administrators. Furthermore, a proper acquaintance with the judicial personnel, so far as it may reveal the intrinsic value of the administration of the criminal law, is impossible unless we consider the surrounding conditions under which the practical, everyday work is performed.

This obvious truth applicable to every legal system has a peculiar significance with regard to the Soviet system. The Soviet régime, we must bear in mind, did not merely inaugurate a completely new system of courts and procedure, but introduced an entirely new personnel into all branches of the judiciary. For even at the very beginning of the new régime when members of the Tzarist courts were not expressly barred, they themselves refused to participate in the new judicial machinery after the issuance of the First Decree on Courts.[1] Even the trained office personnel of the pre-revolutionary Minister of Justice "went on strike" as soon as the soviets seized the power.[2]

The Bolshevik Revolution of November, 1917, not only changed the political form of the government; it openly declared a merciless war upon the upper social strata, which are called "the bourgeoisie", who on the whole were bitterly opposed to the Revolution as well as to the socialist or communist doctrines

[1] *The Weekly*, Nos. 44 and 45, 1922, page 4. D. I. Kurskii, Commissar of Justice, tells in an interview that not a single justice of the peace was willing to continue his work after the First Decree was issued.

[2] *Ibid.*, See the article written by P. Stuchka, who was the first acting Commissar of Justice after the Bolshevik Revolution.

of the Bolsheviks and their allies, the left wing of the Social Revolutionists.[3] The new government boastingly heralded the era of workers' and peasants' rule. But the ranks of the new ruling classes did not contain too great a number of legally trained persons, nor too many intellectuals in general. This condition must be constantly borne in mind when we attempt to visualize the situation as it existed in the period immediately following the Revolution of November, 1917. The personnel of the new judiciary had to be drawn from factory workers and peasants, and from those intellectuals who were connected with, or at least friendly to, the extreme revolutionary parties.

Thus, while at the head of the Commissariat of Justice were placed highly trained, learned jurists, Dr. Shteinberg, and later P. Stuchka, those appointed to the judgeships and other posts connected with the judiciary were for the most part inexperienced, untrained, at best only politically intelligent workers and peasants. The new judges brought to the bench together with their inexperience and awkwardness in handling legal problems the layman's point of view; and this was true both as regards the judges and the co-judges. Contrary to all expectations, as we have already pointed out in another connection, the criminal courts during the very beginning of the Revolution were extremely mild. The emotional expressions which demonstrate the human sympathies of the layman unhampered by any technicalities or adherence to strict requirement of the law were given free play.

It is rather noteworthy that the project for the first revolutionary tribunals at Moscow was drafted not by a jurist but by an historian, Pokrovski. This project, which for a short time was the law governing the revolutionary tribunals in Moscow,[4] provided a maximum sentence of four years' imprisonment.[5] Such

[3]At the beginning of the Revolution, and immediately afterwards, the extreme left wing of the Russian Social Revolutionary Party which was considered a peasant party, co-operated with the Communist.

[4]The official center was first Petrograd, but as communications with other cities were rather irregular, Moscow continued to be a center for itself.

[5]D. I. Kurskii, in the interview cited, see *supra*, Note 1, states that the fact that the mild attitude of the Moscow Revolutionary Tribunals "proves that historically we were forced to resort to terror by the mad animosity of the counter-revolution".

an attitude on the part of the layman revolutionary is quite comprehensible. The socialist theory has always maintained that the criminal is nothing more than a victim of the circumstances and environment under which he lives. As society creates the circumstances and furnishes the environment, society is chiefly to be blamed for the anti-social conduct of its member, the criminal, and the latter is looked upon as an unfortunate person deserving pity rather than scorn.[6] We are told of a characteristic instance where one of the new judges, a woman and an old revolutionary party worker, freed professional criminals brought before her upon their "word of honor".[7] But the heightened moral tone during the hey-day of the Revolution soon disappeared; the class-war ceased to be merely a phrase—it became a sad reality.

I. SOCIAL AND EDUCATIONAL CHARACTERISTICS OF THE JUDICIARY

We have already indicated that the Revolution erected new courts with a bench of laymen as judges. What were the outstanding characteristics of this new judicial personnel? We have scant information at our disposal to present an accurate picture of the situation prior to January, 1923, when the reorganization of the entire system took place. Our inquiry will therefore primarily be directed to the period following the passage of the First Judiciary Act of 1922.

As we look at Tables Nos. 8 and 9 we note that the vast majority of the judges in both types of courts were recruited from the ranks of workers and peasants. This fact has persisted with almost mathematical exactness. Any other composition of the courts would be fiercely decried as making tribunals unfit and untrustworthy to exercise their functions as administrators of revolutionary law. Since according to communist theory, class division, with its concomitant class struggle, has its origin in the

[6]Dr. Shteinberg, the first Commissar of Justice under the present régime, who, together with his social revolutionary group, broke away from the communist in 1918, spoke with enthusiasm about the humane attitude of the first Soviet revolutionary tribunals towards all defendants, including counter-revolutionists. Even the latter were looked upon as unfortunate creatures who were reared in moral darkness, and were, therefore, morally not to be held accountable. This was told by Dr. Shteinberg to the writer when the former visited this country in 1928.

[7]I. Rostovskii, *The Weekly*, Nos. 44 and 45, 1922.

Table No. 8

SOCIAL STATUS AND EDUCATION OF THE JUDGES OF THE PROVINCIAL COURTS

Social Status	1923[8] %	1924[9] %	1925[10] %	1926[11] %	1927[12] %	1928[13] %	1929[14] %
Workers	34.	34.7	30.1	37.2	34.9	41.2	46.
Peasants	36.	36.3	34.2	35.2	24.7	11.6	12.
Clerks, Intellectuals, etc.	30.	29.	35.7	27.6	40.4	47.2	42.
Education							
Higher Education	17.	14.9		16.6	15.7	5.9	
Secondary Education	21.	23.2		18.8	18.4		6.6
Elementary Education	62.	61.9		64.6	65.9		74.8

Table No. 9

SOCIAL STATUS AND EDUCATION OF THE JUDGES OF THE PEOPLE'S COURTS

Social Status	1923[15] %	1924[16] %	1925[17] %	1926[18] %	1927[19] %	1929[20] %
Workers	26.5	29.5	33.9	32.8	32.8	16.3
Peasants	49.5	56.	54.5	52.2	38.2	22.8
Clerks, Intellectuals, etc.	24.	14.5	11.6	15.	29.	60.9
Education						
Received Higher Education	9.9	6.3		4.	3.7	6.
Secondary Education	14.6	13.4		15.7	13.6	45.
Elementary Education	75.5	80.3		80.3	82.7	

[8] Brandenburgskii, *The Weekly*, No. 24, 1923.

[9] Official Report on Courts for 1924, pages 9, 10.

[10] *The Weekly*, No. 47, 1925.

[11] Official Report for 1925, pages 20, 22.

[12] These figures are taken from a table prepared for the writer, at his request, at the Commissariat of Justice in Moscow, and was signed by Khlebnikov, the director of the statistical department of the commissariat.

[13] *The Weekly*, No. 46, 1929, pages 1075, 1076. Besides the 5.9% of university graduates, 17.2% of the judges had taken law courses.

[14] *The Weekly*, No. 6, 1929, pages 123, 124.

[15] For the data on the social status, see *The Weekly*, Nos. 51 and 52, 1923.

[16] Official Report for 1924, page 12.

[17] *The Weekly*, Nos. 48 and 49, 1925.

[18] See *supra*, note 11.

[19] See *supra*, note 12.

[20] *The Weekly*, No. 6, 1929, pages 123, 124.

early environment of the individual, the atmosphere in which one is born and reared is of the utmost importance in determining one's propensity towards one or the other of the warring camps —the proletariat or the bourgeoisie. Soviet leaders are apparently content that the majority of the judges are *born into the workers' and peasants' class.* Usually the statistical data show the social status of their ancestry rather than their own. If we study the occupations pursued by the judges prior to their appointment to the bench, the representation of peasants is far below that of other occupations or professions. Judges who were born in peasant homes comprised 35.2% of all the judges in the provincial court and 54.5% in the people's court during 1926, while only 7.4% and 15.9% respectively were peasants by prior occupation. On the other hand, the percentage of clerks, intellectuals, etc., by prior occupation was much greater than the ratio of those belonging to the same groups by birth.[21]

It is, of course, to be expected that the social status of the judges may correspondingly indicate their educational level. Under conditions existing before 1917, the so-called lower classes had little, if any, opportunity for education. What the above tables reveal is the rather amazing fact that in spite of the numerous short-term law courses established in many centers, in addition to the regular courses of law at the universities, together with the general dissemination of education throughout the country, the educational standard of the judiciary has not changed to any considerable extent since 1923.

When we discuss the personnel of the judiciary we cannot restrict ourselves to the judges exclusively. The procurators and inquisitors are an inseparable part of the entire judicial machinery. From Table No. 10 we observe that the number of workers by occupation appointed to the position of procurator and assistant procurator has been consistently growing; the representatives of the non-laboring professions and occupations have been somewhat diminishing. Another point to be noted is the small number of

[21]In 1926 the provincial courts had 27.5% and the people's courts 14.7% of all their respective judges, persons who had been born in homes of clerks, intellectuals, etc., while with regard to occupations prior to their appointment, the figures stood 54.5 for the people's and 52% for the provincial courts.

those actually tilling the soil who are entrusted with a responsible position in the procuracy in a country predominantly peasant. Table No. 11 indicates the education received by the members of this branch of the judiciary. As we have pointed out before, grouping by occupations is a reasonably accurate guide to the educational level of the class as a whole. The constant increase of workers necessarily carries a corresponding decrease in educational standards.

Table No. 10

SOCIAL STATUS OF THE PROCURATORS AND THEIR ASSISTANTS

Procurators	1923[22] %	1924[23] %	1925 %	1926[24] %	1927 %
Workers by birth......	27.7	30.8	36.8	21.2	23.1
Workers by occupation.	...	20.1	19.3	38.6	40.8
Peasants by birth......	32.7	38.4	35.1	36.4	38.4
Peasants by occupation.	...	1.6	1.7	3.5	6.1
Clerks, Intellectuals, etc., by birth	39.6	30.8	28.1	42.4	38.4
Clerks, Intellectuals, etc., by occupation	78.3	78.3	79.	57.9	53.1

Assistant Procurators	1923 %	1924 %	1925 %	1926[25] %	1927 %
Workers by birth......	23.	29.5	34.6	14.6	17.5
Workers by occupation.	...	22.1	27.4	29.	32.1
Peasants by birth......	23.4	31.5	34.2	38.7	44.1
Peasants by occupation.	...	7.	9.2	8.3	7.
Clerks, Intellectuals, etc., by birth............	53.6	39.	31.2	47.7	38.
Clerks, Intellectuals, etc., by occupation.......	...	70.9	63.4	62.7	60.9

[22]See *supra*, notes 8 and 15.

[23]*The Weekly*, Nos. 48 and 49, 1925, covering the years of 1924 and 1925.

[24]Official Report of the Procuracy for 1926, page 5, covering the years of 1926 and 1927.

[25]The data with regard to the assistant procurators are to be found in the same places as that of the procurators, as indicated, *supra*, notes 22, 23 and 24.

Table No. 11

EDUCATIONAL STATUS OF THE PROCURATORS AND THEIR ASSISTANTS

Procurators	1923[26] %	1924[27] %	1925 %	1926[28] %	1927 %
Higher Education......	44.2	...	...	19.3	12.2
Secondary Education ..	26.7	...	...	29.8	28.6
Elementary Education..	29.1	...	...	50.9	59.2

Assistant Procurators	1923 %	1924 %	1925 %	1926 %	1927 %
Higher Education	39.	...	...	23.6	23.8
Secondary Education ..	19.7	...	...	22.1	21.
Elementary Education..	41.3	...	...	54.3	55.2

Table No. 12

SOCIAL STATUS OF THE SENIOR INQUISITORS AND THEIR EDUCATION

	1923[29]	1924[30]	1925	1926[31]	1927[32]
Workers	...	...	...	8.6	6.7
Peasants	35.	...	...	30.	19.1
Intellectuals, Clerks, etc.	65.	...	...	61.4	74.2
Higher Education....	44.5	48.2	...	45.6	45.6
Secondary Education.	...	24.	...	29.4	24.2
Elementary Education	...	27.8	...	25.	30.2

[26] *The Weekly*, Nos. 51 and 52, 1923.

[27] We have no complete data for 1924 and 1925. We know, however, that in 1925 there was a further decrease of 10% of procurators with a higher education, and 6.2% of assistant procurators, compared with 1924. See N. Logovier, *The Weekly*, Nos. 48 and 49, 1925. This fact clearly indicates the constant diminishing of persons with higher education appointed to the office of the procurator.

[28] Official Report, page 6, covering the years of 1926 and 1927.

[29] Brandenburgskii, *The Weekly*, Nos. 24, 51 and 52, 1923.

[30] Official Report on Courts, 1924, page 10.

[31] See *supra*, note 11.

[32] See *supra*, note 12.

Table No. 13

SOCIAL STATUS OF THE PEOPLE'S INQUISITORS AND THEIR EDUCATION

	1923[33] %	1924[34] %	1925[35] %	1926[36] %	1927[37] %	1928[38] %
Workers	17.	...	20.8	19.7	16.9	15.3
Peasants	42.	...	44.8	43.5	29.9	22.
Clerks, Intellectuals, etc.	41.	...	34.4	36.8	53.2	62.7
Higher Education	24.	25.7	...	18.8	17.4	16.7
Secondary Education	..	23.9	...	27.9	23.2	...
Elementary Education	..	54.3	...	53.3	59.4	...

We are still to concern ourselves with the third group of the judiciary, the senior and people's inquisitors who serve as a highly important link in the pre-trial proceedings. A glance at Tables Nos. 12 and 13 shows that at the outset Soviet authorities drew to the office of the senior inquisitors the most able and intelligent group available. As early as 1923 there were 44.5% among them who had received a university legal education. This was a group of the former, experienced jurists.[39] The high educational quality of these semi-judicial officers has been maintained up to this day. Furthermore, even to the office of the people's (district) inquisitors persons were appointed who had a far higher educational average than those who filled the ranks of the people's judges. It is also interesting to note that 36% of the senior and 13.1% of the people's inquisitors received their university legal education prior to 1917.[40]

[33] *The Weekly,* No. 24, 1923.

[34] See *supra,* note 30.

[35] *The Weekly,* No. 47, 1925.

[36] Official Report on Courts, Moscow, 1926, page 20.

[37] See *supra,* note 12.

[38] *The Weekly,* No. 46, 1929, pages 1075, 1076. Besides those who receive a higher education 15.5% of the inquisitors had taken law courses.

[39] Ya Brandenburgskii, *The Weekly,* Nos. 51 and 52, 1923.

[40] From among the provincial judges only 12.1%, had graduated from a university prior to 1917, while in the people's court the percentage of the latter group is only 1.9%. See Report on the Court for 1925, Moscow, 1926, page 22.

PERSONNEL OF THE SOVIET JUDICIARY AND ITS ACTIVITIES

In attempting to establish for ourselves a clear notion of the important characteristics of the personnel of the judiciary, we must remember that the Soviet republic embraces a very broad area in character ranging from modern industrial cities to remote, mediaeval villages, with a most heterogeneous population differing greatly in their cultural development. To measure according to the average, while the only method conceivable, has therefore its serious limitations. Thus, while there were only 18% of people's judges who received a higher education in 1921,[41] taking the country as a whole, 28% of all the people's judges in the city of Moscow were university graduates.[42] On the other hand, the province of Moscow (outside the city) had only 12% of people's judges with a university education.

The qualifications of the Soviet judiciary have never been deemed ideal or even fully satisfactory in the eyes of Soviet leaders. The comparatively low general educational level of the judiciary has not been, however, deprecated as a serious obstacle. On the other hand, the lack of legal education among the members of the judiciary has apparently been more keenly felt. "We do not care for 'diplomas' ", writes a leading Soviet legal writer, "but our troubles lie in the fact that our higher schools have not given us many learned jurists."[43] Some effort has evidently been made to induce the judicial worker to obtain a legal training. It is not uncommon to find many judges among the students of law.[44]

II. PRACTICAL EXPERIENCE OF THE JUDGES

The next step in our inquiry should be directed towards discovering whether the obvious lack of general education and legal training is to some extent compensated for by practical experience in administering the criminal law. In this connection we may note that the work in the different branches of the Soviet

[41] *The Weekly*, No. 11, 1922.

[42] *Ibid.*, No. 6, 1922.

[43] Ya Brandenburgskii, *The Weekly*, Nos. 48 and 49, 1922.

[44] Among the seventy-three persons who graduated from the so-called higher juridical courses in 1926, 73% had served as members of the judiciary between 2 to 6 years. Six were presidents of the provincial court or procurators; twenty-two have been judges of the provincial court; eight were people's judges, etc. *The Weekly*, No. 24, 1926.

judiciary constitutes in itself an excellent training school. Due to the system which requires periodic revisions, inspections, the sending of circulars of instructions, the arranging of periodic county and provincial conferences of judicial workers where legal problems are discussed, the judicial workers gradually accumulate a body of legal knowledge growing out of the daily work, and thus become better qualified to perform their duties. But for some reason or other the mobility of the Soviet judicial personnel reaches impressive proportions. In 1923, as we know, the new Judiciary Act establishing the provincial court became effective, and judges for these courts were for the first time appointed. For 1924 a considerable number were not reappointed, being replaced by new appointees.[45] But during the first half of 1924, after the yearly appointments were made, many more changes took place. Thus for a comparatively short period, the following numbers from among the personnel of the provincial court resigned or were dropped: Presidents—10 (17.8%; deputy presidents—25 (24%); judges—146 (26.6%); judges in reserve—103 (75.2%); and senior inquisitors—182 (57.4%).[46]

With all these handicaps, the number of experienced judges, however, has grown constantly from year to year. During 1925 only 62% of all the provincial judges and 30.9% of all the people's judges had three years' experience on the bench. Special attention apparently was given to the office of the provincial procurator. For at the end of 1923, 60% of all the procurators had served in the Soviet judiciary for not less than three years.[47] What improviments have been achieved in that direction is illustrated in Tables, Nos. 14, 15 and 16.

These tables are self-explanatory and show decidedly an increase in the number of those who have at least passed through the school of experience. The senior inquisitors who scored the highest average in the educational level represent the largest number also in point of experience. We may observe that on the staff of 1927 not a single senior inquisitor had less than one year's

[45]Thus at the beginning of 1924 the personnel was changed with regard to 4 presidents, 15 deputy presidents, and 101 judges, all of the provincial court.

[46]Official Report on the activities of the different courts for 1924, page 7.

[47]*The Weekly*, Nos. 51 and 52, 1923, page 1192.

practical training, while 57.1% of the entire number had served for over five years.

Table No. 14[48]

PERCENTAGE OF JUDGES WITH REGARD TO LENGTH OF JUDICIAL SERVICE

Year	Up to one year service %	From one to two years' service %	From two to three years' service %	From three to five years' service %	Over five years' service %
	Provincial (and equivalent) Court Judges				
1926	12.9	11.4	19.7	29.5	26.5
1927	1.8	8.1	13.4	30.8	45.9
	People's Court Judges				
1926	24.8	20.1	25.6	17.5	12.
1927	4.4	29.8	23.4	25.3	17.1

Table No. 15[49]

PERCENTAGE OF PROCURATORS AND ASSISTANTS WITH REGARD TO LENGTH OF SERVICE

Year	Up to one year service %	From one to two years' service %	From two to three years' service %	From three to five years' service %	Over five years' service %
	Procurators[50]				
1926	7.	26.3	35.1	26.3	5.3
1927	2.1	...	26.5	46.9	24.5
	Assistant Procurators				
1926	21.3	17.2	26.1	26.9	14.
1927	20.7	11.6	21.3	34.2	12.2

[48]The data for 1926 was taken from the Official Reports on Courts, Moscow, 1926, page 18; the statistics for 1927 are obtained from the tables given to the writer at the Commissariat of Justice. See *supra*, note 12.

[49]All the data used in this table are taken from the Official Report of the Procuracy, Moscow, 1927, page 6.

[50]The elimination of procurators without experience went on gradually. Thus in 1924, 23% of all the procurators had only one year of experience; in 1925 their number was reduced to 12.3% of all the procurators. See N. Logovier, *The Weekly*, Nos. 48 and 49, 1925.

Table No. 16[51]

PERCENTAGE OF SENIOR AND PEOPLE'S INQUISITORS WITH REGARD TO SERVICE

Year	Up to one year service %	From one to two years' service %	From two to three years' service %	From three to five years' service %	Over five years' service %
		Senior Inquisitors			
1926	5.9	8.6	31.	24.8	29.7
1927	...	3.6	9.5	29.8	57.1
		People's Inquisitors			
1926	24.7	17.8	25.4	16.8	15.3
1927	3.8	28.0	22.	25.5	20.7

III. PARTY AFFILIATIONS OF THE JUDICIARY

To complete the characteristics of the judicial personnel, from which we may infer their probable behavior as the administrators of Soviet criminal law, we shall note their party affiliation. A Russian non-Soviet legal writer[52] maintains that the procedure in Soviet courts must be studied only in conjunction with the fact that the entire judicial machinery is completely dominated by the Communist party. The latter fact is indisputably correct. We must not, however, understand it in the sense that the party's grip has been made effective for the mere control of party patronage. The make-up of the Communist party, the only party legally existing in Soviet Russia, resembles more a military-religious order than a political party in our sense of the word. The party member is placed in a responsible position because of his duty to adhere unflinchingly to and to abide unquestioningly by the principles and spirit of the party; he is unqualifiedly committed to all the commands of the army-like organization, and he is subject to stringent party discipline.

An examination of Table No. 17 shows the average of communists in the various branches of the judiciary. All the other members are classified as non-party persons, for no other political

[51] See *supra*, note 48.

[52] Temashev, pages, 222 and 224.

Table No. 17

PERCENTAGE OF COMMUNISTS IN THE JUDICIARY

	1923[53] %	1924[57] %	1925[58] %	1926[59] %	1927[62] %	1928[63] %	1929[64] %
Provincial (regional, circuit, etc.) judges	76.8	81.4	69.1	80.7	82.6	85.6	91.6
People's judges	50.[54]	75.3	83.	82.5	83.9		55.
Procurators	100.[55]			100.[60]	100.	92.9 (Procurators and Assistant procurators)	95. (Procurators and Assistant procurators)
Assistant procurators	78.4			90.3	90.4		
Senior inquisitors	26.[56]	28.4		33.6[61]	34.1		
People's inquisitors	38.		50.	51.7	83.9		85.9

party, as we have already indicated, is permitted to lead an open, legal existence. In studying the foregoing table we observe that all the procurators, without a single exception, are communists. This is not an accident; it is in harmony with an idea fully and consistently carried out. The procurator, as we know, is not a mere prosecutor; he is "the guardian of the revolutionary law". It is the administrative nature of his office which counts above everything else. Such duties and responsibilities as are his should be preferably entrusted to communists. The same tendency we find with regard to the provincial court. While all the judges in this court have theoretically the same judicial power and authority, it is the president or his deputy who shoulders the administrative responsibilities as well as powers. Accordingly, we learn that while the party membership of the provincial courts was 81.4% in 1924, 55 out of 56 presidents were communists, and that all deputy presidents were members of the same party, while 81.1% of all the other judges and only 47.4% of the judges in reserve came from the communist ranks.[65] We may note here in passing that there is an unmistakable definite

[53] *The Weekly*, Nos. 51 and 52, 1923.
[54] *Ibid.*, No. 24, 1923.
[55] *Ibid.*, No. 13, 1923.
[56] *Ibid.*, No. 24, 1923.
[57] Report on the Courts for 1924, page 8.
[58] *The Weekly*, No. 47, 1925.
[59] Official Reports on Courts, Moscow, 1926, page 19.
[60] Official Report of the Procuracy, Moscow, 1927, page 6.
[61] See *supra*, note 59.
[62] See *supra*, note 12.
[63] *The Weekly*, No. 46, 1929, pages 1075, 1076.
[64] *Ibid.*, No. 6, pages 123, 124.
[65] Official Report on Courts for 1924, page 8.

correspondence between party membership and the educational standard. The more educated elements within the Soviet judicial apparatus are, as a rule, drawn from among the so-called non-party elements. While the average for all the members of the provincial court for 1924 who received a university education was 14.9% (see Table No. 8) the average of presidents and deputies, 100% of whom were communists, constituted only 6.6%; while among the judges in reserve, only 47.4% of whom were communists, we find 34.3% university graduates.

IV. SOCIAL AND EDUCATIONAL CHARACTERISTICS OF THE CO-JUDGES

Before leaving the subject of the judicial personnel it is well to make a brief survey of the type of co-judges. True, they are not considered a part of the permanent personnel; nevertheless, during their terms they exercise all the authority of judges and, in theory at least, since they are in the majority, decide the case.

First, as to the general type of co-judges. Due to incessant propaganda carried on to induce women to participate in public life, the number of female co-judges is constantly increasing. In 1925, of all the co-judges 15.4% were women; they constituted 18.6% in 1926, 19.5% in 1927, and 20.4% in 1928. As can be expected the vast majority of the co-judges are peasants and workers. The following comparative table for four years indicates how the various large occupational groups have been represented.

Table No. 18

SOCIAL STATUS OF THE CO-JUDGES

	1925[66] %	1926 %	1927 %	1928[67] %
Peasants	60.2	61.6	58.3	57.3
Workers	20.8	18.2	16.8	18.3
Soldiers	2.3	2.3	2.	2.
Clerks, etc.	16.7	15.5	...	22.4

[66] P. Alimov, *The Weekly*, No. 34, 1927. In this article, Alimov, a member of the Commissariat of Justice, states the comparative data for 1925, 1926 and 1927.

[67] *The Weekly*, No. 35, 1928.

Though no qualification is required, the educational level of the co-judges is somewhat higher than that of the average villager or city worker.

Table No. 19[68]

EDUCATIONAL STANDARD OF THE CO-JUDGES

	1925 %	1926 %
Higher education	0.5	0.5
Secondary education	7.8	7.8
Elementary education	77.6	77.6
Slightly literate	11.7	11.7
Illiterate	2.4	2.4

As we are constantly reminded that the Communist party dominates the courts, the question is to what extent do they control the party affiliation of the co-judges. The table below indicates that the percentage of communist sitting as co-judges is far below the percentage we found among the appointed judges.

Table No. 20[69]

PARTY MEMBERSHIP OF CO-JUDGES

	1925 %	1926 %	1927 %
Members of the communist party or candidates for membership	21.	18.2	18.
Non-party members	79.	81.8	82.

While the data presented above afford us a general view of the co-judges as a whole, the difference between the status of the co-judges at people's and provincial courts in the city communities on the one hand, and rural communities on the other presents such a wide variance as to present really a different type of persons. A glance at the tables below will be instructive.

[68]See *supra*, notes 66 and 67.

[69]*Ibid.*

Table No. 21[70]

SOCIAL STATUS OF THE CO-JUDGES (1925) IN THE PROVINCIAL AND PEOPLE'S COURTS

	Peasants %	Workers %	Soldiers %	Clerks, etc. %
Provincial court	11.5	49.8	3.8	34.9
Provincial court when going on circuit	20.7	33.0	2.0	44.3
People's courts in cities..	21.6	43.8	3.8	30.8
People's courts in villages	76.3	11.3	1.8	10.6
General Average .... (See Table No. 18)	60.2	20.8	2.3	16.7

This table undoubtedly points out that the co-judges, as a rule, are recruited from the predominant group of a given locality. Thus while 21.0% of the co-judges at the people's courts in the city districts were peasants, 76.3% of the latter served as co-judges in the village districts. The percentage of clerks serving in the provincial court is steadily growing. In 1926 it was 36%; in 1927, 37% and in 1928, 38.9%.

It is rather significant that more than one-third of all the co-judges carefully picked for the provincial and circuit courts, which are considered the pillars of the dictatorship of the proletariat, are neither workers nor peasants.

A wide difference between the city and village co-judges in people's courts is also to be observed as to the percentage of communists, women, and illiterates, as illustrated by Table No. 22.

Table No. 22[71]

PERCENTAGE OF CO-JUDGES WHO ARE:

	Communists %	Women %	Illiterates %
Provincial Court	68.7	15.8	1.2
Provincial Court when out on the Circuit	67.2	13.8	..
People's Court in the Cities...	32.1	26.7	1.0
People's Court in the Village..	13.3	13.7	3.0

[70]Official Reports on Courts for 1925, Moscow, 1926, page 165.
[71]*Ibid.*

The great number of communists among the provincial court co-judges is quite natural. Unlike the co-judges of the people's court, those of the provincial court are, as we know, carefully picked from among the more politically intelligent city workers since the latter are the backbone of the ruling Communist party. For the same reason we find more communist co-judges in the city districts of the people's courts, while their number is negligible in the village districts, there being comparatively few communists among the peasant population.

V. CONDITIONS AFFECTING THE ACTIVITIES OF THE JUDICIARY

The foregoing survey acquaints us with the general character of the personnel of the Soviet judiciary. For a more comprehensive understanding, however, of the Soviet administration of the criminal law, which is the aim of our inquiry, we must turn our attention to a study of the surrounding conditions in the light of which the entire picture of the judiciary and its functions may be more illuminated.

The judiciary of the first few years of the present Soviet régime labored under most unfavorable conditions. An economically ruined country in which there incessantly raged a bitter civil war was hardly fertile soil for a normal development of a new judicial system carried on by an entirely new personnel. The complete breakdown of transportation facilities in a tremendously large country hopelessly isolated remote places from the centers whence some instruction and guidance might have come.

By 1922, when the Soviet-Polish wars had ceased, the civil war had been ended, and the devastating famine brought under some control, more attention was given to the judiciary. Country-wide revisions and inspections instituted revealed the utter unfitness of many of the new personnel charged with important duties. The fanaticism of the orthodox Bolsheviks had led them to assume that the bare fact that a person was a worker or a peasant, preferably the former, by occupation or even by birth inherently qualified him to do any difficult task. With a religious zeal befitting Fundamentalists, it was believed that the magic class-conscience would make up for lack of intelligence, education and experience, and would inevitably lead to the glorious goal of the Revolution.

When a check-up was made a different situation was discovered. A report of investigations conducted in thirty-six provinces and regions, out of more than fifty, states that 1,446 persons in the service of the judiciary were dismissed and held for court for misfeasance in office. Among these 988 were such responsible officials as judges, inquisitors and court secretaries. But this work, we are told, was not yet considered a complete clean-up.[72] Most of the graft received by the officials was in the form of food products. One-half pound of black bread to a court secretary, in one case, was a bribe to advance the case on the trial list. Such a fact presents a vivid picture of the pitiful economic conditions under which these new worker-judges labored. "Salary is paid out four months after due", one complains. "It is already the fifth month since we received any salary",[73] writes another. We may safely presume that in the central parts of the country, the situation was much better, but remote places in Russia are not few.

With the re-organization of the judiciary at the beginning of 1923, more normal conditions began to prevail. The re-established means of transportation of course helped to minimize the backwardness of the numerous remote small towns and villages. Simultaneously the people's courts, which up to 1923 were subject to but little control, were brought under the immediate supervision and control of the newly created provincial court.

In connection with the general conditions under which the members of the judiciary worked, we must take into consideration their economic welfare. Complaints were occasionally made that the judiciary were greatly underpaid, even according to Soviet standards; that government employees in other branches were better remunerated. At the beginning of 1924 the salaries received by the people's judges ranged from 33 to 80 rubies per month in one province *(Wyatka)*, to 69 to 94 in another province[74] *(Yaroslov)*. Members of the procuracy on the other hand received 38 to 60 rubles a month while less responsible officials

[72]B. Zenkovich, *The Weekly*, No. 17, 1923.
[73]*The Weekly*, Nos. 24 and 25, 1922.
[74]Official Reports on Courts for 1924, pages 28 and 29.

were paid 100 to 120.[75] The fixed rates varied from place to place. Thus, during 1924, the people's judges in the city of Moscow earned 135 rubles a month. The obviously poor economic position of the judiciary has received a marked improvement in recent years. At the beginning of 1926 the salaries received by people's judges ranged from 60 to 170 rubles and those of the people's inquisitors from 45 to 135 rubles a month.[76] In 1928 the writer was informed that the people's judges and inquisitors received 180 rubles per month in the city of Moscow while those in the province of Moscow, outside the city, earned 160 rubles; the salary for the provincial judges was 200 rubles, and that of the president of the court and his deputy 225 rubles a month.[77] It is interesting to note that in 1912 when the actual purchasing value of the ruble was many times higher than it is today, the justice of the peace received a salary of 2000 rubles a year, and the president of the conference of the justices of the peace 4,200 rubles a year.[78]

With all this in mind we may pursue our inquiry further to discover how heavy is the burden placed upon such a judiciary laboring under the described conditions, and to what extent it is able to cope with the innumerable intricate problems connected with the administration of the criminal law.

VI. THE PERSONNEL OF THE ORGANS OF INVESTIGATIONS

Before attempting to answer these questions, let us digress for a moment in order to discuss briefly the personnel of the organs of investigation and their qualifications. In describing the personnel of the judiciary we omitted any discussion as to the personnel of the police and the bureau of criminal detection, which are not an integral part of the judiciary nor subject to the direct control of the Commissariat of Justice. Nevertheless, they

[75]P. Alimov, *supra*, note 66.

[76]Report for 1925, page 13.

[77]The presidents of the court, usually being communist, cannot receive more than the maximum salary a member of that party may draw. This is known as "Partmax", for brevity, and varies in different sections of the county. It was fixed at 225 rubles a month for those living in the city of Moscow.

[78]The president received a yearly salary of 2700 rubles, for board 750, and for quarters 750, the justice of the peace received 1500 rubles as salary, and 500 for board.

often perform, as we know, important functions in pre-trial proceedings, particularly in less serious offenses.

On the whole, the general qualifications of the personnel of the organs of investigation is far from satisfactory, even from the Soviet point of view. An All-Union inspection has established that "In the organs of investigation are recruited persons who for some reason have not been able to find employment for themselves in any other place."[79] The average salary they receive ranges from 30 to 35 rubles a month. It is therefore not surprising to find that during 1927 the procuracy instituted criminal prosecution against 2727 members of the organs of investigation. The Department of the Workers' and Peasants' Inspection, an all-powerful controlling commissariat, in summing up the results of its nation-wide check-up on the activities of the organ of investigation, frankly stated that it found "serious defects in the police and in the bureau of criminal detection, and that the qualifications of their constituents were inadequate."[80] An effort is, however, being made to raise the standard of these criminal investigators. In almost every administrative department courses to train the members for police work are established. But with all this, the qualifications of the organs of investigation as well as the quality of their performances still remain on a low level. Of all the criminal cases these organs have completed in 1926 and 1927, only 34.2% in the former and 25.2% in the latter year were finally submitted for trial by the higher authorities, while the vast majority of the cases were simply dismissed.[81] We may now turn back to our inquiry into the productivity of the criminal judicial machinery.

VII. ACTIVITIES OF THE JUDICIARY

For the purpose of a proper consideration of our present problem we shall follow up the evolutionary process of the criminal cases in their sequence as they normally pass through the various stages in the administration of the criminal law.

[79] *The Weekly*, Nos. 37 and 38, 1928.

[80] *Ibid.*, No. 26, 1928, page 751.

[81] *Ibid.*, Nos. 37 and 37, 1928, page 994. In one hundred cases referred by the police to the inquisitor only 41.9% of all the witnesses examined by the organs of investigation were summoned again by the inquisitor, the rest of them had nothing to do with the case. See *The Weekly*, No. 30, 1928, page 831.

We shall, therefore, have our starting point at the very bottom of the ladder, the organs of investigation. They, of course, take jurisdiction over numerous cases, either for a complete investigation or for a short, temporary one. These cases are almost always transferred in due course to the people's inquisitors, for the purpose of a preliminary inquiry or for holding for court or a discontinuance. Of all the cases these organs of investigation, the police and the bureau of criminal detection, transferred to the inquisitors during 1927, only 15.7% finally reached the courts with accusatory conclusions; 67.9% were sent to the court with recommendations to discontinue; 5.9%, less serious cases, the inquisitors themselves dismissed and 10.4% were returned to the same organs for additional investigation.[82] These figures are used by Soviet writers to indicate the fruitlessness of the labors of the police, which wastes its time and energy with very little results.

The next and by far the more important step in the process is the work of the inquisitors. The latter, as we recall, have two different functions—first, to supervise all cases completely investigated by the police; second, to conduct preliminary inquiries in the more serious offenses. What is the extent of their work and to what degree are they able to perform their tasks?

In 1923 there was an average of 124 cases for each people's and senior inquisitor of which only 69 were completed; in 1924, during the first six months, the average had increased to 146 cases for each inquisitor, with 102 completed.[83] As the number of inquisitors with practical experience had increased, they were seemingly better equipped to complete a greater percentage of the cases on hand. Thus for each 100 cases in which a preliminary inquiry was to be conducted, they completed 83.6% in 1924;[84] in 1925, 89.8%;[85] in 1926, 88.1% and in 1927, 89.9%.[86]

[82]B. Zenkevich, *The Weekly*, No. 30, 1928, page 831.

[83]Official Report on Courts for 1924, page 70. These figures cover the activities of both the senior and the people's inquisitors. For if we take the works of the latter separately, they have completed 216 cases for the first six months of 1928. *The Weekly*, No. 11, 1926, page 323.

[84]E. Tarnovsky, *The Weekly*, No. 38, 1926.

[85]*Ibid.*

[86]A. Rodnyanski, *The Weekly*, No. 32, 1928, page 887.

Let us now observe what happened to the great number of cases which passed through the apparatus of inquiry of the inquisitors. Table No. 23 indicates that the number of cases in

Table No. 23
RESULTS OF ALL THE CASES COMPLETED BY THE INQUISITORS

	1923 %	1924 %	1925 %	1926 %	1927 %
Held for Court..........	34.	31.7	39.9	47.7	49.
Dismissed or Discontinued	38.	48.6	44.4	41.6	42.5
Transferred to the proper district	..	19.7	15.7	10.7	8.5

which sufficient information was collected by the inquisitors to justify holding the accused for court has been constantly growing. The idea is now clearly gaining headway that the inquisitors should not embark upon a formal preliminary inquiry unless there is what we should term a strong *prima facie* case.

A letter of instructions issued by the Commissariat of Justice and the Supreme Court jointly[87] speaks emphatically of the necessity of refraining from taking up preliminary inquiry without good reasons. Unfounded charges of the commission of a crime, the latter warns, must be weeded out. Moreover, no one should come under the jurisdiction of the inquisitor and an inquiry conducted unless the charge against him contains "on its face a considerable indication of an obvious crime". The mere taking jurisdiction must be so well supported by facts that the logical outcome of every inquiry should be the accusatory conclusion.

While the data presented above point to the greatly improved quality of the inquisitorial work, it is perhaps due to the fact that the quantity of the cases handled by them has been greatly decreased[88] since 1924. At the beginning of 1926 there were in the entire R.S.F.S.R., outside the autonomous republics, 1609 inquisitorial districts, averaging 51,186 people to each district.[89] In

[87] *The Weekly*, No. 33, 1928, page 919.

[88] In 1925 each inquisitor had an average of 182 cases, while in 1926 the average dropped to 106 cases.

[89] Report on Courts for 1925, page 10.

1927 there were 1,664 districts.[90] But the number of criminal cases to go through the procedure of the minute preliminary inquiry have diminished, as has already been indicated, from year to year. Thus, during 1926, the people's inquisitors completed inquiries in 148,087 cases, which made up an average of 88.4 for each inquisitor, while in 1927, only 122,825 cases were completed, or an average of 73.3 for each inquisitor.[91] But though the efficiency of the inquisitor had decreased, this did not cause the inquisitors' dockets to become crowded for the total number of cases received by them had dropped to a greater ratio.[92]

As the status of a person undergoing a preliminary inquiry is markedly affected thereby, the necessity to expedite the proceedings had been persistently urged. Though the law requires that the preliminary inquiry should be completed within two months, this aim has never been fully achieved. During the first half of 1926, only 61.8% of all the cases under preliminary inquiry were completed by the inquisitors within the two-months' limit, while in the second half of 1927, 66.3% of all the cases were completed within two months. Again, if we take the same two periods, we find that the inquiries lasting from two to four months were 25.8% and 19.% respectively. On the other hand, cases in which the preliminary inquiry lasted more than four months averaged 14.2% for the last six months of 1927, and 12.4% for the first half of 1926.[93] It seems, however, that special attention has been directed towards expediting the inquiry of cases in which accused persons are held without bail. Out of all such cases in the hands of the people's inquisitors in 1926, 84.9% were completed within two months, while the percentage of those cases not completed even within three months was 6.6%.[94] Cases where the inquiry is conducted by the senior inquisitors moved, strangely enough, much more slowly. Thus for 1925 and 1926, we have the following data:

[90]*The Weekly*, No. 32, 1928, page 883.

[91]*Ibid.*, page 882.

[92]During 1926 the inquisitors received 139,384 new cases, and only 116,632 during 1927.

[93]*The Weekly*, No. 33, 1928, page 904.

[94]Report on Courts for 1925, pages 130, 131.

Table No. 24

INQUIRY BY SENIOR INQUISITORS COMPLETED

	1925 %	1926 %
Within two months..................	65.6	57.1
Within three months................	13.2	16.5
Over three months..................	21.2	26.4

This may perhaps be explained by the fact that the senior inquisitors investigate only the more complicated cases.

The significance of the inquisitors' inquiry is predicated upon the idea that it uncovers crimes and discovers those guilty of their commission and establishes every material fact from which the court may judge and decide. Therefore, the real test for the inquisitor's achievements is the number of convictions attained and upheld, based upon his inquiry, as compared with the number of crimes he uncovers.

The preliminary inquiry which lasts sometimes for months is also designed to be a process of filtration. Those cases which contain, in the judgment of the inquisitor, positive proof of guilt are to proceed on their road to the trial; the rest are discontinued either by the inquisitor, the procurator or the court. Only where there appears such positive proof of guilt are cases completed with an accusatory conclusion and forwarded to the procurator for his approval.

The aggregate number of these serious cases which reach the procurators were disposed of by him in the manner set forth in Table No. 25.

Table No. 25[95]

	1926 %	1927 %
Accusatory conclusion of the inquisitor affirmed..	75.9	83.2
Affirmed in effect, but accusatory conclusion re-drafted	7.	4.2
Returned to the inquisitor for additional inquiry..	12.2	8.1
Forwarded to the courts with recommendation to discontinue proceedings	4.9	4.5

[95] *The Weekly*, No. 33, 1928, page 906.

The data presented in this table might lead us to the conclusion that the apparatus for preliminary inquiry has been considerably strengthened and has become a more perfected instrument, though in the estimation of the procuracy only 10% of all the inquisitors are very well qualified technically, the qualifications of 65.3% are considered satisfactory while 24.7% are designated as poorly qualified.[96] The constantly improving quality of the inquisitors' activities in the eyes of the procuracy is noteworthy. Out of all the cases the inquisitors forwarded to the procurators in 1923 with accusatory conclusions attached, the latter flatly rejected the accusatory documents and recommended that the proceedings be dismissed in 20% of all the cases.[97] In 1924 the percentage of such direct disagreement between the inquisitor and the procurators dropped to 15.5%;[98] and gradually diminished from year to year until it was reduced, as the foregoing table indicates, to only 4.5% for 1927.

The next chronological event in the development of a criminal case takes place in the courts prior to or at the trial.

The number of criminal cases received by the people's court, which takes jurisdiction of the overwhelming majority of all criminal cases, grew immensely from 1923 to 1925, crowding the dockets of the court to the point of overloading its capacity. In 1925, the number of cases began to decrease rapidly. The aggregate number of cases received at the people's court is as follows:

1923[99]	1,724,205 cases.
1924[100]	1,966,131 cases.
1925	1,250,371 cases.

How did the people's judges at that time cope with this enormous flow of cases? In 1923 each district (or court) disposed of an average of 78 cases a month, while in 1924, the amount of judicial work was increased so that the average for each court reached 95 cases disposed of each month. In some districts the efficiency was much greater, 140 to 170 cases a

[96]*Ibid.*, page 905.
[97]*Ibid.*, No. 16, 1924, page 376.
[98]E. Tarnovski's report to the fifth conference of the judicial officials.
[99]*The Weekly*, No. 7, 1926.
[100]Report on court for 1925, pages 79, 80 and 81. The figures are given for 1924 and 1925.

month being cleared off the dockets.[101] The dockets of the people's court were still overcrowded at the beginning of 1925, for the increase in efficiency did not keep pace with the influx of new cases. The situation was improved during 1925; though the average of cases disposed of by each court was not more than 94 a month (slightly less than in 1924), the new cases that came in amounted on the average to only 94 a month for each court. At the beginning of 1926, there were 2,700 people's judges, or one judicial district to a population of 30,503.[102]

As we have already learned, cases forwarded to the courts are not necessarily put on trial. There is the preliminary process of elimination or sifting performed at the so-called administrative session. How that system operates can best be told by Table No. 26.

Table No. 26

CASES AT PEOPLE'S COURTS

	1924 %	1925[103] %	1926[104] %
Tried on the merits	63.7	51.6	...
Dismissed on various grounds	25.9	32.5	32.5
Returned for additional inquiry	2.9	3.	5.9
Transferred to the proper jurisdiction	7.5	12.9	12.9

By cases "tried on the merits" is apparently meant cases in which a verdict of guilty or not guilty is rendered. Many cases not dismissed at the administrative session reach the trial but, after testimony is heard, may be dismissed on legal grounds or returned for additional investigation. Thus the percentage of cases which come up for trial is greater than the number of those cases actually tried to a conclusion on their merits.

Out of all the cases which finally reach the trial at the people's court, the percentage of convictions and acquittals is as follows:

[101] Report for 1924, page 64.
[102] Report for 1925, pages 9, 10.
[103] *Ibid.*, page 83.
[104] *The Weekly*, No. 31, 1928, page 853.

Table No. 27

CASES TRIED AT PEOPLE'S COURTS

	1924 %	1925[105] %	1926[106] %	1927[107] %
Convictions	81.	73.8	...	...
Acquittals	19.	26.2	25.4	25.6

We turn now to the provincial, circuit and regional courts, as tribunals of original jurisdiction. Here, too, we observe a similar development. During 1923 each court received a monthly average of 116 cases, distributed among a number of judges holding sessions separately, which in the first half of 1924 grew to 189 cases a month for each court.[108] Nevertheless 91% of all the cases received were cleared from the dockets. In the following two years the provincial courts increased their efficiency, while at the same time the number of incoming cases had diminished.

During 1924, 163,688 new cases were received by the provincial, circuit or regional courts, while 157,917 were tried or otherwise disposed of; in 1925, 129,505 new cases came in, and out of these 132,695 cases were completed.

The cases in the provincial, circuit or regional courts were disposed of in the manner indicated by Table No. 28.

Table No. 28

CASES IN PROVINCIAL, CIRCUIT AND REGIONAL COURTS

	1924 %	1925[109] %	1926[110] %	1927[111] %
Tried on their merits	24.5	27.9	...	...
Dismissed or discontinued	66.1	59.9	49.3	48.4
Returned for additional inquiry	5.6	5.6	...	6.3
Forwarded to the proper jurisdiction	3.8	6.6	6.6	...

[105]Report for 1925, page 137, states the data for 1924, 1925.
[106]B. Zenkevich, *The Weekly*, No. 35, 1927.
[107]*The Weekly*, No. 30, 1928, page 830.
[108]Report for 1924, page 58.
[109]*Ibid.*, page 108, states the figures for 1924 and 1925.
[110]*The Weekly*, No. 13, 1928.
[111]*Ibid.*, No. 4, 1928, page 102. (Article by A. Ikovski).

Of all the cases that reached the trial, as explained above, 17% resulted in acquittal in 1924, 21.9% in 1925,[112] and 26.2% in 1927.[113] Thus, we see, the percentage of acquittals increased from year to year. Every increase in the percentage of acquittals at the trials, or discontinuance before the trial, is taken by the Soviet legal authorities as an indication of the ineptness of the inquiring apparatus. Such a conclusion is well justified. Unlike our own system, where the indictment is based exclusively upon the testimony presented against the accused, the Soviet system, we recall, requires those engaged in conducting the preliminary inquiry to perform as complete an investigation as is practically possible, amounting to a preliminary trial. The inquisitor is not to draw any accusatory document and the procurator is not to approve it, unless they are convinced that the act is criminal in its nature and merits punishment,[114] and that the accused is the person who committed it. It therefore follows logically that anything short of a conviction reflects to some extent, at least, upon either the judgment or the qualifications of those who deliberated on the fate of the case prior to the trial.

We have seen the approximate length of time it takes for the completion of the preliminaries. How quickly, we may ask, do the courts bring a case to a point of determination? This question is seemingly one of great concern to Soviet higher judicial authorities. The latter openly declares war against any tendency to drag a case for a long time, as was quite usual, not to say customary, both in old and new Russia.

[112]Report for 1925, page 136.

[113]*The Weekly*, No. 13, 1928, page 398.

[114]Not every criminal act deserves a punishment. A note to section 6, and section 8 of the Cr. Code, 1926, grant to the courts and the procuracy discretionary powers not to prosecute, or not to inflict any punishment in some instances, though a law has been violated.

The note to section 6 states that though a certain act is forbidden by the Code, the commission of such act, nevertheless, shall not be deemed socially dangerous, and therefore a crime, if it was insignificant in its nature and without harmful consequences.

Section 8 provides that if at the time of the preliminary inquiry or the trial the alleged criminal act lost its socially dangerous character, though it was such when committed, due to the change in the criminal law or in the socio-political circumstances or if in the opinion of the court the defendant at that moment cannot be considered a socially dangerous person, no measure of social protection (punishment) shall be applied.

In the first half of 1927, 51.4% of all the cases listed with the people's courts were completed within one month from the time they were brought to court.[115] This is, of course, a general average for the entire Federated Republic. Thus, to cite a striking example, the people's courts of the Far East had completed only 44.8% of all the cases within one month,[116] while on the other hand the people's courts of the City and Province of Moscow completed 80% of all their cases within fourteen days, and 45% within seven days[117] from the time they were brought to court.[118]

In the provincial and circuit courts cases are apparently not so quickly tried. Only 17.5%, however, of all the cases were not brought to a conclusion within three months.[119] In a circular letter of instructions issued by the Commissariat of Justice on January 30, 1929, the courts were required to carry out the following schedule: Every case which reaches the people's court in a city must be tried in two weeks, and every case in a village, in one month, every case which reaches the provincial, circuit or regional court must be completed within one month at the latest.[120]

We may now briefly sum up the process of elimination which takes place from the time a crime is being investigated up to the final affirmation of a conviction, taking the latest data available.

1. Of all the cases investigated by the organs of investigation, the inquisitors, who are to supervise the activities of the former, dismissed outright 67.9%. Of course, some of these dismissals were recommended by the police themselves.

2. Of all the cases in which a preliminary inquiry was conducted by the inquisitors, 42.5% were dismissed because the inquisitor did not discover the person who committed the crime, or for a number of other reasons.

[115] *The Weekly,* No. 13, 1928, page 400.

[116] *Ibid.*

[117] *Ibid.*, No. 11, 1928, page 338.

[118] In 1926 the revision conducted by the Commissariat for Peasants' and Workers' Inspection established that outside of the city of Moscow, it took two to five months to have a case completed. See B. Zenkevich, *The Weekly,* No. 35, 1927.

[119] *The Weekly,* No. 13, 1928, page 398.

[120] *Ibid.*, No. 5, 1929, page 120.

3. Of the cases in which the preliminary inquiry resulted in an accusatory conclusion—that is, when the inquisitor after listening to the testimony of the accused and his witnesses became convinced that he had as a matter of fact committed an act which is a crime not of trifling nature—the procurators dismissed 4.5%.

4. Of all the cases that reached the provincial and circuit courts either through the procurator, when the inquisitor had drafted an accusatory conclusion, or through the latter when a discontinuance or a dismissal was recommended, 59.9% were discontinued.

5. Out of all the cases sent to the people's courts either to continue the proceedings, or by the procurator, where a preliminary inquiry was conducted, 32.5% were dismissed.

6. Of all the cases which survived the different stages of elimination, and were at last brought to the trial court, an average of 25.6% resulted in acquittal in the people's courts, and 26.2% in the provincial and circuit courts.

7. Finally, of all the cases tried on their merits, the cassational instances reversed 10% of the verdicts rendered in the people's courts, and 9.1% at the provincial and circuit courts.

Chapter XII

IMPRESSIONS AND OBSERVATIONS

Of the various proceedings in the administration of the criminal law in Soviet Russia only the trial and the cassational session, by reason of their being open and public, afford to the curious and unbiased observer an excellent opportunity to see the Soviet system of criminal procedure in actual operation, to watch the translation of the abstract theory into reality. How this reality compares with the theories we have studied, what we generally observe, and how these observations impress us, are questions which inevitably come to our mind.

A. Impressions of a Court Trial

I. THE COURT ROOM

The first impression one receives upon entering a Soviet "Temple of Justice" is somewhat startling. The rooms where court sessions are held are devoid, with a few notable exceptions, of the impressiveness one is accustomed to in this country. The court room is not infrequently an ordinary low-ceilinged chamber with glaring holes in the broken plaster, and the paint faded to a nondescript shade. The furnishings usually consist of a small table placed on a slightly elevated platform, three crude wooden chairs for the judges and one chair to the left of the platform for the court secretary who takes notes of what occurs at the session. The two tables below the platform for the use of the procurator and the advocate and ordinary wooden benches for the public complete the equipment.

The tables are usually covered with what was once, before it faded, red cloth, the revolutionary emblem, but not infrequently cloth of dark green is substituted. Wall decorations, which may aid in creating the dignified atmosphere of a court, are totally absent. A huge portrait of Lenin hangs over the rostrum, and occasionally an additional picture of another revolutionary leader is the only other adornment on the walls. The total absence of any flag, coat-of-arms, etc., is notable as it is universal.

II. THE PUBLIC

The extreme unattractiveness of the court room does not, however, deprive it of the peculiar court atmosphere which is, after all, not dependent solely upon the spaciousness of the room, or its gorgeous appointments, but upon the attitude of those who frequent it, notably the public.

As a rule, the Soviet courts are crowded. There are first those who are, in one way or another, immediately concerned with the outcome of a particular case. But there are always many spectators, especially in the smaller towns, who come to the court room as a diversion from their daily occupation and worry. At any rate, the presence of the public at the trial sessions is conspicuous. This is not so for obvious reasons at the cassational sittings. The lively stage-like performance of the trial, with all its episodes of human interest which are so alluring to the average person, is lacking at the hearing of the appeal (complaint).

The public present at the trial are not passive observers who see, listen and go home to resume the duties of their daily life. Not the Russian. There are always animated, impassioned discussions on foot, as soon as the judges retire to deliberate on the verdict. The merits of the case receive a remarkably keen analysis during these improvised debates in which the defendant, if not under guard, may and usually does join. Thus, simultaneous with the rendering of the enforceable verdict within the judges' chamber, the public gratuitously shapes its own verdict based solely on what it deems proper and just under the circumstances.

It was the good fortune of the writer to join *incognito* in those highly stimulating, free-for-all discussions, and thus get a glimpse of what the public thinks, how it reacts towards the court and its decisions. For the discussions once started are never brought to a completion by the mere announcement of the verdict by the court. The debate continues outside the court room, but this time the main attention is concentrated on the verdict rendered and the sentence imposed.

Generally speaking, the attitude of the public towards crimes and criminals is not far removed from that taken by the government. The mere fact that one has done something which is forbidden by statute does not necessarily make his deed vicious or contemptible. One who has committed simple larceny, for example, is not a criminal, in the moral sense, in the eye of the public nor in the eye of the court. On the other hand, the embezzler of public funds is deemed a socially dangerous character deserving the severest punishment. From what we have observed, the public usually considers the verdicts of the court just and the sentences imposed meet with its approval.

Whatever justification there might have been for Professor Sorokin's assertion in 1924,[1] that the population scorns Soviet justice and "does not consider it as justice at all", the state of affairs in 1928 unmistakably showed that the people as a whole took a very positive attitude towards the courts, the dispensers of justice.

III. THE JUDGES

The clang of a bell announces the entrance of the judges into the court room, and all those present rise. The same procedure is repeated when the court retires at the close of the session. This somewhat obsolete formality which is severely criticised in the Soviet legal press adds, however, a bit of solemnity to the otherwise prosaic atmosphere.

Were it not for the position the permanent judge occupies at the table (he sits between the two co-judges) one could not distinguish between the judge and the temporary co-judges, as no uniform, gown or regalia is worn. The typical Russian *rubashka* (shirt) buttoned up to the neck, or any other shirt, sometimes without a coat, is the ordinary summer costume of the judge. Nevertheless, the simplicity of appearance does not in the least detract from the authoritative determination emanating from the bench. The public in the court room is apparently fully conscious of the fact that the three plain looking persons at the table yonder are judges whose decision carries weight, and whose sentences will be strictly enforced.

As a rule, the behavior of the presiding judge who conducts the session is earnest but simple, without any sign of stiffness or rudeness. The power of the court is not brought into play

[1]"The Soviet Codes and Soviet Justice," by Pitrim Sorokin, *Michigan Law Review*, Vol. 23.

unnecessarily. But there are, of course, exceptions. At least in one instance the writer observed a people's judge, who wore a heavy, typically Ukranian moustache, exhibiting all the strikingly repulsive characteristics of the old type Russian *chinovnik,* a word quite inadequately translated into "official".

IV. THE DEFENDANT

In striking contrast to the wholesome atmosphere saturated with the spirit of delightful plainness and utter lack of officialdom, is the custom of having the defendant, who was in custody awaiting trial, guarded throughout the trial by two officers with their swords removed from their scabbards held in position ready for action. This survival of old Tzarist Russia makes a painful impression. Being wholly unecessary as protection, it is an unjustifiable show of brutality.

A defendant, however, who has not been in custody prior to trial is seated unguarded on one of the first row benches designated as the "bench of the accused" (*skamya pudsudimikh*).

A remarkable feature is the active part taken by the defendant at his own trial. As he is invariably asked by the presiding judge whether he wishes to interrogate the witnesses, the defendant, as a rule, fully avails himself of this right. On several occasions the writer was profoundly impressed by the remarkably clever cross-examination conducted personally by a simple-looking defendant.

The active participation of the defendant at his own trial often makes one forget that the life or liberty of a person is at stake, and alleviates the tension of the court atmosphere. One may even get the illusion that the defendant is merely assisting the court in determining his own fate which is, of course, not the case.

V. THE PROCURATOR AND THE ADVOCATE

Neither the procurator nor the advocate occupies the central position of the trial, as is common in our courts. Their rôle at the trial is of a decidedly subordinate character. In many trials, especially in the people's courts, the proceedings are conducted in the absence of either the procurator or the advocate.

In the absence of the twelve men, good and true, there is no one susceptible to the passion and zeal, as well as ingenuity, displayed by attorneys on either side at our jury trials.

Of the two "assistants" to the court, which the procurator and the advocate are in theory, the procurator is notably the one who is nearer to the court by his appearance, training, social or party affiliations, and his approach to problems to be solved by the court; he is the product of the new political and social régime. The advocate, on the other hand, not infrequently sounds a complete disharmony by his attire, appearance and manner of speech. He is often a person of a different sphere, politically as well as psychologically. The pro-Soviet sentiment often displayed by advocates, who are invariably far removed from the philosophy of the soviets, does not sound sincere or convincing and is sharply rebuked by soviet leaders themselves.

The sworn-attorney of the old régime, who but over a dozen years ago was seated among the distinguished and mighty on the social olympus of Russian life, cuts a pitiful figure. In spite of his constant profession of loyalty to a political system which dethroned his profession, his mere presence at the court is only tolerated. The political party in power is unhesitatingly distrustful of any old-time intellectuals in any branch of state or social activity. The mere institution of the college of advocates is said to be the result of "a compromise in principle with the old bourgeois order".[2]

VI. OBSERVING THE COURT IN ACTION

In the surroundings above described the Soviet court can be seen in action.

On the whole the rules of procedure prescribed by the Code are fairly well observed, though some important rules appear less impressive, or even absolutely valueless, when applied in practice. A striking illustration is the right of the defendant not to testify. A great number of cases are tried without the participation of defense counsel, and, therefore, there is no one to advise the defendant of this particular right. But even an advocate, when present, would hardly advise his client to withhold his story of the

[2]Krylenko, *The Judiciary and the Law*, 1927, pages 8 and 9.

case for fear that he would be charged with imitating the bourgeois lawyer, a sin too heavy for any Soviet advocate to bear. Furthermore, in the absence of a jury, the court would quite naturally draw a strong inference against an accused who would not testify.

As the Soviet trial knows of no game of wits to be played between the prosecutor and the defender, a characteristic that no observer can fail to notice, one would imagine the whole proceedings to be an extremely dull affair. But quite the contrary is true. The liveliness of the trial is mainly due to the vividness and rapidity with which the public proceedings are carried on. In the complete absence of any objections to the introduction of testimony, the story of a case is unfolded with amazing frankness and dispatch. The witnesses, mostly plain folks, often portray in their simple, striking manner a vivid, graphic picture of a crime with all its illuminating background and surrounding circumstances.

The discard of any legal niceties in the admission of evidence has actually destroyed any shield of technicalities behind which a criminal might escape conviction. He must stand or fall on the merits of the case. But the unrestrained admission of evidence tending to show the so-called circumstances and surroundings necessarily creates too wide an opening and, perforce, tends to prejudice the mind of the slightly trained judges, and in particular the inexperienced, temporary co-judges against the defendant, and sometimes perhaps in his favor.

The sincere desire to establish the truth about the case, and dispose of it in accordance with the Soviet policy of crime and punishment is eminently evident. But to achieve this aim it would require a great number of legally trained judges. The lack of such judges is obviously a serious handicap to the entire system. The effort made in recent years to improve the quality of the judicial personnel has apparently not been without accomplishment. Here and there one can observe a trial judge exhibiting unusual skill in disposing of knotty problems in the most simple, unpretentious manner.

We may note that simplicity in discharging judicial duties has become a cardinal requirement. Any tendency to indulge in trival legal niceties is derisively termed *Kruchkotvorstvo,* that is the invention of a mental catch or trick. It is rather amusing to observe how some judges and procurators display, perhaps unconsciously, a propensity to indulge in refined points and the use of legalistic language.

B. Cross Currents Within the Soviet System

Nothing is more striking and fascinating to the student of the Soviet administration of the criminal law than to observe the combative cross currents within the very system.

The Soviet political thought is unmistakably clear. It consciously rejects the western ideas of justice; it strives to annihilate the entire body of procedure developed by the liberal forces on the continent of Europe. Every arrangement which has the earmark of the so-called bourgeois world is *ipso facto* condemned as objectionable. The entire political and social structure, including the courts and the procedure therein, must be basically new, different—proletarian.

In conflict with this conscious striving for the new, there is alive within the soviets, a force which is nourished by the well established principles upon which the judicial systems elsewhere in Europe have been built. Whether it is the force of sheer tradition, or the inner logic upon which those principles are founded, is immaterial. This force has unquestionably had a remarkably great influence upon the shaping of the Soviet judicial structure and its procedure; it has tended to check and modify the would-be anti-bourgeois judicial system.

It may be that the western ideas of justice, worked out during many years and tested by experience, have injected themselves into the Soviet judicial system because the very desire of the soviets to establish an orderly form of courts and procedure necessarily collided with the theoretical design for a purely proletarian court, a mere docile agent of the government.

There is apparently a wide inconsistency between the Soviet theoretical abstraction which boldly denies the distinctiveness, not to say sanctity, of the judiciary, and the method and manner by which the various Soviet codes concerning the judicial system are prepared, analyzed and enacted. For if the judiciary is on the identical basis with other governmental agencies, and serves merely as an instrument in the hands of the ruling class for the oppression of its enemies, why should the courts alone have detailed, formal norms of procedure, why the establishment of rigid guaranties of the rights of the different parties, notably the defendants, why the minutely prescribed trial procedure, the open and public hearings? The truth is that whatever the Soviet theory concerning the judiciary may be, the Soviet courts are called upon to deal with judicial questions in a judicial way. The similarity between the innumerable rules of procedure in the present system and those in existence in pre-revoluntionary days, in spite of the many deeply rooted differences, is indicative of the wide gap between the theoretical conception of the Soviet court and its true character.

N. V. Krylenko in his persistent manner asserts that "the courts are a mere orderly form of vengenance" and in the fact of its being orderly lies the *"differentia specifica"*[3] of the court. But the mere attempt to have the court act in an orderly form, that is, in accordance with the carefully prescribed rules, as pointed out, has inevitably led them to further compromises. Thus Krylenko maintains that "We have built our judiciary so * * * as to give the judges within certain limits a guarantee of independence". Furthermore, "in this respect we say that after all not everything is bad with the bourgeois legislation, and that something of that system we have to borrow."[4] The "borrowing", one may conjecture, takes place because the judicial ideas of the western word, usually termed bourgeois, or liberal, still exert a remarkably great influence on Soviet judicial legislation. In advocating a new criminal code, Krylenko states that he expects opposition within "our own midst, among us jurists because in many of us the old principles of the liberal school is strongly entrenched."[5]

A mere cursory review of the history of the Soviet legislation concerning the judiciary plainly reveals that the presence of the ideas of the liberal school have been discovered soon after their annihilation has triumphantly been declared.

[3]Krylenko, *The Jud. System,* page 16.
[4]Krylenko, *The Judiciary and the Law,* 1927, page 43.
[5]*The Weekly,* 1928, No. 23, page 664.

The judicial system inaugurated in the first days of the Revolution was later, we recall, denounced as having been tainted with the bourgeois spirit. The People's Court Act of 1918, was at that time widely proclaimed as the legislation which gave birth to the true proletarian courts. This self-contentment was, however, short lived, for it was unequivocally admitted that the influence of the burgeois procedure proved to be more than powerful.[6] The various codes enacted during 1922 were a great achievement of the Soviet judicial system. They were the product of a more mature and deliberate consideration worked out and drafted carefully after the civil war had been over, and political safety and quiet had reigned. These codes were prepared under the direct supervision of the stalwart of the stalwarts, N. V. Krylenko. Surely no section, or even phrase could have been inserted without his unqualified approval. In 1928, however, Krylenko explained that the codes of 1922 fully reflected a compromise between the "ideas of the liberal-bourgeois jurisprudence" which demands formal guaranties for those who come before the court, and the principle that the court is a weapon in the hand of the ruling class to combat the enemies of the proletarian revolution.[7] Even where the Union adopted its Guiding Principles for the Judiciary "there were compromises made on matters of principle with the old bourgeois order".[8]

It is interesting to note that when the first Soviet Criminal Code was enacted in 1922 an English legal journal wrote: "What strikes the practitioner at once is its comparative commonplaceness; the whole reads rather like the Digest of Criminal Law." Furthermore, "altogether the code seems severely orthodox as a legal exhibit."[9]

The mysterious "liberal ideas" constantly at work apparently modified even the most cherished doctrine of the Soviet judiciary, the proletarian class character of the court. As one would expect, some of the Soviet courts took the meaning of the class court doctrine too literally. But the plenum of the Supreme Court of the R.S.F.S.R. has in one of its letters of instruction complained

[6]Krylenko, *The Judiciary and the Law*, 1928, page 10.
[7]*Ibid.*, page 16.
[8]Krylenko, *op. cit.*, *supra*, note 4, page 8.
[9]*Solicitors' Journal*, 1925, Vol. 69, page 802.

that not all the judges have fully comprehended the meaning of the class point of view in deciding cases. "The courts must remember", the instruction states, "that the carrying out of the class attitude concerning the penal policy consists not in convicting the 'nepman' or the '*Kulak*' [rich peasant], and not in acquitting the toiler, or the poor or middle-class peasant, but in the clear understanding of the social danger of the act committed by the citizen brought to trial, appraised from the point of view of the interests of the proletariat as a whole."[10]

Once we visualize the contradictory currents within the system, we may comprehend the intricate inner mechanism of the judicial structure, built upon a compromise between two strikingly opposing tendencies. One of the most outstanding characteristics of the Soviet judiciary, the abolition of the jury and its substitution by co-judges is also, it would seem, a direct result of those conflicting theories. One tendency would strive for a court of judges only, while the other would demand a trial by jury—the co-judges arrangement is the logical compromise. It is frankly stated that "there was a time when our people's courts and the rôle of the people's co-judges were looked upon as analagous to a court with a trial by jury."[11] At this point we may note that the trial by jury in the Russian judicial system has never been as fundamental an institution as it has been with us. In pre-revolutionary days, the justices of the peace, the municipal courts and the courts presided over by the *zemski* chief[12] which tried less serious cases never had jury trials. Beside these courts, the judicial *palata* tried grave offenses without a jury.[13] But even in the Tzarist circuit courts, not all cases were entitled to a trial by jury.[14]

The Soviet régime has wiped out the Tzarist judicial structure and has built up a new one. But its newness, in reality, is confined only to the personnel. Otherwise, it is still to a considerable extent the Russian system, which was in turn based upon the French system, modified and adapted to the basically new political and social order.

[10]Letters of Instructions for 1925, No. 2, *The Weekly*, 1925, Nos. 31 and 32.

[11]Krylenko, *op. cit., supra*, note 4, page 55.

[12]See appendix No. 8, pages 381, 384 and 385.

[13]*Ibid.*, pages 393 and 394.

[14]*Ibid.*, page 389.

APPENDIX

Appendix No. 1

U.S.S.R., ITS CONSTITUENT REPUBLICS AND THEIR AUTONOMOUS PARTS

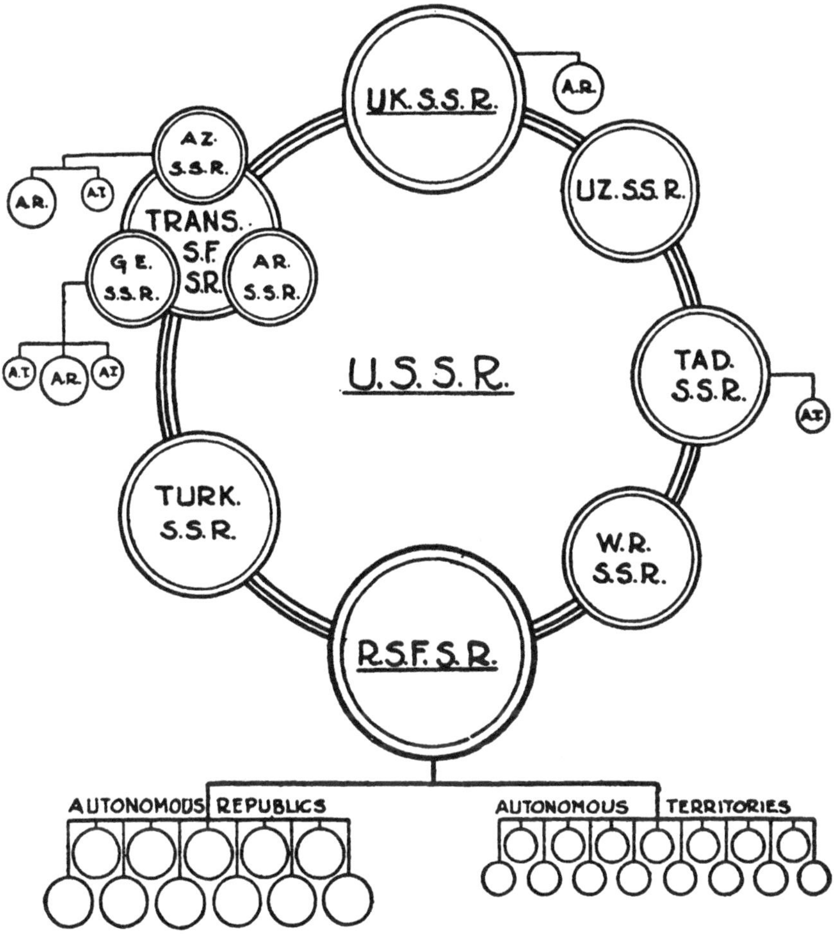

A.R. = AUTONOMOUS REPUBLIC
A.T. = AUTONOMOUS TERRITORY
Az.S.S.R. = AZERBAIJAN SOCIALIST SOVIET REPUBLIC
Ar.S.S.R. = ARMENIAN SOCIALIST SOVIET REPUBLIC
Ge.S.S.R. = GEORGIAN SOCIALIST SOVIET REPUBLIC
FOR OTHER ABBREVIATIONS, SEE INTRODUCTION PAGES 1 AND 2

Appendix No. 2

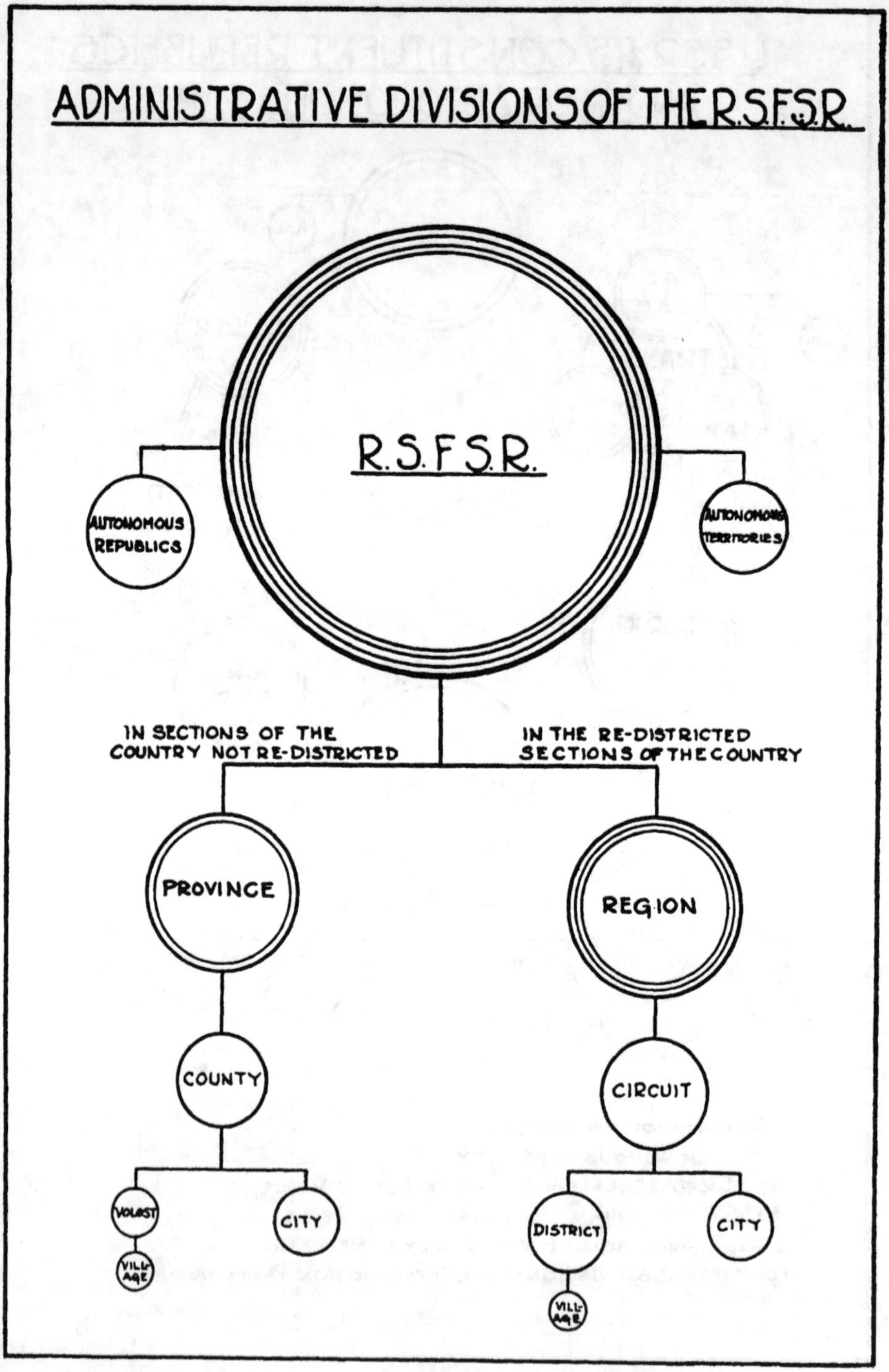

Appendix No. 3

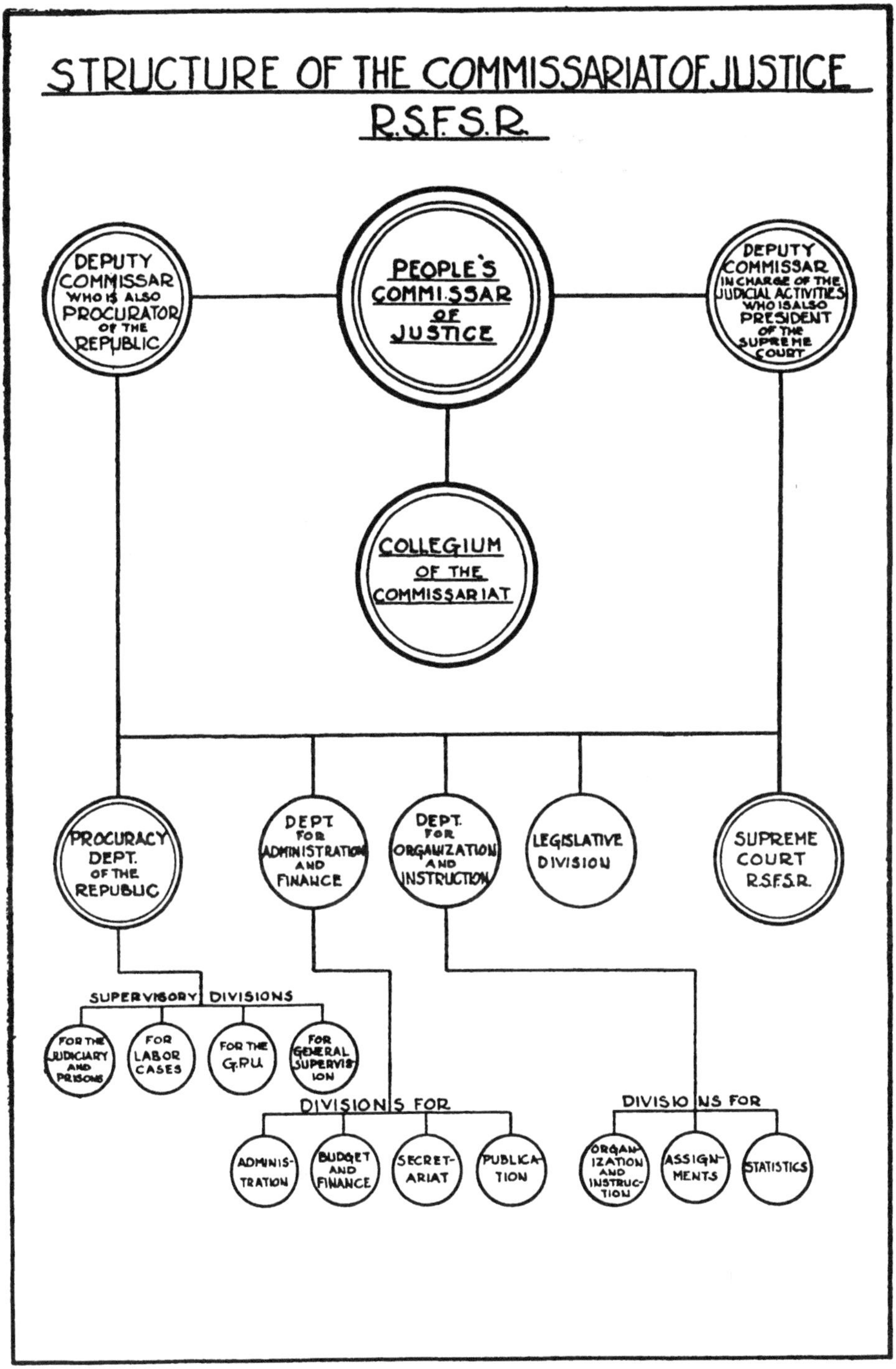

Appendix No. 4

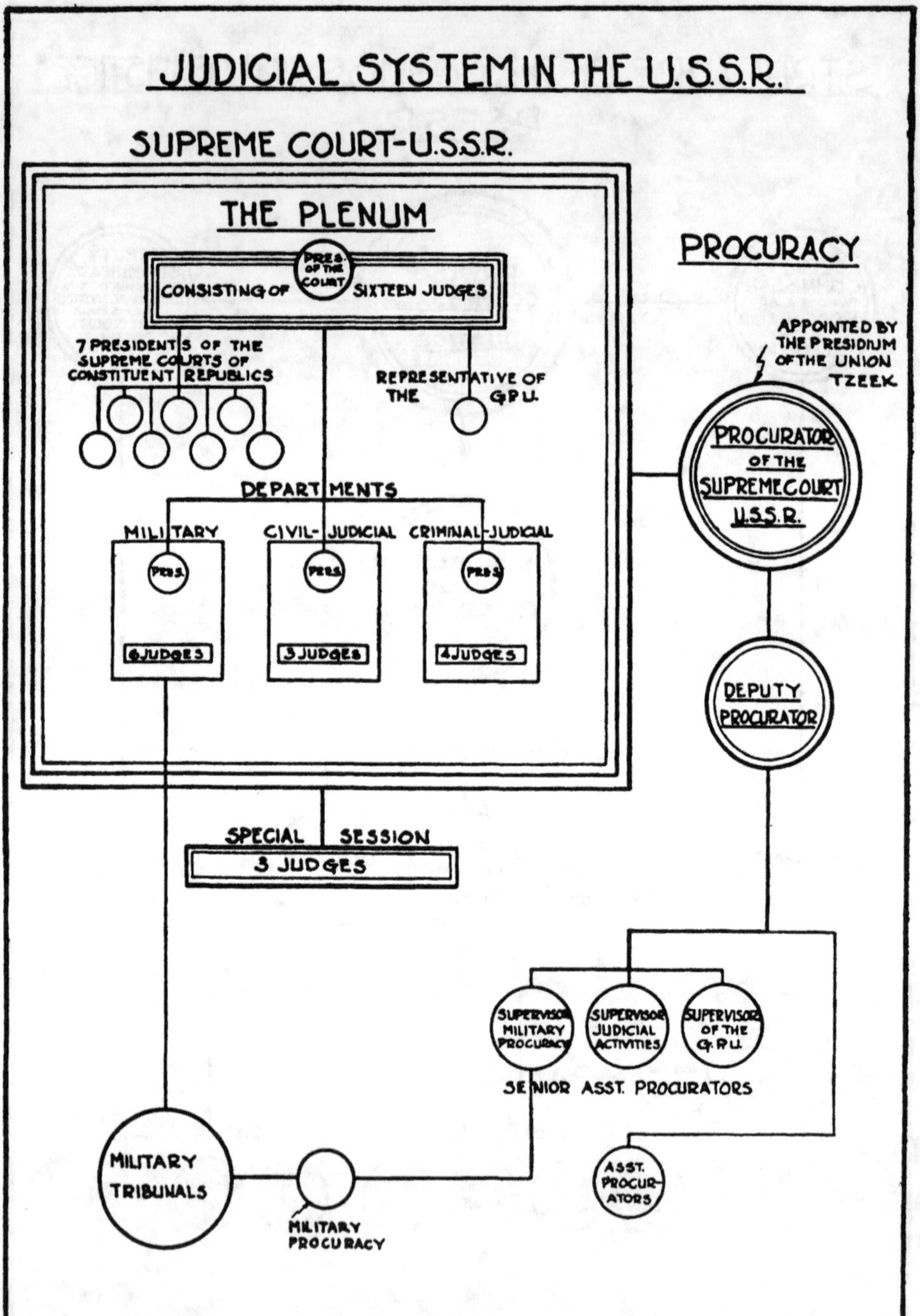

Appendix No. 5

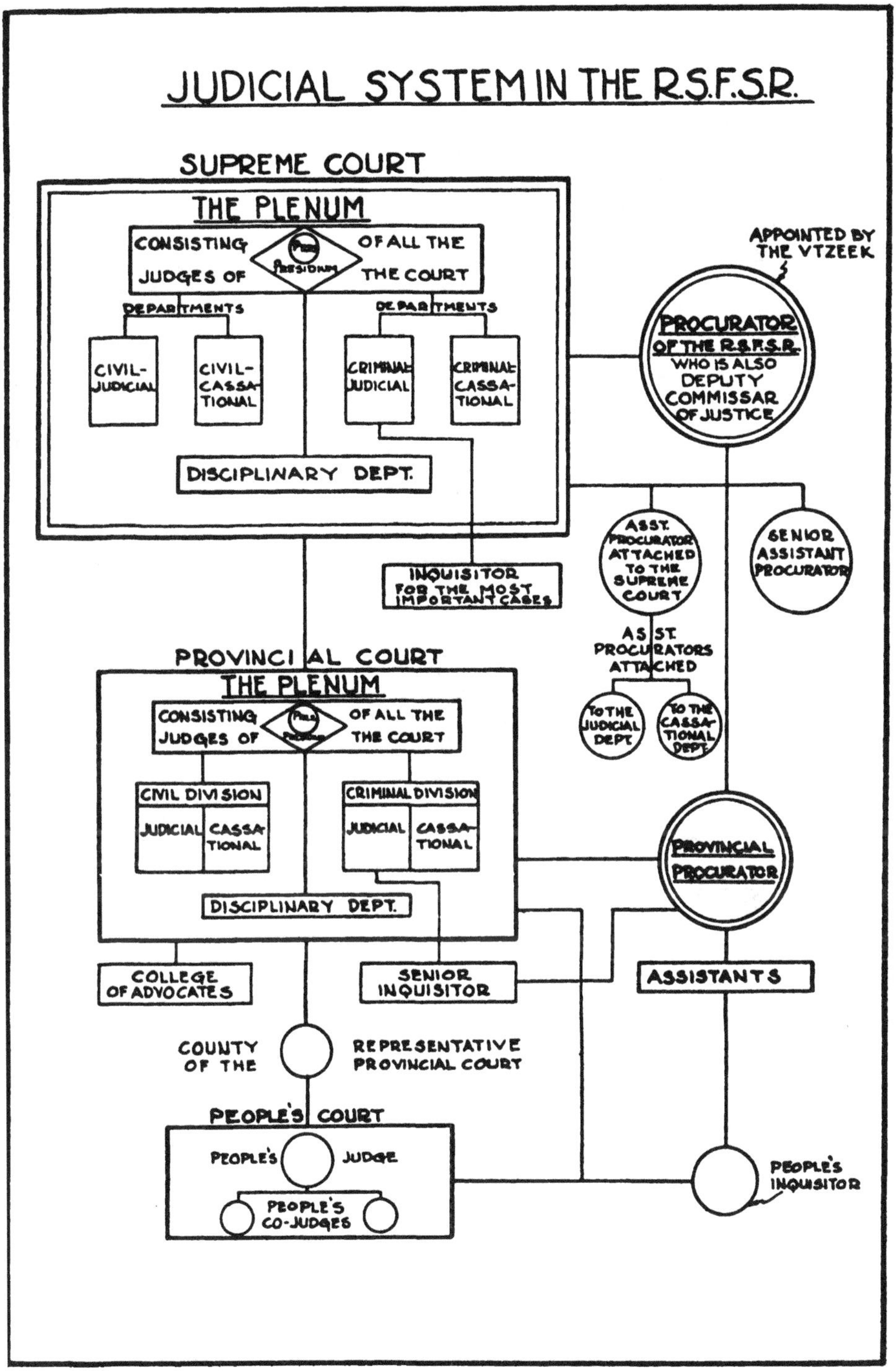

Appendix No. 6

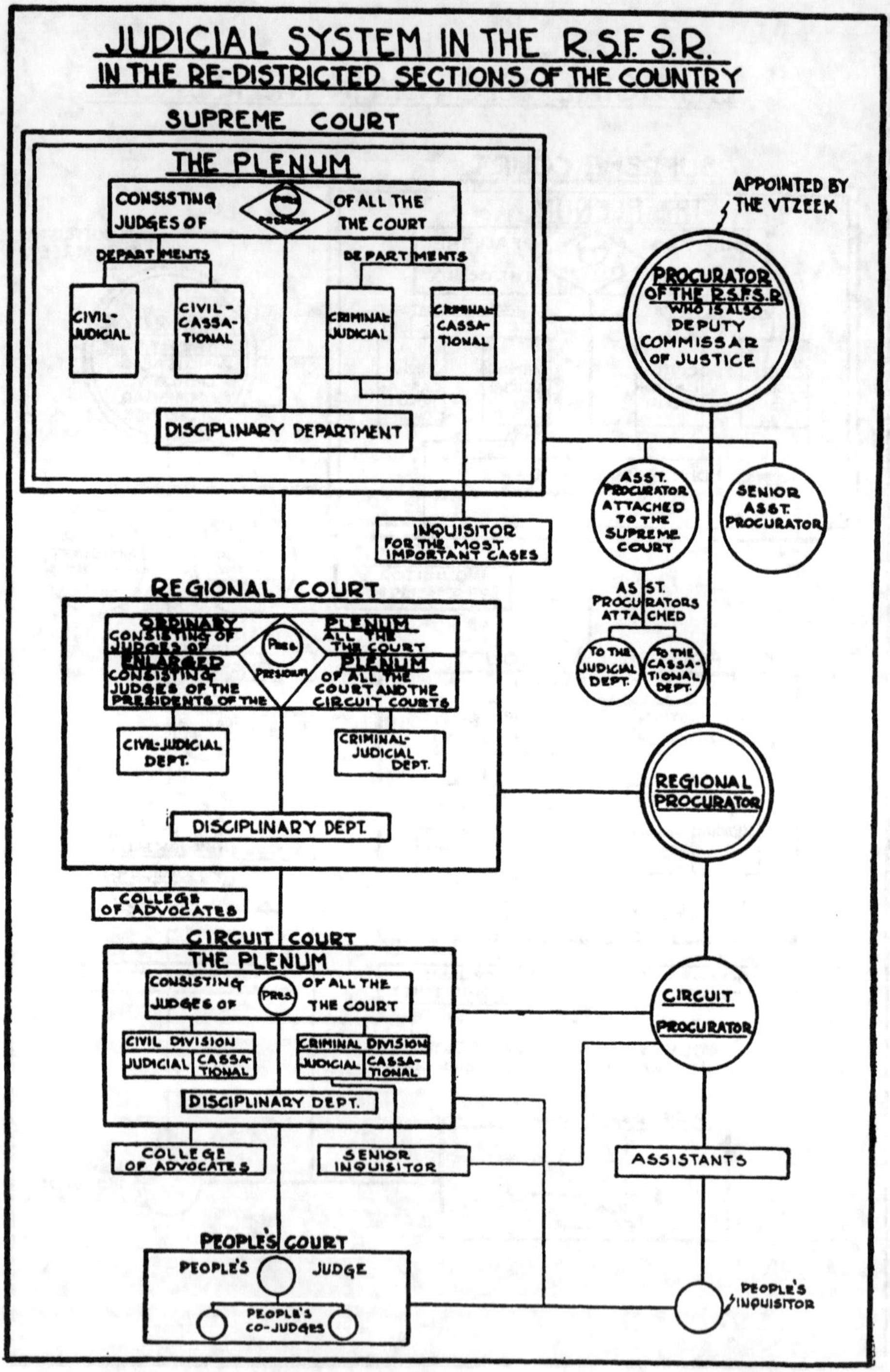

Appendix No. 7

SUMMARY OF THE 1931 PROJECT FOR A NEW CODE OF CRIMINAL PROCEDURE[1]

On August 30, 1931, the Commissariat of Justice of the R.S.F.S.R. published in its official organ a project of a new Code of Criminal Procedure, and invited discussion of it by all Soviet judicial workers.

While the draft has, of course, no legal force at present and may, perhaps, never be enacted into law without important modifications,[2] it is, however, an extremely significant document because it discloses in no uncertain terms the tendencies prevalent among Soviet judicial workers. These tendencies reflect the general political mood of Soviet leadership today. We shall, therefore, briefly summarize the salient changes and innovations advanced by this Project.

At the outset we note the rather remarkable fact that the proposed Code marks at many points a return to an earlier period of the present régime. Unlike the law in existence since 1923, and the proposed Codes of 1927 and 1928, this terse Project (134 sections compared with the 465 sections of the present Code) contains four rather lengthy sections of high-sounding political declamation and declaration of faith.

These four sections, termed "basic statutes", really form the cornerstone upon which the framers of the Project intend to build up the system of criminal procedure in the near future. The opening sentence of the "basic statutes" proclaims: "The Code of Criminal Procedure of the R.S.F.S.R. shall be based upon the general aim of the Proletarian Revolution and the general basis of the Soviet criminal policy as outlined in the Criminal Code of the period of transition to communism."[3] It then declares that during this period it is necessary to mobolize the creative activities of millions of workers in the cause of socialist development and

[1] *Proekt Ugolovno-Protzessualnovo Kodeksa* R.S.F.S.R. Soviet Justice (*Sovetskaya Ustitziya*) No. 24, 1931.

[2] The Projects for a new Code of Criminal Procedure advanced in 1928 were continuously discussed in legal circles and the press. Only at the close of 1929 were few sections of the proposed code enacted into law.

[3] Project for a New Code, *op. cit., supra,* note 1, section 1.

to combat the stubborn opposition of the remnants of the capitalist class. The Code of Criminal Procedure, therefore, aims to create "necessary conditions" for carrying out these purposes through the court, the procuracy and the organs of inquiry. Among these conditions are "class vigilance . . . flexibility and speed."[4]

The fundamental principles advanced in the declaratory sections of the proposed Code narrow down to the basic thought that the Soviet régime is in the midst of building up the socialist structure and that the population of the country is sharply and irreconcilably divided, with respect to criminal law, into two clearly distinguishable antagonistic camps. On the one hand the remnants of the incorrigibly hostile capitalist groups—the counter-revolutionists—and on the other hand the laboring people, who, though inherently friendly to the aims of communism, find themselves among the violators of the Soviet order by reason of old entrenched habits, or lack of social discipline and self-restraint. It logically follows that the criminal judiciary is to "apply, on the basis of revolutionary law, severe and merciless measures of repression towards elements hostile to socialist development." But at the same time the judiciary is "to exert a disciplinary influence with regard to crimes committed by the laboring masses."[5] It is, therefore, quite natural to have the proposed Act announce that "The court, the procuracy and the organs of inquiry are bound to rely in their work upon the masses and to seek the co-operation of the laboring elements, and of the first line of the active groups of the proletarian collectives."[6]

With the above in mind we proceed to summarize the outstanding characteristics of the proposed law.

I. JURISDICTION OF THE COURTS

A feature, highly characteristic of the entire Project, is the division between "counter-revolutionary and similar" crimes on the one hand and all other crimes on the other. The same division is made with regard to jurisdiction. "All criminal cases shall be tried at the people's court" except "counter-revolutionary and similar crimes" which are to be tried at the regional court or its

[4] *Ibid.*, section 2.
[5] *Ibid.*, section 2, subsections a and b.
[6] *Ibid.*, section 3, subsection a.

equivalent.[7] The Supreme Court is given, as heretofore, original jurisdiction over certain persons.[8] This places the people's court in the same position it occupied prior to the Judiciary Act of 1922.[9]

II. PRELIMINARY INQUIRY

The functions of the police, as an organ of preliminary inquiry, are considerably broadened. It conducts such inquiries under the direct and *actual* supervision of the people's inquisitor in all cases except "counter-revolutionary or similar" crimes, which are subject to the exclusive jurisdicton of the inquisitor.[10] The preliminary inquiry in all cases must be completed within one month. But this period may be extended to two months by the district procurator, and to three by the regional procurator.[11]

The procuracy receives complete, unqualified control over the preliminary proceedings, the procurator having the discretionary power to assign any case to any organ of inquiry, or to conduct it himself.[12]

Measures to secure the attendance of the accused or of the defendant are reduced to only three—signed promise not to leave the jurisdiction, guaranty by a person or a group, and the taking into custody,[13] *i. e.*, holding without bail (to apply our term). While the power to hold the accused in custody is carefully circumscribed by restrictive provisons, an excepton is made with regard to those accused in "counter-revolutionary or similar" crimes, who may be held without bail if the official in charge of the inquiry "considers it unwise to leave the person at large due to his 'class danger.' "[14] This harsh provision is somewhat tempered by the proviso that the "organs of inquiry and the procuracy are subject to disciplinary responsibility for holding one in custody without sufficient grounds as provided in this section of the

[7]Unlike the Code in existence the Project enumerates all the courts including territorial courts of the autonomous territories, and the superior courts of the autonomous republics.

[8]Project, *op. cit., supra,* No. 1, sections 54, 55 and 57.

[9]See *ante,* p. 25.

[10]Project, *op. cit., supra,* note 1, section 15.

[11]*Ibid.,* section 17.

[12]*Ibid.,* sections 10 and 15.

[13]*Ibid.,* section 41.

[14]*Ibid.,* section 41, second paragraph.

Code."[15] The organs of inquiry are subject to criminal responsibility for applying violence, threats, etc., in obtaining evidence.[16]

By the terms of the proposed law the procurator, and in some instances his assistant, the inquisitor, decide the question of holding for trial, suspending or discontinuing the case. The proposal that the procuracy shall have complete control over proceedings prior to trial is consistently carried out, though some of the leading figures within the Soviet judiciary are strenuously opposed to it.[17]

III. THE TRIAL

In connection with trial, the most striking feature of the Project is the abolition of all distinction between procedure in the people's court and in the higher type of courts of original jurisdiction. Thus, the exceptional characteristics of trial in the provincial or similar courts, circumscribing the rights and privileges of the defendant, as provided by the present law, would apply also to trial in the people's court. On the whole the provisions are more stern and severe save only with respect to the defendant's right to counsel. We recall that the defendant does not now have an absolute right to engage counsel at the provincial and similar courts. The Project, however, provides: "The Court shall permit the participation of defense." The right of the defendant to engage counsel would, therefore, be absolute even in the provincial, regional or similar courts. The Project further provides: "The participation of defense counsel shall be obligatory"[18] in specified instances, of which one is the defendant's illiteracy, a condition not included in the existing law.

Unlike the Code in force, the Project grants to the trial court the discretionary power to change the "formulation of the accusation", apparently even if the new charge is of a more serious nature. The court is required to refer the case for further inquiry, after it has changed the charge, only if it would otherwise be impossible for the court to decide the case properly.[19]

[15] *Ibid.*, section 41, third paragraph.
[16] *Ibid.*, section 20.
[17] See *ante*, pp. 130 and 131.
[18] Project, *op. cit.*, *supra*, note 1, section 62.
[19] *Ibid.*, section 88.

As a complete departure from Russian tradition, the trial court may limit the duration of final speeches.[20]

In rendering the verdict "the court shall give weight to all the data in the case, the personality of the defendant, the existing laws and the general policy of the Proletarian Government."[21]

Another highly characteristic provision requires the courts to arrange for the trial of cases at workingmen's clubs, trade unions' quarters and other places where the presence of the worker is assured "in order to mobilize the toiling masses for war on crime or shortcomings that obstruct socialist development, as well as for the purpose of strengthening discipline and the new forms of communal life among the toilers."[22]

IV. CRIMINAL REVIEW

Fundamental and striking changes are proposed by the Project with regard to criminal review.

First, no complaint is allowed where the sentence consists of a public reprimand, a fine, or an order to make restitution, not exceeding the sum of 100 rubles, or 500 rubles in the case of the non-laboring classes. A complaint may be permitted, however, even in these cases on the petition of social organizations or governmental organs.[23]

Second, in "counter-revolutionary or similar" crimes the court of cassation has the power to decide whether to permit the participation of the parties at the cassational hearing.[24]

Third, the Project apparently contemplates the creation of a special Department of Supervision of the Supreme Court to review legally binding verdicts and decisions which are brought from the regional, territorial or superior courts. The proposed law also assigns to the presidium of the regional, territorial and superior courts the power to review legally binding verdicts by way of supervision, a power which is now lodged in the plena of the respective courts. The presidium of the court, as we know, is a small body while the plenum is composed of all the judges of the

[20] *Ibid.*, section 91.
[21] *Ibid.*, section 97.
[22] *Ibid.*, section 70.
[23] *Ibid.*, section 109.
[24] *Ibid.*, section 111.

court. This change is apparently suggested in order to achieve desired speed.

At this point it is well to emphasize the fact that the Project contemplates a complete return to the practically abandoned "three story" system of courts. It seems to presuppose the abolition of the province, leaving the region or the territory, which are both of the same standing, as the only significant administrative unit, while discarding the circuit, which is the subdivision wthin the region. Such an arrangement existed in the re-districted sections of the country up to 1926, and proved completely unworkable.

What may be the fate of this Project is purely conjecture. While, on the whole, it probably gives expression to the ideas which are at present dominant in Soviet life, it undertakes to settle so many controversial points that it is unlikely to become law in its present form.

Appendix No. 8

CRIMINAL JUDICIAL SYSTEM IN IMPERIAL RUSSIA

A. Criminal Courts

The criminal courts in Imperial Russia may be divided into four distinct systems: (1) courts of the peace, (2) *zemski* courts, (3) general courts and (4) courts of cassation.

I. COURTS OF THE PEACE SYSTEM

The courts of this system acted in a limited field dealing for the most part with petty offenses. Cases which properly originated in this type of court would never reach any other system for purposes of retrial or appeal. The characteristics of these courts were that cases were always tried here summarily and that one justice sat in cases of original jurisdiction, and a conference of justices of the same court sat as a court of appeals.

a. *Courts of the Peace*

This type of court was created in Russia during the great era of reforms in the sixties of the last century. It was a part of the new judicial system, the main principles of which were worked out by a commission and confirmed by the Tzar in 1862,[1] and were finally enacted into law in November, 1864.[2] These courts of the peace which began to function only in a part of the Empire in 1866 took the place of courts which had apparently both judicial and executive functions. This new system, according to a Russian scholar of that day, "was to lay down first of all the new rule of division between the judiciary and that of the administrative and legislative functions."[3]

The law provided that each county *(uyezd)* was to comprise a separate district of the peace with justices holding court at the

[1] A. Kornilov, *Modern Russian History*, Vol. I, p. 101, (N. Y., 1916).
[2] Statute on the Judiciary, *Fund. Laws*, Vol. XVI.
[3] Th. M. Dimitrief, *Judicial Reform (Sudebnaya Reforma) Collected Works*, Vol. II, p. 469, Moscow, 1890.

county seat and in other cities as well.[4] Each district was divided into sections with one justice assigned to each section.[5] In addition to the sectional justices of the peace there were honorary district justices of the peace.[6] The latter, as the name indicates, were not, properly speaking, office-holders. No particular section was assigned to them. They received no remuneration for occasional services, nor any sum to cover possible expenditures.[7]

The honorary justice was, nevertheless, in duty bound "whenever he was within the district to take up any case subject to the jurisdiction of a justice of the peace, at the request of both parties."[8]

The sectional justice selected, with the consent of the assembly of the justices, his seat within the territorial limits assigned to him and there he conducted his judicial business.[9] He received a salary and all expenses connected with his official duties. Ordinarily these sums were paid out of the imperial treasury, but in a few large cities they were paid out of the city treasury.[10] If the sectional justice declined to receive any remuneration for his services he was styled "honorary sectional justice of the peace", which name he carried so long as he took charge of his section without receiving a salary.[11]

Both honorary and sectional justices were elected for a term of three years,[12] at the regular session of the county assembly of the landed nobility,[13] or at the provincial assembly of the same nobility if less than twelve electors were present at the county gathering.[14] While it was not required that the justices should be learned in the law, there were a number of requirements for eligibility to that office. They had to be "residents of the county, not younger than twenty-five years of age; they had to possess either a university or secondary education or three years' service

[4]Statute on the Judiciary, *Fund. Laws,* Vol. XVI, section 12.
[5]*Ibid.,* section 15.
[6]*Ibid.,* section 16.
[7]*Ibid.,* section 50.
[8]*Ibid.,* section 46.
[9]*Ibid.,* section 41.
[10]*Ibid.,* section 44.
[11]*Ibid.,* section 45.
[12]*Ibid.,* section 23.
[13]*Ibid.,* section 24.
[14]*Ibid.,* section 25.

in such capacity as would give them practical knowledge in the conduct of judicial affairs."[15] In addition they had to satisfy a property qualification. The statute just quoted described in great detail the amount of land a person had to control, either owning it himself or through his wife or parents, in order to qualify for the office of justice. This made the justices substantial landowners.

A sectional justice had to give all his time and attention to judicial matters within his section. It was specifically provided[16] that the sectional justice might not hold any other office of a governmental or social nature except an honorary position in a charitable or educational institution. The honorary justice, on the other hand, was permitted to hold, with few exceptions, any other office.[17]

The offenses which were subject to the jurisdiction of a justice of the peace were numerous, and are set forth at great length in a special act on punishments inflicted by the justices of the peace.[18] According to this act the scope of the court's power and its position as a criminal tribunal can sufficiently be understood from the fact that it had jurisdiction of all the offenses which were punishable, according to the penal code by:

"1. Rebuke, remark or reprimand;
2. Fine of not higher than 300 rubles ($150.00);
3. Detention for not more than three months;
4. Imprisonment for not longer than one year and six months."[19]

b. *Assembly of the Justices of the Peace*

The gathering of all the justices of the peace, sectional as well as honorary, of each district comprised a court of the highest resort for courts of the peace and was styled the "assembly of the justices of the peace". The assembly was presided over by one of

[15] *Ibid.*, section 19.
[16] *Ibid.*, section 42.
[17] *Ibid.*, section 49.
[18] *Fund. Laws*, Vol. XV, p. 3798.
[19] *Ibid.*, section 1, and see also Statutes on Cr. Procedure, section 33 (1864).

the justices selected for that purpose,[20] who served in that capacity for three years.[21] The assembly was essentially a court of appeals for cases brought from the justices of the peace within the district. It enjoyed an extraordinary power of review to an extent entirely unknown in our common law system. In addition to its appellate jurisdiction, the assembly of the justices of the peace was also vested with the power to receive and decide by way of cassation complaints and protests against legally binding judgments of the justices of the peace, when no appeal would lie.[22] The assembly had the power to decide also jurisdictional disputes between justices of the same district.[23] As the highest court in the court of the peace system, it had the power to exercise direct supervision over all the justices of the peace in the given district.[24] Notwithstanding all these powers the time and place for its conference were decided, not by the court itself, but by the county assembly of landed nobility, and, in a few of the largest cities of the Empire, by the City Councils.[25] (City Councils were composed of the landed nobility and wealthy merchants.) In cases of necessity, however, the president judge of the assembly himself was allowed to call an extra session.[26] To facilitate the handling of the business the assembly could divide itself into separate groups. The president judge presiding over one group, while presidents *pro tem,* were to be elected to preside over the other groups.[27] But not less than three justices were to participate in each case to be decided by the assembly.[28] Another important feature of the assembly was that the assistant procurator of the circuit court had to be present at its sessions.[29]

II. *zemski* COURT SYSTEM

These courts arrived upon the heels of the peculiarly Russian *zemstvo*[29a] institution. Although other persons besides peasants

[20]Statutes on the Judiciary, *Fund. Laws,* Vol. XVI, section 17.
[21]*Ibid.,* section 53.
[22]*Ibid.,* section 51. See also Statutes on Cr. Procedure, *Fund. Laws,* Vol. XVI, section 176.
[23]Statutes on Cr. Procedure, *Fund. Laws,* Vol. XVI, section 37.
[24]Statute on the Judiciary, section 64.
[25]*Ibid.,* section 52.
[26]*Ibid.,* section 54.
[27]*Ibid.,* section 55.
[28]*Ibid.,* section 56.
[29]*Ibid.,* section 58.
[29a]The *zemstvo* was a peculiar Russian institution organized in 1864 as

came within their jurisdiction the peasantry were the objective for the establishment of the whole chain of *zemski* courts as well as other courts which shared a similar authority over portions of the population who were not to come under the jurisdiction of the purely *zemski* courts.

The *zemski* courts were instituted only in certain portions of the Empire. But wherever they functioned they superseded the courts of the peace system and the entire jurisdiction of the latter was distributed among three different courts of the *zemski* type. This fact made this type of courts a complicated one. Except in the matter of jurisdiction they had the same characteristics as the courts of the peace system, described above. In a few isolated instances, however, an appeal from one of these courts could be taken to another system, instead of the usual form of appeal to a territorial assembly of judges of the same system.

a. *Municipal and* Zemski *Courts*

Municipal and *zemski* courts were created simultaneously by the statutes of 1889. In forty-three provinces of the Empire the new system was inaugurated. This judicial system consisted of sectional *zemski* courts in the rural districts,[30] municipal courts in the larger cities of the same territories, with but few exceptions, and county assemblies.[31] This new judicial system which was established "for the purpose of creating a firm local authority concentrated in the hands of the nobles",[32] superseded the justices of the peace courts. The counties which became subject to the new statutes were divided into *zemski* sections[33] and each section had a resident sectional *zemski* chief.[34]

a result of the abolition of serfdom in 1861. It was made up of the landed nobility with some representation of the peasantry. Usually the more liberal minded elements of the nobility were active in the *zemstvo* institutions. The *zemstvo* aimed to ameliorate the condition of the peasantry. It maintained model farms, farm schools, elementary education in the village, hospitals, etc.

[30]Statute as to the supervision of Peasants' Affairs, *Fund. Laws,* Vol. IX, book III, section 1.

[31]Rules as to the Judiciary in the regions where the *zemski* chiefs were established. *Fund. Laws,* Vol. XVI, section 4.

[32]A. Kornilov, *Modern Russian History,* Vol. II, p. 263.

[33]Statute, *op. cit., supra,* note 30, section 2.

[34]*Ibid.,* section 5.

The criminal jurisdiction of these courts extended, with few exceptions, over all the offenses handled by the justices of the peace.[35] Besides judicial powers the chiefs had great powers of supervision over all the institutions of the peasantry.[36] They could even dismiss from office untrustworthy village clerks or officers.[37] The *zemski* chiefs were appointed by the governor *(Gubernator)* upon the advice of the province or county marshal of nobility. The appointee's name was then sent for confirmation to the Minister of the Interior[38] who had the power to reject the candidate and ask that another one should be appointed.[39] The governor picked the name of the appointee from a special list of persons who were eligible for such office, which list was compiled and kept by the county marshal of nobility.[40] To be eligible for such an appointment a person had to be a provincial marshal of nobility or a local nobleman who met a certain qulification of land-ownership. In addition it was necessary for the appointee to possess a university education or to have served one year in one or more of a number of specified institutions, all of which were connected with the supervision of peasants' affairs.[41]

The municipal judges had, so far as judicial powers were concerned, the same authority in their respective large cities as the *zemski* chiefs in their rural sections. "The power of the judge was vested in a single person and he was to be known as a municipal judge."[42] The judges were appointed by the Minister of Justice,[43] who could dismiss a judge on the recommendation of his advisory board.[44] To be eligible for the office of municipal judge a person had to have a university law degree. In addition, he was required to have an experience of not less than three years' service in a judicial capacity not lower in rank than that of secretary of a circuit court.[45] As the legal qualifications for a municipal

[35]Rules, *op. cit., supra,* note 31, section 162.
[36]Statute, *op. cit., supra,* note 30, Vol. IX, section 23.
[37]*Ibid.,* section 29.
[38]*Ibid.,* section 13.
[39]*Ibid.,* section 14.
[40]*Ibid.,* section 11.
[41]*Ibid.,* section 6.
[42]Rules, *op. cit., supra,* note 31, section 5.
[43]*Ibid.,* section 6.
[44]*Ibid.,* section 7.
[45]*Ibid.,* section 6. (See also Statutes on the Judiciary, sections 202, 203).

judge were much higher than those of the *zemski* chiefs, he enjoyed a higher standing in the judicial ranks. Thus, he was dismissed or disciplined in the same manner as a judge of the circuit court.[46] He was also invited to sit on the circuit court bench if one of its judges was absent.[47] In his own court, the municipal judge was to be guided by the same rules and regulations prescribed for *zemski* chiefs.[48]

b. *The County Assembly*

In each county there was a county assembly.[49] The judicial session of the assembly consisted of the county marshal of nobility, the county member of the circuit court, the municipal judges, and the *zemski* chiefs of the county.[50]

The county assembly sat as a court of appeals on cases which had properly originated either in the municipal courts or in the courts of the *zemski* chiefs.[51] The assembly was given the additional important power of reviewing a legally binding judgment by way of cassation.[52]

The presence of the assistant procurator of the circuit court was required at all the judicial sessions of the assembly. He was to be there in order to state his opinion and give his conclusions whenever necessary.[53]

c. *The Provincial Board*

The same law which created the *zemski* chiefs and the county assemblies also instituted the provincial board.[54] Though the functions of this board were primarily administrative, it nevertheless exercised some important powers of judicial review in cases which were brought from the county assemblies.

Each province had a provincial board.[55] The board was made up of the governor of the province, who presided, the

[46] *Ibid.*, section 11.
[47] *Ibid.*, section 18.
[48] *Ibid.*, section 16.
[49] Statutes, *op. cit., supra*, note 30, section 64.
[50] *Ibid.*, section 67.
[51] *Ibid.*, section 81.
[52] Rules, *op. cit., supra*, note 31, section 240.
[53] Statute, *op. cit., supra*, note 30, section 70.
[54] See *supra* note 29.
[55] Statute, *op. cit., supra*, note 30, section 96.

lieutenant-governor, the provincial marshal of nobility, two special members, and the procurator and the president of the circuit court.[56] The two special members, who had very important duties to perform, since they had to prepare a case for the consideration of the board, were appointed by the governor who sought the advice of the provincial marshal of nobility.[57]

The procurator took part in the sessions of the board only in order to state his opinions and conclusions, but did not participate in the vote on the judgment to be rendered.[58]

Besides extensive powers of supervision vested in the provincial board, the law also provided, that complaints and protests against legal binding judgments of the county assemblies were to be taken to this board.[59] The board had then the power to reverse such final judgment[60] and send the case back to the county assembly.

d. *Volost Court*

The volost court was of very little importance as a criminal tribunal. It was a kind of small village court immediately subordinate to the *zemski* chiefs. It had jurisdiction over very slight offenses of a purely local nature involving peasants only. A striking illustration of the nature of its criminal jurisdiction was its power to punish a breach of an oral contract by which one peasant agreed to give his labor and in return received money in advance in bad faith and then refused either to serve or to return the money.[61] These courts were supervised by the *zemski* chiefs or the county assemblies, the latter appointing the presiding judge.[62] In general its power to punish was limited to a rebuke in open court, a fine of not more than thirty rubles, and detention up to fifteen or, in a few exceptional cases, up to thirty days.[63]

[56] *Ibid.*, section 97.
[57] *Ibid.*, section 99.
[58] *Ibid.*, section 98.
[59] Rule, *op. cit., supra,* note 31, section 240.
[60] Statute, *op. cit., supra,* note 30, section 116.
[61] Volost Courts, Statutes as to the Peasantry, *Fund. Laws,* Vol. IX, section 127.
[62] *Ibid.*, section 113.
[63] *Ibid.*, section 143.

III. GENERAL COURT SYSTEM

The general court system had jurisdiction over more serious offenses. The statutes seem to treat them separately under the term "General Judicial Places".[64] Cases which properly started in one of those courts had their final appeal, as distinguished from cassation, within the limits of that type. Cases were tried either summarily or by jury, or with representatives of the castes, according to the nature of the case. The striking features of the general courts were that not less than three judges sat in every case, a preliminary inquiry was held in most cases, and appeals were taken to an entirely different court of a much higher standing.

a. *Circuit Court*

The most significant court of original jurisdiction in Imperial Russia was the highly dignified circuit court.

A circuit court was given jurisdiction over a wide territory embracing several counties. It consisted of a president and numerous judges.[65] The whole court was then divided into small divisions with a vice-president presiding over each division.[66] But not less than three judges, including the president, were to sit at each judicial deliberation.[67]

The jurisdiction of the court extended over all serious offenses, since the law provided,[68] that it should take jurisdiction over all criminal offenses excluded from the jurisdiction of the justices of the peace, the county member of the circuit court, the municipal courts, and the *zemski* chiefs. This court was the only one in the Empire which had the system of trial by jury. Even here, trial by jury was had only in very grave cases, where a verdict of guilty would carry with it forfeiture of all rights of the accused incidental to his particular guild or his caste, or of all his special rights and privileges.[69]

[64] *Fund. Laws*, Vol. XVI. The heading over the book II reads: "Rules of Procedure in the General Judicial Places."

[65] Statutes on the Judiciary, *Fund. Laws*, Vol. XVI, section 77.

[66] *Ibid.*, section 78.

[67] *Ibid.*, section 140. See also Statutes on Cr. Procedure, *Fund. Laws*, Vol. XVI, section 595.

[68] Statutes on Cr. Procedure, *Fund. Laws*, Vol. XVI, section 200.

[69] *Ibid.*, section 201.

The court had a regular seat, usually in the largest city of the circuit, and held its sessions in a specially designated court building.[70] But the circuit court for the hearing of criminal cases held court also in other cities within its circuit; sometimes going to the place where the alleged crime was committed.[71]

The president, vice-president and the judges of the court were appointed by the highest authority of the Empire, the Tzar, upon the presentation of the Minister of Justice.[72] To be eligible for such a position a person had to be a graduate of a university law school.[73] In addition, to be eligible as president or vice-president of the circuit court a person must have served, prior to his appointment, as a member of the judiciary for a period of three years in a rank not lower than that of procurator or judge of the circuit court.[74] The qualification for a judge of the court was satisfied by three years' previous judicial service in the rank of secretary of the court.[75] A person was also qualified for judgeship if he was a sworn attorney of ten years' standing.[76]

A very important feature was that the tenure of office of all judgeships in this court was for life. The statutes did not specifically provide for life tenure, but the latter was undoubtedly fixed indirectly by the provision that "The president, vice-president and members of the judiciary [in the circuit courts] may neither be relieved from office without their petitioning therefor, nor transferred from one place to another withouut their consent."[77] To the above rule there were certain necessary exceptions. Thus a judge could be asked to resign after he had been seriously ill for over a year and if he refused be would be dismissed.[78] Judges could also be transferred from one circuit to another in cases of extreme necessity, and then only upon the decision of the full session of the court and with the approval of the Minister of Justice.[79] There were also provisions allowing the

[70]Statutes, *op. cit.*, *supra*, note 65, section 137.
[71]*Ibid.*, section 138.
[72]*Ibid.*, section 212.
[73]*Ibid.*, section 202.
[74]*Ibid.*, section 206.
[75]*Ibid.*, section 203.
[76]*Ibid.*, section 204.
[77]*Ibid.*, section 243.
[78]*Ibid.*, section 229.
[79]*Ibid.*, section 227.

dismissal of a judge in cases where he was fined or penalized by a court even for an offense not connected with the judicial office,[80] or a temporary suspension from office if he was under indictment.[81] It may be safely said that members of the general judiciary were to enjoy a tenure of office during good behavior.

The trial session of the circuit court consisted of not less than three judges, one presiding, and twelve jurors, one of whom was the foreman and was required to be able to read and write.[82]

Three weeks before the opening of the jury sessions the drawing of jurors took place. The president judge drew thirty names from the jury list and three from the list of candidates for jury service.[83] Three days before trial began the defendant was served with a list of the names of the judges, procurator, and the jurors who were to participate in his trial.[84] This was necessary in order that the defendant might prepare a challenge for cause against a judge, the procurator or a juror. The defendant, as well as the procurator, or the private prosecutor were also allowed three peremptory challenges of jurors.[85]

The jurors could actively participate at the trial, for they had the same power as the judges to examine witnesses, or parties at any time and could take notes during the trial.[86]

At the end of the trial (the defendant or his attorney had always the right to close) the foreman of the jury was given a number of specific questions, prepared and read by the presiding judge.[87] These questions the jury was asked to answer briefly, for example, "yes, it happened", "yes, premeditated", etc.[88] The jury was urged to reach a unanimous answer to each question, but a majority decided. In case of a tie the answer favorable to the defendant was to stand.[89] The jury was to state whether the defendant deserved leniency in the event of a conviction.[90]

[80] *Ibid.*, section 295.
[81] See *supra*, note 76.
[82] Statutes on Cr. Procedure, *op. cit.*, *supra*, note 23, sections 595, 658 and 670.
[83] *Ibid.*, section 550.
[84] *Ibid.*, section 589.
[85] *Ibid.*, sections 655 and 656.
[86] *Ibid.*, sections 672 and 674.
[87] *Ibid.*, section 801.
[88] *Ibid.*, sections 811 and 812.
[89] *Ibid.*, section 813.
[90] *Ibid.*, section 814.

A recommendation of leniency reduced the punishment by one or two degrees.[91]

The verdict of the jury was not subject to an appeal, but could be carried, on legal grounds, to the court of cassation. But if the trial court unanimously deemed the verdict of guilty unjustifiable, it could grant a new trial with a different jury. The verdict reached at the second trial was final.[92]

The circuit court also tried criminal cases without a jury. In this event the verdict reached by the three judges was appealable to the judicial *palata*.

b. *County Member of the Circuit Court*

At the time the new judicial institutions, *zemski* chiefs and the municipal courts, were organized another judicial office sprang into being—the county member of the circuit court.

The law provided that each county should have at least one county member, and certain specified counties, two or three members, of the circuit court.[93]

The county member was to perform a number of judicial functions. He was to have original jurisdiction over offenses which were formerly assigned by law to the jurisdiction of the justices of the peace, and which by the law of 1889 were not made subject to the jurisdiction of *zemski* chiefs or municipal courts.[94] The county member administered justice according to the rules of procedure prescribed for the justices of the peace.[95] Appeals from the few cases tried by the county member were heard by the circuit court at the place where the case had originated.[96]

c. *The Judicial Inquisitor*

The judicial inquisitor was considered a member of the circuit court and was assigned to a designated district within the circuit.[97] All the qualifications for eligibility to a circuit court judgeship applied to the inquisitor. But a person could also be

[91] *Ibid.*, section 828.
[92] *Ibid.*, section 818.
[93] Rules, *op. cit., supra*, note 31, Vol. XVI, part 1, section 26.
[94] *Ibid.*, section 20.
[95] *Ibid.*, section 30.
[96] *Ibid.*
[97] Statute, *op. cit., supra*, note 65, section 79.

appointed to that office if he was on the list of candidates for a judicial office.[98] Persons who were university law school graduates could be named for this list by the chief president of the *palata*, and were considered in the service of the government.[99] The functions of the inquisitor will be discussed later.

d. *Judicial Palata*

The judicial *palata* was a court of appeals of the highest standing. Cases appealed from the decisions of the circuit court were removed to the judicial *palata*.[100] Like all other Russian appellate courts it had tremendous reviewing powers and often approached the point of an actual retrial of a case, since it could summon and examine witnesses, experts, etc.[101] The appeal was heard in open court in the presence of the public.[102]

Each judicial *palata* had jurisdiction over a large region, embracing several provinces.[103] The court was divided into a number of departments,[104] civil, criminal, etc. Each department was made up of a president and a fixed number of judges.[105] But no judicial session could be held with less than three judges.[106] The judge appointed to preside over the full session of the *palata*, where all the judges of every department participated, was styled the chief president of the *palata*.[107]

The judges of the court were appointed by the same authority and in the same manner as the judges of the circuit court were appointed.[108] The required qualifications for eligibility for office were also the same as for the circuit court.[109] But the length of previous judicial service and the rank of such service which were conditions precedent to the appointment of president or vice-president of a circuit court were prescribed for an ordinary judge of the *palata*. To be eligible for an appointment as president of

98 *Ibid.*, section 205.
99 *Ibid.*, section 407.
100 Statutes on Cr. Procedure, *Fund. Laws*, Vol. XVI, section 877.
101 *Ibid.*, section 879.
102 *Ibid.*, section 884. See also section 620.
103 *Ibid.*, section 110.
104 *Ibid.*, section 111.
105 *Ibid.*, section 112.
106 *Ibid.*, section 140.
107 *Ibid.*, section 113.
108 See *supra*, note 72.
109 See *supra*, notes 73 and 74.

the *palata* one had to serve for not less than three years, prior to the appointment, in a judicial rank not lower than either procurator or judge of the *palata,* or president or vice president of the circuit court.[110]

While the judicial *palata* was essentially a court of appeals it had some important original jurisdiction. By special statute a great variety of offenses, which may properly be denoted as offenses against the government, were transferred to the original jurisdiction of the *palata.*[111]

There was no trial by jury in this court; but in the trial of certain grave offenses where a verdict of guilty would carry with it forfeiture of the special rights and privileges of the accused, or the rights he enjoyed through his guild or his caste, the tribunal was made up of judges of the *palata* and representatives of the different castes. The full court consisted then of the president and three judges of the *palata,* the provincial marshal of nobility, the local city mayor, and the elder of one of the *volosts* within that county.[112] This peculiar form of a court was in no sense in its nature or structure a jury trial. The so-called representatives of the castes were, in any given case, additional judges, since they participated in the rendering of the judgment and their votes were counted as those of the judges.[113] A judgment thus rendered was not subject to an appeal,[114] but was subject to review by way of cassation. As a high tribunal of original jurisdiction the *palata* held court in different cities within its region.[115]

Besides its other powers the *palata* exercised great authority in matters of supervision. It had the final word in deciding jurisdictional disputes between circuit courts.[116] Its supervisory powers were so extensive that it could on its own initiative pass upon the validity of a decision of a circuit court to discontinue a criminal case.[117]

[110]Statute, *op. cit., supra,* note 65, section 207.
[111]Statute, *op. cit., supra,* note 100, section 201 (1906).
[112]*Ibid.,* section 1105.
[113]*Ibid.,* section 1106.
[114]*Ibid.,* section 1106.
[115]Statutes on the Judiciary, *Fund. Laws,* Vol. XVI, section 138.
[116]Statutes, *op. cit., supra,* note 100, section 232.
[117]*Ibid.,* section 529.

IV. DEPARTMENT OF CASSATION

The jurisdiction and functions of this court of cassation made it a type entirely unknown in our system of criminal courts. It was not a court of appeals but of supervision and interpretation. It took jurisdiction when there was no ground for appeal, and cases from courts of the peace, the *zemski* courts or the general courts, might eventually reach the court of cassation.

The idea of a court which would be the highest court of law with powers of cassation and supervision was borrowed from the French system of jurisprudence.[118]

The statutes of 1864 provided: "Within the Governing Senate there shall be instituted, for purposes of supervising the judicial system, a Supreme Court of Cassation with two departments—one for criminal, and one for civil cases."[119] The purpose of the Departments of Cassation was not to decide cases on their merits, but to ensure the correct interpretation of the law and its uniform application by the judiciary over the entire Empire.[120]

The Departments of Cassation were to have their seat at the Capitol,[121] which was then St. Petersburg. Each department consisted of (1) a session of the full department, and (2) sessions of separate divisions of the department. The plenary session consisted of not less than seven senators or judges, including the presiding senator; the separate divisions were made up of not less than three senators, the senior member presiding.[122]

The senators were appointed directly by the Tzar on his own initiative,[123] without any presentation by the Minister of Justice. For this position persons were appointed who had served not less than three years either as head procurator or assistant procurator of the Senate, or president, judge or procurator of the judicial *palata*.[124]

The judicial jurisdiction of the Department of Cassation extended to all legally binding judgments, which were not appealable. The statute provided: "Complaints and protests by way of

[118]Th. M. Dimitrief, *op. cit.*, *supra*, note 3, p. 505.
[119]Statute on the Judiciary, *Fund. Laws*, Vol. XVI, section 114.
[120]*Ibid.*, section 5.
[121]*Ibid.*, section 115.
[122]*Ibid.*, section 140.
[123]*Ibid.*, section 216.
[124]*Ibid.*, section 208.

cassation are permissible only against final judgment, which can not be brought by way of appeal."[125] Every judgment rendered by a court having appellate jurisdiction, as well as judgments rendered by a circuit court with a jury, were considered final or legally binding. All complaints and protests from such final judgments were taken to the Criminal Cassational Department, where such "final judgments may be changed by way of cassation."[126]

The Department of Cassation was the only[127] tribunal in Imperial Russia to interpret the law. Such an interpretation of the law required a session of the full department and once given served "as a guide for the uniform application of the law."[128]

"The court to which a case was returned from the court of cassation for a new trial had to follow the exact interpretation of the law as laid down by the Senate."[129]

The hearing of a case brought by way of cassation was conducted in open court.[130] The same was true with the announcing of the decision of the Senate.[131] The decision of this highest tribunal in all matters subject to its jurisdiction could "under no circumstance be subject to any complaint."[132]

B. The Preliminary Inquiry

The general function of the judicial inquisitor was to conduct all the preliminary inquiries in criminal cases subject to the original jurisdiction of the circuit court.[133] The inquisitor had to have "a legal basis and a sufficient ground to institute a preliminary inquiry".[134] Once an inquiry was set on foot the powers of the inquisitor were extensive. He could examine witnesses and documents, inspect places, arrange for medical investigation

[125]Statutes on Cr. Procedure, *Fund. Laws*, Vol. XVI, sections 905.
[126]*Ibid.*, section 855.
[127]While the assembly of the justices of the peace had some power of cassation its decision was binding only on the case before them. It had no authority to interpret the law generally. This power was vested in the court of cassation.
[128]Statutes on Cr. Procedure, *Fund. Laws*, Vol. XVI, section 916.
[129]*Ibid.*, section 930.
[130]*Ibid.*, section 918.
[131]*Ibid.*, section 926.
[132]*Ibid.*, section 937.
[133]*Ibid.*, section 249.
[134]*Ibid.*, section 262.

and inspection,[135] question the accused,[136] conduct a so-called "neighborhood inquest"[137] and intercept the mails of those under suspicion.[138] The inquisitor had also the authority to take such measures as would ensure the presence of the accused at the inquiry or the trial. He could, therefore, order that the suspect be kept under guard or admitted to bail, or allowed on parol, etc. The duty of the inquisitor was not merely to establish the facts which would lead to a conviction. On the contrary, "He must without prejudice investigate all the favorable circumstances of the accused, as well as the unfavorable ones."[139] To carry out these powers the law provided that the inquisitor might call upon the civil and military authorities to cooperate with him,[140] and that "all legal demands made by the inquisitor on the police force, governmental agencies or private persons must be carried out without delay."[141]

The important limitation on the powers of the inquisitor was that once an inquiry was started he could not on his own authority discontinue the case. This could be done only by the authority of the circuit court.[142]

The inquisitor, to be sure, was not the final authority in matters touching his official duties. His every act and decision during the long process of investigation was subject to appeal and reversal. Notwithstanding this he wielded a tremendous power over the fate of all those subject to his inquisitorial jurisdiction.

C. Prosecution

There were two methods of prosecution in Imperial Russia:—the less significant method was by private prosecution, the other by public prosecution. The statute provided that "Judicial prosecution shall be conducted either by officials of the government or by private persons."[143]

135 *Ibid.*, section 336.
136 *Ibid.*, section 398.
137 *Ibid.*, section 454.
138 *Ibid.*, section 368.
139 *Ibid.*, section 265.
140 *Ibid.*, section 272.
141 *Ibid.*, section 270.
142 *Ibid.*, section 277.
143 *Ibid.*, section 2.

I. PUBLIC PROSECUTION

A separate unit which functioned within the scheme of the general judiciary was the well-organized procuracy. This organization consisted of head procurators, procurators and assistants all of whom were under the supervision of the Minister of Justice who was termed the Procurator-General.[144] The head procurator *(Oberprocuror)* and his assistants were connected with the work of the Department of Cassation.[145] Each unit of either the judicial *palata* or the circuit court had a separate procurator and a number of assistant procurators.[146]

The procurator of the circuit court was subordinate to the procurator of the judicial *palata,* the appellate court of that group, while the procurator of the *palata* together with the head procurator of the Department of Cassation were directly subordinate to the Minister of Justice.[147] Out of the number of assistant procurators of the circuit court a few were assigned to the court itself, while the rest were assigned to different cities within the circuit.[148] This was necessary since the procurator had to perform a number of duties outside the courts.

The head procurator of the Department of Cassation and his assistants, the procurators of the *palata* and their assistants, and the procurators of the circuit court were all appointed by the Tzar on the presentation of the Minister of Justice.[149] The Minister of Justice, upon presentation of the procurator of the *palata,* appointed the assistant procurators of the circuit court.[150] The qualification for eligibility to the various offices of procurator were the same as for corresponding offices in the general judiciary,[151] except that the length of experience in judicial affairs required for the procuracy was much higher. The length of previous judicial service required as a condition precedent to the appointment of the different ranks in the procuracy was as follows: Not less than four years for the office of assistant procu-

[144]Statutes, *op. cit., supra,* note 119, section 124.
[145]*Ibid.,* section 127.
[146]*Ibid.,* section 125.
[147]*Ibid.,* section 129.
[148]*Ibid.,* section 126.
[149]*Ibid.,* sections 219, 221.
[150]*Ibid.,* section 222.
[151]*Ibid.,* section 202.

rator of the circuit court; not less than six years for the office of procurator of the circuit court or assistant of the *palata;* not less than eight years for the office of procurator of the *palata* or assistant head procurator and not less than twelve years for the office of head procurator of the Department of Cassation.[152]

The procuracy was, in fact, in its every-day activity, the agency for public prosecution and the representative of the Empire at the more serious criminal cases. In theory, however, the organized nation-wide procuracy was not merely to prosecute and to seek a conviction, but "to see that a case proceeds correctly and that the judges shall have all the means to base their judgment on exact data."[153]

So far as actual prosecution was concerned, the procuracy did not take part in any case which was subject to the jurisdiction of the courts of the peace or the *zemski* systems. The statute provided that in criminal cases within the jurisdiction of the general judiciary, that is, in the circuit court and the judicial *palata,* prosecution should be placed upon the procurators and their assistants.[154] But for the performance of duties connected with the procuracy which extended beyond the realm of actual prosecution, the assistant procurator of the circuit court was required to be present at the sessions of the appellate courts of the peace system and the *zemski* system, which were the district and county assemblies.[155] His duty was to explain the importance of the testimoney and to point out the law which ought to be applied.[156] Such function of the assistant procurator can hardly be conceived of as an act of prosecution. He did not prepare the indictment, he was not present at the original trial of the case, nor was he present at the appeal to seek a conviction. On the other hand, the procurator could protest a judgment only if it was favorable to the defendant.

A study of the different statutes touching upon the duties and powers of the procuracy indicates that every member of the procuracy was a more important judicial officer and ranked higher than any judge of the court with which he was connected.

[152] *Ibid.*, section 210.
[153] Th. M. Dimitrief, *op. cit., supra,* note 3, page 503.
[154] Statutes, *op. cit., supra,* note 125, section 4.
[155] See *supra,* notes 29 and 53.
[156] Statutes, *op. cit., supra,* note 125, section 166.

The procuracy was entrusted with enormous powers. The procurator supervised directly every move in the preliminary inquiry conducted by the inquisitor;[157] he could be present at every stage of inquisitorial proceedings;[158] he had the power to set free any person unlawfully held under guard.[159] It was the procurator or his assistant who directed the course of proper proceedings after the preliminary inquiry was completed. The procurator had the authority to decide whether any given case should be dropped or discontinued, or the accused held for trial.[160] When the procurator decided to proceed with the case he stated his conclusions in the form of an indictment, or a document of accusation *(obvenitelniiakt)*.[161]

Upon the presenting of formal indictment, which in serious case had to be approved by the procurator of the *palata,* the procurator of the circuit court, the usual court for original jurisdiction became the prosecuting attorney in that case. But even then the law clearly forbade him to display zeal in seeking a conviction. The statute provided, that "the procurator must not present the case from one angle only, stressing the points which will convict the defendant, and he must not exaggerate the value of the testimony against the accused and the seriousness of the crime."[162] If at the trial, after testimony was presented, the procurator thought that the defendant ought to be acquitted, he was in duty bound "not to uphold the indictment".[163]

In describing public prosecution in Imperial Russia, we might add that there was sometimes a form of public prosecution also in the lesser courts—justice of the peace and *zemski* courts —to which the activities of the procuracy did not extend. The police as well as other administrative organs of the government could act here as prosecuting agencies.[164] This was not, strictly speaking, public prosecution, but as the complaint was usually brought by a police official against a person who committed a

[157] *Ibid.*, sections 249, 278.
[158] *Ibid.*, section 280.
[159] *Ibid.*, section 10.
[160] *Ibid.*, section 510.
[161] *Ibid.*, section 519.
[162] *Ibid.*, section 739.
[163] *Ibid.*, section 740.
[164] *Ibid.*, section 740.

minor offense, the police official who appeared in court was the prosecuting witness against the defendant.

II. PRIVATE PROSECUTION

Private prosecution was the usual or ordinary form of prosecution at the minor courts. This method of prosecution in these courts was informal and was instituted by an ordinary complaint which could be brought orally or in writing.[165] But there were also a number of offenses in the jurisdiction of the circuit court which were not subject to public prosecution.[166] In these cases the parties could settle the case out of court at any time before a judgment was rendered. There was still another type of offenses, of which rape was an instance, which could not be instituted by the procuracy unless the injured party made a formal complaint,[167] but which could not be settled by the parties out of court once a prosecution had been started. In such a case after the prosecution was initiated by private prosecution, the procurator took over the functions of a prosecuting attorney.[168]

Where a case was presented before the circuit court by private prosecution the private complaint took the place of the document of accusation.[169]

III. CIVIL CLAIMANT *(grazhdanski istetz)*

An interesting feature in the procedure of the Russian criminal law was the participation of the civil claimant, *i. e.*, the injured party in the criminal proceedings of the case, for the purpose of recovering damages.

The law stated: "Any person who has suffered as a result of the offense, and who does not have the right of a private prosecutor,[170] may be recognized as participating in the capacity of a civil claimant in the criminal proceedings, provided he makes a declaration seeking compensation during the proceedings of the

[165] *Ibid.*, section 45.
[166] *Ibid.*, section 5.
[167] Penal Code, *Fund. Laws*, Vol. XV, section 157.
[168] Statutes, *op. cit.*, *supra*, note 125, section 5.
[169] *Ibid.*, section 526.
[170] This could take place either in the minor judiciary where the police authorities, themselves, started the prosecution, or in a case subject to public prosecution only, as most cases in the circuit court were.

criminal case."[171] Once such a declaration was made the civil claimant became an actual party to the case, so far as the recovery of a money judgment was concerned. The defendant was then confronted with a struggle against two parties—the prosecutor and the civil claimant simultaneously. During the conduct of the preliminary inquiry, the civil complainant, or his attorney, had a right to bring his witnesses, to be present at all the preliminary proceedings, examine the accused and the witnesses, submit corroborative testimony with regard to his claim, and demand copies at his own cost of all the official protocols.[172] With very few exceptions he was treated through all the stages of the proceedings as a party plaintiff in the criminal action. Thus he was informed by the court when the document of accusation was filed, and he also received copy of it.[173] The civil claimant could add names of witnesses to be supoenaed by the court as could also the procurator and the defendant.[174] In conformity with his position, the civil claimant, or his attorney, participated in the final argument before the court and the jury. He was to make all necessary statements and declarations, and prove all the circumstances which had a bearing upon his demand for compensation. But he was not to touch the criminal responsibility of the accused.[175] The civil claimant could also appeal from a judgment against his claim.[176] The judgment rendered by the trial court in a criminal case contained also a provision as to the compensation asked by the civil claimant.[177]

To make the procedure more effective, the civil claimant could request the inquisitor to attach property of the accused so as to secure the satisfaction of a possible money judgment which might be later obtained in the criminal court. If the inquisitor thought the reasons good for so doing he would petition the court to that effect.[178]

This effective remedy given by the law to the civil claimant was in addition to a separate remedy by civil action. The injured

[171] Statutes, *op. cit., supra*, note 125, section 6.
[172] *Ibid.*, section 304.
[173] *Ibid.*, section 559.
[174] *Ibid.*, section 560.
[175] *Ibid.*, section 742.
[176] *Ibid.*, section 859.
[177] *Ibid.*, section 776.
[178] *Ibid.*, section 305.

party did not have to make a civil claim, or if one was made and he failed to appear at the trial,[179] the criminal case proceeded without the civil claim; the injured party, however, did not lose his right to proceed in a civil court.

D. Attorneys

There were two kinds of advocates, as they were commonly called, in Imperial Russia—sworn attorneys and private attorneys.

1. SWORN ATTORNEYS *(presyazhni povereni)*

The sworn attorney was the only advocate who was considered a member of the highly dignified and much respected legal profession. To become a sworn attorney a person had to be a graduate of a university law school, and must also have either practiced law for five years as an assistant to a sworn attorney or have been connected for the same length of time with the judiciary in such work as would give him a knowledge of legal practice.[180]

Every sworn attorney was registered with a particular judicial *palata* and had to select a place of residence within the area under the jurisdiction of such *palata*.[181]

Something akin to our bar association, but with greater power and influence in shaping the profession, was the council of the sworn attorneys. At each judicial *palata* a regional council was organized for the purpose of supervising all the sworn attorneys within that region.[182] When a city outside the seat of the *palata* had not less than ten sworn attorneys, they could organize a branch of the regional council at the circuit court.[183]

The statutes described with great detail all the steps necessary to organize such a council. The main points were that not less than twenty attorneys signed a petition to the *palata*, and the latter appointed one of its judges to supervise the formation of the council. The judge was to preside until the organization of the council was completed, a president elected and a list of all its members turned over to the procurator of the *palata* and then

[179] *Ibid.*, section 594.
[180] Statutes on the Judiciary, *Fund. Laws*, Vol. XVI, section 354.
[181] *Ibid.*, section 356.
[182] *Ibid.*, section 357.
[183] *Ibid.*, section 366.

published for general information.[184] The council was the board of admission to membership of the profession. A person desirous of becoming a sworn attorney had to file an application with the council submitting all the documents necessary to prove his eligibility to membership.[185] The council had the authority to approve or reject the application.[186] In the former case the candidate seeking admission was sworn in, and his name was entered on the rolls of the sworn attorneys (hence the name sworn attorney).[187] Besides the duties of passing on applicants for admission to the profession, the council was entrusted with the power to take up complaints against its members, to appoint advocates to represent poor litigants, to appoint attorneys to represent persons who applied to the council for that purpose, to fix the amount of an attorney's fee when there was no written agreement between the advocate and his client, and to levy fines on attorneys for offenses charged on complaints made by clients or by the council itself.[188]

There were a great number of duties and obligations prescribed for the members of the profession, and the council saw that the advocate behaved in accordance with the rules. For a breach of duty, the sworn attorney was responsible to the council, the latter having the power to discipline its members by warning, rebuke, suspension from practice for a term of not more than one year, expulsion from the ranks of the sworn attorneys, and, in extreme cases, citing the member to the criminal courts.[189] To take any of the above-mentioned steps, the decision had to be reached in the presence of not less than half of the entire membership, and by a vote of not less than two-thirds of those present.[190] The attorney thus disciplined could appeal to the judicial *palata,*[191] the latter's decision being the final disposition of the matter.[192] Among many other restrictions placed upon the attorney he "was forbidden to buy or in any other similar way

[184] *Ibid.*, sections 358, 362 and 363.
[185] *Ibid.*, section 379.
[186] *Ibid.*, section 380.
[187] *Ibid.*, sections 381, 382.
[188] *Ibid.*, section 367.
[189] *Ibid.*, section 368.
[190] *Ibid.*, section 375.
[191] *Ibid.*, section 376.
[192] *Ibid.*, section 377.

obtain a power of attorney. * * * All such agreements were void and rendered the attorneys liable in accordance with the rules of the councils."[193] He was also prohibited to appear in court as counsel against his parents, wife, children, brothers, sisters, uncles and counsins.[194]

To keep a firmer control over the activities of the advocates, the law provided that "each sworn attorney must keep a list of all cases entrusted to him, and present it to the council at first demand."[195]

II. PRIVATE ATTORNEYS

A private attorney was one who, upon applying to a particular court, received a certificate as private attorney. Such certificates could be issued by the courts of the peace, circuit court and the judicial *palata*. The certificate permitted the holder to practice only in the judicial unit from which it was issued.[196] Thus certificates obtained from the assembly of the justice of the peace entitled one to practice in all the courts of the peace under the jurisdiction of the assembly.[197] Though the statute creating private attorneys speaks only of civil cases,[198] there is no doubt that private attorneys were allowed to appear in criminal cases. In the case of the circuit court, the important criminal court of original jurisdiction, the law specifically provided that "the accused has a right to select as his advocate a sworn attorney or a private attorney * * * ."[199]

In general the private attorney enjoyed neither any special rights nor any degree of professional dignity. They usually practiced in the smaller communities and before the minor judiciary.

[193]*Ibid.*, section 400.
[194]*Ibid.*, section 401.
[195]*Ibid.*, section 406.
[196]*Ibid.*, section 406.
[197]*Ibid.*, section 406.
[198]*Ibid.*, section 406.
[199]Statutes on Cr. Procedure, *Fund. Laws*, Vol. XVI, section 565.

INDEX